ORDINARY HORROR

ORDINARY HORROR

THE AESTHETICS OF DEFORMATION FROM LEOPARDI TO FERRANTE

Andrea Capra

STANFORD UNIVERSITY PRESS
Stanford, California

Stanford University Press
Stanford, California

Library of Congress Cataloging-in-Publication Data
Names: Capra, Andrea, 1991- author
Title: Ordinary horror : the aesthetics of deformation from Leopardi to Ferrante / Andrea Capra.
Description: Stanford, California : Stanford University Press, 2026. | Includes bibliographical references and index.
Identifiers: LCCN 2025050522 (print) | LCCN 2025050523 (ebook) | ISBN 9781503647459 cloth | ISBN 9781503648142 paper | ISBN 9781503647657 ebook
Subjects: LCSH: Italian literature—20th century—History and criticism | Italian literature—Themes, motives | Horror in literature
Classification: LCC PQ4088 .C28945 2026 (print) | LCC PQ4088 (ebook)
LC record available at https://lccn.loc.gov/2025050522
LC ebook record available at https://lccn.loc.gov/2025050523

Cover design: Jan Šabach
Cover art: Unsplash

The authorized representative in the EU for product safety and compliance is: Mare Nostrum Group B.V. | Doelen 72 | 4831 GR Breda | The Netherlands | Email address: gpsr@mare-nostrum.co.uk | KVK chamber of commerce number: 96249943

Printed and bound by CPI Group (UK) Ltd, Croydon, CR0 4YY

Est mortalibus insitus horror

—LUCRETIUS, *DE RERUM NATURA* V.1165

CONTE

ACKNOWLEDGMENTS

This book's gestation lasted several years, spanned numerous locations, and both emanated from and affected different stages of my life. Although differently named back then, *Ordinary Horror* was born at Stanford. There, I found a most extraordinary community of friends who variously contributed to this project: Daniele Biffanti, Björn Buschbeck, Alberto Comparini, Phoebus Cotsapas, Donatella D'Aguanno, Jacopo Dalmasson, Corey Dansereau, Griseldo Dule, Gabriel Ellis, Nelson Endebo, Allie Gamble, Daniel Hernandez, Helen Krueger, Melih Levi, Ben Libman, Maria Massucco, Thomas McDonald, Andrea Ottolini, Mareike Reisch, Lorenzo Rota, Mitch Therieau, Declan Thompson, Leonardo Velloso, and Victoria Zurita. Paulina Choh's caring critical eye has been invaluable. Emily Goodling provided crucial feedback in the earlier stages of this project. Romina Weinberg has been a most trusted reader and interlocutor.

Among the Stanford faculty, I wish to honor Sepp Gumbrecht, Robert Harrison, and Laura Wittman, who skillfully shepherded this project and also provided support and mentorship. Shane Denson's and Thomas Harrison's commentaries left a profound mark on *Ordinary Horror*'s development. I am also indebted to Russell Berman, Amir Eshel, Marisa Galvez, Roland Greene, Mark Greif, Héctor Hoyos, Joshua Landy, Sarah Prodan, and Fred Turner.

My three years at Princeton were crucial for developing this book. I thank the Society of Fellows in its entirety, and in particular Célia Abele,

Yelena Baraz, Rhea Dexter, Michael Gordin, Dimitrios Halikias, Chloe Howe Haralambous, Marcus Lee, Bailey Sincox, Lieke van Son, and Beate Witzler. Guy St. Amant's feedback on my manuscript brought clarity and analytic rigor where it was lacking. Along with their intellectual contributions to *Ordinary Horror*, Federico Marcon, Gaetana Marrone-Puglia, and Christy Wampole have been steady sources of support on both an academic and personal level. Sandra Bermann, Jeff Dolven, Pietro Frassica, Florian Fuchs, Simone Marchesi, Meredith Martin, Michele Morelli, Serguei Oushakine, Matteo Parisi, Effie Rentzou, Nigel Smith, and Thomas Trezise have influenced this book with their suggestions, reflections, and intellectual presence. I'm also grateful for the community that I found as Faculty in Residence of New College West, and in particular to AnneMarie Luijendijk and Jo Wagner.

Timothy Campbell, Paola Gambarota, and Alessia Ricciardi's participation in my manuscript workshop gave me the opportunity to rethink some crucial aspects of *Ordinary Horror*. To Benjamin Bratton I owe the idea of coining a term to describe my approach to horror—the term I ultimately picked became the title of this book. Liara Roux's comments rendered my manuscript sharper. I also want to mention here the contributions provided by Franco Baldasso, Sophie Barstein, Fabio Camilletti, Patrizio Ceccagnoli, Emanuele Coccia, Maria Pia De Paulis, Markus Gabriel, Alessandro Giammei, Serenella Iovino, Anton Ivanov, Antonio Lucci, Marco Malvestio, Maria Anna Mariani, Paolo Pecere, Gabriele Pedullà, Stefano Serafini, Maurizio Serra, Peter Sloterdijk, and Sandy Waters.

Two anonymous readers provided frank, insightful, and, most importantly, useful feedback. Lys Weiss's elegant copyedits improved the manuscript. I thank Erica Wetter at Stanford University Press, and the rest of the team, for having believed in this project.

At New York University, where *Ordinary Horror* reached its final form, I found an intellectual community that welcomed me with open arms. I am grateful to my colleagues in the Italian Studies department—in particular to Nicola Cipani, Alison Cornish, David Forgacs, Ara Merjian, Eugenio Refini—and to Emily Apter, for having engaged with my work since we first spoke in 2023. I also owe a special debt of gratitude to all the students who thought with me about horror at Stanford, Princeton, and NYU.

Writing about ordinary horror means writing about a topic that in different capacities affects each one of us. This led to numerous conversations over the years, at times in the most implausible settings, with people whose names I forgot or perhaps never knew in the first place. I would like to thank all my unnamed interlocutors for their observations, or the retelling of their own encounters with horror, as they enriched my thinking about this quintessentially human experience.

Some of chapter 3's ideas appeared as "Descartes at War: Curzio Malaparte and Primo Levi" in *Modern Language Notes* 139 (2024): 108–31. An earlier and shorter version of chapter 5, "To Dissolve and to Shatter: The Role of Horror in Elena Ferrante," was published in *Italian Quarterly* 61, no. 239–40 (2024): 88–109.

INTRODUCTION

HORROR BEYOND HORROR

What is horror? The word evokes natural catastrophes that we hope to avoid, as well as a popular genre rife with supernatural elements. A fictional entity like Dracula brings horror to mind, but so does the concrete reality of a terminal illness. Horrifying events take place in haunted houses, but no less in war zones. What is horrible can be so close that it casts our life into crisis, or as far removed as it is in a work of fiction consumed for entertainment. No matter the chosen perspective, horror is one and many: from the Latin *horrēre* (to shiver, to stand on end), it commands attention to something both extreme and unsettling.

Horror also commands attention to itself. In recent years, this genre has grown more visible, diverse, and refined. Stephen King's staggering success complements the canonization of H. P. Lovecraft.[1] The ongoing cult fixation on horror B-movies like *Night of the Living Dead* or *Re-Animator* coexists with art-horror productions such as *The Babadook* or *Midsommar*.[2] Must-watch TV series like *The Walking Dead* echo the award-winning horror video game franchise *Resident Evil*. This public interest has paralleled scholarly research, and the field of horror studies, once relegated to the margins of the academically acceptable, has gained increasing legitimacy.[3] The genre's typical motifs have generated a range of compelling interpretations: zombies are revealed as an allegory of mindless consumerism; witches, a symbol of rebellion against patriarchy; vampires, a representation of the elite's extractivism.[4]

This, however, is just half of the story. Horror is not limited to aesthetically mediated situations, such as reading a book or watching a movie; it is a concrete possibility that may take hold of our lives at any time and through numerous circumstances. Such circumstances usually differ from those depicted in horror literature or cinema. How many among us have been chased by a masked serial killer? Likely fewer than those who have dealt with cancer. Horror, then, is not only a *genre* with its standardized motifs but also an *experience* emerging from a sprawling set of sources. The former evokes an entertainment industry with increasingly large audiences, as well as an academic field; the latter, though arguably closer to our lives, remains something that most people would rather not deal with firsthand, and an elusive subject of inquiry.[5]

But perhaps there is something to be gained by learning what Medusa's true face looks like. In *The Philosophy of Horror*, arguably the most important book in horror studies, Noël Carroll affirms that his task is to study *art-horror*—"that is, 'horror' as it serves to name a cross-art, cross-media genre."[6] I take the other path, and instead explore what I call *ordinary horror*—that is, the more commonplace and plausible horror that one may encounter in everyday life.[7]

Horror and the ordinary may seem an incongruous pairing, but by focusing on horror *beyond* the horror genre, I contend that this experience is, in fact, part of the ordinary.[8] This claim could strike my readers as counterintuitive: if anything, horror seems to imply extraordinary circumstances. To address this ostensible paradox, it is worth considering the extraordinariness of certain ordinary circumstances. Imagine the following: you are reading this book, and your phone rings. You pick it up, and someone informs you that a loved one has died in a car accident. All of a sudden, everything changes: you are frozen in place, the temperature becomes unbearable, the chatter around you oppressive, and your heart rate ramps up. At a loss for words, you ask yourself: how can *this* be happening? Your world shatters as an event beyond your control unravels the comfortable nest of predictability that you thought yourself embedded in, revealing your powerlessness since there is nothing you can do to change the present circumstances. You know that fatalities on the road are ordinary occurrences, and a quite common cause of death. But regardless of their statistical frequency, this event, as it directly affects your life, acquires the aura of extraordinariness.

The word "horror" encapsulates the nature of the experience I have just described. In our ordinary way of talking about such events, the same term and its derivatives can be used productively: it would indeed be horrible if you picked up the phone and were told that a loved one had been killed. Moreover, that horrific day might haunt you for years to come. The same can be said for countless other occurrences, such as sexual violence, financial downfall, or certain medical diagnoses; these are just some examples of how horror can emerge in our world and thus in our language as well.

Few people, if any, go through life without experiencing something horrible. Widespread as this experience may be, it is difficult to convey its subjective magnitude. Can one truly retell what it felt like to see a loved one wither away in a hospice? Is it possible to express to others what it meant to live through a devastating earthquake? After such an event cast one's life into crisis, the gap between an experience and its retelling becomes starkly apparent.

This matter is of particular interest for literary texts. If one of their distinctive features is a desire to portray the human experience in all its complexity, the intersubjective opacity that shrouds moments of horror becomes a charged question, to be addressed by the writer and the critic alike: how may horror be adequately addressed on a narrative level, in a way that conveys its experiential thickness and the subjective upheaval it carries?

This question already projects us beyond the horror genre: if horror can intrude into ordinary life, why should we confine its manifestations to a specific genre? Similarly, the presence of horror does not necessarily define a book or a movie in its entirety: for example, if a novel contains a rape scene, it does not mean that it belongs in the "horror fiction" section of a library, even though a consensus about the horrifying nature of the act should not be hard to achieve.

The complexity of the topic is apparent: horror is a recognizable genre that encompasses motifs such as monsters and haunted houses, but is also the word at the center of a lexical family that we use to describe events ranging from genocide to terminal disease. It can be the defining feature of a book, or just one of the many experiences portrayed within it. It is a sought-after form of entertainment, or something that we hope to avoid for as long as possible. For all these reasons, too, horror is one and many.[9]

Rather than viewing horror's multiplicity as an intractable blockage that condemns us to silence, I see it instead as a point of departure and an opportunity to better understand what we mean by this term. In his *Philosophical Investigations*, Ludwig Wittgenstein writes that a philosophical problem has the form: "I do not know my way about."[10] This book provides an orientation within the problem of horror beyond the horror genre: it is an attempt at making better sense of what ordinary horror is, its significance for our time, and its representation in the arts.

In lieu of applying a ready-made theory to a corpus, my method does the opposite and finds in what is not typically associated with horror the building blocks for thinking of it outside of the boundaries of a genre. If horror truly haunts our lives and therefore our literature, it will also be found in the area of the literary world that I know best. Accordingly, I take modern Italian prose as my site for fieldwork, and there learn how to read for ordinary horror. Addressing the horror hiding in plain sight in a canon typically not associated with it unveils what is unique in Italian ordinary horror, and how this experience manifests in a tradition where the horror genre has been left to the margins of high literature.

In offering a blueprint to analyze the presence of horror in works not part of the eponymous genre, this book teaches how to see texts under a new light. While focused on Italian authors, the interpretative framework provided here is not limited to the Italian tradition. With a broad reach, *Ordinary Horror* paves the way for further comparative and transmedial inquiries. By placing texts first and remaining receptive to what arises during our encounter with them, I encourage close attention to the specific nature of the material under scrutiny. We must avoid essentializing horror in order to recognize its cultural, historical, and subjective particularities, alongside the distinct ways that different canons and media represent it. This heterogeneity should be taken not as a hindrance, but as symptomatic of the richness of the matter at hand. *Ordinary Horror* seeks to be a starting point rather than an endpoint, opening a discussion rather than closing it.

To lay secure foundations for the study of horror beyond the genre, I will now elaborate on the three main argumentative thrusts of these opening paragraphs: first, the relationship between horror and the ordinary; second, the interrelation between horror's phenomenology and aesthetics; and third, horror's presence in modernity and modern Italian literature.

THE ORDINARINESS OF HORROR

The complexity in approaching horror outside the boundaries of the genre can make the topic seem too vast to be approached at all. Indeed, where might one begin? If the study of the genre rests on a recognizable canon and a set of established methodologies, the analysis of more ordinary forms of horror can seem like a hopelessly vague scholarly endeavor. To overcome this potential blockage, this book starts from what we already know: that horror may manifest in our lives, in our ordinary experiences, and therefore in ordinary language as well.

To elucidate the productiveness of this point of departure, I turn to the work of British philosopher of language J. L. Austin and in particular to his 1956 paper "A Plea for Excuses." This essay shows how examining everyday excuses illuminates the subtlety and precision of ordinary language in clarifying human actions and intentions. But I invoke it here less for its topic than for its rare methodological intervention, as it provides guidelines on how to analyze ordinary language and where such a study may lead. In discussing the relevance of the subject of excuses from a philosophical point of view, Austin invites his audience to reflect on "*what we should say when*, and so why and what we should mean by it." Austin considers this a methodological invitation: it is "*one* philosophical method," among others, to approach a problem that troubles us.[11] For him, ordinary language—the everyday ways people speak and use words in real-life situations—is a formidable repository of knowledge and a most reliable starting point from which to address philosophical questions.

Austin states that when problems are addressed from this perspective, "we are looking again not *merely* at words (or 'meanings', whatever they may be) but also at the realities we use the words to talk about: we are using a sharpened awareness of words to sharpen our perception of, though not as the final arbiter of, phenomena."[12] Ordinary language reveals and develops our understanding of reality rather than being something we arbitrarily append to it: there are likely good reasons, he suggests, if we use certain terms to speak about certain phenomena. A careful consideration of "*what we should say when*" goes beyond linguistic analysis, as it compels us to think more thoroughly about the phenomena that we are talking about in the first place. For this reason, Austin calls this method "linguistic phenomenology," while conceding that the formulation "is rather a mouthful."[13]

This is a point of departure, a "*first* word." As Austin repeatedly underlines, ordinary language "is not the last word: in principle it can everywhere be supplemented and improved upon and superseded."[14] Far from being a fatalistic bowing down to the given, an analysis of ordinary language is a descriptive rather than prescriptive endeavor, one that seeks to clarify something readily present to us that we still approach in an uncertain, confused manner. It is a preliminary analysis, to be supported by other forms of inquiry.

To bring Austin's question to bear on the topic of this book, we may ask: when should we use the word "horror," and what do we mean by it? Within the context of literary criticism, this question also turns into an invitation to pay close attention to texts that bring to mind horror without quite belonging to the genre. Unwinding this thread allows us to attain a heightened awareness of how we use this term, which, in turn, sharpens our understanding of horror itself.

This approach may come across as impressionistic and lacking in sophistication, but this assumes that focusing on the ordinary is intellectually flat. This need not be the case. After decades of high theory's intoxicating abstractions, a return to the ordinary is opening up a refreshingly immediate and relatable way of thinking about literature. In her 2015 book *The Limits of Critique*, Rita Felski contends that the hermeneutics of suspicion championed by deconstruction, new historicism, and poststructuralism have promoted an adversarial approach to literature, narrowing the critic's field of vision by privileging the treatment of texts as objects to be decoded for hidden power structures, ideologies, or repressed meanings.[15] While this is surely productive, Felski argues that other methods are possible and should be pursued with similar vigor. In *Uses of Literature*, Felski proposes the category of "recognition" as one such way of paying attention to how and why a reader develops an emotional engagement with a text. A reader, she writes, may feel "addressed, summoned, called to account by a text."[16] Through a similar process we may also recognize, or be addressed by, the horror present in what we read: if a particular scene comes across as horrifying, there are probably good reasons for it, even if those reasons are initially unarticulated. This itself can be a starting point that, in giving us pause, raises a host of questions for further inquiry.[17]

Echoing Felski's work, I believe that one of the limits of critique is that it may make one suspicious of the ordinary. If what truly matters is hidden, and if the critic's gaze ought to be trained to plumb such depths, are we willing to meaningfully engage with and respect what stands in front of our eyes? Along similar lines, Toril Moi explicitly argues for the groundbreaking potential of focusing on the ordinary in the study of literature. In her *Revolution of the Ordinary: Literary Studies after Wittgenstein, Austin, and Cavell*, she invites readers to pay renewed attention to the concrete, context-rich ways people actually speak and write, to ground literary analysis in the complexity and spontaneity of how meaning operates in human life and literary texts. Drawing from the philosophers of language explicitly named in her book's title, Moi argues that criticism often stems from the question: "Why this?"[18] Before anything else—before methodological disputes and disciplinary quirks—it is a sense of confusion that often sets an inquiry in motion: "If the critic doesn't have a problem, if nothing really puzzles her about the text, she really has no reason to investigate it. A reading is an attempt to get clear on something."[19]

To address Moi's "Why this?" we may start from Austin's "*what we should say when.*" A problem that troubled me was how in certain texts a realistic descriptive framework was momentarily suspended by scenes that departed from verisimilitude—the sun suddenly turned into a rotten orange, a platoon of soldiers into zombies. Why this? What might this strange disturbance in a text's realism indicate? I found my way out of this confusion by thinking through what the passages that gave me pause brought to mind and sought to represent. My readers will surely have already guessed that I relate these passages to horror. This is not because I experienced it upon reading them—a claim difficult to generalize and substantiate—but because, in ordinary language, the word *horror* felt appropriate to describe what was present on the page. For example, even if I am not always and necessarily horrified while reading about the Holocaust, I will most likely grant that the word *horror* can be meaningfully used in relation to it.[20]

From this precritical response to a text, a critical analysis can begin: while first I did not know my way about a given matter, now I have managed to forge a path ahead. The term "ordinary" in my book's title also suggests a connection with the concrete, the relatable, perhaps even the already known. The instantiations of horror that I will discuss are all plausible ones in the context of a life, as they take place in texts that do not portray any fantastical creatures or supernatural happenings. From this perspective, I am following the Wittgensteinian invitation to bring a word back to its everyday use[21]—the word "horror" in this case, beyond the horror genre. To be sure, our use of the word "horror" in relation to a genre is also part of ordinary language. Yet this is half of the story. *Ordinary Horror* approaches the other half, the one that connects more directly with our everyday experiences, and thus what we are familiar with already.

In his Dewey Lecture, Hilary Putnam addresses the relevance of ordinary language when thinking about the ordinary facts of our lives and why he believes that literature plays a crucial role in this regard:

> If asked *why* I think our ordinary concepts are important, I would have to respond with a question: If "ordinary language" is just something to be sneered at, then is the whole vocabulary we have for describing the world of human agents to be either despised or else replaced by the "Newspeak" of some social science? To me it seems clear that the descriptions of human life we find in the novels of Tolstoy or George Eliot are not mere *entertainment*; they teach us to perceive and describe what goes on in social and individual life. And such descriptions require the many subtle distinctions that ordinary language has made available to us. The question of the relevance or irrelevance of "how we speak" is not just a question for philosophers, although it is that too. It is a question for philosophers, because once ordinary language is laughed out of the room, philosophical theories are no longer held responsible at all to the ways we actually speak and actually live; but it is a question for more than just philosophers, because, at bottom, contempt for ordinary language is contempt for the humanities.[22]

The humanist should not shy away from the ordinary; indeed, the analysis of the latter is one of the most valuable tasks the former can accomplish, and literature, Putnam reminds us, is a rich venue to learn more about the ordinary facts of human life. While contempt for ordinary language is arguably contempt for the humanities, I believe, echoing Felski and Moi's debates regarding the hermeneutics of suspicion, that a similar contempt may be found in literary criticism that overlooks ordinary ways of relating to texts: if the immediately available content of something that we read strikes us and gives us pause, that in itself can be a point of critical departure that should be granted full scholarly legitimacy. At times, Wittgenstein writes, "the aspects of things that are most important for us are hidden because of their simplicity and familiarity. (One is unable to notice something—because it is always before one's eyes.) [. . .] We fail to be struck by what, once seen, is most striking and most powerful."[23]

Among the many possible uses of literature, one is to provide the material to carry out what Wittgenstein calls a "grammatical investigation." This concept refers to the careful study of how words are used in everyday language in a way that clarifies how they gain their meaning from context, patterns of life, and shared human activities.[24] Literary texts provide a rich repository of material to start a grammatical investigation and thus orient ourselves in relation to a problem. The context-rich ways in which these works depict the complexity of human life can be a site for fieldwork, from which we may learn more about the interrelation between ordinary language and ordinary experiences.[25] Moi writes: "a grammatical investigation investigates whatever it is that makes us puzzled and confused."[26] This book undertakes such an investigation into the presence of horror in modern Italian literature beyond the horror genre, and thus in our lives as well. It is just one approach among others; to invoke Austin once more, this is a starting point, as a grammatical investigation can take many forms and directions.

Readers may still wonder whether one can legitimately study an experience through literature. Would it not be wiser to restrict myself solely to textual analysis and avoid mixing literary depictions of horror with its lived manifestations? While my primary object of study is indeed the former, I follow Putnam in affirming the insight literary works provide into the latter—that is, "what goes on in social and individual life." Rather than a category error, I consider this joint approach a way to better understand not only horror in itself but also how this experience is narrated. These are two sides of the same coin: experiences are subjective, shrouded by intersubjective opacity, and become intelligible and communicable through narratives.[27] While this is by no means the only method of analysis, we should not dismiss literature's capacity to enrich our understanding of horror. To this end, each chapter of *Ordinary Horror* contributes to an incrementally nuanced taxonomy of this experience through a text-driven engagement with its literary depictions.

To understand how literature helps us make sense of this experience,

I will now articulate two key methodological choices: the analysis of individual horror *scenes* rather than horror *books*, and the study of what I term the "aesthetics of deformation" as a key literary technique for conveying horror's subjective magnitude.

HORRIFYING MOMENTS, SCENES OF DEFORMATION

The thought experiment of learning about the death of a loved one illustrates a key consequence of horrifying events: they make your experience of the present radically change. As horror takes hold of your life, the room closes in around you, you become lightheaded, perhaps slightly nauseous. The surrounding world remains the same and yet it *feels* different. Structurally similar shifts take place under many different circumstances: if I received particularly good news upon waking up, the walk to my office would become more pleasant. The opposite is also true: if I had a terrible day, being on an overcrowded train would be a much more unpleasant experience than it already is.

These are all distinct ways of phenomenologically engaging with the world. For the purposes of this book, I take phenomenology to be a descriptive discipline that provides an account of the structures of consciousness as they manifest in our immediate, first-person perception. Its focus is our experience of the world, with "world" here meaning the all-encompassing background against which our experiences arise, as the realm of possibilities that surrounds us and in which we live.[28]

Phenomenology does not disdain the ordinary; in fact, it takes the ordinary as foundational for its methods. Edmund Husserl, its originator, called upon philosophers to "go back to the 'things themselves'"[29]—that is, to focus on how phenomena actually appear in experience. But isn't this also an invitation to pay attention to the ordinary? If we understand Husserl's dictum as a call to examine the ways things are given in experience, and to shift from what he terms a "natural attitude" (the everyday stance in which we take the world and its objects for granted) to a "phenomenological attitude" (the reflective stance that suspends prior assumptions to investigate how phenomena are constituted in consciousness), then we must largely rely on ordinary language, even if just as a starting point. This shift of attitudes utilizes a methodological bracketing, suspending assumptions and judgments in order to explore the structures of consciousness underpinning a given situation. Yet, in undertaking it, we must be cautious not to throw out the baby with the bathwater and thus remove ourselves from the everyday world entirely. In other words, by doing phenomenology we *build* upon the ordinary, rather than *dismiss* it. This is because ordinary concepts and ordinary language are essential to describe ordinary experiences.[30] As Moi writes, "If we take phenomenology to be a way of doing philosophy which brackets questions of essence and ontology, and instead tries to grasp phenomena as they appear to human consciousness through thick descriptions, ordinary language philosophers will find its procedures, if not its underlying metaphysical commitments, congenial."[31]

After departing from the ordinary, phenomenology returns to it with new insight and a clearer understanding. The phenomenologist starts from and develops the common-sense knowledge that our experience of the world is not neutral and that, depending on contextual factors, the same situation can be colored in a variety of ways. This book focuses on the phenomenology of horror—in other words, it studies how we experience the world when we are held by horror's grip and what the underpinnings of this experience are.[32] It is important to keep in mind that these questions do not belong solely to the sphere of phenomenology, as they could also be meaningfully addressed by more naturalistic accounts of consciousness, such as those provided by biochemistry or neurophysiology. But while the knowledge that being horrified involves a particular response from my amygdala or a prolonged release of cortisol is surely meaningful, this does not address the qualia of horror—that is, the subjective dimension of what it is like to be horrified, its distinctive texture as this experience restructures our perception of both self and world in that moment.

To further clarify the magnitude of this phenomenological shift, I turn to what Martin Heidegger termed *Ereignis*, which in German means "event, incident, or occurrence." In Heidegger's philosophy, *Ereignis* is an event through which Being suddenly and radically discloses itself, appropriating the perceiving subject into a new mode of relating to the world. His reflections on the topic are difficult, scattered throughout his production, and mutate considerably in a period that ranges from 1919 (his first mention of the concept) to the last years of his life.[33] Yet, a key feature of *Ereignis* is that it "reorders and centers my world anew"[34]—it is something overpowering, "something irremediably excessive"[35] that alters the very parameters of subject and world, provoking a rupture in our experience of reality.

In Heidegger, *Ereignis* signifies a crisis that forces us to transcend ourselves, and is colored by tints of renewal or disclosure; it is a break toward something, not mere destruction.[36] But what if that was not the case? What if an event—a horrifying event—could not be redeemed or repurposed? While I will repeatedly caution against overdetermining horror's consequences, I consider this experience an event that involves a break from everyday reality. Heidegger too emphasizes the shock (*Erschrecken*) that an *Ereignis* involves:[37] as an event unfolds, our ordinary suddenly becomes extraordinary.

A moment of horror transposes us out of familiar phenomenological coordinates via a radical shift in how we relate to the world. Horror, as I will argue, unveils the latent fragility, unpredictability, and uncontrollability of human existence. Before considering the aesthetic implications of thinking about horror in terms of *Ereignis*, the gap between phenomenology as it relates to living subjects and the kind of phenomenological analysis that I apply to literary texts must be addressed.

Phenomenological analysis thirsts for sources that give an account of the experiential thickness of being in the midst of life.[38] Echoing Putnam, I believe that literary texts are one such source. The kind of phenomenological analysis that I apply to literature, crucially, is not that of reception theory in the vein of Hans Robert Jauss or Wolfgang Iser.[39] I maintain the importance of such work in relation to horror—both within and beyond the horror genre—although it comes with substantial perils when it seeks to generalize its findings to a multiplicity of readers. More narrowly, I propose to adhere more closely to the text and to the text only: rather than the reader's phenomenological response, I am interested in the phenomenology depicted on the page. Otherwise said, to meet my critical goals I need not posit a horrified reader; all I need is a horrified character or narrating voice for recognizing the horror present on the page. This approach sidesteps the difficulties inherent in presupposing a horrified response to a text that depicts something horrific: depending on contextual factors, I may or may not be directly horrified upon reading about cancer or the Holocaust, yet still grant that the word "horror" can be meaningfully applied to both. In so doing, ordinary language intersects with my phenomenological approach and provides a backstop against essentialization. Simultaneously, it also allows me to group together texts that may not consistently rely on the word "horror" to describe what is happening on the page: the death of a loved one can be described as terrible, mournful, devastating, or profoundly unsettling, yet each of these descriptors may point toward an experience that partakes of the structure and semantics of horror without necessarily being named as such.

Being receptive to the phenomenology on display in a text involves paying close attention to it and to its oscillations: as our lives are characterized by experiential diversity, so too is much of the literature we read. A plausible multiplicity of rich descriptions of characters and their actions is a defining feature of literary narratives and makes Hector's bravery coexist with the horror he experiences facing Achilles at the gates of Troy. At the same time none of these experiences can, in principle, be said to be the defining feature of a book: as already noted, if a novel describes a horrifying rape, it does not necessarily mean that we will find the book in the "horror fiction" section of a library.

To pinpoint and zoom in on the conspicuous yet not totalizing presence of horror in texts beyond the horror genre, I propose an approach that I term *reading for scenes*. This approach sets aside questions of genre to focus on *what* is narrated in a specific passage rather than *where* the passage occurs. Reading for scenes is a close-reading practice that involves an in-depth analysis of the selected passages as they narrate specific events or situations: to follow this method means to embrace a kind of localism, as reading for scenes grants analytical value to a passage even if that moment is atypical or tangential to the text's main thrust.[40] Literary scenes, of course, are constitutive of novels or memoirs, but they also crop up in other forms of writing, such as philosophical texts, where they can manifest as anecdotes, fictional dialogues, or brief vignettes. Here, too, reading for the agile and focused approach of scenes allows me to address the dynamics present in such passages, without presupposing their presence in the rest of the work.

In this book I select scenes of horror, and, without essentializing this experience or extending it to the rest of the text, I pay close attention to what is horrifying whom, when, and why, and consider how this experience is depicted in the selected passage. The local and descriptive approach of reading for scenes allows me to register the horror present in a given passage as the reader encounters it. In setting aside the analysis of hidden meanings or repressed emotions—to echo a title by literary critic Heather Love—my method of reading for ordinary horror stays close to a text, without necessarily having to go deep in order to function.[41]

This approach does not dismiss questions of genre, or the study of a text as a unitary whole; on the contrary, it coexists with them. Without claiming to exhaustively interpret a work in its entirety, reading for scenes privileges the close-reading of specific passages to reveal their inner workings and thus expand our understanding of the analyzed sources. In so doing, it also validates our experience as readers of being struck by a specific moment of a text, something that may not reflect our overall attitude regarding that work in its totality.

Moi's invitation to start a critical journey via the simple question "Why this?" resonates with the form of critical engagement I am proposing. A particular scene may give us pause, and demand further scrutiny from us. Moi suggests something similar; in discussing how a section of a text may implicate the reader and command from them a specific form of attention that translates into a critical analysis, she writes: "In this situation, there is no recipe for how to begin, or for where to go. All we can do is to find a 'blur or block from which to start,' as Cavell puts it in *The Claim of Reason*. That 'blur or block' may be a passage or a theme that haunts us, to which we always return, something that grabs our attention and refuses to let it go.'"[42]

Reading for horror scenes across different authors also makes the critic receptive to patterns that could go unnoticed if encountered in isolation. This allows me to build bridges between texts by identifying common literary techniques that weave together authors otherwise difficult to analyze comparatively. One of the key results of this inquiry is the identification of a technique embraced by a number of canonical modern Italian authors to depict moments of horror: the departure from verisimilitude and the interpolation of deforming descriptions into an otherwise realistic framework. By "deforming," I refer to a momentary breakdown of the descriptive standard established by the text: this could mean, for instance, a realistic scene where the sun transforms into a rotten orange or a group of soldiers into the living dead. Crucially, these transformations are not permanent, and the previous descriptive standard is soon recuperated—indeed, if the sun remained a rotten orange, or truly was one, the text could not be considered realistic anymore.

I call this momentary breakdown of realism *aesthetics of deformation*—a term that I use to encompass the departures from verisimilitude also present in a host of literary techniques ranging from Viktor Shklovsky's defamiliarization or Tzvetan Todorov's fantastic to those typical of Expressionism or the grotesque.[43] Even if only for a scene, the text mutates its features, becomes disquieting, and what we would expect to find in a horror book appears in works not part of that genre: just as horror can all of a sudden take hold of someone's life, so it can also become a scene's most salient element. A text's aesthetic oscillations mirror how horror may manifest in our everydayness: instead of being something that can be controlled or contained—even by a genre—it is an event, an interloper that manifests itself when and where we may not expect it, in literature and in our existence as well.[44]

Aesthetics and phenomenology also connect insofar as the aesthetics of deformation is a way of reflecting the phenomenologically upending nature of horror: just as an event may rip apart the safe predictability of our present, a deforming description rends a tear in the fabric of a text. The thought experiment that opened this introduction highlights this connection: as soon as you receive that phone call, does your present *feel* the same way as it did a few seconds ago? To be sure, nothing external has changed: if someone took a photo of the room where you are sitting before and after the call, the two images would only minimally differ. But for you, as the subject in the grip of horror, the world could not be any more different. Via the aesthetics of deformation, a literary text can give a sense of the magnitude of this phenomenological shift—a shift that remains mostly unseen by external observers.

If horror is an event (*Ereignis*) in which the world is ruptured and reconstituted, then literary texts that portray this process may deform their narrative world to represent the experience. A horrifying event does not merely slot into a stable reality like a puzzle piece; instead, it unravels and reshapes the reality experienced by the subject. A realistic narrative that suddenly splinters into surreal description, temporal disjunction, or unreliable perception can be read as mimetic of a moment of horror: the *form* of the story breaks to signal that the very *world* of the story is breaking.

I present these ideas here for propaedeutic reasons: they establish a foundation of conceptual underpinnings, methods, and stakes that the following chapters will explore and expand upon. To summarize: first, I am using an ordinary understanding of the word "horror" to identify a set of literary sources; second, I am seeking to better understand what ties those sources together through close-reading of scenes; third, I am identifying a shared aesthetic based on deformation; fourth, I am explaining that aesthetic through an appeal to phenomenology. To conclude this introduction's preparatory work, the following section explains the focus on works from modern Italian literature and provides a chapter overview.

MODERN ITALIAN HORROR

As a scholar of modern Italian literature, I chose this canon to learn how to read for ordinary horror. This choice in part responds to practical concerns: my knowledge of Italian literature allows me to better pick and contextualize my sources, identify the meaningfulness of patterns whose relevance I might otherwise not fully recognize, and more surely trace intertextual connections between authors. While *Ordinary Horror* reveals the subtle yet pervasive presence of this experience in a canon not typically associated with it, a key question must first be addressed: what is distinctive about horror in modernity? And, in turn, how can this help us to better understand how horror manifests in modern Italian literature?

The horrors of modern history have not gone unnoticed. Around the midpoint of the twentieth century, Theodor W. Adorno and Max Horkheimer memorably and tragically observed that the wholly enlightened Earth was radiant with triumphant calamity.[45] Today, the proliferation of recording and sharing devices combined with the hyperconnectedness of our societies results in our nervous systems experiencing a constant influx of horrifying stimuli: if we are lucky enough to be sheltered from it in our everyday lives, all it takes is scrolling through our feeds for us to be exposed to the horrors manifesting elsewhere, including point-of-view recordings of armed conflicts and school shootings, footage of environmental disasters and forced displacements, reportage about teen suicide and terminal diseases.[46] From this point of view, too, horror is part of the ordinary, as a presence that keeps casting an unsettling shadow over our world. In the light of this, according to Peter Sloterdijk, the thinker of our epoch should "pause beneath the petrifying gaze of Medusa and contemplate it as an icon of present-day being."[47] But what, exactly, makes an event horrifying, and Medusa one of the goddesses of modernity? Rather than listing the horrors of our world, I seek to answer these questions.

This book understands horror as "the experience of forced powerlessness."[48] To experience horror means to see one's world cast into crisis by something that renders the subject incapable of meaningfully affecting a negative present situation: if you picked up the phone and someone told you a loved one had died, your impotence would be one of the salient features of the experience. If warfare did not strip people of agency and inflict unwanted suffering, we would not speak of its horrors. If there were an easy treatment for cancer, it would not be a horrible disease. This applies to the horror genre, too: if Leatherface could easily be stopped, *The Texas Chainsaw Massacre* would not be a horror movie. Attending carefully to horror's contextual specificities does not imply that each instantiation of this experience differs entirely from others. Indeed, the very fact that ordinary language permits diverse circumstances to be recognized collectively as horrifying suggests that something binds them together from an experiential point of view.

As horror confronts us with the limits of our control, this experience acquires a particularly troubling flavor in modernity, a period whose goal is encapsulated by the Cartesian dictum of becoming "masters and possessors of nature"[49]—here understood as a desire for control over the world and its circumstances. Modernity's desire to extend the reach of human agency and, in turn, diminish the space of impotence, uncertainty, and the absence of control has been the subject of in-depth studies by philosopher Stephen Toulmin. Toulmin argues that from the seventeenth century onward the standards of deterministic predictability set by Newton's laws of motion have been extended to other spheres of human life and aimed at the creation of "Cosmopolis," a society as rationally ordered as Newtonian physics. The breakthroughs and paradigm shifts of modernity seemed to promise, to paraphrase Galileo, the deciphering of the book of nature, which would lead, in the words of Descartes, to its mastery and possession. Newton, Galileo, and Descartes, alongside other figures such as Bacon and Condorcet, are the fathers of what, according to Toulmin, is modernity's main tendency: the rearrangement of human knowledge and life according to an agenda of prediction and control.[50]

Although coming from a different disciplinary standpoint, statistician Nassim Nicholas Taleb offers a similar take on the topic, defining modernity as "humans' large-scale domination of the environment, the systematic smoothing of the world's jaggedness, and the stifling of volatility and stressors." "Modernity," he continues, "corresponds to the systematic extraction of humans from their randomness-laden ecology—physical and social, even epistemological."[51] In the words of sociologist Hartmut Rosa, modernity is "structurally driven toward making the world calculable, predictable, and controllable in every possible respect."[52]

These attempts have undeniably led to some staggering successes, as the ages-old tendency of mankind to exert control over its environment saw a dramatic acceleration in recent centuries, in addition to a qualitative leap ahead thanks to technoscientific breakthroughs. This tendency promoted a shift in episteme in the affected societies—that is, a shift in how a community's framing of its collective knowledge influences politics, individual choices, and ways of thinking.[53] In modernity, solutionism became more and more the rule of the land: to a phenomenon corresponds a scientific explanation; to an illness, a specific treatment; to a cause of risk, an insurance policy.[54] To be increasingly in control of the world and its circumstances involves expecting that control to further expand; but as control expands, one may also become less and less accustomed to unexpected events and believe oneself to be sheltered from them more than warranted.[55]

While Jürgen Habermas approaches the question of modernity from a different standpoint, his description of this period as an "unfinished project"[56] applies here as well: the ever increasing complexity of the world keeps frustrating modernity's domesticating attempts. This complexity is also a feedback loop produced by modernity itself, since technoscience functions both as a territorializing and deterritorializing force. As suggested by Rosa's book title, *The Uncontrollability of the World*, we are still dealing with this very uncontrollability, despite our undeniable progress in operating on and engineering the ecosystems with which we interact.

The study of ordinary horror is thus of particular interest in the modern period, as this experience undoes some of this epoch's main presuppositions: against the desire for ever increasing mastery over the world and its circumstances, horror's forced powerlessness acts as a somber reminder that the reach of our control is limited, that we remain exposed to events whose magnitude can unravel our lives, and, ultimately, that the house of modernity is still haunted by what it sought to exorcise.

Thinking of horror in modernity thus acquires a new relevance as a topic of scholarly inquiry. Beyond referring to the analysis of a genre that develops in this era, it points to an experience that in modernity has a uniquely disturbing flavor. From this perspective, too, horror returns to the ordinary, the common, and the widespread, evoking not only a current enshrined as canonical in certain traditions such as the Anglo-German ones, but an experience woven in the very fabric of modern literature across canons. *Ordinary Horror* focuses on the Italian canon and, through this change in perspective, reveals horror's conspicuous yet overlooked presence in it.

Italian literature's relation with horror is indeed complex. While horror radiates from the canon's origins through Dante's *Inferno* and Boccaccio's depictions of the plague, this term is not typically associated with the highest expressions of modern Italian literature.[57] As if to symbolize how its presence may be attributed to foreign influences, Italian uses two different words to refer to "horror" as an experience and as a genre: while the Italian word "*orrore*" is used for the former, the latter is addressed with the English loanword "horror." In analyzing the relation between Italian modernity, modern Italian literature, and modernity at large, Alessandra Aloisi and Fabio Camilletti argue that modern Italian culture represents "the encounter between the legacy of Classical antiquity, Catholic religion, and philosophical rationalism," thereby "rooting cultural identity in the worship of aesthetic 'measure,' the refusal of superstition, and philosophical/theological rigour."[58] While this could in part explain why a horror writer of the caliber of Mary Shelley or Edgar Allan Poe does not feature in the highest echelons of the Italian canon, once we shift our attention to *orrore* a different way of approaching this tradition becomes possible, and this experience acquires a newfound centrality therein.[59]

Ordinary Horror focuses on a host of canonical Italian authors, none of whom is typically associated with horror. Rather than reassessing forgotten names or unearthing overlooked movements, this book shows the importance of ordinary horror in the making of modern Italian literature—effectively reading parts of the canon uncanonically. A central wager of this project is that horror is not simply present in each of the authors analyzed, but should be considered a key component of their production. At times, this focus will formalize and expand on something already beyond the contentious, such as the connection between Primo Levi's writings on the Holocaust and horror; at other times, it will articulate more subtle links, such as the connection in Anna Maria Ortese's work between horror and poverty. In so doing, *Ordinary Horror* parallels recent attempts at identifying the presence of subterranean currents in Italian literature, such as the fantastic, the gothic, or the weird;[60] crucially, however, it identifies in horror an experience that overtly manifests in key Italian authors rather than a genre or a mode that remained overlooked in, at the margins of, or dismissed by the Italian canon.

Five interconnected chapters develop a taxonomy of horror's characteristics alongside its presence in modern Italian literature. Moving from the nineteenth century with Giacomo Leopardi to the twenty-first century with Elena Ferrante, this book with its broad chronological scope and diverse canon studies the presence of horror across various individual experiences, historical periods, and stages of societal change. Covering eight authors whose production spans more than a hundred years, *Ordinary Horror* uses polyphony as a means both to counter the establishment of a singular normative model of horror and to foster innovative connections between writers through their engagements with horrifying experiences. Chapters 1 and 5, each devoted to a single author, open and close the arc of this book through dialogue with one another. Chapters 2, 3, and 4 each feature a dyad of authors; through the lens of ordinary horror, they provide a comparative examination of figures rarely, if ever, studied in tandem. These couplings are asymmetrical and echo the interplay between melody and countermelody in music: the first and main author, whose analysis constitutes the bulk of the chapter, introduces one or more central themes, while the second author adds nuance or a contrasting perspective. This dynamic avoids the establishment of a normative model and fosters a richer, more layered exploration of horror's characteristics, including its temporality and its impact on the affected individual.

Ordinary Horror starts with the nineteenth-century polymath Giacomo Leopardi. Drawing primarily from his philosophical diary *Zibaldone*, I elevate Leopardi as the central figure of my understanding of horror. Through his work, I establish this book's framework on three levels. First historically, by identifying the desire to maximize control over the world and its circumstances as a primary characteristic of modernity, which Leopardi deems unattainable given the complexity of reality considered from our incomplete and fallible perspective. Second phenomenologically, by describing states when a present situation throws the subject's habitual assumptions and perceptions of reality into crisis, emphasizing that a darkening of our world is a possibility that can never be excluded from our experiential horizon. Third aesthetically, by demonstrating how literary descriptions can convey the way the same situation, due to contextual factors, can cause turmoil for one person while being perceived as neutral by others; tracing a path through Leopardi's work, I illustrate how even an Italian garden in bloom can become horrifying under specific circumstances. In defining horror as "the experience of forced powerlessness," this chapter also distinguishes it from the sublime: in the latter, the subject is in a position of safety concerning what overwhelms; in the former, what overwhelms directly and negatively affects the subject.

After chapter 1 sets the book's tone by emphasizing the role of powerlessness in horror, chapter 2 turns to the beginning of the twentieth century with Carlo Michelstaedter and Luigi Pirandello to study the temporality of this experience. Michelstaedter's *Persuasion and Rhetoric*, a philosophical work from which I analyze literary scenes, depicts transient instances of horror through moments of crisis and nightmares, which the subject soon overcomes without suffering any long-lasting consequences. Conversely, with Pirandello's essay "On Humor" and the novels *The Late Mattia Pascal* and *One, No One and One Hundred Thousand*, I show how a single moment of horror can also have enduring effects for the subject experiencing it. I thereby distinguish the present-centered nature of horror from the dialectics between past and present that inform trauma, and caution against essentializing horror's temporality and repercussions on a life. This chapter also addresses how Expressionism intersects with my aesthetics of deformation, and shows that horror can erupt even in the protected lives of the socially elite despite the bulwarks of socioeconomic privilege. The growing popularity of insurance policies in the early twentieth century, thematized in both Michelstaedter and Pirandello, allows me to introduce what I term the "safety fallacy" (the overreliance on the control one believes one exerts over life) and discuss how it creates a false impression of security—an impression that horror undoes.

Chapter 3 moves from the downfall of individual hubris to an event that seems to have made horror widespread—World War II. Taking up Curzio Malaparte's wartime novels *Kaputt* and *The Skin* and Primo Levi's writings on Auschwitz, I focus on their reactions to situations so horrifying as to appear unbelievable. If chapter 2 conceptually revolved around the question "how can this be happening *to me*?" here the emphasis shifts and the question becomes: "how can this be happening *at all*?" Drawing from Taleb, I discuss horror's relation to "black swan" events. These are rare, unpredictable events that carry an enormous impact. In particular, I triangulate horror, "black swan" events, and an intertext present in both Malaparte and Levi: the figure of René Descartes. With Malaparte as an anti-Cartesian and Levi as a self-proclaimed Cartesian, I examine how horrifying "black swan" events challenge the Cartesian project of becoming master and possessor of the world. The undoing of the Cartesian subject—the modern subject par excellence—enables a better discussion of the role that horror plays in modernity. Unspooling this thread, I show that even when horror appears commonplace and foundational for the examined historical context, it maintains a subjective strain: a victorious army like the Americans in 1944 Naples, just like the SS in Auschwitz, can be in the midst of the horrifying without their worlds being cast into crisis.

Chapter 4, featuring Anna Maria Ortese and Giuseppe Berto, steps into the postwar period of economic growth and increasing national cohesion to explore some of the unexceptional and everyday ways horror may belong to existence in peacetime. These authors' works do not feature the outlier events present in Malaparte and Levi's; instead, this chapter centers on sources of horror that are widespread yet, precisely because of this, are also banal and mundane, such as poverty and illness. Ortese's collection of short stories and literary reportage, *Neapolitan Chronicles,* depicts a postwar Naples where part of the population's living conditions are nothing short of horrifying even in the absence of extreme circumstances such as warfare. The chapter discusses how Ortese's twisting of horror tropes, such as that of the haunted house, sought to disrupt processes of habituation and normalization that might render acceptable living conditions that should remain unacceptable. With Berto's autobiographical novel *Incubus,* conversely, I analyze this author's attempts to make tolerable a situation that inherently seems to resist habituation, and discuss why novelty, the overwhelming, and unpredictability feature prominently in horror's phenomenology. Focusing on scenes of the novel that describe how illness provided a recurring source of horror, I show how our own self and body, rather than what lies outside of us, may be enough to turn our existence into a nightmare.

Turning toward Elena Ferrante's work, chapter 5 begins within the

toes; this one is injured in its bark and afflicted by the air or by the sun penetrating the wound; that other one has a damaged trunk, or roots; that other has many dry leaves; that other one has its flowers gnawed at, nibbled; that other one has its fruits pierced, eaten away. That plant is too warm, this one too cold; too much light, too much shade; too wet, too dry. One cannot grow or spread easily because there are obstacles and obstructions; another finds nowhere to lean, or has trouble and struggles to reach any support. In the whole garden you will not find a single plant in a state of perfect health. Here a branch is broken by the wind or by its own weight; there a gentle breeze is tearing a flower apart, and carries away a piece, a filament, a leaf, a living part of this or that plant, which has broken or been torn off. Meanwhile you torture the grass by stepping on it; you grind it down, crush it, squeeze out its blood, break it, kill it. A sensitive and gentle young maiden goes sweetly cutting and breaking off stems. A gardener expertly chops down trunks, breaking off sensitive limbs, with his nails, with his tools. (Bologna, 19 April 1826.) Certainly these plants live on; some because their infirmities are not fatal, others because even with fatal diseases, plants, and animals as well, can manage to live on a little while. The spectacle of such abundance of life when you first go into this garden lifts your spirits, and that is why you think it is a joyful place. But in truth this life is wretched and unhappy, every garden is like a vast hospital [*vasto ospitale*] (a place much more deplorable than a cemetery), and if these beings feel [*sentono*], or rather, were to feel [*sentissero*], surely not being would be better for them than being. (Bologna, 22 April 1826)[1]

Which one is the true garden? Is it the one in bloom that we would expect on an April afternoon, or is it the one unveiled through Leopardi's words as a "*vasto ospitale*"? Both, and neither, at the same time. The factual existence of a garden tells us little about one's experience of it. According to Leopardi, our way of being in the world is characterized by instability. On the one hand, Leopardi subscribes to a form of empiricism that makes experience "alone mother of cognition and knowledge" (*Zib.* 417–18). On the other hand, a host of what Leopardi calls "passions" affect the perceiving subject: they are transitory moods, attunements to specific situations, and momentary inclinations.[2] For Leopardi, entering a garden means navigating a kind of reality characterized by a not-fully-controlled encounter between sensory experiences and transient passions. This interplay gives rise to what can be called, with a slight anachronism, his phenomenology.

Vegetation is a surprisingly frequent motif in phenomenological writings, perhaps because of its widespread presence around us, which we take as a given and thus as a useful point of departure for a study of the structures of our consciousness. In his *Ideas Pertaining to a Pure Phenomenology and to a Phenomenological Philosophy*, Edmund Husserl starts from a "blossoming apple tree" and "the freshly green grass of the lawn" to describe the relation between natural and phenomenological attitude.[3] In a similar vein, Jean-Paul Sartre, in his précis "Intentionality: A Fundamental Idea of Husserl's Phenomenology," takes the example of a tree to state that "our consciousness of things is by no means limited to our knowledge of them." Noting that we can love, hate, or even fear a tree, Sartre emphasizes that it is through intentional relations—the fact that our consciousness is inherently relational, connecting to the world around it through various forms of awareness and emotions—that we discover things "in their horror and their charm."[4]

The French philosopher's mention of horror is fitting in this context, as the *Zibaldone*'s garden is indeed horrifying. Leopardi's description of it contains an abundance of horror genre motifs: gruesome dismemberments, torture instruments, and the vocabulary of slashing and crushing. But a garden is not that—or at least not *only* that. An Italian garden in late April is more commonly imagined as a spectacle of beauty than a torture chamber. What, then, can make such a place so unsettling to someone's eyes?

The reflection that Leopardi pens on April 22, right after the garden's description and continuing that same block of text, provides some clarity in this regard. He concedes that a garden is prima facie something that cheers the spirit with the abundance of life it displays. Yet, under more careful scrutiny, this vitality is revealed as a cover-up for a "*vasto ospitale*," which is to say a place of widespread suffering. While this belief is here asserted rather than elucidated, in his *Zibaldone* Leopardi develops the idea that sentience is linked to suffering, and, most important, that suffering is the quintessence of sentience. As I will argue, powerlessness in relation to this inescapable state of affairs is the foundational aspect of Leopardi's metaphysics of horror and the underpinning of what he calls the "horrible [*orribile*] mystery of things and of universal existence" (*Zib.* 4099).[5]

Sentience is what makes Leopardi's garden horrifying: "if these beings feel [*sentono*], or rather, were to feel [*sentissero*], surely not being would be better for them than being" (*Zib.* 4176–77). The garden is not horrifying in itself; it becomes so through a perceiving subject who either experiences at first hand the dynamics Leopardi describes or reckons such dynamics as horrifying. In the latter case, the reckoning may be due to the face-value disturbing nature of the passage or to the suspicion that the garden is the objective correlative of a more widespread condition affecting the observer. But no matter the chosen perspective, there is a link between an experiencing subject and a horror: without the former, the latter cannot exist. For this reason, *Ordinary Horror* resists the temptation to essentialize the experience, focusing instead on the contextual elements that constitute it. Rather than asking *what* is horrifying, a more flexible and accurate framework should consider *what* horrifies *whom*, *when*, and *why*.

Leopardi's garden is far removed from our everyday experience of the same: as is clear every time I teach this passage, the idea of a garden as a torture chamber is one that most people reject, considering it no more than a rather conceited philosophical exercise of a bleak mind. It is precisely for this reason that I take it as a fitting image to open a study of horror beyond the horror genre. I contend throughout this book that there is nothing inherently horrifying; rather, horror is a context-dependent experience without a fixed referent. I will initially explore this claim via a path through Leopardi's work, one that will elucidate why under certain circumstances even a garden may turn horrifying.

Leopardi's worldview is one in which sentient life is preyed upon by overwhelming and overpowering forces. In particular from the Romantic era onward, the experience of being dwarfed by that which greatly exceeds the subject has become associated with the sublime. According to Immanuel Kant's canonical analysis, the sublime arises when we encounter something so immense or powerful that it transcends our comprehension, leading us to feel diminished. While the sublime's phenomenological premises of fear, awe, and being overwhelmed can be considered negative, Kant repurposes this experience as a validation of human capabilities. Rather than powerlessness in itself, for Kant these feelings underscore the mind's capacity to conceive remarkably vast or powerful phenomena, and the experience ultimately leads to an affirmation of human reason and the moral law within.[6]

Yet, not all situations are so easily controllable. Safety and separation are two crucial circumstances that must be preserved for a phenomenon to be experienced as sublime: if storms and volcanoes can appear so, it is precisely because they are at a distance. Conversely, the condition that Leopardi describes with his garden is one whereby that which overwhelms and overpowers *directly* and *negatively* affects sentient beings. To him, what he describes is not a sublime atrocity exhibition to be observed from a position of serene detachment; on the contrary, it compels an acknowledgment of our horrifying position therein, as subjects caught in a blind cycle of creation and destruction.

Through an analysis of the sublime and horror's shared phenomenological point of departure and subsequent divergence, this chapter defines horror as "the experience of forced powerlessness." This split suggests consequences that extend beyond phenomenological analysis. Because its underlying dynamics revolve around the possibility of overcoming—and thus, at least in part, taming—the overwhelming, the Kantian sublime coheres with this book's understanding of modernity as a project aimed at reducing the space of the uncontrollable. Leopardi, as we shall see, provides a more sober assessment of modernity's project: while the reach of human control over the world and its circumstances is undeniably extending, this should not make us believe that mankind is destined to become "master and possessor of nature"[7]—to evoke the dictum of he who, with Kant, is the philosophical father of Western modernity, René Descartes.

If the sublime is thus symptomatic of modernity's tendency to tame, control, and ultimately render into an aesthetic object, from a safe distance, even that which overpowers the human, the powerlessness that horror evokes and responds to acts as a somber reminder that there are situations one cannot quite control. Indeed, whereas the sublime is predicated upon leveraging or at least resisting that which overwhelms, horror denies such repurposing of the negative into the positive. If the former involves a degree of hopefulness that borders upon optimism, an analysis of the latter compels us to focus on a more pessimistic worldview. Where the sublime found its thinker in Kant, I will make the case that Leopardi provides the necessary building blocks for thinking of horror beyond the horror genre.[8]

I lay down these building blocks in this chapter's first section, which centers on the *Zibaldone,* to explore the radical horror of Leopardi's metaphysics, underpinned by what he calls the "horrible mystery of things and of universal existence." I here discuss why, for Leopardi, suffering is an inescapable aspect of the human condition, and why this realization can cast one into a state of crisis that may radically alter one's perception of reality. The next section then defines horror as "the experience of forced powerlessness" through a comparative analysis with the sublime, examining the overlaps and divergences between these twinned experiences in their aesthetics and their status in modernity. Finally, the third section wraps up the chapter and opens the way to the ones ahead by focusing on Leopardi's retellings of his encounters with a force so immense and powerful as to escape comprehension, in a horrifying way: nothingness.

HOW TO MAKE A GARDEN HORRIFYING

Living beings possess a limitless love for themselves, which they express by seeking their own good. Leopardi calls this *piacere* (pleasure), no matter how masochistic or selfless it may appear. Living beings crave a *piacere* of such nature that would quench their thirst for it once and for all. Yet, their capabilities of experiencing and retaining *piacere* are limited, as is the *piacere* they may actually attain in life. This is the origin of the dissatisfaction one experiences right after achieving *piacere*, a dissatisfaction that makes one's desires immediately shift to something else. Such is the mismatch between one's longing for an absolute, limitless *piacere*, and the limited nature of the mental and physical organs entrusted to experience it.

This is a very succinct summary of Leopardi's *teoria del piacere* (theory of pleasure), which he began to elaborate as early as February 1821 (*Zib.* 646–50), and which underpins his philosophy from that point on. According to his immanent philosophy, no transcendent scenario can be a future resolution for the conundrum of desire: living beings seek a *piacere* that is relative to their current condition (*Zib.* 3489), such that it "is no more possible that mortal man should truly desire the happiness of the Blessed than that the horse should desire that of man, or the plant that of the animal" (*Zib.* 3499). In fact, "man cannot go beyond matter, even by a single degree, with his intellect, imagination, or any other faculty or any other sort of ideas, and if he believes he has gone beyond it and conceived or had an idea of any kind of something that is not material, he is quite mistaken." Consequently, if one thinks that one desires something otherworldly, "he is mistaken, he does not desire it, it merely seems to him that he does" (*Zib.* 3503).

This regulatory norm in Leopardi's epistemology governs what can legitimately be thought: "Our mode, our faculty of reasoning, is right and capable of truth, if it restricts itself to the order of things that we know or are able to know, and that in some way pertain to us, and to the things that have some relation to that order" (*Zib.* 1644). Leopardi's materialism thus deems poorly formulated any desires apparently tied to realms of transcendence not directly knowable to us. There may be other forms of existence, but they are outside our epistemological reach. Speaking of them is equivalent to discussing the idea of spirit, meaning "*a substance which is not one of those we know or are able to know or to conceive of*" (*Zib.* 4207). Not unlike what Wittgenstein will write in his *Tractatus Logico-Philosophicus*, Leopardi suggests that "of what one cannot speak, about that one must be silent."[9] Indeed, the *piacere* that human beings crave—and the suffering from its lack—is enclosed within the horizon of earthly life. Speculating about an afterlife or transcendent scenario where *piacere* will be fulfilled once and for all is inconclusive, inconsistent, and, at most, a device of domination wielded by religious powers (*Zib.* 3507).[10]

For Leopardi, we exist in a state of perennial dissatisfaction, incapable of reaching that fulfillment of *piacere* we so desperately desire. But then, what can we hope for? Why is our condition of such pitiful nature? Leopardi calls this the "horrible mystery of things and of universal existence" (*Zib.* 4099). In the same *Zibaldone* entry, Leopardi notes that this matter is thematized in his 1824 *Dialogue of Nature and an Icelander*, from his *Moral Essays* (*Operette morali*)—a collection of philosophical dialogues and fictional essays he composed between 1824 and 1832.

The *Dialogue* tells the story of an Icelander who, convinced since his youth of the vanity of existence and the impossibility of achieving true happiness, has sought his entire life to escape suffering. After having abandoned human society in order to avoid petty fights over equally petty matters, he spends the rest of his time looking for a place where he may live frugally and serenely—a failed quest, frustrated by unceasing encounters with inhospitable weather and natural catastrophes, with dangerous wildlife and poisonous creatures, with maladies and ultimately the deterioration of his own body in old age. Almost by accident he encounters Nature herself, a colossal goddess with a "face as beautiful as it was terrifying," to whom he voices his struggles.[11] Nature replies that this world is not made for the well-being of mankind and that everything that exists participates in an endless cycle of creation and destruction. Such statements do not surprise the Icelander, who holds no illusions about the insignificant position of mankind in the grand scheme of things. Yet, he asks, if the world is not made for mankind, and if everything is caught in this blind cycle, "who is gladdened or who is benefited by this most unhappy life [*vita infelicissima*] of the universe, preserved by the injury and death of all those things that go to make it up?"[12] Such is the mystery that the Icelander seeks to make sense of. But right after articulating this question, he dies for unknown reasons. With his death, the dialogue reaches its conclusion, leaving Nature's answer unspoken.

To understand why Leopardi connects this text to the "horrible mystery of things and of universal existence," let us quote in its totality the entry where this sentence appears:

> It is not possible to explain better the horrible mystery of things and of universal existence (see my "Dialogo della Natura e di un Islandese," especially the end) than by saying that not only the range, compass, and power of our reason are insufficient and even false, but also its fundamental principles themselves. For example that principle, which once rooted out puts an end to every discourse, every line of reasoning, every proposition, and the very faculty we have through them to form and conceive of truths, that fundamental principle "A thing cannot both be and not be" seems absolutely false when you consider the palpable contradictions there are in nature. Effectively being, and not being able to be happy in any way, because of an innate impotence which is inseparable from existence, rather not being able not to be unhappy, are two truths as well demonstrated and certain about man and every living being as any truths can be according to our principles and experience. Now being, linked as it is with unhappiness, and linked to it necessarily and essentially, is something in direct contradiction with itself, with its perfection and particular end, which is happiness alone, and is damaging to itself and inimical to its own being. Therefore the being of living creatures is naturally, essentially, and necessarily in contradiction with itself. Such a contradiction is evident as well in the essential imperfection of existence (an imperfection which is demonstrated by

> and part of the necessity of being unhappy); that is in being, and being necessarily imperfect, that is with an existence not as it should be. (*Zib.* 4099-4100)

For Leopardi, to exist means to be unhappy. This is because of our thirst for *piacere*, without any possibility of quenching it once and for all. And while to exist means to be in a state of perennial tension between desire and the impossibility of its fulfillment, no justification for such unhappiness can be discerned from mankind's frame of reference—no greater good is in sight, and no transcendent reward can truthfully be hoped for.

Leopardi's understanding of the law of noncontradiction suggests that beings must be able to satisfy their seeming raison d'être. According to Leopardi, the striving toward an attainment of *piacere* is the quintessential characteristic of living creatures. Yet, instead of being able to fulfill their desire for *piacere*, they each are stuck in a perennial quest for fulfillment of such *piacere*—a quest inherently doomed to failure. Leopardi cyclically returns to this topic (*Zib.* 4137, 4168-69), and reaches the conclusion that "the end of man, the greatest good of man, his happiness, do not exist" (*Zib.* 4168). What, then, is to be made of the "horrible mystery of things and of universal existence"—that is, the question, also voiced by the Icelander, regarding whom this all benefits?

In a note of the *Zibaldone* written during his stay in Bologna—approximately a month before penning the garden passage that opened this chapter—Leopardi voices an answer to this question, an answer he terms "terrifying, but true [. . .] supreme, and terrible":

> Man (and likewise the other animals) is not born to enjoy life, but only to perpetuate life, to communicate it to others who come after him, in order to preserve it. Neither he himself, nor life, nor anything in this world is properly for him, on the contrary his entire being is for life.—A terrifying, but a true proposition and conclusion of all metaphysics [*Spaventevole, ma vera proposizione e conchiusione di tutta la metafisica*]. Existence [*esistenza*] is not for the existent being [*esistente*], does not have for its end the existent being, nor the good of the existent being; if there is any experience of good, that is purely by chance: the existent being is for existence, entirely for existence, this is its only real end. Existent beings exist so that existence exists, the individual existent being is born and exists so that existence continues and so that existence may

> be preserved through him and after him. All this is clear from seeing that the true and only end of nature is the preservation of the species, and not the preservation or the happiness of individuals; which happiness does not even exist at all in the world, not for individuals nor for the species. On the basis of this we have necessarily to arrive finally at the general, summary, supreme, and terrible conclusion mentioned above. (Bologna, 11 March 1826) (*Zib.* 4169)

Leopardi distinguishes between "*esistente*," that which exists as individually determined and can sense, and "*esistenza*," that which is above any singular determination. Every existent being exists to perpetuate existence, but nothing in existence, if not by sheer chance, exists for the good of existent beings: this, for him, is "terrifying, but a true proposition and conclusion of all metaphysics." Looking back at the *Dialogue of Nature and an Icelander*, Nature's answer to the Icelander would have confronted him with the realization that there is no *esistente*-centered reason for the "wretched life [*vita infelicissima*]" of everything that exists.[13]

This answer to the "horrible mystery of things and of universal existence" is, according to Leopardi, "terrifying" and "terrible." Crucially, these negative descriptors make sense only if they refer to a sentient being—an *esistente* in Leopardi's lexicon. Rather than being horrifying per se, the cycle of creation and destruction becomes so for the individual who is subject to it.

Leopardi adduces several reasons to explain why this condition is profoundly disquieting. One is the impossibility of fulfilling human beings' greatest good: the achievement of *piacere*. Another is the meaninglessness of this cosmic configuration, which Leopardi, as I will address in the concluding section of this chapter, describes as the nothingness that envelops him. A third and crucial reason is that this cycle of creation and destruction results in a profusion of suffering that affects each living being.

Suffering indeed plays a central role in Leopardi's worldview. While much of existence is insensible, not everything is. Leopardi writes: "The whole of nature lacks sensation, with the exception of animals. And they alone are unhappy, and not being is better for them than being, or rather not living than living. Less unhappy, though, the less sensitive they are (both species and individuals) and vice versa" (*Zib.* 4133). This is because existent beings' goal of achieving a satisfactory *piacere* is unfulfillable and, in fact, illusory, as their real purpose is preservation of existence. Having thus established a direct correlation between being sentient and being unhappy, he argues that "sensitive beings are naturally *souffrants* [suffering], a part of the universe that is essentially *souffrante*. Since they do exist and their species perpetuate themselves, it must be said that they are a necessary link in the great chain of beings, and in the order and the existence of this universe as it is, to which their harm is useful, since their existence is harmful to them, being essentially a *souffrance*" (*Zib.* 4133).

Be it directly via the hardships of life or indirectly through the privation of *piacere*, sentient beings suffer by their own nature. What this suffering accomplishes is nothing but the preservation of existence, and it fulfills no purpose for the direct good of existent beings. As existent beings, we cannot step outside of our materialistic and individual frame of reference, ruled by the *teoria del piacere*, and thus cannot find true fulfillment in the goal of preserving existence. Because of our condition, while sentient life is indeed a minuscule part of existence writ large, we cannot avoid ascribing to it the utmost importance: "animals in relation to the sum total of all other beings, and to the immensity of the whole universe, are nothing. And if we consider them as the principal part of everything there is, the beings most worthy of consideration, and so not as the tiniest but greatest part, because great in value if small in extension, this judgment of ours comes from the way we consider things, weigh up the relations between them, appraise them comparatively, assess and regard the great system of everything" (*Zib.* 4134).

For Leopardi, the "mystery of things and of universal existence" cannot be analyzed from a position of serene detachment, and is shown as "horrible" once considered in the light of the meaningless suffering inherent to sentient life. Blaise Pascal, in his *Pensées*, wrote: "*Le silence éternel de ces espaces infinis m'effraie* [The eternal silence of these infinite spaces frightens me]."[14] The pronoun "*me*" is here key. The emptiness of the cosmos is not horrifying per se: it becomes so if there is someone who experiences such emptiness as disquieting. For this reason Pascal uses the demonstrative adjective "*ces* [these]" to refer to "*espaces infinis*": they are those the subject can meaningfully relate to, rather than any infinity or any space whatsoever. The same can be said for Leopardi's analysis of existence: its functioning turns horrifying once we consider our frightful position therein. This is because—and I here momentarily indulge in the splatter motifs of the horror genre—the cogs of existence are lubricated by the blood of the existent beings it crushes.

A similarly gruesome style, as my reader will remember, characterizes Leopardi's description of a garden "in a state of *souffrance*." We can now return to that passage to better comprehend its underpinnings and reflect on its significance for thinking about horror beyond the horror genre.

Let us enter, once again, Leopardi's garden:

> Go into a garden of plants, grass, flowers. No matter how lovely it seems. Even in the mildest season of the year. You will not be able to look anywhere and not find suffering. That whole family of vegetation is in a state of *souffrance*, each in its own way to some degree. Here a rose is attacked by the sun, which has given it life; it withers, languishes, wilts. There a lily is sucked cruelly by a bee, in its most sensitive, most life-giving parts. Sweet honey is not produced by industrious, patient, good, virtuous bees without unspeakable torment for those most delicate fibers, without the pitiless massacre of flowerets. That tree is infested by an ant colony, that other one by caterpillars, flies, snails, mosquitoes; this one is injured in its bark and afflicted by the air or by the sun penetrating the wound; that other one has a damaged trunk, or roots; that other has many dry leaves; that other one has its flowers gnawed at, nibbled; that other one has its fruits pierced, eaten away. That plant is too warm, this one too cold; too much light, too much shade; too wet, too dry. One cannot grow or spread easily because there are obstacles and obstructions; another finds nowhere to lean, or has trouble and struggles to reach any support. In the whole garden you will not find a single plant in a state of perfect health. Here a branch is broken by the wind or by its own weight; there a gentle breeze is tearing a flower apart, and carries away a piece, a filament, a leaf, a living part of this or that plant, which has broken or been torn off. Meanwhile you torture the grass by stepping on it; you grind it down, crush it, squeeze out its blood, break it, kill it. A sensitive and gentle young maiden goes sweetly cutting and breaking off stems. A gardener expertly chops down trunks, breaking off sensitive limbs, with his nails, with his tools. (Bologna, 19 April 1826.) Certainly these plants live on;

> some because their infirmities are not fatal, others because even with fatal diseases, plants, and animals as well, can manage to live on a little while. The spectacle of such abundance of life when you first go into this garden lifts your spirits, and that is why you think it is a joyful place. But in truth this life is wretched and unhappy, every garden is like a vast hospital [*vasto ospitale*] (a place much more deplorable than a cemetery), and if these beings feel [*sentono*], or rather, were to feel [*sentissero*], surely not being would be better for them than being. (Bologna, 22 April 1826) (*Zib.* 4175–76)

Having reconstructed a path that started from the author's *teoria del piacere*, then focused on his distinction between existent beings (*esistente*) and existence (*esistenza*), and finally led to Leopardi's reflections on the role of suffering in sentient life, we can now better understand why the garden of the *Zibaldone* is "in a state of *souffrance*."

Leopardi's take on matter's sentience is ambiguous and a complex topic in the author's reception. On the one hand, Leopardi writes in the *Zibaldone* that "*matter thinks and feels* [la materia pensa e sente]" (*Zib.* 4251). On the other hand, just a hundred pages before, he states: "The whole of nature lacks sensation, with the exception of animals" (*Zib.* 4133). In the garden passage, this ambiguity is reflected in the verbal tenses Leopardi employs. He writes: "if these beings *feel* [sentono], or rather, *were to feel* [sentissero]" (my emphasis), with the verb "*sentire*" oscillating between the present indicative and the subjunctive imperfect—a tense used to express uncertainty. The garden's plants may or may not truly sense; if they did, they would be better off not existing given the suffering inherent to sentient life.

It is ultimately beyond the scope of this study to ascertain whether for Leopardi matter in its entirety thinks and feels. What counts here is that we can consider the garden passage as a thought experiment: if matter as a whole did sense, Leopardi seems to ask, how could one render the suffering that would be ubiquitous in a place teeming with life?

Leopardi portrays a garden where each existent being participates in a collective scream of agony. In it, a pollinating bee turns into a pain-inducing creature. The sun and the wind become agents of destruction. Trees are pierced and gnawed. Stepping on the grass is akin to crushing a body and spilling its blood. A girl's plucking of flowers is compared to limbs being rent and torn. A gardener is revealed as a torturer. Overall, this is a scene rife with splatter tropes that contemporary readers likely connect to the horror genre.

In many languages, including English and Italian, the word "horror" is indeed associated with the eponymous genre. Yet, although Leopardi is no horror author, in describing his garden passage one may, with reason, resort to that term or its cognates. I do not believe that a word's multiplicity of uses should cause any concerns in discussing literary matters, because this is how ordinary language works. We use the word "horror" in numerous mundane scenarios: I can say that I am going to watch a horror movie tonight, such as Ridley Scott's *Alien*, and at the same time use the same word or its derivatives to describe something particularly troubling that I experienced, such as the horrible turbulence that I was subjected to on my flight to San Francisco, or to discuss one of the many tragedies unfolding around the globe, such as the horrors of war. "Horror" should be considered a polysemic word in literary studies, too, one that can be used to label a horror genre work like H. P. Lovecraft's "The Call of Cthulhu," and whose use also sheds light on the underpinnings of Leopardi's garden. While the use of the word "horror" is canonical in relation to the former, its usefulness and appropriateness in talking about the latter author are key claims of this chapter.

The reasons are several. To begin with, a clear connection exists between Leopardi's metaphysics of horror—according to which suffering is inherent to sentience—and the author's horror-inflected style in this page of the *Zibaldone*: the latter serves the purpose of conveying the former. It does so by departing from commonplace descriptions of a garden and turning an idyllic space into something more akin to a torture chamber. The outcome recalls the third and rightmost section of Hieronymus Bosch's *Garden of Earthly Delights*, where an idyllic scene, chiefly present in the first section of the triptych but also partly preserved in the second, is replaced with a hellish landscape. But whereas Bosch's paintings are surreal and depict supernatural creatures such as devils and reanimated skeletons, Leopardi's garden does not feature anything otherworldly: it preserves its natural elements, which are, however, described from a deforming slant, one that portrays them as if they sensed and therefore suffered. This is because, rather than an aberration or a strange flight of the mind, Leopardi's garden of horrors is symbolic of a horrifying condition that his system extends to all living beings—us humans included.

For Leopardi, this condition is inescapable: sentient life is underpinned by a kind of suffering whose sole outcome is to preserve existence writ large. Given such a state of affairs, Leopardi speaks of a "horrible mystery of things and of universal existence." But if this is really the case, would life look any different from a torture chamber? Leopardi's garden serves as a mirror of our condition. If one embraces Leopardi's metaphysics, the profusion of life that defines a garden changes its colors: upon focusing on the link between existing and suffering, the wonder of all wonders, that beings *are*, turns into the horror of all horrors.[15]

This shift is rendered by his descriptive deformation of what a "normal" garden in April would look like: the plants and the flowers one expects to find there are preserved, but they appear disquieting—disquieting just like Leopardi's worldview, underpinned as it is by an inextricable link between sentience and suffering. Leopardi's garden carries the consequences of this connection to an extreme: if one were to consider reality through this lens only, this is how a garden might appear. Most of us do not embrace this perspective, or at least not all the time. Precisely for this reason, I argue, Leopardi chooses an estranging and striking description of a garden to mark the horrifying nature of this realization, when it becomes the ruler of someone's perception of reality.

While in this chapter I consider Leopardi to be a thinker of the horrifying, this is not to suggest that horror is all we find in this author. Leopardi is interested in how humans dwell in the world. Indeed, his *Zibaldone* thematizes a range of experiences, from boredom to love, from friendship to rage.[16] He authored satirical poems and love poetry, but also treatises on topics as disparate as astronomy, sociology, and philology.[17] In Italy, Leopardi is a core component of any school curriculum. And a remarkable sense of wonder about the world belongs to his writings, as also encapsulated by Leopardi's most famous poem, *Infinity*, where the speculation about what may lie beyond a hedge kindles the imagination of the author, leading him to a metaphorical shipwreck that is described as "sweet."[18]

Just as our lives are characterized by phenomenological heterogeneity, so too does Leopardi's production contain a remarkable range of experiences, analyzed in their complexity and poetically distilled, which contributed to his canonization as one of the greatest Italian authors of all time. In the light of this, I contend that horror is a key feature of Leopardi's work, and, in fact, a central aspect of his worldview. Thus, horror diffuses throughout Leopardi's pages, sometimes hidden, sometimes more overtly present. But while horror is certainly a feature of the *Zibaldone* passage I am focusing on, it is worth asking the following: what precisely causes *this* garden, at *this* point of the *Zibaldone*, to look like *this*?

It is difficult to provide a satisfactory answer to this question, particularly given the fragmentary nature of Leopardi's philosophical diary. The notes before and after the garden passage discuss language and poetry, and are thus different in both content and form. The letters that Leopardi wrote in the period around April 19 and 22, 1826, are also distant from the bleakness of the entry analyzed here. It is wiser to err on the side of caution, and refrain from overdetermining the circumstances that led Leopardi to write this passage. But as we saw, there is a clear link between Leopardi's philosophical system and the way he describes a garden in bloom, and it is worth delving into this connection further.

I believe that Leopardi's garden represents a moment when a realization we normally keep at bay can no longer be held at a safe distance. For example, I am aware that on any given day something terrible could happen to my loved ones. Yet, in my daily life, I must brush these concerns aside in order to function. There are moments, however, when this awareness becomes acute—perhaps upon learning of someone's death from an aggressive illness. A similar dynamic, only more extreme in its consequences, underpins the *Zibaldone* passage: it represents what a garden might feel like if one were to compulsively fixate on the suffering that characterizes everything that exists.

Imagine that you fully agreed with Leopardi's worldview. One day, as you are approaching a garden, you start ruminating on the ubiquity of suffering around you, as it affects each and every part of matter. Haunted by this idea, you obsessively think about it, until your experience of reality changes as a consequence. What you previously brushed aside so as to go about your day now acquires towering dimensions, at least in your mind. In entering a garden, your experience of it shifts: the walk that you did countless times without paying too much attention to the pollinating bees and stalks of grass is now affected by your thinking, which alters how you phenomenologically relate to that place. Just as Antoine

Roquentin's surroundings in Sartre's *Nausea* mutate and horrify upon his realizing the true essence of a chestnut tree (a presence up to that point completely inoffensive),[19] so would your experience of the world turn into something much more disquieting once the idea of ubiquitous and inescapable suffering is let run loose, affecting your present and altering the very framework through which reality is disclosed to you. This transformation highlights a fundamental tension in perception itself: as certain aspects of the world come into focus, others necessarily retreat into obscurity. Sloterdijk comments on the dialectic between concealment and unconcealment in Heidegger by stating that "in the clearing, it becomes manifest that not everything is manifest. The manifestation is never complete—and the suspicion against what is veiled and not appearing is in principle never to be put to rest."[20] That is to say, neither a chestnut tree nor a garden is ever fully revealed to us: our perception of phenomena is partial and provisional, insofar as perception, phenomenologically speaking, is not a passive reception of complete information but an active, interpretative act that is open to reconfiguration.

It is, I believe, quite purposeless to wonder whether Leopardi truly had some sort of hallucination that made a garden in Bologna appear as a torture chamber. It is also beside the point to ask if Leopardi really entered a garden in April 1826. Instead, I am proposing here a less biographically oriented claim: with this passage, Leopardi depicts a garden as if his assumptions about the links between suffering and existence were the ruling factor of one's perception of reality. In other words, Leopardi is providing an aesthetic rendition of a metaphysical claim. He does so by stepping away from verisimilitude, and deforming what a standard description of a garden would look like. In this book I propose the term *aesthetics of deformation* to describe and group together similar descriptive techniques, and I will return to it in this chapter's next section.

For the time being, it is important to emphasize that Leopardi's view in this passage is not from nowhere: it posits an observer who is, at a minimum, sensitive to the suffering around them, or, ideally, one aware of being part of the cycle of creation and destruction that the garden represents. Without any of these preconditions, the garden would not be disclosed as a torture chamber. The aesthetics of this passage from the *Zibaldone*, therefore, both evokes and responds to phenomenological matters: the gruesome scenery Leopardi pens on the page is not one to be observed from a position of serene detachment; in fact, it compels us to consider our horrifying position therein. We too, as sentient beings, are "in a state of *souffrance*," interned in a "vast hospital" of which the garden is a symbolic representation. Once this set of realizations rules one's perception of reality, the true horror of Leopardi's garden can appear.

Its horror is also due to the inescapability of the condition the garden represents. According to Leopardi, there is no way for existent beings to extract themselves from the rulings of existence. There is no way out of this "vast hospital," if not through death itself.[21] The best we can do, for him, is to live a life that allows us to distract ourselves from this realization, and thus momentarily forget about our condition.[22] But this is not always possible, as there are moments when it is difficult to keep at a safe distance the awareness of the "horrible mystery of things and of universal existence." In those moments, something that would otherwise be kept under control manifests itself in all its horror.

These points underscore why a study of horror should focus not on normative claims but on specific situations. Horror is context-dependent: even a canonically horrifying object like a corpse may not be perceived as such by, for instance, an autopsist at work. To clarify and elaborate this dynamic, let us delve into the connections between horror and another context-dependent experience underpinned by the overwhelming, fear, and awe: the sublime. A comparison of these two experiences will help establish my definition of horror in terms of forced powerlessness.

HORROR OR: THE FLIPSIDE OF THE SUBLIME

In June 2022, as I was about to leave California after finishing my PhD program and head to the East Coast, I spent a week in Death Valley with a friend. In that season the desert is unforgiving, with the average daytime temperature above 100°F. There are summer days, however, when the air gets cooler and the sand turns into mud because of a monsoon. While extremely rare, monsoons can take place in Death Valley, but they are difficult, usually impossible, to predict. One day we noticed that the sky, typically crystal clear, had begun darkening, and the winds picked up—two clear signs of a summer thunderstorm. In a matter of minutes it began raining, and intensely so, for a short while. Once it stopped, we decided to drive to Dante's View—one of the highest peaks in the area, part of the

Black Mountains—to see the desert after the rainfall, and perhaps catch a super-bloom.

We reached Dante's View as the storm was raging in front of us, in the valley below. With a spectacle nothing short of sublime, gusts of wind were raising vortexes of sand, and the golden halo of sunset tinged the dark clouds and filtered through, blending with the raindrops pouring down. At the bottom of Death Valley, the water reacted with the salt flats of Badwater Basin, raising fumes caused by the mixture of hot surface, cooler rainwater, and surrounding air. While salt itself does not evaporate, the rain hitting it kicks small salt particles up into the air, which remain suspended by the heat and the evaporative updrafts of the water. From our vantage point we could see the sunset, the bright white salt, the dark storm clouds, and the air shimmering from the heat—their colors blending together, ruptured by lightning and thunder.

We snapped out of our daze upon realizing that the monsoon, rather than being ahead of us, was in fact moving our way. The rain we had previously experienced was just the first sign of what was to come. At an elevation of 5,500 feet, and surrounded by a barren landscape, we were perfectly poised to become lightning rods, not to mention the danger of flash flooding along the steep roads on our way back downhill. In a matter of seconds, sublime wonder was overtaken by fear. Our safety now called into question, we dashed to the car, and eventually made it back to our home base in Tecopa, just outside of Death Valley.

In his *Critique of Judgment*, Kant defines the dynamic sublime in terms of might. He writes: "Nature considered in an aesthetic judgment as might that has no dominion over us, is *dynamically sublime*."[23] That might has no dominion over us is here crucial: Kant concedes that thinking of nature as might involves looking upon it as "an object of fear," but, he continues, one may look upon a phenomenon "as *fearful*, and yet not be afraid *of* it." This takes place if and only if "our own position is secure." However, once safety is called into question, one enters a phenomenological territory different from the one of the sublime: the subject "flees from the sight of an object filling him with dread; and it is impossible to take delight in terror that is seriously entertained."[24]

What I experienced in Death Valley mirrors Kant's description of the phenomenological transition from the sublime to fear. The monsoon was at first a mighty phenomenon that had no dominion over me: looking at it from my position of safety on Dante's View, I experienced the storm as an aesthetic object rather than a direct threat. In accordance with Kant's reasoning on the topic, that phenomenon's might, unfolding in front of me in that dramatic landscape, made it more appealing: "provided our own position is secure, [its] aspect is all the more attractive for its fearfulness." However, the monsoon did turn into an object of fear when I realized that I was about to be hit by the storm while in a dangerous location. To use Kant's formulation, I "seriously entertained" the possibility of being in danger, and fled.

My story had a positive ending: flight was successful, and my phenomenological barycenter moved from sublime wonder, to fear, and finally to relief once I was back in Tecopa. But what if a positive resolution had not taken place? Among the myriad things that could have gone wrong, what if I had been unable to find my car keys, and the monsoon had washed over us in all its might? With these questions, I am extending Kant's reflections on the sublime by asking what happens when withdrawing from that which threateningly overwhelms is not an option, or is not successful. Kant leaves this implicit question unanswered; it is precisely where he stops that I want to continue, and where horror begins.

Upon realizing the impossibility of flight, my experience of the storm would have shifted again. In the face of nature's might, I would have been powerless. My powerlessness would have been forced, rather than deliberate: I did not want to be there, not anymore at least, for I wanted to flee but could not. My trip to the desert had been thus far characterized by mastery over my surroundings: thanks to a car and air conditioning, I could safely visit Death Valley during the otherwise inhospitable summertime. But all of a sudden, if something had gone wrong, my mastery would have been replaced by the absence of control regarding what was happening.

Kant notes that sublimity "does not reside in any of the things of nature, but only in our mind, insofar as we may become conscious of our superiority over nature within, and thus also over nature without us (as exerting influence upon us)."[25] To paraphrase in more overtly phenomenological terms, we establish an intentional relation with something, and this relation is constitutive of the sublime: something is not sublime *in itself*, but instead *for us*, under specific circumstances. Such circumstances include the preservation of a safe distance from that which may overwhelm and overpower us. But what if that distance is suddenly erased? What if instead of our *being* in control, we suddenly realize that, in reality, a situation *escapes* our control, overwhelmingly and threateningly so?

I propose to use the word "horror" to describe this experience of forced powerlessness. Indeed, I can easily imagine myself using the word "horror" in ordinary language to retrospectively describe, if I survived, what I could have experienced in Death Valley: it surely would have been horrible, and horrifying, to be stuck on top of Dante's View during a storm, with neither shelter nor protection. This use of "horror" does not ascribe any specifically horrifying qualities to the monsoon: a monsoon is not horrifying in itself; rather, it becomes so for someone experiencing it under specific circumstances. For these reasons, and despite the standardized motifs of the eponymous genre, I consider horror an experience without a fixed referent.

If the might of a monsoon may evoke horror, or at least the possibility thereof, a garden appears much less threatening. Yet, the path traced through Leopardi's *Zibaldone* allows us to understand why even a garden can be horrifying: the forced powerlessness in the face of the suffering that belongs to sentient beings' existence underpins the metaphysical horror that diffuses through Leopardi's pages. In turn, this horror starkly manifests itself in the *Zibaldone*'s analyzed passage, which depicts the experience of being in a garden under specific, unsettling circumstances.

While being in a garden in bloom differs greatly from standing on a mountain peak in Death Valley during a monsoon, both of them can turn into horrifying situations. In turning horrifying, such different situations would share certain phenomenological underpinnings, with the crucial one, I argue, being the forced powerlessness provoked by a situation that escapes the subject's control. A garden or a monsoon would not be, respectively, beautiful and sublime anymore, or at least not only. Instead, they would mutate into something much more disquieting in the affected subject's perception. This would take place through a novel intentional relation established between subject and phenomenon, one provoked by a change in contextual circumstances.

But can a simple shift in circumstances render something horrifying? To argue for this position, I turn to a short 1949 text by Martin Heidegger, "The Point of Reference," where the German philosopher ponders what happens when something is transposed out of its previous essence. The piece chiefly concerns the shrinking of time and space through technological advancement such as telecommunications or airfare, which for Heidegger generate an illusory form of proximity—one that promotes no true nearness insofar as it "washes [everything] together into the uniformly distanceless." After a brief, somewhat sibylline mention of the cataclysmic effects of the atomic bomb in relation to the sociopsychological dynamics of his epoch, Heidegger reflects on what he calls "*das Entsetzliche*": "What is this clueless anxiety waiting for, if the horrible [*das Entsetzliche*] has already occurred? The horrifying is what transposes all that is out of its previous essence. What is so horrifying? It reveals and conceals itself in the way that everything presences, namely that despite all overcoming of distance, the nearness of that which is remains outstanding."[26]

In this dense quotation, Heidegger describes the unsettling transposition of some*thing* out of its previous essence to a nearer horizon. Some*thing* gets closer, but in doing so it does not become more decipherable or controllable. Some*thing* gets revealed in getting closer, but that *thing* also becomes more concealed insofar as its nearness does not equal its integration into a homely context. Distance has been overcome, but this newly acquired nearness makes everything even more disturbing. A previous and more controllable essence is now gone: what remains is a nearness that is in fact outstanding, as it does not promote any increase in handiness. This nearness reveals something new about the essence of that *thing*, in a way that one could not experience from afar. "*Das Entsetzliche*" takes hold of one's present once the collapse of distance between oneself and some*thing* results in a nearness that remains disturbingly outstanding—a nearness that makes that *thing*, whatever it may be, an unresolved matter. In so being, some*thing* that was either inoffensive or dealt with at a safe distance, like a garden, a chestnut tree, or a monsoon in Death Valley, suddenly causes a disturbance in the subject's world.

A transposition of essence helps clarify how something may mutate into a source of horror. Consider that I can at any point think about cancer, torture, or warfare without any of these phenomena casting my world into crisis, even in the full awareness that someone, somewhere, is directly being affected by them right now. Indeed, I know that these phenomena exist, and I believe that I am correct in using the word "horror" in ordinary language to describe them. Yet, as I now think and write about them, I am not horrified. This rather obvious point carries relevant implications. The key is that cancer, torture, or warfare are not horrifying per se, but instead may become so depending on how I relate to them at a given moment. Things would indeed change if any of these phenomena began directly affecting my life—either because of a diagnosis or because I started obsessing about this possibility. At that point, something that I had kept at a safe distance before would now appear under a different, more disturbing light. Under such circumstances, my present would be cast into crisis: what appeared remote or manageable would now be outstanding and overwhelming. This would render me powerless; the secure mental home and space of autonomy I imagined myself to possess would suddenly be shown to be an indefensible playground for forces beyond my control. Such a transposition of essence is content-agnostic, meaning that given certain circumstances and personal dispositions, it can take place for any given phenomenon. It can apply to cancer and monsoons, but also to the chestnut trees in Sartre's *Nausea* and the garden in bloom in Leopardi's *Zibaldone*. While none of them is a priori horrifying, all of them can become so.

This approach shifts the emphasis from an object of horror to a horrified subject. In systematically arguing for the context-dependence of horror, it provides a paradigm for understanding this experience that does not need to rely on horror-genre motifs such as the presence of repellent creatures, supernatural elements, or extreme situations. Through a focus on its phenomenological underpinnings, it also frees horror from being overdetermined by cultural codes: corpses and esoteric rituals can surely evoke horror, but not necessarily. Simultaneously, this approach opens up the space of the horrifying, and makes it cohere with how we use this word already: if seeing a loved one being consumed by a disease is generally something that brings horror to our mind, a theory of this experience must accommodate this matter of fact, as it is reflected by ordinary language, or be subject to revision.

Only through a more flexible paradigm of horror can I argue for its relevance regarding Leopardi's work, and vice versa. Leopardi indeed does not *write* horror fiction, nor, strictly speaking, does he philosophize *about* horror; rather, it is the outcome of his philosophy that *is* horrifying.[27] His metaphysics leads to a worldview that renders his very philosophy a source of horror once its outcomes are no longer kept at a safe distance. For this reason, he calls his way of looking at reality "grim and wretched, yet alone truthful": those affected by it "find and feel everywhere nothingness and emptiness, and the vanity of human cares and desires and hopes, and of all the illusions so inherent in life that without them it is not life" (*Zib.* 103).

I will return to Leopardi's remarks on hopelessness, vanity, and nothingness in the next and final section of this chapter. For now, I will return to the sublime, and consider how this experience has been, especially since Kant, of interest for aesthetic reasons. Indeed, the sublime is not only an aesthetic experience, but also an experience rendered through specific aesthetics—be it in painting, poetry, music, or literary writings. Can the same be said for horror?

The garden of torments from the *Zibaldone*, in my reading, is symbolic of a particular phenomenological orientation—an orientation affected by a set of metaphysical beliefs that rule the subject's perception of reality. While such a way of phenomenologically dwelling in a place is in its essence incommunicable given that individual experiences involve a degree of intersubjective opacity, this does not necessarily lead to silence. Since my words cannot truly make you experience what being in Death Valley during a monsoon was like, I entrust them with the task of working around that gap. I do so by relying on the tools of the literary trade, such as narrative, symbol, and metaphor, in the full awareness that I am creating a linguistic simulacrum of an experience rather than providing you with the experience itself. This, I believe, is what Leopardi's garden passage does, and the way that it works.

To this end, it relies on what I am calling aesthetics of deformation: a term that I use to describe how the description of an object or a situation does not follow conventional standards, but instead embraces a more disquieting and unsettling style, just as happens in the *Zibaldone*, where a gardener is rendered as a torturer and the plucking of some flowers as an act of gruesome mutilation. As I will show in the following chapters, structurally similar aesthetics of deformation underpin the scenes of horror present in a number of canonical Italian texts that are not part of the horror genre. Their presence disrupts (be it just momentarily) the realistic framework in which they are embedded and unsettles the very stability of that framework. In doing so, they mirror what may happen in our everyday life once it is shaken by a horrifying event that shatters the comfortable predictability of our daily predicament and casts our world into crisis.

The experience of horror, like the sublime, can be rendered through specific aesthetics. In so doing, I do not wish to overdetermine, and ultimately propose a normative framework for, what an aesthetic rendition of horror is or should be like; rather, I am providing a scaffolding to think of horror that remains open to reconfigurations, also depending on the medium or the canon analyzed.

At the same time, I contend that, aesthetic divergences notwithstanding, a common phenomenology of the experience of horror can be identified, one that centers on matters of forced powerlessness. In phenomenological terms, I am here beginning an eidetic reduction that will continue throughout this book—that is, I am here starting to identify the essential, invariant structures of a particular experience by bracketing out the variable, contingent details of individual instances. The aesthetics of deformation represents the phenomenology of this experience by conveying the upheaval that an event of horror triggers, both in our perception of the world and within a literary text.

Beyond the aesthetic and the phenomenological, there is another, more elusive area of overlaps and subsequent divergences between the sublime and horror worth dwelling upon. The sublime can be connected to modernity's tendency to tame, control, and ultimately render into an aesthetic object, from a safe distance, even what overpowers the human. From this perspective, it should not be surprising that this concept became central in Western thought especially from the eighteenth century onward, at the onset of modernity. Whereas the sublime is tied to a certain domestication of that which exceeds us, horror evokes and responds to the opposite, as it erupts when a given phenomenon can no longer be kept at bay and forcefully renders powerless the subject exposed to it. But if so, what can be said about horror's relation to the modern epoch? And how does it differ in these regards from the sublime?

In this book's introduction I observed that the twentieth century was, in many regards, a horrifying century. The twenty-first, too, has arguably opened under the same banner: terrorist attacks coexist with state-run warfare, the specter of worldwide pandemics is once again haunting us, geopolitical tensions are increasing and so is the risk of nuclear holocaust. But the argument for the uniquely horrifying nature of the recent past falls flat when one considers that horrifying events have been present throughout human history. Indeed, to mention only a few large-scale events from Western history before the twentieth century, the word *horror* aptly describes the eruption of Mount Vesuvius in 73 AD, the fourteenth-century Black Death, or the Atlantic slave trade. The list goes on and will never be fully integrated with the horrors that left no traces or have been buried by the sands of time.

The claim that the twentieth century was a uniquely horrifying century is also undermined by the rather trivial observation that we cannot know what past horrors felt like for those who experienced them. Was the Black Death somewhat comparable to Hiroshima and Nagasaki's nuclear explosions for those who suffered through it? Was it a "half-Holocaust" on a hypothetical horror-scale? Such questions sound preposterous and meaningless for good reasons, aside from being outright offensive to the memory of those affected by similar catastrophes.

While one could try to identify certain quantifiable metrics for a study of horror—for instance, by analyzing death tolls or the frequency and nature of the word used in describing a given event—it remains dubious what such a classification would accomplish. Furthermore, as I argue, ordinary horror not only concerns lists of casualties or widespread destruction but may also reside in more personal matters, such as poverty or the illness affecting a loved one, and hence constitutes a diffuse, subtle presence in human history and in our lives as well.

Since a quantitative approach to horror presents us with more questions than answers, this book addresses the topic through a phenomenological outlook that seeks common experiential denominators for a host of different instances of the horrifying. Yet, while mindful of the intricacies of speaking of horror in historical terms, does a phenomenological approach allow us to say something cogent about horror's relevancy for a specific epoch?

I believe so. If horror is indeed defined by powerlessness, it is my contention that this experience acquires a peculiarly troubling flavor during the modern period. As I began emphasizing from *Ordinary Horror*'s first pages, one of modernity's quintessential characteristics is a certain rebelliousness against human impotence and passivity. The progress of our civilization over the last few centuries reflects this attitude, seen in endeavors as different as modern medicine's reclaiming of human lives in the face of diseases and child mortality, or the crowning of the dream of human flight through aviation. Modernity's battle-ready attitude turned a good part of what was once ruled by chance or seemingly undefeatable natural laws into a winnable struggle against all odds.

It should thus not be surprising that the sublime became a central philosophical and aesthetic category of the modern period: if volcanoes and storms are not symbols of the numinous anymore but cannot be domesticated quite yet, they may as well become phenomena whose observation from a safe distance can constitute a matter of personal uplift and aggrandizement. Indeed, while Kant's understanding of the sublime is underpinned by the presence of limits—with the sublime being triggered by that which we do not have the capacity to understand or control—the presence of such limits is what human reason needs in order to become aware of its capacities and, ultimately, its superiority over nature.[28]

This is a risky game to play, as it calls for a degree of flirtation with what exceeds us. For this reason, Edmund Burke, whose work profoundly influenced Kant's, conceded in his 1757 essay on the topic that the sublime contains "some degree of horror."[29] The key element here is that horror must be kept at a potential level: while an erupting volcano may upend my reality, so far it does not since I am safe from it, and therefore I can experience this phenomenon in a positive light.

While my focus up to this point has been on what Kant calls the dynamic sublime, this logic also applies to the other form he theorizes: the mathematical sublime, which refers to the feeling of awe that arises when confronted with something so immense that it overwhelms our capacity to comprehend it.[30] A clear starry night, revealing to us an infinity of celestial objects unfathomably distant from our planet, can, for instance, trigger this kind of sublimity. But, remembering Pascal's *effroi* in the face of the universe, one runs the risk of leaving such a contemplative state profoundly unsettled, as here too the sublime requires a degree of insulation—this time under the form of holding steady to a certain sangfroid in dealing with similar cosmic vertigos.

The mathematical sublime arguably encapsulates part of modernity's ethos: if black holes and the images produced by the James Webb Telescope awe our imagination, it is because we have expanded our world through tools that disclose phenomena otherwise inaccessible. From this perspective as well, there is a clear link between the sublime and horror, with technoscientific advances also engendering new venues for the latter to erupt—nuclear weapons' otherworldly mushroom cloud manifests the thin line that separates these two experiences, and aesthetics, too, perhaps more disturbingly than anything else.

Two conclusions may be drawn at this point. The first is that the sublime cannot be conceived without a flipside of horror, as the overwhelming effects that belong to the former may, under certain circumstances, turn into the powerlessness that characterizes the latter. The second is that while the sublime's significance for modernity also lies in how it repurposes what exceeds the human, thereby providing a way of exerting indirect control over it, horror's everlasting and ever shifting presence acts as a somber reminder that our house is still haunted by what it sought to exorcise in its struggle against impotence and the absence of control. These two interconnected experiences are thus uniquely relevant for the modern context. And while the sublime has been thoroughly analyzed in aesthetics and other fields, horror, beyond the horror genre, remains a less discussed object of study despite its widespread presence around us.

I have been arguing for Leopardi's relevance in understanding horror's presence in our world, and his intuitions on the topic are not limited to the metaphysical concerns explored in the previous section. To him, horror is so foundational to human existence that it creates the need for a social contract. As he writes in *Broom* [*La ginestra*], one of his later poems, it is "horror [*orror*] / that first joined mortals in a common pact [*strinse i mortali in social catena*] / against unholy nature [*empia natura*]."[31]

In the beginning was horror: it is this primordial experience that first brought mankind together. Society, for Leopardi, is thus a form of partial insulation against this experience, a sort of collective bracing aimed at minimizing the powerlessness-inducing circumstances in which an individual, if left on their own, would be prey to nature's rulings.

Whereas the mention of a "*social catena*" led to an abundance of debates regarding Leopardi's political beliefs,[32] the word "*orror*" has not generated the same interest. There is a certain irony in this critical tendency, as it mirrors Leopardi's bitterly sarcastic diagnosis of his own time: an overemphasis on sociopolitical, context-dependent matters and a neglect of the most troubling, foundational elements of the human condition, alongside a privileging of optimism and hope for progress over pessimism and a lucid confrontation with the most disquieting aspects of human existence.

Indeed, while *Broom* is surely a poem about human resilience, it is also one that is cast against the backdrop of the possibility of the catastrophe, and in fact its inevitability—the eruption of Mount Vesuvius, on whose slopes the flower that gives this poem its title grows against all odds.

The form of insulation provided by what Leopardi calls "*social catena*" has grown progressively tighter in the modern period. This took place not only through technoscientific advancements but also via the implementation of insurances and social policies such as the welfare state, as I will elaborate in chapter 2. From this point of view, Taleb provides an apt definition of what modernity is and does: according to him, it represents "humans' large-scale domination of the environment, the systematic smoothing of the world's jaggedness, and the stifling of volatility and stressors."[33]

Horror, then, stands as that which most decisively upends—be it only momentarily—this paradigm of control. The strengthening of a "*social catena*" against "*orror*" is what, for Leopardi, creates the impression of an inexorable march of the "*magnificent, progressive destiny* [magnifiche sorti e progressive]" of humankind. But no matter how closely knit, this "*social catena*" is one that our "cruel nurse [*dura nutrice*]"—Nature, existence—can with a single whim "suddenly and totally annihilate."[34]

Leopardi's words, more than defeatist or reactionary in their essence, echo what sociologist Karen Cerulo calls "positive asymmetry." In her *Never Saw It Coming*, she defines positive asymmetry as "the tendency to see the best and background the worst," which Cerulo identifies as "an overwhelming perceptual pattern" active, in particular, in developed and insulated societies.[35] From this perspective, not only do we legitimately seek to avoid horror in our lives; perhaps more disturbingly, we also refuse to fully acknowledge the magnitude of the latent yet concrete possibility of its eruption in our everydayness. This is, to an extent, a matter of self-preservation: if I catastrophized all the time—if I feared getting hit by a brick falling from a roof every time I left my apartment—I would be paralyzed and incapable of doing anything. We posit the existence of a nest of predictability that rules our life and act accordingly, as when I presuppose that no bricks will hit my head upon leaving my home, no matter that this could indeed happen at any time. For the most part, the way reality unfolds coheres with how I forecast it from within my nest of predictability, and things go according to the plan.

There are situations, however, when something *does* go wrong, and, after our nest of predictability is shattered, we are cast into a state of crisis. In accordance with the disciplinary norms of phenomenological analysis, this book privileges the descriptive rather than the prescriptive, and I here do not wish to make any claims about why things may go wrong and what one should do in those circumstances. Instead, I want to focus on those horrifying moments as they happen and are retold, those moments when someone is engulfed by a generalized sense of powerlessness and forced to reckon with the illusory nature of our positive asymmetries: the worst is indeed happening, and right in front of us. Leopardi's philosophy moves from similar premises, as it identifies and emphasizes horror's foundational, everlasting presence in our lives and societies, despite modernity's various attempts at the domestication of existence.

If the sublime's repurposing of that which overwhelms into an aesthetic is a continuation of the Cartesian project of ever increasing mastery over the world and its circumstances, horror pokes a hole in this dream: from a shared phenomenological point of departure, the latter experience leads the subject to a state of forced powerlessness instead of the self-aggrandizement provided by the former. Accordingly, whereas the sublime borders on a form of optimism against all odds that underpins modernity's project, horror responds to the more pessimistic observation that, in the end, there are situations one cannot control.

This is particularly troubling for an epoch underpinned by what Leopardi calls "*computisteria*."[36] With this futuristic-sounding word (at least by early nineteenth-century standards), Leopardi refers to the tendency of assessing matters through calculation, hence through forecasting and prediction. As he writes in his *Zibaldone* with reference to geopolitical events and military confrontations, in the modern epoch "resistance depends on calculation as to the forces, resources, hopes for success, injuries, and benefits at stake in yielding or in resisting," to a point that "the fate of the world is decided in *computisteria*" (*Zib.* 1005–6). This echoes, only to pull it from the realm of the speculative to the one of reality, Gottfried Leibniz's "*calculemus*"—that is, the belief that at some point in the future "whenever controversies arise, there will be no need of more disputation than what occurs between two philosophers or calculators. It will be sufficient to pick up their pens, sit down at the desks (*abacus*) and say to each other [. . .] : *let us calculate*."[37]

As I have shown elsewhere, Leopardi looked with skepticism at the feasibility of this project, and in particular at its generalization to all aspects of human life.[38] His doubts are epistemological: rather than arguing for the existence of something ontologically incomputable in reality, for Leopardi it is dubious that we will ever be able to reach a comprehensive understanding of the interconnected, complex, and nonlinear systems we seek to domesticate, one that would render them fully operable and controllable.

This becomes particularly clear in the sarcastic *Announcement of Prizes Offered by the Academy of Sillographes*, from the *Moral Essays*, where Leopardi criticizes what today we may call technological solutionism: the belief that any given phenomenon can be turned into a technical problem for which a technical solution exists.[39] In this text, Leopardi's irony is directed at how a fictional Academy describes as inevitable and self-evident the creation of three automata that, learning from the knowledge amassed in published books, would encapsulate at the highest degree the virtues of friendship, courage, and fidelity. Leopardi's sarcasm toward the Academy is rooted in the fact that, for him, these aspects of human life so far evade the reach of mankind's full understanding and thus the hope of artificial synthesis. While Leopardi does not seem to rule out the possibility of a progressive clearing of such epistemological fog, nothing should make us believe that this will necessarily happen—contrary to the Academy's belief that modern society will inevitably move from the invention of the lightning rod (*parafulmini* in Italian) to that of some "parajealousy, paracalumny, paraperfidy or parafraud."[40]

Written before the heyday of positivism and its subsequent discontents, Leopardi's intuitions about the developing episteme of modernity have been validated by time, and by more recent treatises on the topic as well. In his *Cosmopolis: The Hidden Agenda of Modernity* and *Return to Reason*, philosopher Stephen Toulmin has extensively argued for the central role in modernity of calculation and computation in creating the impression of a stable, predictable cosmos that functions according to rules fully knowable by mankind through quantitative methods—methods that can be deployed to analyze and govern society and everyday life as well. The underpinnings of this project, as argued by Toulmin, reflect what the American pragmatist John Dewey identified as the quintessential trait of Western thought since the time of ancient Greece, the so-called "quest for certainty" that reached in modernity its epoch of fullest articulation and implementation.[41] Progress in this quest has gone hand in hand with technoscientific advancements, and the past few decades have been no different. Today, data analytics, artificial intelligence, and predictive algorithms are increasingly used to forecast various aspects of human life and the natural world, as Igor Tulchinsky and Christopher Manson argue in *The Age of Prediction*, a book that maintains a careful equilibrium between optimism and an awareness of the challenges that this may bring. With reference to the three automata of his *Announcement of Prizes* and from the onset of the nineteenth century, Leopardi well foresaw the increasingly prevalent role of computation and technology in modernity's attempts to reduce unpredictability, maximize forecasting, and domesticate the future.

Against the backdrop of the growing tide of modernity's episteme, Leopardi focuses on horror as a central metaphysical, societal, and experiential category. In an epoch increasingly characterized by the desire to make the world controllable, horror's forced powerlessness stands as that which ruptures the apparent linearity and inevitability of this process. In showing the fragility and, in part, illusory nature of modernity's positive asymmetries, it acts as a somber reminder that things can go wrong, that our autonomy may be stripped away from us, and our world can be cast into a sudden state of crisis. The phenomenological underpinnings that the sublime needs to keep at a safe distance—the sense of being overwhelmed, the fear and the awe—acquire in horror towering and uncontrollable dimensions: the optimistic wager of repurposing into an aesthetic object and a matter of personal aggrandizement that which exceeds the human leaves space to the pessimistic realization that, after all, we are not safe, nor can we ever become fully so. If the question "how can this be" may belong to the experience of both horror and the sublime, only in the former does it become symptomatic of a collapse of modernity's hopes for prediction, forecasting, and control.

What is there to be done against the "*orror*" that Leopardi identifies as a foundational experience of mankind? While the creation of a "*social catena*" seems desirable, Leopardi does not suggest any way out from the grip of the at times latent, at times overtly present horror that belongs to the human condition. The inevitability of our encounter with this experience mirrors the fate of the flower that gives title to Leopardi's poem *Broom*, a flower destined, eventually, to be annihilated by the "subterranean fire" of Mount Vesuvius.[42] The best that we can do, Leopardi suggests, is to face our condition with dignity and lucidity, and take the broom as symbolic of this attitude: "far wiser and less fallible / than man is, you did not presume / that either fate or you had made / your fragile kind immortal."[43]

This is no antidote: a heightened awareness of horror's presence in our world does not necessarily lead to an improvement in our chances of avoiding or dealing with it. Horror is the blow we cannot parry, and thus, for this reason too, a context-dependent experience: just as what could have been a source of horror in the past may not be so anymore, what we become adjusted to and handle better ceases to be a horrifying matter and moves us to a different phenomenological territory. From this perspective as well, horror may be deemed a foundational experience of mankind: ever adaptive to our current predicament, it stands as the experiential correlative of that which cannot be controlled and can cast our world into crisis.

While I am claiming that Leopardi should be considered a thinker of the horrifying similar to Kant's standing in relation to the sublime,[44] it remains dubious whether philosophizing about horror renders one better prepared to deal with it. Leopardi's personal writings give us the opportunity to read about how someone convinced of horror's foundational, everlasting, and inherent presence in our world reacted to its sudden eruption in his life. In concluding this chapter, I analyze Leopardi's retellings of his repeated encounters with something so immense and overpowering as to escape comprehension in a horrifying way: nothingness.

HORROR NIHILI: CONCLUSION

Is *horror vacui* the same as *horror nihili*? While the former, in Aristotelian terms, refers to nature's alleged distaste for the void, the latter's evocation of nothingness addresses humanity more directly, and our fears as well. What *horror vacui* suggests in terms of spatial emptiness, *horror nihili* infuses with a darker tonality: if dealing with an empty zone appears to be a feasible task, can the same be said about confronting nothingness itself? Nature may indeed abhor a vacuum, but the same is not necessarily true for human beings. Nothingness goes beyond the existentially neutral, as it evokes an absence of a disquieting kind: there is something unsettling about this word and its cognates (to annihilate; annihilation), as if a past or future threat were looming large.

Leopardi's reflections on nothingness are extensive, in a way that made him both a precursor and, according to Italian philosopher Emanuele Severino, the culmination of a certain strain of nihilism in Western metaphysics.[45] Nothingness is a central concern in Leopardi's thinking, so much so that he comes to define it as "principle of things, and indeed of God." The most important reason for his sweeping affirmation is that no-thing is absolutely necessary, "that is, there is no absolute reason why it cannot not be, or not be in a specific way, etc." (*Zib.* 1341). Nothingness and radical contingency go hand in hand: everything could be otherwise, because everything emerged from a state of complete indeterminacy. Since nothing is absolute and absolutely true, even the alleged perfection of God himself is illusory: just like any other idea, the idea of God, too, is grounded in pure possibility, which is to say in nothingness. For Leopardi everything comes from nothingness and goes back to it, with nothingness being the only "true infinity" (*Zib.* 4174).[46]

In Leopardi's writings, reason becomes nothingness's unlikely bedfellow. Whereas in ancient times mankind could still hold steady to what Leopardi calls *illusioni* to secure a degree of happiness and a system of values (*Zib.* 51), modernity's election of reason and its demystifying powers as the sense-making tool of the epoch led to an epistemic sea-change.[47] The upheaval provoked by this novel state of affairs revolves around reason's function, which, for Leopardi, is chiefly a negative one: "reason is an instrument of destruction rather than construction," which excels at showing the groundlessness of previously held beliefs (*Zib.* 4192), no matter the stabilizing role of such beliefs.[48] Reason resembles an autoimmune disease: the immune system developed to cast out falsities threatens mankind itself by attacking those very layers that once facilitated a state of happiness and spiritual grandeur. The "knowledge of the truth [*cognizione del vero*]" that reason promotes is what unveils the false nature of *illusioni* (*Zib.* 168, 4135), but in destroying them, according to Leopardi, we are left without our most effective existential defense mechanism and engine of greatness (*Zib.* 4135–36).[49] This process leads to a worldview that is "grim and wretched, yet alone truthful": those who embrace it "find and feel everywhere nothingness and emptiness, and the vanity of human cares and desires and hopes, and of all the illusions so inherent in life that without them it is not life" (*Zib.* 103).[50] With a line of argumentation that anticipates nihilism by several decades, reason is termed "the true mother and cause of nothingness" (*Zib.* 2941) and what validates in modernity the ancient adage *vanitas vanitatum et omnia vanitas.*

The literature on Leopardi's philosophical reflections on nothingness is substantial, and I will refer the interested reader to those contributions for a thorough exploration of the topic.[51] Instead, I want to delve into Leopardi's recollections of his own personal encounters with it. This may sound like a paradox: how can one retell an encounter with that which is no-thing? But the phenomenological approach of this book allows for a circumvention of this problem, as here, too, the focus is on a horrified subject rather than a horrifying phenomenon.

This is also the approach taken by Leopardi himself. Consider the following letter that he wrote to his friend Pietro Giordani in 1819—that is, before the passages from the *Zibaldone* analyzed in this chapter and the writing of the *Moral Essays* as well:

> I am so dazed by the nothingness that surrounds me that I do not know how I have the strength to take up the pen to respond to your letter from the first. If I were to go mad at this moment, I believe my madness would be to sit perpetually with astonished eyes, mouth agape, hands between my knees, neither laughing nor crying, nor moving except by force from wherever I might be. [. . .] And I am so terrified by the futility of all things, and the condition of humanity, with all passions dead, as they are extinguished in my soul, that I am beside myself, considering that even my despair is nothingness.[52]

The letter describes a twenty-two-year-old man utterly powerless against the nothingness he perceives around himself, whatever "nothingness" may be: while awe and being overwhelmed certainly belong to the experience Leopardi describes, instead of turning into a sublime device of self-aggrandizement they here underpin a state of paralysis. Much as awareness of the suffering inherent to sentience was the trigger for the horrification of a garden in the *Zibaldone* passage of April 1826 that opened this chapter, Leopardi, in his private correspondence, admits being unable to keep at bay the thought of the vanity—the nothingness—that envelops "all things," his desperation included.

Just a few months afterward, Leopardi returns to the topic in another letter to Giordani, dated March 6, 1820. In it, he laments that reason's "barbarous teaching" is that "human pleasures and pain are mere deceptions." Conversely, "the suffering that comes from the certainty of the nothingness of things is always and solely right and true."[53] This form of lucidity, however, is hardly sustainable. T. S. Eliot, a Leopardian likely unbeknown to himself, would later write similarly in his *Four Quartets* that "humankind / Cannot bear very much reality,"[54] which is here Leopardi's message as well: were we to constantly hold the gaze of nothingness, the outcome would be insanity. But instead of being a departure from reality, such "madness" would be "reasonable in every respect," and underpinned by the most crucial component of modernity's episteme: the reliance on reason itself.[55]

Given this state of affairs, forgetfulness is key: "everything in this world is done out of simple and continual forgetfulness of the universal truth that everything is nothing." In the absence of a degree of separation from nothingness—without a form of insulation from the horrifying—society itself would break down, and suffer the same paralysis Leopardi reported experiencing himself: "there is no other truth but nothingness, and this thought, and having it continually in the soul, as reason would have it, must necessarily and directly lead us to the state of being I have described."[56]

In the *Zibaldone,* too, around the same time when he wrote these letters, Leopardi insists on the hollowing effects of nothingness, as it drains from within the subject touched by it: "All is nothingness in the world, including my despair [. . .] Even this pain of mine is vain, nothing. After a certain time it will pass and turn to nothing, and leave me in a universal emptiness, a terrible apathy that will not even let me lament" (*Zib.* 72). The quasi-stoic tone of this note, already undermined by an apathy described as "terrible" that Leopardi foresees in his future, is shattered just a few pages later by nothingness's sudden and uncontrollable presencing in his life: "I was frightened to find myself in the midst of nothingness, a nothing myself. I felt as if I were suffocating, thinking and feeling that all is nothing, solid nothing" (*Zib.* 85). This encounter possesses no redemptive, enlightening elements, nor does it provide any kind of self-betterment or hardened resilience: horror simply takes over, engulfing Leopardi's present and casting his world into crisis, rendering him powerless.

While it has been argued that Leopardi's philosophical stance on nothingness changes over the years, at times in contradictory ways to the point of becoming inconsistent,[57] what remains constant throughout is a sense of the horrifying effects on the subject held by its grip[58]—be it only for a fleeting moment when the thought of the nothingness that precedes, follows, and envelops everything that exists cannot be kept at bay anymore. This is a recurring theme in Leopardi's writings, one that spans from these early *Zibaldone* notes to much later ones, and from the letters Leopardi wrote to Giordani in 1819 to the poems he would compose in the last years of his life.[59]

At this point, it should be clear that Leopardi's work is of a hopeless kind more than a hopeful one. If reason made us immune to the soothing power of *illusioni* and cast us adrift in a cosmos whose meaninglessness we can now recognize with lucidity, Leopardi would also grow disillusioned with love—this "ultimate illusion," as he defines it in the poem *To Himself*.[60] Nothing can be done to change this state of affairs, nor can anything truthfully be hoped for. This condition underpins what he calls the "horrible mystery of things and of universal existence" (*Zib.* 4099)—a formulation that should now appear even more foundational of Leopardi's thinking.

Nothingness also functions as a limit:[61] it represents an insurmountable barrier for mankind's resolution, and for modernity's battle-ready attitude as well. It erases the possibility of foundational meaningfulness, one that would perpetuate itself in time and constitute a solid grounding for our species. For the anti-Platonist, materialist, and atheist Leopardi, nothingness signifies that anything could be otherwise, that everything will eventually cease to be, and that nothing, in the end, truly matters. It is an abyss that spans our past and future, and in so doing affects our present as well.

From a Kantian perspective one may consider the infinity of nothingness as an instantiation of the sublime. In fact, Leopardi too, in his *Zibaldone*, offers a similar take, writing that in certain literary masterpieces "the spectacle of nothingness [. . .] seems to enlarge the reader's soul." But in the same note, Leopardi carefully emphasizes that a degree of separation must exist in order for nothingness to be repurposed as a device of self-aggrandizement. This separation is provided by the aesthetic mediation of a work of art, as our experience of it would radically differ if we encountered the same phenomenon "in the reality of things" (*Zib.* 260). It is in this lived confrontation with nothingness that Leopardi invites us to consider the horror beneath it, as some of his personal writings pull the topic from the realm of aesthetics and metaphysics to that of phenomenology.

Yet, if horror requires something more than an aesthetic device to erupt into a life, this does not mean that aesthetics plays no role. A different perspective is possible, one that focuses on the role of aesthetics in *describing* an experience, rather than in *provoking* it. Otherwise said, while I share Leopardi's doubts about the possibility of using literary tools to reliably horrify a reader, I do not mean to suggest that they cannot be used to describe the horror that may take hold of someone's present. In fact, this is exactly what I have argued Leopardi does in the garden passage here thoroughly analyzed, as he deforms, twists, and upends the standard descriptors of a situation in order to convey a shift in attitude—a horrifying one—regarding it. This book will present several other examples of a similar reliance on an aesthetics of deformation to recount the sudden eruption of horror into a life.

Leopardi's take on horror focuses on its presence and effects in everyday life, rather than seeking to evoke it via monstrous creatures or otherworldly situations. I take the garden passage from the *Zibaldone* that opened this chapter as symbolic of this attitude: there is no need to look far beyond the plausible, Leopardi seems to suggest, to find the motifs that today we associate with the horror genre. The gory, the repellent, the painful, the powerlessness and the absence of control that we connect to horror are not to be found in twisted flights of the mind only: they are all around us, in plain sight, if one looks carefully enough.

If considered from this perspective, Leopardi's garden of tortures becomes an invitation to consider the ordinary world under a more disquieting light. Written in April 1826, that passage is the concluding part of a longer block of text. In it, Leopardi goes beyond the contextually circumscribed and the singular instantiation of the horrifying by expanding the state of affairs symbolized by his torture garden to existence writ large:

> Everything is evil. That is to say everything that is, is evil; that each thing exists is an evil; each thing exists only for an evil end; existence is an evil and made for evil; the end of the universe is evil; the order and the state, the laws, the natural development of the universe are nothing but evil, and they are directed to nothing but evil. There is no other

> good except nonbeing; there is nothing good except what is not; things that are not things: all things are bad. All existence; the complex of so many worlds that exist; the universe; is only a spot, a speck in metaphysics. Existence, by its nature and essence and generally, is an imperfection, an irregularity, a monstrosity. But this imperfection is a tiny thing, literally a spot, because all the worlds that exist, however many and however extensive they are, since they are certainly not infinite in number or in size, are consequently infinitely small in comparison with the size the universe might be if it were infinite, and the whole of existence is infinitely small in comparison with the true infinity, so to speak, of nonexistence, of nothing. (*Zib.* 4174)

We have come full circle, as the mention of nothingness closes the paragraph that begins the garden passage that opens this chapter. While this quoted segment does not describe a moment of horror per se, it encapsulates, perhaps better than any other page by Leopardi, the hopeless, relentless, and foundational nature of the "horrible mystery of things and of universal existence" that his writings variously address. Everything is evil, for Leopardi, because everything is stuck between the hammer of suffering, represented by the torture garden, and the anvil of nothingness, discussed in this section.

The horror of this condition is not always present to us. Here, too, forgetfulness is key, and positive asymmetries certainly belong to an episteme like the modern one, whose goal is to exert an ever increasing control over the world and its circumstances: it is indeed expedient, if not outright necessary at times, to focus on the garden in bloom rather than the one "in a state of *souffrance*." Leopardi was aware of this, and mourned until his death the modern loss of those *illusioni* that made life sweeter.

Beyond this lamentation for a vanished obliviousness to the frightful position we dwell in, Leopardi invites us to keep in mind the fragility inherent to the control we exert over our lives. But, as sung in *Broom*, this awareness does not necessarily lead to a kind of preparedness that involves the overcoming of the catastrophe. Despite modernity's bulwarks, we remain exposed to events that may all of a sudden cast our world into a state of crisis—even only through a momentary, heightened awareness of our precarious ontological condition, one inherently bound to suffering and surrounded by nothingness.

Just as in a horror story, there is no reason to assume that things will ultimately go well. This is a profoundly unsettling statement, which Leopardi invites us to reckon with even if it runs against what we modern individuals are bound to believe, eager as we are to stick to our positive asymmetries as members of increasingly insulated societies. In a similar spirit, the penultimate page of the *Zibaldone* displays an entry that reads as a bitter acknowledgment of the difficulties inherent to our condition: "Two truths that men will generally never believe: one, that we know nothing, the other, that we are nothing. Add the third, which depends a lot on the second: that there is nothing to hope for after death" (*Zib.* 4525).

Indeed, no one truly believes in horror stories—do they?

TWO

NOT IN CONTROL: CARLO MICHELSTAEDTER AND LUIGI PIRANDELLO

In January 1892, Norwegian painter Edvard Munch wrote in his diary an entry that reads as eerily similar to the garden passage from the *Zibaldone* of Leopardi, addressed in the previous chapter:

> I was walking along the road with two friends. The sun set. I felt a tinge of melancholy. Suddenly the sky became a bloody red. I stopped, leaned against the railing, dead tired and I looked at the flaming clouds that hung like blood and a sword over the blue-black fjord and the city. My friends walked on. I stood there, trembling with fright. And I felt a loud, unending scream piercing nature.[1]

This verbal description finds its pictorial rendition in Munch's *The Scream*, with which it is frequently juxtaposed according to the author's intentions. This most famous canvas depicts a horrified world, where familiar phenomena—the sky, a bridge, the water—assume disquieting traits. In the middle of *The Scream* stands a humanoid figure whose abnormally elongated hands are placed by the face; in constituting the work's focal point, it draws the viewer's attention to a figure from which the rest of the painting both emanates and returns. Indeed, this person—Munch himself, as we gather from his aforementioned diary note—is subject to the horrified world sprawling around him, but is also its conjurer: both in the diary entry and in the painting, the two men in the background who keep walking seem oblivious to the mutation reality undergoes, their figures remaining straight in contrast to the queer shapes of Munch's body. Nature may indeed be screaming, just as in Leopardi's garden, but its shriek can be heard only by those attuned to it.

I use the concept of aesthetics of deformation to group together descriptive techniques constituted by a deviation from verisimilitude, as when a work of art embraces an unsettling style while remaining anchored to a baseline realism. Both Leopardi's garden and Munch's *The Scream* operate within this aesthetic framework, as they deform reality without the interpolation of any supernatural elements, but rather by teasing out the horrifying elements lurking beneath the ordinary. In both instances, the phenomenological orientation of what is depicted belongs to an individual who experiences a moment—or the event (*Ereignis*)—of horror. The aesthetics of deformation provides an outlet to convey the otherwise subjective experiential twist taking place, as it marks a shift that has made someone's reality more disquieting than the norm.

In art history, Expressionism is the current with which this approach most naturally aligns. Starting from the end of the nineteenth century, Expressionism infused the representation of the external world with a personal twist: against Naturalism and Impressionism's attempts at providing a snapshot of what is out there, it sought to bring to the fore the fundamental role that subjectivity plays in shaping one's experience of reality, in particular when it appears as a troubling matter.

Munch's production, and especially *The Scream*, encapsulates much of what Expressionism is and does. It is important to keep in mind that according to his diary note, the horrification of the world the author describes and depicts is forced rather than willed. As with Leopardi's garden, Munch is not seeking out a certain experience, nor can he exert any control on it: all of a sudden a shift takes place, one that alters how he relates to his surroundings. This shift consummated, his world is cast into crisis—a phenomenological crisis rendered aesthetically through a tear in the fabric of realism, one that makes the world *appear* otherwise, because it *feels* otherwise.

Powerlessness, a crucial element in my understanding of horror, is at the core of Expressionism. In the words of literary critic Thomas Harrison, this current "comprises a vision of history as nightmare, an obsession with mortality and decay, a sense of human marginalization from the autonomous developments of culture, and the responses they spur."[2] The common denominator of these components is that they all underpin a worldview in which man is largely prey to overpowering forces active in history and metaphysics. Orthogonal to a Cartesian view of ever increasing mastery over the world and its circumstances, Expressionism brings attention back to those morbid and disquieting aspects of reality that largely resist our control.

If Leopardi's bleak worldview found few sympathizers in the early nineteenth century, by the beginning of the twentieth Expressionism would bring similar instances to the forefront of European artistic milieus. Such transition is not to be divorced from historical events, and it is no coincidence that the looming sense of crisis pervading society at the time led to a reassessment of what Leopardi had ironically termed, decades earlier, the "*magnificent, progressive destiny*" of mankind.[3] The gathering of the dissonant, overcharged forces of the early twentieth century would soon erupt in the cacophonies of the battles of the Marne and Verdun, to resurface again just a few years afterward, thundering from the devices of mass communication employed by totalitarian regimes, and eventually echoing through the Gestapo's torture chambers, and more.[4] To quote Sloterdijk's pithy formulation, in the twentieth century "wonder changed its colors to alienation and horror,"[5] as it became increasingly clear that the wholly enlightened earth was radiant with triumphant calamity.[6]

I shall return to history's horrors in the next chapter. For now, I will delve into the cracks of early twentieth-century optimism, particularly concerning the lives of members of the up-and-coming class of the bourgeoisie, which increasingly positioned itself at the center of the economic, political, and social world. Expressionism represented a rejection of the bourgeois values that prevailed at the turn of the century; this took place, among other things, through the rebuttal of realism and naturalism, a critique of materialism and rationalism, the focus on themes such as alienation and decay, and an anti-establishment attitude. More pointedly, Expressionism's distortions of reality troubled the desires of the bourgeois class for stability and progress by showing that things can suddenly go wrong, and become soaked in a more horrifying light. Despite the veneer of composure belonging to an apparently well-ordered and predictable world, Expressionism suggests that something more disquieting lurks underneath.

Expressionistic artworks depict a multiplicity of instances of ordinary horror, and they frequently do so through the techniques that belong to the aesthetics of deformation. Given this, it would be tempting to extend the category of Expressionism through time, and make of it a transhistorical artistic sensibility akin to what Italian critic Gianfranco Contini defines as "metaphorical expressionism."[7] Yet, I believe that a more balanced approach is one that extends through time an experience rather than an artistic current, as it is cumbersome to argue for the transhistoricity of a movement presented in many contexts as chronologically quite well defined; historical categorizations exist also because they do useful work in schools, textbooks, museums, and beyond. Conversely, acknowledging the transhistorical nature of an experience is a less contentious position. Such experience will surely change through time and express itself differently in different contexts, but this does not alter the fact that there is an experience that we call horror, just as there is one we call love, that belongs to our way of being in the world, historical contingencies notwithstanding. Accordingly, instead of considering the representation of horror through deforming aesthetics as something that makes a work of art belong to the current of Expressionism, it seems more expedient to flip this perspective, and instead argue that horror is a common experience that found in Expressionism a remarkable venue for aesthetic articulation, but not the only one. Crucially, this does not flatten out the complexities of Expressionism and make of it a mere artistic vessel for the horrifying; instead, my claim simply points to how the representation of horror is a frequent and crucial feature of this movement, without claiming it to be the only one.

Embracing this perspective helps explain how certain motifs of Expressionism, such as its aesthetics and thematic fixations, are found in contexts and authors typically not associated with this current. Italy, for instance, is not the first country that comes to mind in talking about Expressionism, and for good reason. But in the Italian canon, too, there are figures whose production reflects the concerns this current evokes and responds to: such is the case for the two early twentieth-century protagonists of this chapter, Carlo Michelstaedter and Luigi Pirandello.[8]

Coherent with the "reading for scenes" approach of this book, this chapter focuses on these two authors' depictions of moments when a sense of a safe and predictable everydayness shatters, leaving space for a more disquieting landscape. Whereas for Leopardi this state of affairs is tied to metaphysics and is largely the outcome of his philosophy, in Michelstaedter and Pirandello the horrified individuals are bourgeois men scarcely interested in speculative matters but convinced of leading a safe and stable life. Both authors emphasize how this belief is largely bolstered by the increasingly central role played by societal devices, such as insurance policies, in creating the impression of a form of preventive control over moments when things go wrong. Against the backdrop of this apparent tightening of what Leopardi called the "*social catena*," Michelstaedter and Pirandello show that even those who seem furthest removed from the horrifying, surrounded as they are by layers of insulation, remain exposed to events that may upend their lives and bring to their world the unsettling totalities characteristic of Expressionism.

The few existing comparative analyses of Michelstaedter and Pirandello focus either on the similarities between their binomial philosophies (*persuasione* [persuasion] and *rettorica* [rhetoric] in the former, *vita* [life] and *forme* [forms] for the latter) or on their shared status as symptomatologists of their times, in particular concerning their critiques of metaphysical truth.[9] My analysis, instead, compares and contrasts how both authors explore and describe the very moments when certainties about how things ought to unfold collapse, leaving one feeling powerless. This allows me to introduce what I term the *safety fallacy*: the exaggerated sense of control one believes one exerts over one's own life. This fallacy, I will show, creates a false impression of security—an impression that horror undoes.

Building on the previous chapter's discussion of horror—its phenomenological and historical contours, and its connection to powerlessness in modernity—this chapter examines a crucial aspect of the experience: its temporality. A pattern typical to the horror genre involves a breakthrough event that affects the plot from that moment on, such as the appearance of a monster. While effective in seizing an audience's attention, this is not necessarily how horror behaves in ordinary life, where this experience can be a temporally limited episode or a situation that quickly turns out to be less troublesome than initially thought, such as an in-flight turbulence or a diagnostic error. Moreover, and mindful of the concept of positive asymmetry discussed previously, we may also dismiss a horrifying episode once it recedes from the forefront of our attention, even if the possibility of its resurfacing still looms large.

My interest in Michelstaedter lies precisely in his depictions of moments of horror that his protagonists quickly snap out of and promptly seek to forget. Analyzing these scenes helps us understand horror as a present-centered experience, and distinguish it from a past-oriented one like trauma. But just as I argued in chapter 1 that there is nothing fixed about what can horrify, there is no certainty that one can quickly snap out of this experience and forget about it. A phenomenology of horror must thus also include those cases where a single instantiation of the horrifying leaves long-lasting repercussions. To explore this point, the last section of this chapter turns to Pirandello's work to analyze how a single moment of horror can radically destabilize a subject, thus making them more susceptible to future eruptions of the same experience.

A MOMENT OF SHATTERING: CARLO MICHELSTAEDTER

On Monday, October 17, 1910, twenty-three-year-old Carlo Michelstaedter finished writing *Persuasion and Rhetoric*, his idiosyncratic dissertation on these two concepts in Plato and Aristotle, now recognized as a philosophical masterpiece of the Italian twentieth century. A few hours earlier, he had argued with his beloved mother Emma about her birthday celebration, which he had apparently forgotten about. At 2:00 p.m. that same Monday, sitting at his desk, Michelstaedter shot himself—twice, according to the local newspaper.[10]

Ever since, his suicide has become a subject of speculation: why did such a physically healthy, artistically gifted, and scholarly talented young man take his own life? It was a "metaphysical suicide" according to some: for them, Michelstaedter's gesture represented the purest outcome of his nihilistic philosophy.[11] For others, Michelstaedter's deteriorating mental health had eventually actualized his suicidal tendencies.[12] In recent years, a more intermediate position has been suggested: just as Michelstaedter's life should not be read as the embodiment of philosophical convictions inevitably leading to self-annihilation, too decisive a separation between his suicide and way of thinking about life results in equally reductionist analyses.[13] This latter position is arguably the least dogmatic one: instead of closing the case, it maintains that some enigmas may remain unsolved.

What is horrifying in a suicide? In many cases, it is the indecipherability of this act and the questions it leaves behind—for a corpse can surely be a disquieting matter, especially when surrounded by a halo of opacity.

Detective fiction is a good example of our desires to dissipate the shroud of fog surrounding a death: a basic assumption of this genre is that to a corpse belongs a mystery, which can, at least in theory, be unraveled with success. Indeed, the most powerful tool available to Edgar Allan Poe's Auguste Dupin, the archetype of the fictional detective, is his ratiocination—the skill of solving mysteries through a complex process combining logic, observation, and inference.

But not all deaths, and perhaps especially not self-inflicted ones, lead to a neat resolution; there are circumstances under which a corpse assumes darker tonalities. This is true even in detective fiction, as seen in H. P. Lovecraft's horror tales, where the police officers tasked with solving a case end up facing the limits of their reasoning. John Legrasse in "The Call of Cthulhu" or Thomas Malone in "The Horror at Red Hook" both stop short of reaching a point of denouement when the threads of a story are drawn together, and its workings are explained or resolved. Instead, their investigations raise question after question, overwhelmingly so, and climax with events that frustrate the detectives' ratiocination instead of comfortably wrapping up a plot by unraveling its mysteries.

The suicide of a young person often does not lend itself to clear and distinct explanations regarding its underlying causes: it is what lies beneath it that constitutes one of the most unsettling elements of the act. In his essay "The Michelstaedter Enigma," Thomas Harrison asks: "What would it have taken for Michelstaedter to continue to live?"[14] Harrison speculates that if Michelstaedter had embraced his artistic side, he could have found a way of productively marshalling the ghosts of his life. This may well be. But Harrison's question implies looking ahead: it involves either the awareness of one's talents as potential sources of fulfillment over time, or at least a praxis that seeks to repurpose dysphoria into euphoria. In other words, Harrison's question implies thinking in terms of a future, which may not be possible for someone who is considering committing suicide.

Suicide forecloses the possibility of a future; it is the most radical answer to a state that cannot be endured any longer. Perhaps more pressingly than negating what may come, suicide wishes to annihilate what is currently taking place. From this perspective, too, horror and suicide are closely connected. Contrary to anxiety's presupposition of a partly indeterminate, menacing or disquieting element ahead in time, horror confronts the subject with what is happening now: horror erupts when some*thing* escapes our control and cannot be kept at bay anymore—be it a thought or a situation. Such an event may, in turn, cast someone's present into crisis, as this newly established intentional relation both evokes and responds to a state of forced powerlessness.

Suicide, too, evokes and responds to a state of crisis, as it entails an act so disruptive as to call into question one of the most basic tenets of human life: self-preservation. Horror's relation to suicide is thus twofold: on the one hand, those alive may be horrified by such an act for a number of reasons; on the other hand, it is likely that the person who commits suicide was also held in horror's grip, in a way that made their present untenable. Seized by the forced powerlessness characteristic of this experience, one may seek a way out of it through death itself.

If we focus on the horror underneath Michelstaedter's taking of his own life, a better suited question is, what did it take for Michelstaedter to *cease* to live? What situation was so unsustainable as to call for the annihilation of the present itself? There is, of course, no final answer. In the case of Leopardi, I argued that his garden passage represents a moment when the outcome of his metaphysics is revealed in all its horror. This did not lead Leopardi to suicide, although the topic is certainly present in his pages, and is, in some way, a specter that haunts his thinking.[15] Could it be that a similar dynamic, just more extreme in its outcome, played a role in Michelstaedter's suicide? Could his suicide have stemmed, at least in part, from a momentary collapse of the safe distance between how he *thought* about life and how he *lived* it?

Michelstaedter's philosophy is indeed distinctively concerned with issues of volition, fulfillment, and awareness.[16] In his dissertation he repurposes the Platonic and Aristotelian concepts of *persuasione* and *rettorica* into the two cornerstones of his thinking. *Persuasione* means the full possession of oneself, as in coherence of words, thoughts, and deeds: in Michelstaedter's terms, "persuaded is *he who has his life within himself*."[17] This condition, however, is unattainable: "the way of persuasion [. . .] is hyperbolic" (*PR*, 47). *Persuasione* can never fully be achieved, as long as words and acts are conditioned by desires, hopes, or fears that dwell in the future. This projection onto the future, Michelstaedter argues, is part of the human condition and collides with the presentness of *persuasione*.

If *persuasione* is unachievable, *rettorica*, conversely, permeates everything as the system of beliefs and apparatus of institutions that pretends that *persuasione* can either be achieved or has been achieved already. In being so, *rettorica* is what gives false meaning to everything that does not have any meaning in itself; similar to Leopardi's *piacere*, *rettorica* makes one turn from thing to thing, with everything becoming a means for something else. Whereas *persuasione* signifies meaningful stillness, *rettorica* implies meaningless motion.

The letters and notes Michelstaedter left behind document a struggle between *persuasione* and *rettorica* in his own life.[18] Michelstaedter's insistence on knowing the reasons behind the way we act reads as symptomatic of the inseparability with which he connected speculations and deeds: for him, one's life must be lived according to one's own philosophy rather than considering the latter an abstract appendage of the former. If theory and praxis should thus be entangled, the unattainability of *persuasione* leaves its thinker in a frustrating position, one painfully aware of a lack, if not a flaw, in their own existence.

We can speculate—and only speculate—that Michelstaedter's suicide also responded to a breakdown of his balancing act between the awareness of his lack of *persuasione* and the necessity to keep this awareness under control. Thrown off balance by the events of his life, such as the argument with his mother and his own likely depressive tendencies, Michelstaedter may have succumbed to the suddenly untenable realization of his own insufficiency in practicing his philosophy. Yet, regardless of our desire to find a conclusive explanation for his actions, it is crucial to emphasize that any assertions concerning the reasons behind Michelstaedter's death must remain within the territory of the hypothetical and presuppose a layer of opacity. Indeed, Michelstaedter's suicide resembles more a horror tale than a detective story.

Instead of focusing on the reasons underlying Michelstaedter's taking of his own life, I am here interested in reading this act as a moment of severe crisis that spun out of control, and tragically so. Chilling as it may sound in hindsight, thinking about and depicting similar moments of horrifying crisis is something that Michelstaedter did in the months leading to his suicide: *Persuasion and Rhetoric* includes passages that momentarily set aside the philosophical tone of the book to provide thick descriptions of figures dealing with situations that they suddenly experience as untenable.

In the following discussion, I focus on the crucial role that horror plays in a selection of passages from Michelstaedter's masterpiece, and on why he resorted to the depiction of this experience in a philosophical work. Two scenes in particular depict men whose conviction of knowing what they do, and the control they believe themselves to exert over their lives, is shown either to be precarious, or to collapse altogether. In these scenes *rettorica*'s veil of reassuring illusions is torn, and the subject must confront their powerlessness in the face of a given situation. Through an analysis of these moments, I explore horror's temporality and propose a distinction between its present-centered nature and the past-oriented focus of trauma.[19]

Just like everyone else, I am aware that at some point I will die. My knowledge of this is syllogistic: since human beings are mortal, and I am reasonably confident of being a human myself, it follows that I too am mortal, despite the fact that I have never empirically tested this hypothesis.

For the most part I have made my peace with this and go about my everyday life without excessive concern that at some point I will face death. But what if someone told me that tomorrow I would surely die? If I trusted them, this news would cause massive repercussions in my life, because knowing I will be no more would cease to be a future concern that I can more or less easily bracket and would instead color my present as perhaps its most defining element. Nothing would change, ontologically speaking: I have always known that I am mortal and that I could die at any moment, potentially within the next few hours. Yet, the newly discovered awareness that tomorrow I would certainly be dead would likely start affecting my present, and turn it into something much more unsettling. This revelation would become an event (*Ereignis*), something that alters the very parameters of subject and world, with a process similar to the one that, in the previous chapter, made Leopardi's garden appear as a torture chamber once the idea of the ubiquity of suffering could not be kept at bay anymore.

Why would the knowledge of my soon-to-occur death horrify me? An answer is that it would strip me of any sense of agency concerning my future as I would become powerless to shape it. Upon becoming aware of my incumbent death, my ontologically unchanged present would undergo a phenomenological shift—that is, my world would change, because of a modification in how I intentionally relate to it. This would likely involve a reassessment of my priorities: instead of preparing for next week's class,

I might choose to spend time with my loved ones or perhaps drive to the ocean. Here, too, one could say that nothing has fundamentally changed: I could very much do these activities right now if I really wanted to, but instead I continue doing something else—something such as working on this chapter, a task that right now I experience as laborious and yet see as a necessary step toward the completion of my book (a desirable and, in fact, desired goal). That we behave in such ways is no surprise: oftentimes we do things *now* because they will have effects *later*.

How much of our thoughts and actions stem from the future, more than from the present? In other words, how much of what we do would change if we knew that we would not be alive in a matter of hours? From this point of view, death seems to act as a reagent, something that alters a situation if added to it, teasing out what would be left hidden otherwise. We owe to Heidegger one of the most significant explorations of the unconcealing powers of what he considered one's ownmost, nonrelational, and uttermost possibility of being, as in what he termed "being-towards-death."[20] But before him, Michelstaedter, too, made the case for death's revelatory powers.[21]

Michelstaedter's *Persuasion and Rhetoric* is an atypical philosophy book, one intermixed with mathematical formulas, diagrams, untranslated passages in German or ancient Greek, fictional dialogues, apologues, and other oddities. Here, I will focus on scenes where its style momentarily shifts from the philosophical to the literary, as figures of speech and thick, rich descriptions of characters, atmospheres, and situations take over the otherwise analytic, albeit idiosyncratic unfolding of the text.[22]

In one of these literary scenes, Michelstaedter stages an experiment aimed at revealing whether someone can truly be said to have made *persuasione* the key element of their life, an experiment for which the preceding paragraphs have already set the stage: what if someone was told that tomorrow they would surely be dead?

> Do you say you are persuaded of what you do, no matter what? Yes? Then I tell you: tomorrow you will certainly be dead. It doesn't matter? Are you thinking about fame? About your family? But your memory dies with you, with you your family is dead. Are you thinking about your ideals? You want to make a will? You want a headstone? But tomorrow those too are dead, dead. All men die with you. Your death is an unwav-

> ering comet. Do you turn to god? There is no god, god dies with you. The kingdom of heaven crumbles with you, tomorrow you are dead, dead. Tomorrow everything is finished—your body, family, friends, country, what you're doing now, what you might do in the future, the good, the bad, the true, the false, your ideas, your little part, god and his kingdom, paradise, hell, everything, everything, everything. Tomorrow everything is over—in twenty-four hours is *death*. (*PR*, 37–38)

In *Persuasion and Rhetoric*, Michelstaedter frequently and freely addresses his reader, as he seeks to promote a first-person confrontation with the matters he philosophizes about.[23] If the revelation of one's incumbent death can likely overwhelm the affected individual, stylistically speaking this is rendered by an equally overwhelming enumeration of what will be lost with one's passing. To a multiplicity of questions ("Are you thinking about fame? About your family?"), "death" is the only given answer ("But your memory dies with you, with you your family is dead"), which is repeated multiple times—similar to a recurring thought one cannot escape. Forms of mental association, be they through opposition ("the good, the bad, the true, the false, [. . .] paradise, hell") or contiguity ("your body, family, friends, country, [. . .] your ideas, your little part"), are all leveled by the foreclosure of tomorrow ("Tomorrow everything is over—in twenty-four hours is *death*"), which goes so far as to affect "god and his kingdom," too.

This need not be the case: as is typical of Michelstaedter's binomial philosophy, rather than univocal the consequences of this revelation are affected by the split between *persuasione* and *rettorica* in how someone conducts themself. If the former is what rules a life, "what you do, which is all inside you at the point of your doing it, cannot be taken away by anyone," not even by death itself, insofar as authentic *persuasione* involves words, thoughts, and deeds cohering and acquiring meaning in the present. Conversely, since the latter is predicated upon the importance of a future whereby volition can unfold, the certainty of incumbent death will shake the very existential foundations of someone held steady by *rettorica*'s grip. At the gap between these two attunements to life, death acts as a reagent: if the foreclosure of the future casts someone into a state of crisis, one's alleged *persuasione* will be exposed as false.

A state of crisis is indeed how the analyzed passage from *Persuasion and Rhetoric* continues. In it, Michelstaedter's prose acquires expressionistic tonalities to depict the horror that suddenly takes hold of a man becoming aware that "in twenty-four hours is *death*":

> Well . . . [well . . .] [*Allora* . . . *allora* . . .] then the god of today is no longer yesterday's, no longer the country, the good, the bad, friends, or family. You want to eat? No, you cannot. The taste of food is no longer the same; honey is bitter, milk is sour, meat nauseating, and the odor, the odor sickens you: *it reeks of the dead*. You want a woman to comfort you in your last moments? No, worse: *it is dead flesh*. You want to enjoy the sun, air, light, sky? Enjoy?! The sun is a rotten orange, the light extinguished, the air suffocating. The sky is a low, oppressive arc . . . No, everything is closed and dark now. (*PR*, 38)[24]

The repetition of the conclusive coordinating conjunction "*allora*" emphasizes that the present paragraph should be understood as a direct consequence of the previous one—that is, the novel awareness of one's incumbent death. What was about to disappear is now pulled back to the subject's consciousness only to be rendered via what I call the aesthetics of deformation: starting from what is close and immediately perceptible by the subject, such as his hunger, increasingly negative adjectives describe how food at first tastes just vaguely different, then turns bitter, and finally becomes nauseating. With an emphasis on the phenomenological thickness of this experience, the aura of death affects the senses of smell and touch, too, resulting in the food "*reek[ing] of the dead*," and the body of a woman feeling like "*dead flesh*." Expanding away from the subject's immediate vicinity, the surrounding world, too, twists as if depicted in an Expressionist canvas, with the sun turning into a rotten orange, the air becoming unbreathable, the sky morphing into an oppressive vault—until the experience reaches its apex and collapses altogether ("everything is closed and dark now").

Michelstaedter presupposes that varying degrees of *persuasione* and *rettorica* would involve substantial differences in how someone experienced being made aware of their incumbent death. For him, and before this was formalized by phenomenology, the way we dwell in the world is not neutral, but instead is affected by myriad contextual circumstances, which lead to an equally sprawling set of possible intentional engagements with reality.[25] As Michelstaedter writes in *Persuasion and Rhetoric*, "Look at the face of a friend you trust and you find a noble visage. You locate the nobility either in the nose or the forehead or 'a certain something of the eyes'; look at him when he has betrayed you and you see a vile mouth, a sinister glance, 'an expression that's just not right.'" In sum, asks Michelstaedter, "What is the experience of reality?" (*PR*, 88–89).

The way we experience reality always involves a certain subjective slant, because our encounter with the world is mediated by our whole persona—that is, by our moods and transitory inclinations, too: "In order to have *objective experience I must watch the things I do not see*, for those that I see, I see by the assent of my entire *persona*," writes Michelstaedter in this regard, with a tone aimed at attacking the positivism of his time (*PR*, 91). Since our experience of reality is thus bent by the weight of subjective circumstances, then, just as a garden can turn into a torture chamber, there is nothing fixed about the way we experience food, someone else's body, or even the sun. If I am claustrophobic, my experience of entering a small room is not simply awareness of four walls close to each other: it is a sense of oppression, whereby the four walls and the space they contain become in my consciousness something else—something more.

In order to describe how subjective circumstances are affecting in a horrifying way the present of a man just made aware that in twenty-four hours he will be dead, Michelstaedter resorts to literary prose and creates the scene here analyzed. It is a *literary* scene centered on the protagonist's phenomenology—that is, a scene that brackets claims to neutrality or objectivity, and instead focuses on describing how a given subject experiences the world at a given point. The aesthetics of deformation at play in it do not presuppose any strong ontological claims concerning the nature of the phenomena present on the page: it is neither about the sun *truly being* a rotten orange nor about it *truly appearing* as such; more narrowly, this description refers to a shift taking place in how the subject phenomenologically relates to the sun, a shift that, given the use of the negative descriptors employed by Michelstaedter, evokes and responds to a negatively charged, unexpectedly disturbing novel state of affairs.

The phenomenological thrust of the page is emphasized by the continuation of the scene:

> But the sun shines, the air is pure, everything is like before, and yet you speak like a man buried alive, describing his tomb. And persuasion? You are not even persuaded of the sunlight; you cannot move a finger,

> cannot remain standing. The god who kept you standing, made your day clear and your food sweet, gave you family, country, paradise—he betrays you now and abandons you because the thread of your φιλοψυχία [philopsychia] is broken. (*PR*, 38)

The world darkens only for the subject experiencing it as such. This shift consummated, as if buried alive, the unnamed man finds himself utterly powerless in relation to the present circumstances. Different from Leopardi's philosophical approach, in which horror was largely the outcome of a set of metaphysical beliefs argued throughout his work, this scene presents a sudden transition in someone's life from a state of normalcy to a world turned upside-down due to a change in what Michelstaedter calls φιλοψυχία, "philopsychia." Central to his lexicon, Michelstaedter translates this Greek word as "love of life, cowardice" (*PR*, 20), and it stands in for a force that closely resembles what Giacomo Leopardi and Arthur Schopenhauer—both known to Michelstaedter[26]—respectively called *piacere* and *Wille*. Philopsychia is what moves the individual from one object of desire to another, without ever allowing for the full satisfaction that would equal *persuasione*. Death severs the thread of philopsychia, and in so doing pulls the rug from under the feet of those whose life is ruled by a constant projection onto the future. Conversely, "he who for one instant wants his life to be *his*, only for an instant to be persuaded of what he does, must take possession of the present, *to see every present as the last*, as if death were certain afterward, *and to create his own life by himself in the obscurity*" (*PR*, 39, original emphasis).

Michelstaedter's insistence on the presentness of *persuasione* is mirrored by the presentness of horror: if the former refers to a complete fulfillment in and by the present, the latter is that which makes of the present an overwhelming state of affairs. This is a point of crucial importance, as it is my contention that horror is indeed a present-centered experience. This formulation may strike my reader as odd: one may wonder, are there any experiences that do not center on the present? This is a sensible objection, which calls for clarification.

By "present-centered" I refer to experiences that fully revolve around what is happening now, and that powerfully compel someone's attention to focus on the ongoing circumstances. High-intensity experiences usually draw the entirety of our persona to focus on them: think of being on a roller-coaster, having sexual intercourse, or escaping from a dangerous situation. It is generally difficult to daydream or space out in those moments, as they lock our attention to what is happening. Horror, I argue, is part of this set of experiences: when it takes over, everything that matters is what is currently taking place, in its overpowering, negative, and disruptive nature. The powerlessness that horror evokes and responds to also lies here, as it means that an individual cannot dismiss or move away from what is commanding their attention.

This is what happens to the man in the scene from *Persuasion and Rhetoric* here discussed: while his incumbent death necessarily involves a projection into the future, the consequences of this realization fold back onto the present. It is the present that becomes oppressive, where the sun becomes a rotten orange, the air unbreathable, and the sky a closed vault. This, crucially, is not a description of what dying may feel like; instead, it describes what it is like to be horrified *now* by the perspective of certain death *then*. If I am horrified by something, it affects me at this very moment—either as what is happening in front of my eyes or as a psychological process impacting my present, as in the currently analyzed passage.

The emphasis on the presentness of horror also allows us to address how this experience differs from trauma, while being potentially interrelated with it. The archipelago of approaches, methodologies, and theorizations on the topic makes clear that trauma resists easy categorizations.[27] Like horror, trauma is part of our ordinary language, as a word that we use effortlessly—perhaps at times too effortlessly—to describe the aftermath of events that leave an individual or a community wounded. This latter element is central to trauma both conceptually and, in fact, etymologically speaking, with the word deriving from the ancient Greek τραῦμα, or "wound." Indeed, the idea of an original, "traumatic" event is a key component of how this word is used, and represents a common denominator that seems to precede disagreements about, for instance, the unspeakability of trauma, which constituted a key component of the first wave of trauma studies but has been challenged by more recent scholarship.[28]

Despite the variety of approaches to it, a fixed element of this experience is what Colin Davis and Hanna Meretoja, building on Cathy Caruth's canonical *Unclaimed Experience*, call trauma's belatedness: "belatedness [is] constitutive of the temporal structure of trauma: trauma is characterized by a delayed response to an overwhelming event that cannot be processed at the time of its occurrence but manifests itself through intrusive thoughts, flashbacks or nightmares."[29] Since trauma necessarily involves a dialectic between a past wound and a present resurfacing, it is worth reflecting on the phenomenology of that initial wound as it is inflicted on a subject—a subject who will become traumatized by it. Indeed, is that initial event, as it happens, the trauma *in itself,* or is trauma the concept that we use to describe that event *in conjunction* with what follows?

Davis and Meretoja underline that "after terrorist attacks, school shootings and natural disasters, it has become commonplace to see horrific events as traumatizing and to offer psychological counseling or 'debriefing' to survivors and witnesses."[30] For the two authors, it is a "horrific event" that creates the wound, the τραῦμα, that will keep festering. Indeed, I contend that horror is a core component of trauma insofar as the former can be the source of the latter: in triggering a moment of shattering that reverberates over time, a horrifying experience sends its shoots into the future. Beyond its impact in the present, the forced powerlessness characteristic of horror in this case would also manifest as the impossibility of overcoming the trauma-inducing event in the first place.

Trauma need not be understood as orthogonal to horror, but can be viewed instead as adjacent to it and in fact, at times, as a twinned experience. Similar to how the initial traumatic event may be described as horrific, the recurring instantiation of trauma, too, can provoke horror, as in the intrusive thoughts, flashbacks, or nightmares mentioned previously. In those moments, and despite the temporal separation from the initial τραῦμα, someone's world is cast into crisis, as it uncontrollably morphs into a disquieting landscape. For these reasons, trauma's overarching temporal dynamics make of horror both a triggering event and an ongoing threat, while simultaneously being underpinned by it.

In chapter 1, I argued that horror is an experience without a fixed referent, and discussed what horror can be *triggered by.* Here, it is important to avoid overdetermining the consequences of this experience—that is, what horror *does.* Coherent with my anti-essentializing thrust, I contend that this experience should not necessarily be linked with trauma. If horror is a present-centered experience, then there is no reason to believe it will necessarily affect the future by assuming the form of a traumatic experience. Indeed, one can snap out of a horrifying experience, given a change in circumstances, and promptly forget about it. This does not take anything away from the horrific nature of such experiences as they happen, because horror's present-centeredness allows for something to be horrifying even if it is then revealed as harmless or does not leave any long-lasting consequences. From a phenomenological point of view, what matters is not where the experience leads, but that a subject, at a given moment, experiences a situation as horrifying.

To avoid overdetermining horror's temporality and outcomes, this chapter includes a second voice in addition to Michelstaedter's. Through an analysis of Luigi Pirandello's work, I will focus on horror's permanence—that is, on horror as an experience that leaves a self shattered, traumatically so. For the time being, however, I turn back to Michelstaedter's *Persuasion and Rhetoric* to further analyze the possibility of horror's transience—that is, I want to consider horror as a moment of shattering that the subject quickly leaves behind. While the scene of horror analyzed in this section allowed me to articulate why horror is a present-centered experience and to trace a distinction between its temporality and that of trauma, the following one will emphasize that horror can indeed be a fleeting experience that leaves no repercussions. Crucially, this also challenges any reassuring hypotheses of horror-induced metanoia, suggesting that we may also learn nothing from this experience, nor will we gain any preparedness for its future resurgences.

Feeling secure is a sought-after condition, one that seems inherent to living a good life. But can we ever be truly and fully secure? If not, is it better to live in the awareness of this lack, or should one instead presuppose oneself to be safe in order to more serenely go about one's existence? In *Persuasion and Rhetoric*'s chapter "Illusion of Persuasion," Michelstaedter addresses this question, examining it through the two counterpoised forces that underpin his philosophy.

Here too, Michelstaedter proceeds *via negativa*, tracing the perimeter of what constitutes a false sense of security. While philopsychia controls the shifting tides of desire and spellbinds one to a future, always future moment of fulfillment, *rettorica* also regulates one's sense of safety by making it appear widespread, all-encompassing, and in fact inherent to life itself: "'If you are here,' he whispers in everyone's ear, 'you are certainly here for the better, and it is timely that Providence put you in this world made for you and looks after your security here.'" But is this really the case? Should we indeed consider ourselves to be a priori safe? After the whispers from this unnamed embodiment of *rettorica*, Michelstaedter steps back into his own voice and adds: "But the dull voice of obscure pain still is not quiet, and again and again it rules, alone and terrible, in the fearful hearts of men" (*PR*, 26).

A humming presence beneath the veneer of control that makes one believe life is fully secure, what Michelstaedter calls "obscure pain" can suddenly take over, and turn one's present into a horrifying matter. If in the previous scene philopsychia was severed by the incumbency of death and the consequent foreclosure of the future, in the following one Michelstaedter describes the experience of a man all of a sudden stripped away from his sense of security and control over life:

> When the light dims, the image of dear things—the screen veiling the external obscurity—becomes more tenuous, and the invisible grows visible; when the weave [*trama*] of illusion thins, disintegrates, tears asunder, then men, *made impotent*, feel themselves in the sway of what is *outside their power, of what they do not know: they fear without knowing what they fear. They find themselves wanting to flee death, having lost their usual way, which feigns finite things from which to flee all while seeking finite things*. (*PR*, 26, original emphasis)

As Thomas Harrison remarks, the Italian word *trama* means both "plot" and "fabric": what here gets torn is indeed the story that one concocts to feel secure, as well as a Schopenhauerian veil of Maya that *rettorica* lays over reality to create the impression of *persuasione*.[31] This *trama* is what *rettorica* weaves to impose an order—of fictitious nature, for Michelstaedter—on a fundamentally unordered and menacing reality, so that a meaningful narration takes the place of the otherwise plotless sequence of acts and desires puppeteered by philopsychia.

However, once the *trama* is torn, the illusion of agency turns into an all-too-real feeling of powerlessness. Those affected by this tear discover that their world is not as domesticated as they believed, as forces beyond their control ("*outside their power*") and understanding ("*of what they do not know*") filter through and take hold of what they imagined to be a safely insulated place: their life. The "*finite things*" that *rettorica* infused with meaning are shown to be empty vessels, with death and finitude functioning as a synecdoche for a creeping, generalized sense of lack of control.

Let us call it the "safety fallacy," this belief in a fully secure existence: the belief, in Michelstaedter's words, "that Providence put you in this world made for you and looks after your security here." This fallacy generally involves a degree of epistemic arrogance—that is, the overestimation of what one knows and can control—alongside the underestimation of the space of uncertainty, or its erasure altogether. Such an illusory form of *persuasione* belongs to the epistemically arrogant individual, whose behavior, as Michelstaedter sarcastically notes, is "*certain and reasonably subordinate* to the end," and whose credo states, "I know what I do because I do it; I don't act by chance but with full consciousness and persuasion" (*PR*, 23).

At its core, Michelstaedter's work is a critique of the safety fallacy. This fallacy is central to the functioning of *rettorica*: without the former, the latter could not push individuals away from a confrontation with their own finitude and existential baselessness by luring them instead to the illusions, norms, and false securities promoted by society. For this reason, the moments in *Persuasion and Rhetoric* when *rettorica* is most clearly shown as illusory take place when someone's safety fallacy collapses. This shakes the foundations of *rettorica*'s apparatuses and in so doing casts the affected subject into a state of crisis, which leads to a moment of horror.

Powerlessness is the defining feature of the experience triggered by a tear in the *trama* of one's life. In the passage's continuation, Michelstaedter compares this state of impotence to the life of children, whose *trama* is less tightly woven than the one ruling adult life: "The weave [*trama*] of children—provisional lives, so to speak—is much less defined, much more varied and disordered, here dense and luminous, there thin and half-dark, half-translucent. They have living joys men no longer know and are much more often than men in the grip of such terrors" (*PR*, 26).

When these "terrors" take hold of a child's life, "things are deformed into strange appearances." Crucially, it is the ordinary aspects of life that deform into something strange, rather than strange things appearing in ordinary life. To give a sense of this, Michelstaedter stages the transfiguration of those who would normally be described as the infant's caretakers: "it seems to children that 'they' scream in a thousand voices and grab them with a thousand hands, and sarcasm sneers in the obscurity with a thousand quivers, and they feel sucked in by the obscurity; they run, wild with terror, screaming to stupefy themselves" (*PR*, 27).

The description of these multi-limbic, quasi-Lovecraftian creatures does not constitute an interpolation of supernatural elements into an otherwise realistic scene; rather, it signals a phenomenological shift in how children relate to their caretakers. The latter are surely "terribly powerful beings" since, in practice, they rule over a great part of the former's life (*PR*, 27), but while this relationship is generally not a troublesome one, sometimes, Michelstaedter implies, children experience their structural powerlessness as disquieting, whatever the reason may be. At that point, once a child is "in the grip of such terrors," even if no real monsters *are* in the room, it *feels* as if they were.

For Michelstaedter, becoming an adult involves, at least in part, considering oneself sheltered from these moments of horror by the tightening of the *trama* we weave around ourselves. The power of the mysterious "they" is replaced by the agency of the individual, now convinced of his safety and autonomy, aware of why he does what he does; the child who was afraid of the dark and not allowed to keep the light turned on at night has now gained access to the switches.

Sometimes, however, the system short-circuits, and the illumination flickers. Despite its tightening in adulthood, Michelstaedter continues, "when the edge of the weave [*trama*] is lifted for reasons beyond men's control, they too know frightful moments," with the use of the synecdoche, by which the plural "men" is employed in lieu of the singular, pointing to the archetypal nature of the experience here described. Those are the moments when the control fallacy cracks, and the "frightful moments" inherent to life, only apparently domesticated by *rettorica*, take hold of one's world: "Dreams come to them in sleep, when the organism, relaxed, lives the obscure pain of singular determinations, for which, in the thinning of the weave [*trama*] of illusion, the obscurity appears more menacing. [. . .] Sarcastic laughter disturbs, ruins, corrupts the tranquil, familiar images they would like to retain in vain, and it weighs upon them with dark images of menace and reproach" (*PR*, 27–28). With a rhetorical thrust similar to that of the previous scene, where food progressively rotted and decomposed once horror became the barycenter of the subject's phenomenology, here too a semantic intensification ("disturbs, ruins, corrupts") parallels the ongoing thinning of the *trama* ("thins, disintegrates, tears asunder" [*PR*, 26]), and in so doing signals the overwhelming nature of the experience. What was once close now feels as if it escapes the subject's reach, while menacing, yet indiscernible thoughts ("dark images") occupy their mind.

As the intensity heightens, the nightmare suddenly ends. Michelstaedter blends external and internal focalization to further dramatize the scene, offering an insight into the protagonist's thoughts:

> They awake, open their eyes wide in the dark . . . and the relieving match gives them peace—the sweet wife is just beside; here the clothes with the body's imprint, here in the pictures the familiar faces of loved ones; all the dear, dear, familiar things. "It's okay. Okay. What time is it? Oh! Late. Gotta get up tomorrow. Damn dreams. God, dreams! Okay. Tomorrow. Let's see if we can get right back to sleep." Reassured, they put out the light again. (*PR*, 28)

Everything is still there as usual: life's nest of predictability reappears, and the feeling of powerlessness is discovered to be nothing but a bad dream. The priority is to fall back to sleep as quickly as possible so that tomorrow can go as planned, and the darkness that first triggered the nightmare is now reclaimed to numb oneself.

Horror was just an interloper, a momentary intrusion into an otherwise domesticated setting—that is, one's bedroom, which here also stands for one's life. The rapidity with which the nightmare ends invites us to consider that horror's temporality is not fixed: if the world horrifies, it does not necessarily do so indefinitely, as a man can experience his world spiraling away only to find it exactly at the same place moments later.

But horror's transience does not mean this experience will not resurface once it has faded into the background. As promptly as the man snapped out of his nightmare, just so can he plunge back into it:

> But the images remaining in the eyes decompose, the plans for tomorrow and the next day cease—man finds himself once more without first name and last, without wife or loved ones, without things to do, without clothes [*senza nome e senza cognome, senza consorte e senza parenti, senza cose da fare, senza vestiti*]. He is alone, naked, with eyes open to the darkness. [. . .] Every sensation becomes infinite; it seems that before your eyes points draw infinitely away; small things become infinitely large, and *the infinite drinks them up.* (*PR*, 28, original emphasis)

In the aftermath of his nightmare, once he has regained the comfort of his safety fallacy, the man is yet again stripped of everything he thought he possessed.[32] Stylistically, this process is mirrored by the repetition of "*senza* [without]," which coordinates a parataxical lexical accumulation of everything that has been taken away from him: powerless, the man must confront the darkness that he arrogantly sought to reclaim for his own agenda. My analysis of Heidegger's "The Point of Reference" in chapter 1 argued that in a moment of horror things can be transposed out of their previous essence and, in so doing, be revealed under a new light. Here, too, Michelstaedter describes a similar transfiguration, one whereby what is close is shown as far distant, and what is small assumes towering proportions: besides spiraling away, things also spin out of control, and conjure up a threatening, all-consuming infinity that echoes Leopardi's nothingness.

Having already blurred the boundaries between third-person plural and second-person singular, in the final section of the scene Michelstaedter stages the demise of this collective embodiment of the safety fallacy by having them hear the whispers of the entity that is causing their world to collapse:

> in anguish they seek a plank with which to save themselves, a solid point; everything decomposes, everything yields, flees, draws away; and the sarcastic sneer dominates all: "Ooooooooohhh . . . nothing, nothing, nothing, I know you're nothing; I know you're nothing; I know where you place your trust and I shall destroy the ground from under you; I know what you promise yourself and your promises won't be kept, just as you have promised and never kept, never kept—because you're nothing, and you can do nothing, I know you can do nothing, nothing, nothing . . ." (*PR*, 28)[33]

Horror twists nearness and distance, past and future, as reality, no matter its alleged stability, turns overwhelming and malign: similar to how the man thought himself to be in full control, now nothing holds anymore as his mental and actual home is shown to be an indefensible territory. The howling repetition of "nothing" undoes his epistemic arrogance, as he begins to doubt the reach of his knowledge and senses the fragility of his condition. Once convinced of the solidity of his life, the unnamed man now feels as if he were "a corpse preserved in an airless environment, which no sooner than exposed turns to dust" (*PR*, 29).

This image wraps up the scene, and the register switches from the literary back to the more overtly philosophical. Whereas the former voice was tasked with phenomenologically describing a world cast into crisis, the latter articulates the reasons behind the man's experience: "In the face of slowly advancing, inexorable time, he feels as powerless to care for his life as a dead man, and he suffers each moment the pain of death" (*PR*, 29).[34] Here, too, powerlessness emerges as a central category in Michelstaedter's work, one inherent to human life from infancy to adulthood, no matter the tightening of one's *trama*.

Later in the paragraph, Michelstaedter returns to the same topic and addresses an error people make in relation to powerlessness: "it rests in the opinions and mouths of everyone when it becomes apparent in specific events, when, as the impotence appears to be caused by determinate things, it too is deemed definite and limited" (*PR*, 29). Michelstaedter's target here is the belief that powerlessness is a discrete outcome of a discrete event. This line of thinking leads back to the safety fallacy, as it presupposes that powerlessness can ultimately be engineered out of a life if the right measures are taken. But this, for Michelstaedter, is a form of fallacious thinking, insofar as it overlooks how "a determinate injury, which men believe limited to this alone, is rather terror at the revelation of the impotency of one's own illusion; it is a certain accident or malady, a death, ruin, catastrophe of given, familiar things: but it is mystery that opens the door to the tranquil, bright room warmed sufficiently for determinate hope, and it sneers: 'Now I'm coming, and here you thought you were safe, and you are nothing'" (*PR*, 31). For Michelstaedter, powerlessness is a constitutive element of the human condition, not merely the outcome of a given happening: disease or financial ruin is a synecdoche for a generalized fragility that belongs to our human nature, as creatures embedded in ecosystems that we do not fully master and that can topple us in unexpected ways. The core of the safety fallacy lies in the phrase "here you thought you were safe," which explicitly references the falsehood of one's beliefs about security and stability: contrary to the reassuring hypothesis of believing oneself to be safe, for Michelstaedter our condition is such that, barring an absolute (and unachievable) state of *persuasione*, horror could eventually seep into a life through a tear in its *trama*, and a powerlessness of a forced kind take hold, be it only momentarily. To convey such a tear in its phenomenological and epistemological repercussions as it unravels one's illusions of safety, Michelstaedter pokes a hole in the fabric of realism with the two expressionistic scenes here discussed, and in so doing leverages his literary talents to advance a philosophical argument.

While describing moments when a fallacious impression of safety is indeed shown as illusory, Michelstaedter is careful not to draw normative conclusions from this experience. Indeed, the affirmation that horror's temporality is not fixed should be understood to mean both that the duration of this experience in itself is not set and that if someone's life horrifies, it does not stay horrified indefinitely. In Michelstaedter's lexicon, if the tear in someone's life "is sewn back up [. . .] men delude themselves again and readapt to some kind of life," so that the nightmares of the night do not carry over to the following day (*PR,* 31).

But this overestimation of one's own security is not a purely individual matter. According to Michelstaedter, modern society promotes a false impression of control over the world and its circumstances, which, in turn, increases the intensity of those moments when the *trama* of a life gets torn. To exemplify this point, in a later section of *Persuasion and Rhetoric* Michelstaedter sketches the comical figure of a man in a "locked vault [*botte di ferro*]," who embodies the safety fallacy promoted by *rettorica*'s individual-centered machinations and societal-inflected apparatuses as well (*PR,* 106).

If not the same individual, this man is someone who shares the same attitudes as the protagonist of the scene just analyzed and parallels *in malo* the absolute security that *persuasione* represents. Yet, whereas in the previously analyzed passage that individual was depicted in a position of fragility, at night and surrounded by darkness, here this man is introduced in the daylight, after "an abundant lunch" as a "portly gentleman" and the highest embodiment of society's *rettorica* (*PR,* 104).[35]

This "man of his time" (*PR,* 107) takes himself to be a learned and tasteful individual who, through self-fashioning and the tools offered by society, believes he exerts absolute control over his life. He describes himself as an "artist [. . .] of the soul," though without indulging in eccentricities, and believes in progress and science because they make human beings "the true masters of creation, [since] no mystery escapes us any longer." His engagement with the arts, philosophy, and the sciences takes place "in its time and place," insofar as "serious life is something else"—whenever he steps into his office, this dutiful bureaucrat relinquishes "personal opinions, feelings, human weaknesses" to fulfill his tasks "with a heart tempered by objectivity." Against each potential future inconvenience, he has set in place a system of prevention: for old age, there is "a pension"; in case of sickness, he belongs to "a welfare fund"; against theft, he is "insured"; and the same goes against "fire," "accidents," and "in case of death" as well. This man lives, as he himself affirms, "secure in a locked vault": a perfectly insulated space, allegedly impenetrable to anything that could make him steer away from the trajectory of his life (*PR*, 106).

Contrary to the individual self-reliance of *persuasione*, his sense of security is a byproduct of a collective orchestration, one enacted via insurance policies and other societal mechanisms. Just as *rettorica* regulates individual life by promoting a desire of self-preservation for itself rather than for the sake of anything meaningful, a similar arrangement, only scaled up, rules society as well—and as one of its members, this man is thus part of an ever improving system whose goal is to progressively eliminate "from the field of life every contingency," according to the belief that "ὁ βίος ὁ μετ' ἀσφαλείας ἥδιστος, 'life with security is the sweetest.'" (*PR*, 111–12).

If Leopardi's "common pact [*social catena*]" in *Broom* evoked a fundamentally unwinnable, yet heroic collective struggle against the rulings of existence,[36] the societal configuration dreamed by this individual is one that does away with any sense of fragility and uncertainty, and is instead convinced of its radical security. While Michelstaedter makes a caricature of this attitude via the man in the locked vault, it is worth noting that a similar ethos is constitutive of early twentieth-century Western modernity—an ethos that Michelstaedter was exposed to, as someone who lived in the Mitteleuropean Gorizia and whose father worked in the insurance industry as the local director of Assicurazioni Generali.[37]

According to Stephen Toulmin, from the seventeenth century onward the standards of deterministic predictability set by Newton's laws of motion have increasingly been expanded to other spheres of human life and aimed at the creation of "Cosmopolis," which is to say a society as rationally ordered and predictable as Newtonian physics.[38] The early twentieth century—Michelstaedter's time—saw a rapid actualization of what had previously remained a theoretical goal, as the increasing implementation of insurance policies, alongside the creation of social welfare, shows how around that period Western societies intensified their systematic extraction of their members from randomness-laden and uncontrollable ecologies. Indeed, most systems of social security were instituted in Western Europe within a few decades: Bismarck's *soziale Sicherheit* in Germany spearheaded this tendency in the late nineteenth century and was shortly followed by France's insurance against work accidents in 1898 and retirement system for low-salaried employees in 1910. A year later, in 1911, Great Britain introduced the National Insurance System. In 1919 Italy ratified the obligatory nature of joint contributions by the state and entrepreneurs to a national welfare system of invalidity and pensions.[39]

Insurance and welfare are two examples of what sociologist James Beniger, with a direct emphasis on matters of agency and lack thereof, called the "control revolution." An ongoing process that began primarily between the 1840s and the 1920s, the control revolution involved "a complex of rapid changes in the technological and economic arrangements by which information is collected, stored, processed, and communicated, and through which formal or programmed decisions might affect social control."[40] This increased emphasis on the collection and deployment of information was, according to Beniger, a response to the crises of control over the world and its circumstances that ensued from the industrial revolution, which relied on the implementation of technologies that disrupted societal homeostasis.[41] Through these changes, Cosmopolis, at the onset of the twentieth century, started becoming more a matter of fact than of speculation, and the control revolution constituted a fundamental catalyst for this process.

Besides the biographical element, Michelstaedter's interest in the topics of safety and control seems to reflect the widespread societal and intellectual impact of these ongoing changes in episteme.[42] Arguably, the very idea of *persuasione* responds to similar matters, although it does so by backgrounding the societal and the relational to foreground the importance of existential self-reliance in order to achieve a genuine sense of security. As Michelstaedter writes, "He who for one instant wants his life to be his, only for an instant to be persuaded of what he does, must take possession of the present, *to see every present as the last*, as if death were certain afterward, *and to create his own life by himself in the obscurity*" (*PR*, 39, original emphasis).

Michelstaedter deemed *persuasione* fundamentally unattainable—mankind can only approach it—and for this reason he employs the mathematical language of asymptotes, hyperbolas, and limits to illustrate his point (*PR*, 47–48, 104–12). In other words, he employs concepts that signal an increasing nearness to a value without reaching it, thus capturing the idea of proximity without coincidence. According to this line of reasoning,

Michelstaedter implicitly concedes that we may never be able to be fully secure if *persuasione* is the only real source of security. Yet, from his reasoning and given the language he employs, it also follows that there are points along the hyperbola that exhibit greater asymptotic proximity to this condition; conversely, others exhibit a greater rate of divergence from the asymptote. It is at these latter coordinates that the man in the locked vault stands, which is to say at the coordinates where the *trama* woven by *rettorica* provides, with the greatest intensity, the illusion of a tightness that translates into the safety fallacy.

My reflections on horror have been cast against the backdrop of modernity's desire to extend the reach of human agency and, in turn, diminish the space of powerlessness, uncertainty, and the absence of control. Horror, as I have been arguing, acquires a peculiarly troubling flavor in modernity precisely as it undoes this episteme, be it only momentarily and for a single individual. For Michelstaedter, too, modern society seeks to overcome once and for all "the inadequate security offered him by the atmosphere" (*PR*, 120)—that is, the exposure to the contingent and the unexpected that are inherent to existence. Increasingly used to systems of prevention that operate at varying degrees of efficacy, the haute bourgeoisie he depicts grew more and more unaccustomed to the idea of not being in full control of themselves, their surroundings, and their lives. This is the safety fallacy that rules the life of the man in the locked vault, who is aptly named "man of his time" to be identified as symbolic of the episteme he represents.

However, as shown in the two literary scenes from *Persuasion and Rhetoric* here analyzed, the locked vault of *rettorica* can crack. Later in the book, Michelstaedter explicitly addresses this topic:

> But when the plot [*trama*] of calculated forces is torn asunder and violence breaks into life and social man finds himself naked before the forces of nature and of man and must resist with the consistency of his body and character, then the pitiful image of the absolute weakness of the man who "finds neither words nor deeds" becomes universal and obvious to all.
>
> This is why the constant effort of society aims at tightening the plot [*trama*] to strengthen it by means of communal weakness and make it secure against every eventuality. (*PR*, 140)

No matter its tightness, the *trama* can indeed be ruptured, and, once that happens, it leaves horrified the individual convinced of its efficacy "against every eventuality." Michelstaedter's *rettorica* is an illusory form of prophylaxis: by promoting the impression of being in full control at all times, it prevents the individual from coming to terms with the fact that no place, not even one's own mind, is fully secure.

However, the fact that the *trama* can be torn does not mean that it will stay so indefinitely: just like the man Michelstaedter depicts, an affected individual may indeed simply fall back to sleep, wake up the next day, and go on living. Similarly, a repaired tear may not leave any meaningful traces: in the two scenes of *Persuasion and Rhetoric* analyzed here, the protagonists do not appear to retain long-lasting effects—be they positive or negative—from what they experienced. Nor does their reality horrify indefinitely: an aberration, even when it causes a complete derangement of the senses and casts one's world into crisis, does not necessarily serve as prelude to a revelation: for this reason Michelstaedter resists both salvaging the negativity of horror by turning it into a springboard for self-betterment, and establishing a direct causation between horror and the woundedness of trauma.

A phenomenology of horror should be similarly prudent with its predicaments: just as there is nothing fixed about horror's temporality, thinking of this experience as necessarily leading to any meaningful changes in someone's life involves an overdetermination of its effects. Horror may indeed not lead anywhere, and we may not be able to retrospectively embed it in a paradigm of sense-making, and herein lies one of the most disquieting aspects of this experience. In dealing with such moments Michelstaedter embraces a distinct literary style to describe what, in the present, refuses the comfort of a *telos* or a reason, and simply casts someone into a state of crisis, without any certainties regarding its outcome. In these cases, it is not about making sense, because horror, in the present, does not make sense for the affected individual: it simply takes over, as an event that unravels and reshapes the reality experienced by the subject.

To resist essentializing horror as an experience of a fixed temporality, I now turn to another early twentieth-century Italian author associated with Expressionism: Luigi Pirandello. Through his work, the analysis will move from transient instantiations of horror to situations where the experience leaves an enduring trace on one's character.

A SHATTERED SELF: LUIGI PIRANDELLO

In 1910, the year of Michelstaedter's suicide, Pirandello turned forty-three. By that point he had undergone a number of severe crises, including the financial ruin of his family and the health collapse of his wife, Antonietta, who would eventually be committed to a mental institution because of her schizoid-paranoia. It has become commonplace to connect these experiences to Pirandello's writings, and likely for good reasons since his production touches on themes such as the precariousness of reality, madness, alienation, and the shattering of one's identity.[43] Increasingly present in early twentieth-century artistic and philosophical discourse, they found expression in Pirandello's work, which became synonymous with some of the most wide-ranging explorations of these themes across literature, theater, and essayism as well, at a time when the epistemic underpinnings of the Belle Époque were being shaken by Darwinian evolutionism, Freudian psychoanalysis, Einsteinian relativism, Nietzschean nihilism, and so forth.

Pirandello's talents in capturing some defining features of his Zeitgeist were recognized by the intellectual world, and he was awarded the Nobel Prize in Literature in 1934. Rather than adding my voice to the already well-established strain of criticism dedicated to emphasizing Pirandello's diagnostic value in relation to his epoch's so-called crisis of reason, this book's phenomenological thrust leads me to focus on how he describes moments of crisis once they manifest themselves in someone's life.

In contrast to the discrete, temporally circumscribed crises in Michelstaedter's work, I here analyze how Pirandello treats a single "horrific event" as an episode rife with future implications—one that destabilizes a subject and produces a traumatizing wound. I will not focus on trauma's overarching temporal dynamics, but rather on those moments when horror takes hold of a life, either as the initial, traumatic moment, or in one of its horrifying recurrences.

Here, too, it is fundamental to underline that, just as there is nothing fixed in what can horrify, the same must be said of what can become a trigger for such repeated occurrences of this experience. There are circumstances that with statistically significant frequency lead from a moment of horror to the emergence of a trauma, which, in turn, leads to cyclical reappearances of horror in the life of a traumatized person: warfare or rape, for instance, come to mind as reliable sources of post-traumatic stress disorder. These are important patterns of correlation, but they do not exhaust the range of possible experiences that can become traumatic. Any event experienced as horrifying can produce rippling effects; Pirandello's work provides a venue for thinking about situations where horror leaves long-lasting repercussions while not being triggered by events typically associated with trauma.

Pirandello's interest in moments when reality gets torn—particularly where the tear leaves long-lasting repercussions—is central to his work. Like Michelstaedter, Pirandello focuses on individuals solidly embedded in their early-twentieth-century episteme of security and stability. But whereas Michelstaedter focuses on the phenomenology of the shattering itself (that is, moments when the *trama* of a life is momentarily torn), Pirandello's conceptual and narrative interest lies primarily in how a single occurrence of one of these events can lead to a shattered self (that is, an unstable subject more prone to the recurrence of the horrifying).

While Pirandello's 1926 novel, *One, No One, and One Hundred Thousand,* reads as the clearest example of his interest in describing the phenomenology of a shattered self, I will first address this topic's underpinnings and importance in the author's work through two texts that became foundational for his oeuvre and reception: *The Late Mattia Pascal* and *On Humor.*

Although Pirandello would reach critical acclaim starting only from the 1920s, he had made a name for himself with the national and international public much earlier, notably thanks to his 1904 novel, *The Late Mattia Pascal.* This book follows the story of Mattia Pascal, the protagonist, who is mistakenly declared dead while on a trip to Monte Carlo, where he had amassed a small fortune at the casino. Faced with the unexpected opportunity to start his life anew, he embraces a new identity under a false name, roams Europe, and eventually settles down in Rome.

The twelfth chapter of the book opens with a memorable exchange between the eccentric thinker and boarding house owner, Anselmo Paleari, and Adriano Meis, pseudonym of the late Mattia Pascal, who is already considered dead by his family and society by this point of the novel:

> "The tragedy of Orestes in a marionette theatre!" Signor Anselmo Paleari came into my room and announced. "Automatic marionettes, the very latest invention. This evening at eight-thirty in Via dei Prefetti, number 54. That's worth going to, Signor Meis."

"The tragedy of Orestes?"

"Yes. *D'après Sophocle*, the poster says. It must be Elektra. Now listen to the curious idea that's occurred to me: if at the climax of the play, just when the marionette who is playing Orestes is about to avenge his father's death and kill his mother and Aegisthus, suppose there were a tear in the paper sky of the scenery [*strappo nel cielo di carta*]. What would happen? Answer me that."

"I don't know," I said with a shrug.

"But it's easy, Signor Meis! Orestes would be terribly upset by that hole in the sky."

"For what reason?"

"Let me go on. Orestes would still feel his desire for vengeance, he would still want passionately to achieve it, but his eyes, at that point, would go straight to that hole, from which every kind of evil influence [*mali influssi*] would then crowd the stage, and Orestes would feel suddenly helpless. In other words, Orestes would become Hamlet. There's the whole difference between ancient tragedy and modern, Signor Meis—believe me—a hole torn in a paper sky."[44]

The passage addresses the crisis of the modern individual, who, after the death of God, dwells in a condition of metaphysical orphanhood, deprived of ethical and epistemological certainties, forced to act out a role whose emptiness has been exposed by modernity's demystifying powers. And indeed, Meis takes Anselmo's reflections as an occasion to pontificate about the puppets' serene existential condition, which he implicitly counterpoises to his own: "Lucky marionettes, I sighed, over whose wooden heads the false sky has no holes! No anguish or perplexity, no hesitations, obstacles, shadows, pity—nothing! And they can go right on with their play and enjoy it, they can love, they can respect themselves never suffering from dizziness or fainting fits, because for their stature and their actions that sky is a proportionate roof."[45] For Meis, the puppet theater represents an enclosed world—no matter if this is just an illusion—where the possibility of meaningful action is preserved, contrary to the "dizziness or fainting fits" of modernity. Here, instead of revisiting this scene's symbolic meanings, I consider the tear in the paper sky as an event in itself, which provokes immediate and massive repercussions in the present. Just like one of the bourgeois men in Michelstaedter, Anselmo's Orestes was sure of his actions: he knew why he was doing what he was doing. However, a tear in Orestes's sky—the *trama* of his life—compromises his resoluteness, once it becomes the ruling feature of his present ("his eyes, at that point, would go straight to that hole"). The tragic hero, swollen by a desire for revenge, suddenly deflates and finds himself powerless, no longer in full control of his life and his actions, incapable of conjuring up the resolution to carry out his vengeance.

This passage describes with comical undertones a moment of forced powerlessness akin to those of the two scenes analyzed in Michelstaedter: similar to the workings of *rettorica*, the "paper sky" functions as a metonymy, referring to a structure that gives the impression of meaning to the characters on stage. In both cases, an unforeseen and overpowering event makes this sense-making structure malfunction.

Contrary to the men of *Persuasion and Rhetoric*, however, this scene does not describe Orestes as held by the grip of horror: the passage lacks phenomenological thickness insofar as Orestes remains an empty figure—a puppet indeed—and the reader is never invited to explore the inner workings of his consciousness once this character realizes that his sky is torn. Conversely, Michelstaedter pens structurally similar moments, but does so by dramatizing the moment of phenomenological crisis the scene depicts through his use of an aesthetics of deformation. One can imagine Orestes, too, experiencing horror, but the Orestes we have access to does not exist except through Anselmo's sibylline words, which are not enough to allow us to further speculate about the tragic hero's intentional states.

Lack of phenomenological thickness notwithstanding, this passage reflects Pirandello's interest in moments when reality becomes overwhelming and casts an individual into crisis. This crisis plays out on two interconnected levels: the first, societal and epistemic, reflects a widespread condition, such as modern subjects' vertigo given their exposure to the "tear" Orestes saw in his sky; the second, personal and phenomenological, reflects how someone might react to the individual instantiation of such "tear."

In his 1908 essay *On Humor* Pirandello articulates the reasons behind his interest in these moments, and emphasizes their importance not only for his artistic production but also, more generally, for the human condition at large.[46] According to Pirandello's immanent vitalism, life is a flux that we seek to crystallize into forms, which are our way of rendering static and univocal what is fluid and relative.[47] Similar to Michelstaedter's *rettorica*, forms grant us a sense of coherence, meaning, and stability, yet they are fictions that we convince ourselves exist in order to safeguard an impression of agency and control over existence.[48] Life, however, keeps flowing despite our attempts at crystallizing it and our desire for control. But at times these forms, which are the riverbanks entrusted with domesticating the flow of life, collapse: "In certain moments of turmoil all these fictitious forms are hit [*investiti*] by the flux and collapse [*crollano*] miserably under its thrust; and even what does not flow under the barriers and beyond the limits—that which is distinctly clear to us and which we have carefully channeled into our feelings, into the duties we have imposed upon ourselves, into the habits we have marked out for ourselves—in certain moments of floodtide, overflows [*straripa*] and upsets [*sconvolge*] everything."[49] Verbs such as "*investiti*," "*crollano*," "*straripa*," and "*sconvolge*" describe an experience in terms of feeling powerless and overwhelmed, despite attempts at pinning down once and for all the flux of life. Rather than just provoking a transitory turmoil, however, Pirandello infuses these moments with a revelatory power that, similar to Heidegger's *Ereignis*, hints at the existence of something else lurking under the veneer of stability provided by the "fictitious forms":

> In certain moments of inner silence, in which our souls strips itself of all its habitual fictions and our eyes become sharper and more piercing, we see ourselves in life, and life in itself, as if in a barren and disquieting nakedness; we are seized by a strange impression, as if, in a flash, we could clearly perceive a reality different from the one that we normally perceive, a reality living beyond the reach of human vision, outside the forms of human reason. Very lucidly, then, the texture of daily existence, almost suspended in the void of our inner silence, seems meaningless, devoid of purpose; and that new reality appears to us horrid [*orrida*] in its sternly detached and mysterious crudeness, for all our usual fictitious relationships, both of feelings and images, have separated and disintegrated it. The inner void expands, surpasses the limits of our body, and becomes a weird emptiness that engulfs us as if time and life had come to a stop, as if our inner silence had plunged into the abyss of mystery.[50]

Reality turns strange once the bulwarks provided by the fictitious "forms" collapse. As if a layer of mystification had been peeled away from someone's eyes, existence now appears "disquieting," "horrid," and assumes expressionistic traits in which what formerly constituted its fabric now deforms and disintegrates.[51] With a process of expansion from the inner workings of a self to the phenomenal world similar to the one described by Michelstaedter for his bourgeois men, a subjective feeling ("the inner void") enlarges to the point of engulfing the subject's surroundings, thus changing their appearance. What Munch described as the scream of existence in the passage that opened this chapter, Pirandello renders as a kind of silence that is mysterious and all-encompassing alike, now taking over the life of the individual who, powerless, is affected by this experience.

For a phenomenological reading, a key verb that Pirandello uses to describe the nature of what is happening is "appears." Like Michelstaedter, Pirandello too does not make any strong ontological claims: he does not affirm that reality *is* horrible; rather, the twist of reality into something disquieting happens within the subject and stems from their experience of one of those "moments of turmoil" that Pirandello analyzes.

In the context of *On Humor*, such moments may act as a prelude to the experience that gives the essay its title.[52] But while Pirandellian humor (*umorismo*) is felt only retrospectively, once a process of reflection unveils the painful underpinnings of a comical experience, my interest here lies in the present force of such events as they happen: it is *during* a "moment of turmoil" that a subject's acts of consciousness may make the world appear disquietingly otherwise.

But the event's present force is not exhausted by the transient unraveling of one's present. Its effects can linger, and a moment of shattering may lead to a shattered self:

> With a supreme effort we then try to recapture the normal consciousness of things, to renew our usual relationship with them, to reassemble our ideas and to feel alive again in the usual way. But we can no longer trust this normal consciousness, these newly recollected ideas and this habitual sense of living because we now know that they are deceptions which we use in order to survive and that underneath them there is something else which man can face only at the cost of either death or insanity. It was only an instant; but its impression lasts for a long time, as a sort of dizziness which contrasts with the stability, itself so illusory, of things: ambitious or miserable appearances. And life, the

> small usual life that roams among these appearances, almost seems to us no longer to be real; it is like a mechanical phantasmagoria. How could we give importance to it? How could we respect it?[53]

A tear in life's fabric exposed its illusory nature, and hinted at something else lurking underneath. Here a garden does not momentarily turn into a torture chamber, nor a dream into a passing nightmare; instead, Pirandello emphasizes the possibility of a more enduring, structural collapse of the subject's sense of stability. While Michelstaedter's bourgeois man concerned himself with regaining his composure to quickly fall back to sleep, Pirandello rules out the possibility of mending the *trama* of a life once a tear of such magnitude unravels one's world. There are situations, he suggests, when it is not feasible to imagine that we will be able to step back into the comfort of our safety fallacy. A horrific event can leave us wounded, incapable of regaining a sense of wholeness and integrity regarding the very fabric of our existence: after such an event has happened, one may wonder, how is it possible to go back to normality?

Pirandello's critical reception has emphasized the backward- and forward-looking aspects of his work: the *diagnosis* of the early-twentieth-century crisis of truth and reason, on the one hand, and the *prognosis* of the shattered and orphaned modern subject, on the other hand.[54] Less attention has been paid to Pirandello's interest in those moments of crisis *as they take place.* Coherent with the descriptive thrust of this book, I thus focus on their unfolding in the present, thematized both in *The Late Mattia Pascal* and, more extensively, in *On Humor*, rather than on their roots or aftermaths.

Pirandello's attention to those "moments of turmoil" is relevant not only for the study of horror, but also for better understanding his production. To this point, the plot of his 1926 novel, *One, None, and One Hundred Thousand,* is set in motion precisely by one of these moments, as it opens and informs the entirety of the book. The protagonist, Vitangelo Moscarda, is made aware by his wife, almost by accident, that his nose is crooked. As Moscarda had thus far believed that he fully knew himself, this unexpected and horrifying realization begins what he describes as "my sickness [*il mio male*]."[55] Over time, he discovers that he appears to others different from how he appears to himself—without there being anything he can do to change this state of affairs, and thus reclaim his former stable self.

This initial moment of powerlessness—the very first scene of the book—casts Moscarda's world into crisis, and sets the plot in motion by fulfilling the same function as the "tear in the paper sky" of *The Late Mattia Pascal*. That is, it creates an opening through which "evil influence" can penetrate into Moscarda's life, and unsettle it. Upon realizing that he indeed looks different from what he had thought, he is "filled by a strange, inner dismay that was also revulsion":[56] his body, and in particular his nose, which at the beginning of the book he describes as "if not actually handsome—at least quite decent," becomes a horrifying source of disgust and bewilderment.[57]

The nature of Moscarda's new reality is such that even familiar presences, like his spouse's body, can become triggers for horror. In the passage of the book where this word and its derivatives occur with the highest frequency, Pirandello describes sexual intercourse between Moscarda and his wife Dida in the following terms:

> "Here, Gengè [Moscarda's nickname]. Sit here. Here, like that. Look me in the eye. What? No? You don't want to look at me?"
>
> Ah, what a temptation to take her face into my hands and force her to look into the abyss of two eyes quite different from those she would want to look at her!
>
> She was there, before me; she grabbed my hair with one hand; she sat down on my lap; I felt the weight of her body.
>
> Who was she?
>
> There was no doubt, in her, that I knew who she was.
>
> And I felt such horror of her eyes, looking at me, laughing and confident; horror of those cool hands that touched me, sure that I was as those eyes saw me; horror of that whole body of hers weighing on my lap, confident in abandoning itself to me, without the remotest suspicion that she was not giving it really to me [. . .]. We were two outsiders, clasped together like this—oh horror—outsiders, not only to each other, but each to his and her self, in that body that the other was holding.
>
> You have never experienced that horror, I know; because you have always and only clasped in your arms your whole world with your woman, without the least suspicion that she meanwhile with you is clasping her world, which is another, impenetrable. And yet, to feel this horror, you would only have to think for a moment of something, any trifle, something you like and she doesn't: a color, a flavor, an opinion

> on this or that; and it would make you perceive more than a superficial difference in tastes, sensations or opinions. [. . .] the world, life, and reality as they are to you, when you touch them, are not hers, for she sees and touches another reality in those same things and in you yourself and in herself; and she is unable to tell you how it is, because for her it is that and she cannot imagine it could be anything different for you.[58]

Six repetitions of the word "horror" underpin this page, with the term always referring to Moscarda's experience of the situation rather than his wife's features in themselves.[59] More than belonging to the external world, horror is an intentional state of Moscarda's consciousness, which informs his phenomenology of the sexual encounter: Dida's eyes are "laughing and confident" and her hands "cool"; yet, Moscarda is horrified by them, with a process similar to the one analyzed in *Persuasion and Rhetoric*, whereby the body of a woman came across as dead flesh for a man who was made aware of his own incumbent death.

To give a better sense of how Moscarda is intentionally relating to his surroundings, Pirandello leans toward free indirect discourse. Dida's body, reified, weighs on Moscarda's knees, "confident in abandoning itself to me," but no possible common experiential ground can be established between the two: the word "horror" placed in dashes between "clasped together like this" and "outsiders" syntactically splits the union that the scene denotatively represents. A phenomenological chasm opens between the two, as Moscarda's habitual perception of his wife changes, as well as his assumptions about her.

But what has changed, exactly? Here, the defining element is that Moscarda cannot keep at bay the present manifestation of the knowledge that one does not experience reality in the same way that others do. This awareness, which diffuses through the book after its first scene, now once again takes over, thus turning intimacy into separation, complicity into suspicion, and transparency into opacity. The initial "tear" conjured up a world where Moscarda is exposed to repeated eruptions of what may cast his present into a state of crisis: a first horrific event left him wounded, and when his trauma resurfaces his world horrifies.

This scene does not belong to what traditionally goes under the name of the horror genre, and for good reason. Indeed, there are no monsters, no gore, no particularly unsettling situation on the page. The horror it describes is instead a less straightforward, perhaps more insidious one, as it plays out within Moscarda's consciousness only. It is one that belongs more to ordinary than to extreme situations, in part because it lacks a clear external referent commonly associated with the genre. No matter the nature of horror, however, the key component that underpins different instantiations of this experience is that they all revolve around a form of forced powerlessness, one that shatters the illusions of being perfectly safe and in control, and in so doing casts someone's world into crisis.

This crisis takes place in the present, because horror concerns the here and now. Pirandello's diagnosis of what has been called the crisis of consciousness of the modern subject plays an important role in his production.[60] So do other elements, such as the vitalism that closes *One, No One, and One Hundred Thousand*, when Moscarda embraces a purely immanent way of living—an outcome that in order to take place may indeed have called for a tear in the fabric of Moscarda's former existence. Crucially, and before it leads to the book's ending, this tear also exposes Moscarda to the "evil influences," the "moments of turmoil" that threaten even well-protected lives such as his, as the wealthy son of a banker.

While it can rightly be argued that these moments metonymically signify the crisis of consciousness that Pirandello thematizes in his production, reducing them to this level of analysis only erases their present value as events in themselves. Speaking about a crisis of consciousness involves thinking of the present situation in terms of the past: what is here and now is assessed in relation to what came before. Conversely, horror blocks any escape from the present situation: what is here and now simply takes over. A fuller understanding of Pirandello's production ought to focus on this latter aspect as much as it focuses on the former.

Besides contributing to Pirandello's scholarship by emphasizing the relevance of such "moments of turmoil" in the author's production, reflecting upon his work sharpens my phenomenology of horror by offering some insights into the temporality of this experience that differ from Michelstaedter's. Whereas *Persuasion and Rhetoric* describes instances of the horrifying that unexpectedly tear the *trama* of a life without necessarily impacting future behavior, Pirandello's work emphasizes the possibility that a single event leads to long-lasting effects.

The possibility of horror's endurance, however, is not necessarily actualized by living a consistently horrified life. More frequently, it may refer to the destabilization caused by a single horrific event that renders a subject more prone to being cast into a state of crisis in unexpected moments and for unexpected reasons. The powerlessness characteristic of this experience also lies in the fact that we cannot quite predict or control when a traumatic wound will start festering again.

This is what happens in Moscarda's life, where horror becomes not ubiquitous but instead a latent presence that can suddenly erupt and take over. Horror becomes part of the ordinary: an experience among others, the color of a kind of intentional engagement with the world, a plausible interloper rather than an exceptional one. Leaving aside the baggage of standardized motifs typical of the eponymous genre, a crooked nose, too, just like a garden, can be a source of horror if certain circumstances are met. Pirandello's writings invite us to consider that, just as there is nothing fixed in what can horrify, the temporality of this experience too is an open matter: while a horrific event may not necessarily lead to a traumatic wound, this hypothesis ought never to be put to rest—this holds true for Moscarda, and for ourselves as well.

NOT SAFE: CONCLUSION

Pirandello, interviewed in 1936, grouped together Friedrich Nietzsche, Otto Weininger, and Carlo Michelstaedter as three thinkers who "wanted to make form and substance coincide absolutely at every instant, and they were broken and overwhelmed."[61] Pirandello's language echoes that which he had used thirty years before in *On Humor* to describe the phenomenology of moments of great turmoil, when a given situation takes over and casts someone's world into crisis by collapsing their points of reference, certitudes, and safety. Nietzsche went insane in Turin, and Weininger shot himself in 1903, at the age of twenty-three; Michelstaedter too was twenty-three when he committed suicide in 1910: three seekers of a way beyond the ordinarily human, they were all pulled back by their confrontation with something that, at some point, made their present unendurable.

In this chapter I read Michelstaedter and Pirandello as two authors whose production engages, from both an aesthetic and conceptual perspective, with what I call ordinary horror. In so doing, I am not offering an exhaustive reading of their work, which seeks to close the case of their reception by offering a moment of resolution—in literary criticism, as for

Michelstaedter's suicide, one cannot presuppose a moment of ratiocination leading to a conclusive denouement. More narrowly, I instead propose to consider the experience of horror as a fundamental element, among others, in these two authors' production.

The horror present on their pages is not one where a threat comes from a masked serial killer, a monstrous creature, or a supernatural happening. It is instead of a more ordinary nature, of a kind that we may plausibly expect to encounter in our own lives, such as the specter of incumbent death, the possibility of finding oneself alone and destitute, or simply the newfound awareness that one does not look like what they thought. Michelstaedter's and Pirandello's descriptions of these moments rely on the aesthetics of deformation that I connected to Expressionism, and thus run parallel to the disquieting landscapes typical of the horror genre. But instead of the spectacular horror that the latter typically relies on, these authors invite us to think about more subtle and pervasive instantiations of this experience—cutting across socioeconomic conditions and layers of insulation in taking hold of individuals from the rising bourgeois class who thought they were in full control of their lives.

At a time when systems of prevention and safeguards against the unexpected were becoming increasingly embedded in the fabric of society, Michelstaedter's *rettorica* and Pirandello's *forme* conceptualize the desire to impose complete order on what they considered to be a fundamentally unordered reality. For both, such attempts are ineffective and misguided at best, delusional and fallacious at worst. They lead to what I have termed the safety fallacy: the exaggeration of the control one believes oneself to exert over one's life. In both, unforeseen events poke a hole in this fallacy and confront the subject previously under its spell with a situation that renders their present uncontrolled and uncontrollable.

The present is the temporal fixation of horror, as an experience that commands attention to the here and now. This, however, does not mean that its temporality is fixed, and with Michelstaedter and Pirandello I propose to consider two different approaches to this matter: short-lived in the former, and leaving long-lasting traces in the latter. Michelstaedter's protagonists eventually snap out of the experience, or at the very least its overcoming is presented as possible; Pirandello, conversely, writes about subjects who are destabilized by a confrontation with their lack of control, and from there onward, with increased frequency, see their world cast into crisis by a variety of triggers. Be it as a transient moment of shattering or an event that leads to the enduring fragility of a shattered self, horror's presence in our lives is multifaceted: a balanced perspective ought to resist overdetermining its unfolding and instead emphasize that the possible, yet not inevitable, outcomes range from trauma and metanoia to no changes whatsoever in the affected subject.

Differences in temporality notwithstanding, horror stands as an event that provokes a tear in the fabric of a life. Before any other conclusions may be drawn, the very existence of a tear proves that such fabric can be torn in the first place. In other words, the minimum consequence of horror is to show that the solidity of our life is not to be taken for granted, no matter how unlikely a rupture of our everydayness appears or how safe we feel.

Michelstaedter and Pirandello, at the onset of a century when the control revolution was making ample strides toward the ideal of "Cosmopolis," stage the individual confrontation with the horrifying discovery of not exerting full control over the world and its circumstances. Powerless, their characters ask: how can this happen *to me*?

In the twentieth century, this question would become increasingly widespread and acquire pressing societal relevance. But it was no longer, or at least not only, merely about the personal crisis of an individual. Rather, in the light of the historical happenings of the time, that discrete horror was subsumed by a larger, existential question that implicated everyone: how can this happen *at all*?

To explore this point, through the works of war veteran Curzio Malaparte and Holocaust survivor Primo Levi, the following chapter moves from the downfall of individual hubris to an event that seemed to have made horror widespread, commonplace, and foundational for a given historical context: World War II.

THREE

STRUCTURAL HORROR: CURZIO MALAPARTE AND PRIMO LEVI

On December 10, 1948, the United Nations ratified the Universal Declaration of Human Rights. Its Preamble affirms the "inherent dignity" and "equal and inalienable rights of the human family," which constitute the "foundation of freedom, justice, and peace in the world." This document was born out of historical necessity, as a response to the atrocities committed during World War II, in particular by Nazi Germany, when "disregard and contempt for human rights" led to "barbarous acts which have outraged the conscience of mankind." The thirty articles of the Declaration enshrine a set of rights and freedoms that cannot be stripped from any individual. In its intent, the Declaration is a bulwark against what World War II had unleashed, namely, the horror that countless people experienced during the war. In opposition, this document establishes as a common denominator the concepts of human liberty, dignity, and equality—concepts that World War II showed as precarious and not self-evident.[1]

In chapter 1, I discussed why the horrification of the world is a hypothesis never to be excluded from our experiential horizon. Through Giacomo Leopardi, I rooted this stance in phenomenology, and we traversed a broad, metaphysical realm to consider how, once they can no longer be kept at bay, certain ideas such as that of the ubiquity of suffering can trigger horror—understood in this book as "the experience of forced powerlessness." In chapter 2 we transitioned from the abstract to the individual, and explored the temporality of horror. In particular, I focused on moments when individuals who believed they could exert full control over their lives saw their certainties shattered by horrifying events. Moving away from the abstract and the individual, I here consider World War II as an event that seems to have made horror structural—that is to say, commonplace and foundational for the examined historical context. My focus, however, will not be on the war in its historicity; instead, war is here the condition of possibility for a state of phenomenological crisis for those exposed to it. In this way, I also intend to speak beyond the historical situatedness of World War II, and reflect on what makes armed conflicts horrifying, also as revealed by the presence of formulations such as "the horrors of war" in ordinary language.

The two protagonists of this chapter are Curzio Malaparte and Primo Levi. I begin with Malaparte, to whom most of the chapter is dedicated, and study the form, style, and content of his journey through World War II as chronicled in his 1944 *Kaputt* and 1949 *The Skin*. With Malaparte I discuss how literature can provide a phenomenological account of world collapse by intertwining "possible" and "impossible" events. However, it will become clear that a world cast into crisis calls into question the boundaries between these two categories. Levi, too, describes a world in crisis, and brings this a step further: *If This Is a Man*, published in 1947, and his 1986 collection of essays, *The Drowned and the Saved*, guide the reader through the experience of having to accept the existence of the "impossible" as constitutive of the Lager (Nazi concentration camps). Chapter 2 conceptually centered upon the question, "how can this be happening *to me*?" However, in analyzing a scenario where horror seems to be widespread, a more appropriate question becomes: "how can this be happening *at all*?" Both authors confront this latter interrogation, subjectively as well as historically.

The disparities between Malaparte's and Levi's lives, works, and receptions cannot be overstated.[2] Whereas Malaparte is one of the most controversial figures of the Italian canon, often trafficking in murky ethical waters and a fascist even before fascism seized power, Levi was a partisan and a direct witness to the Holocaust who subsequently offered important testimony on a national and international stage. Without overlapping or equating two different experiences of the war, I contend that such a comparison is less reckless than it may initially appear. Both authors depict a world in a state of profound crisis. This crisis is, first, epistemological, with a strong emphasis on the failure to "make sense" of what they are experiencing. This leads to a set of aesthetic consequences, as each must deal with how to represent circumstances so far removed from everyday life as to come across as "impossible." I address these topics through the most striking (and strikingly overlooked) link between Malaparte and Levi: the figure of René Descartes, whose presence forms a surprising yet substantial intertext shared by Malaparte and Levi.[3] At first glance, Descartes and World War II may appear to be unlikely bedfellows. But Descartes's philosophy also concerns itself with preventing or overcoming a state of crisis, and both Malaparte and Levi focus on Cartesianism's shortcomings in dealing with the state of crisis triggered by World War II.

Neither author offers a comprehensive discussion of Descartes's philosophy. As I show, Cartesianism is for them synonymous with a kind of rationalism that overextends Descartes's inferential method from the sciences to touch on domains such as history and human behavior. While flawed,[4] this understanding of Cartesianism becomes for both an epistemological and aesthetic device: faced with the upheavals of World War II, Malaparte and Levi employ the literary medium to narrate the failure of the Cartesian subject's final project, stated at the end of the *Discourse on the Method*, to become "master and possessor of nature," here understood as the desire for control of mind over matter, of man over history and its circumstances.[5]

Malaparte and Levi chose the literary medium to represent a reality that acquires infernal traits, and their works are rife with Dantean intertextualities. Their hells, however, are phenomenological rather than ontological in nature: they are states wherein the (Cartesian) subject must bear their condition without mastering it, thus leading to their forced powerlessness. This will further my phenomenology of horror in several ways: first, by showing how horror maintains a subjective strain even when it appears to be structural, since both authors depict figures who are in the midst of the horrifying without being affected by it; second, by exploring, in dialogue with Adriana Cavarero's concept of horrorism, why horror implies siding with, or being, the victim; third, by discussing horror's relation to a set of events that statistician Nassim Nicholas Taleb calls a "black swan"—unpredictable events that carry extreme impact and are often rationalized by hindsight only; and fourth, by considering whether literary prose can provide a unique vantage point for the retelling of horror, in light of these authors' choice to use the literary medium as testimony.

I begin with the story of the dog Spin from *Kaputt*, which introduces some of the main themes of the chapter. We will follow Malaparte through the war, moving from *Kaputt*'s Eastern front to the Italian peninsula of *The Skin*, with a crescendo that will lead us to his anti-Cartesian hell: the city of Naples. We then shift perspective, descend one step further into this Inferno, and look through the eyes of a Cartesian in hell, with the second part of this chapter focusing on Levi's imprisonment in Auschwitz.

AN ANTI-CARTESIAN HELL: CURZIO MALAPARTE

Kaputt's chapter "The Mad Rifle" tells the story of Spin, the three-year-old dog of the Italian ambassador in Belgrade, Francesco Mameli. The narrated events take place on April 6, 1941, ten days after the Yugoslavian government (a signatory of the Tripartite Act) was overthrown in an anti-German coup. The coup provoked the Axis invasion of Yugoslavia, which resulted in days of bombardment of the capital by the aircraft of the German Luftwaffe and the Royal Yugoslav Army as well, in a fight for control of the city.

Spin is a hunting dog, well accustomed to rifles, shots, and shouts. Despite Spin's familiarity with loud noises, the explosion of a massive bomb is not comparable to a gunshot: Spin's life, as soon as the bombing begins, is cast into crisis by the sensory upheaval triggered by this novel, mysterious event. This section of *Kaputt* makes use of free indirect speech to ambiguously shift the focus between Malaparte-the-character and Spin, thus moving the reader toward the experiential viewpoint of the dog. Soon after the start of the air raid, Spin is quick to grasp that something is wrong with his world: since the hunting rifles are still hanging in their usual places on the walls, he realizes that the bangs he hears "were not rifle shots, but something abnormal, absolutely beyond the human, beyond nature." As the attack intensifies, the personnel of the Italian embassy, Spin included, are evacuated to a shelter. Once there, seemingly paralyzed by what he experienced, the dog refuses to leave even after the bombardment is over.[6]

For the first time in history, the military technology of World War II allowed armies to unleash semi-targeted, sudden, and massive destruction in the form of carpet bombing, with the first instance occurring as early as September 1939, ravaging the cityscape of Warsaw. The use of bombers made it possible to bypass ground obstacles and enemy lines, and thus rendered even cities vulnerable to attack: no place was safe anymore. Spin, who considers war a kind of hunting,[7] is bewildered by this novel development: "The world had collapsed, something terrifying, supernatural, must have happened, something which Spin couldn't make sense of."[8]

In Spin's former world, rifle shots were familiar, benign presences. A loud noise meant that he was on a hunt with his master. These new noises, however, uproot trees and houses alike, as they collapse the sky over the city. The most certain rule that had guided Spin's existence was the causality principle that connected the report of rifle shots with a pleasurable experience, during which he could fulfill his nature and make good use of his hunting skills. This link is now broken, and, in turn, Spin's world becomes hostile, inherently threatening, and unfamiliar, something beyond his control. For Spin, if loud noises no longer mean that he is out hunting, then nothing can be trusted anymore: "He didn't touch food, he stared at the soup with suspicious eyes, those distrustful and pleading eyes of a dog that fears being betrayed by the very hand of its master. No human or natural law existed anymore. The world had collapsed."[9]

In addition to facing a world where his canine sensemaking has been shattered, Spin's forced powerlessness is compounded by the mysteriousness of what is taking place around him: "The darkness in which he found himself, a darkness concerning the events of that terrible day and the reason for that waiting, added to the terror of the massive explosions of the bombs an anxiety far worse than any uncertainty."[10] Those around Spin—the members of the Italian diplomatic corps—experience some distress as well. They voice their concern, although with composure: "it's the end of the world," states prince Ruffo; "it's a real hell," Mameli adds; and according to the first secretary Guidotti, "nature has gone mad." They are pale while they sit in the shelter and smoke their cigarettes.[11] Their experience of the air raid, however, is not one of horror, because they are convinced of knowing what is going on: it is the war—*their* war, as they are successfully reclaiming the city for the Axis forces—and they assume that the bombardment will eventually stop.[12]

Spin, however, is in a more precarious position. No matter his usual courage, the explosions he hears challenge the causal connections of his world: "But the horrible roar that had, that morning, made the world collapse, was not, could not be the friendly voice of the rifle: it was a voice never heard before then, a new, frightening voice." Spin imagines this voice belonging to some "horrifying monster" or "ferocious foreign god" that ended the "reign of the rifle," which, thus far, had ruled his reality "in order and in harmony."[13]

Now that order and harmony are broken, Spin's world loses any remaining sense of stability. He first imagines his master limping around the wastelands of an Earth turned into ashes, burdened by his defeated rifle. The vision intensifies as Spin spirals down into a somber thought loop, and ponders whether the rifle, assuming a new, twisted form, is the source of the explosions: "What if that frightening voice . . . What if the rifle, overtaken by a sudden madness, had started to run through the streets, fields, woods, shores, disrupting nature with its new, horrendous, delirious voice? At this thought, Spin felt his blood freeze."[14]

This is a typical Malapartian descriptive technique: something first causes a crack in the subject's world, a crack that progressively widens, and, like a deforming prism, changes the way the subject experiences his surroundings. The subject is then overwhelmed by the present circumstances as they take over. In order to convey the experience of this horrified world, the author shifts away from verisimilitude and embraces what I call an aesthetics of deformation, which parallels how, from a phenomenological point of view, reality stops "making sense" for the subject experiencing their world cast into crisis.

But the temporality of horror is not fixed, and when the world horrifies, it does not necessarily remain so indefinitely. Indeed, Spin's story has a happy ending. Malaparte suggests that Mameli shoot a rifle in front of his dog, so that Spin can regain access to his former, stable world where explosions come from clear and distinct sources. After the shot, Spin sees that "the rifle, finally healed from its monstrous madness, returned to make its old, familiar voice heard in the pacified nature."[15]

Although Spin's sojourn in a disquieting reality comes to a quick end, in 1941 the rest of Europe was still in the midst of horror. Slightly less than two years had passed since the beginning of World War II, and approximately four more would be necessary to reach the end of the conflict.

Malaparte's coming of age as a novelist took place during this time.

Born in 1898, he was a decorated veteran of World War I, where he fought alongside the French troops in the Legione Garibaldina, suffering damage to his lungs in a chemical weapon attack during the Battle of Ligny; the aftermath of this event likely led to the lung cancer that took his life in 1957. By the beginning of World War II he had already acquired considerable literary fame thanks to his essay *Technique du coup d'état*, where he evaluated the various techniques armed militias used in modern European history to take over governments and analyzed their common elements. The book, published in France in 1931, was quickly banned in Germany and Italy, among other nations. An early member of the fascist movement, he joined the Fasci italiani di combattimento two years before the 1922 March on Rome. Despite his mixed fortunes with the regime, Malaparte remained well within its ranks until the Italian armistice of 1943, when he took the side of the newly formed Badoglio government and aligned himself with the Allied forces.[16]

Malaparte's *Kaputt*, published in 1944, is a first-person narration of his journey through part of World War II. After being a soldier in his early twenties, in his forties he was a witness to this second global conflict as a war correspondent on the eastern front for the Italian newspaper *Corriere della sera*.[17] *Kaputt*, Malaparte writes in the book's preface, presents war as its "objective landscape," the stage upon which its true main character can act out its role. The "chief character" of the book is "Kaputt" itself, "this gay and gruesome monster." According to Malaparte's (pseudo-)etymological explanation, the Jewish "*Koppâroth*" is the root of the German word *kaputt*,[18] which means "broken, finished, gone to pieces, gone to ruin." The "chief character" of the book is the reduction of Europe to "a pile of rubble," and the war is the stage upon which this demolition is performed (*Kaputt*, 3).

Kaputt is not the war novel of a combatant: during World War II, Malaparte did not directly participate in any military actions, nor did he experience the frontlines. The text is instead Malaparte's account of a world in the process of being demolished—a world going *kaputt*, just like Spin's world when the bombing of Belgrade called into question his most foundational assumptions about reality. The war, as "objective landscape," creates the conditions of possibility for chronicling this experience of world collapse.

While critics have described Malaparte's work as expressionistic and surreal, this chapter focuses on the purpose of his style rather than its position in the history of the avant-garde. From this perspective, I contend that Malaparte's aesthetics hints at his epistemological uncertainty and sense of bewilderment concerning the historical circumstances he was experiencing.[19] His account of World War II is not a list of facts. Most of his narration is shaped as a loose reminiscence of past events, which Malaparte evokes while a guest of diplomats, generals, or aristocrats—often as they talk at a lavish banquet, in rooms filled with the fumes of cognac. Rather than a linear narration, *Kaputt* is a set of heterogeneous memories and experiences unified by the "objective landscape" of war.

Kaputt's historical figures and events are placed alongside ones of more ambiguous status. For example, Malaparte likely knew and encountered Prince Eugen of Sweden;[20] similarly, his friendship with the Spanish poet and diplomat Agustín de Foxá is documented.[21] More complex is his status as a witness to the 1941 Iaşi pogrom: while the local Jewish community provided testimony of Malaparte's passage through their city, his presence in the city during the days of the carnage is likely a literary construction.[22] This narrative ambiguity spills over to, and gets compounded by, more surreal episodes: is Malaparte to be trusted when he describes hundreds of horses trapped up to their necks in Finland's Lake Lagoda and flash-frozen by a sudden cold wave (*Kaputt*, 49–60)? What is to be made of his numerous references to cannibalism (*Kaputt*, 15, 34, 254)? Did he really encounter soldiers without eyelids (*Kaputt*, 256)? And did Ante Pavelić, the governor of the Axis-controlled Independent State of Croatia, actually delight his guests with a basket full of human eyes in lieu of a platter of oysters (*Kaputt*, 272)?

None of these latter experiences can be ruled out as impossible in a world going *kaputt*, where the horrors of World War II are the "objective landscape." In discussing the ambiguous status of Malaparte's reportage, Czech author Milan Kundera writes that Malaparte "invented a form that is a totally new thing and that belongs to him alone." Kundera describes the Italian author as an "undetectable spy" who moves through Nazi-occupied Europe, free to interact with important historical figures in informal settings, and in so doing is uniquely positioned to give, as he does, a very early testimony to a number of historical events, such as the cruelty of the Axis lieutenants, particularly against the Jews. Given Malaparte's unique vantage point, asks Kundera, why has no historian ever used *Kaputt* as a source? According to Kundera, it is because *Kaputt* "is a literary work whose aesthetic intention is so strong, so apparent, that the sensitive reader *automatically* excludes it from the context of accounts brought to bear by historians, journalists, political analysts, memoirists."[23]

Malaparte's reader quickly realizes that the book is not a factual account of the war and its protagonists. *Kaputt* explains little; instead, it reveals. What it reveals is Malaparte's experience of witnessing a world being demolished. For this reason, *Kaputt* is the book of a phenomenologist more than of a historian-chronicler. Malaparte is not on a quest for clear and distinct reasons regarding what is happening around him, nor is he seeking to historicize Europe's downward spiral into war. His purpose is to give a phenomenological account of being in a world where the present is so overwhelming as to call into question the final goal of the Cartesian subject: the experience of a world going *kaputt* shows the subject the foolishness of their faith in fully mastering reality and its circumstances, and forces them instead to confront a situation that they must bear without controlling. Horror, as an event, suspends questions of "making sense": it simply takes over, in its overwhelming and threatening nature, thus casting the subject's world into crisis. For those convinced they can master the world, there can be no greater upending than experiencing their forced powerlessness.[24]

Instead of trying to rationalize what is taking place, Malaparte's style and content are aimed at expressing his horror at what he witnessed.[25] This is achieved, as Kundera writes, in a prose charged with an "aesthetic intention" impossible to overlook. To this point, Malaparte's style has often been described as baroque, heavy, and pompous—derogatorily so, until the author's recent rediscovery. More specifically, the story of Spin shows how Malaparte leverages deforming descriptions, such as the one of the rifle going mad, to reveal what it means to experience reality going *kaputt*.

In his dual role as both author and protagonist of *Kaputt*, Malaparte is frequently exposed to the horrors that World War II unleashed. In his retelling of the conflict, against the backdrop of the "objective landscape" of war, a raincloud can become a "ripe tumor" (*Kaputt*, 107), and an approaching storm an "enormous, painfully breathing black lung" (*Kaputt*, 34). Even light, during wartime, can become an unsettling element. Anyone who has ever gone twenty-four hours or more without sleeping knows how the sunlight—that same sunlight we are so used to—feels different after a restless night. Several sections of *Kaputt* are set above the Arctic Circle, when the so-called white nights take place—a natural phenomenon whereby during summertime in high latitudes the sun remains visible throughout the night. Malaparte, born and raised in Tuscany, is unaccustomed to the midnight sun, which he experiences as symptomatic of an upside-down world.

From its opening pages the novel connects the Nordic light to a looming sense of death, but it is in the chapter "Naked Men," set in Lapland, that this theme reaches its apex, and offers an insight into Malaparte's use of the aesthetics of deformation to convey the ordinary horrors of warfare. The chapter describes a banquet hosted by the governor Kaarlo Hillilä. Malaparte sets the stage by describing how the Nordic light fills the dining room where the guests are enjoying their meal, and illuminates the space with "the blinding glare of an operating room" (*Kaputt*, 317–18). Hillilä and the rest of the group, intoxicated after several rounds of cognac, ask Malaparte about his unexpected encounter in an elevator, a few nights before, with the Reichsführer-SS Heinrich Himmler, whom they consider "a genius" (*Kaputt*, 320). Malaparte, who is perfectly aware of the dangers of such conversations, claims that he did not recognize Himmler, and that, in any case, he does not want to have anything to do with him. The narration shifts away from the dialogue and centers again on Malaparte's internal point of view as he observes that the midnight sun is casting a "dead and frozen splendor of chalk" on everything underneath. "Beneath that sky," the description continues, "the trees, the rocks, the grass and the water dropped with a queer substance, soft and slimy" (*Kaputt*, 323).

The "queer substance" is light itself, "that chalky light was the ghostly, dazzling light of the North," which penetrates everything it touches, and changes the way that Malaparte, already unsettled by the conversation about Himmler, experiences his surroundings. Human beings as well undergo this process of deformation, since the light "burns every sign of life, every semblance of humanity [and] gives man the appearance of death."[26] Malaparte focuses on the faces of the other guests and realizes that they are slowly turning into "masks of chalk, blind and dumb. Faces without eyes, without lips, without noses—shapeless and smooth masks of chalk" (*Kaputt*, 323). Everyone in the room who is touched by the Nordic light undergoes the same transformation. Underpinned by the associative thinking typical of *Kaputt*, their featureless and unsettling countenances—their metamorphoses into death masks—evoke Malaparte's memory of something he once witnessed in Sodankylä, which he starts retelling to the participants of the banquet in an attempt to change the conversation topic to something less compromising than his encounter with Himmler.

Malaparte thus reminisces about another night when "the sky [was] white" and everything looked as if it were made of plaster. The midnight sun "looked like a blind eye without eyelashes." He recalls the arrival of an ambulance, followed by some nurses who unloaded the stretchers transported by the vehicle and then deposited them on a nearby lawn. The nurses' dresses and the lawn as well were coated with the light's blinding whiteness. Surprisingly, the stretchers appeared to be carrying "statues of chalk, their heads oval and smooth, without eyes, without noses, without mouths," sculpted as if to represent figures stuck in time while performing "heavy, motionless frozen postures." Eventually a cloud created a fleeting moment of penumbra that sufficed to break the deathly spell cast by the Nordic light:

> Suddenly a gray cloud spread over the sky, and out of the sudden twilight around me, revealing their real shape, emerged the beings and things that before had been merged into that still white glow. The chalk statues on the stretchers were abruptly changed into human shapes by the sudden shadow from that cloud. Those chalk masks were turned into living human features. They were men, they were wounded soldiers. They followed me with their wondering and puzzled glances, for I, too, had suddenly turned before their eyes from a chalk statue into a man—a living man, made of flesh and shadow. (*Kaputt*, 324)

The light recedes, and, once the veil it had cast is momentarily lifted, the protagonists of the scene catch a glimpse of their own mortality, wounds, and fears. In a world gone *kaputt*, Malaparte and these soldiers must bracket the derangement of the ordinary that they witness and experience on a daily basis. Their habituation to the horrors of war is metaphorically represented by the perennial light of the Nordic summer: if Hell is on earth, the sun may as well stop setting. The role of light itself is flipped, as it constitutes an obscuring rather than an illuminating presence, and in so doing covers up a twisted reality instead of exposing it. Once this veil is torn—once, sticking to Malaparte's image, a cloud creates some penumbra—the plaster casts turn (again) into beings made of flesh, human beings who, Malaparte now realizes, are severely disfigured.

In a world going *kaputt*, the encounter with wounded humans is normalized to avoid paralysis in the face of the horrifying spectacle of ubiquitous physical and psychological suffering. This coping mechanism is aesthetically represented by the transformation of the soldiers into plaster casts that cover up their flesh with unfeeling material. But a momentary cloud can provide some shelter from this obscuring light, and once this happens, those involved must face the fact that, despite their resilience and the degree of control they thought they exerted over their surroundings, they neither master nor possess their world. They are all subject to a situation that forces their powerlessness to an extent that commands a recalibration of their horizon of expectations concerning what is happening around them, just as one might eventually stop questioning why the sun is not setting anymore above the Arctic Circle. However, once a cloud breaks the spell of the light, the mutilated flesh breaks free of the plaster casts that kept its horrifying nature hidden.[27]

Malaparte chronicles the experience of being in a world where the present and its categories of sense-making are upended. There, the experience of forced powerlessness becomes the norm. In being so, his work, with its style, form, and content, refuses the pretense of the Cartesian subject to master and possess the world, in particular when the latter is going *kaputt*. Malaparte's technique of blurring the distinction between factual and deformed descriptions of events and objects also calls into question the possibility of keeping reason separate from emotion—which is to say, the possibility that the subject can untether their phenomenological, embodied experience of the world from rational, abstract causal explanations and factual descriptions.[28] If reason would like to make sense of the world's circumstances and master them, Malaparte shows that there are moments when the present simply takes over, and forces the subject, in its entirety, to confront the lived situation without being able to assert their dominion in the face of what is happening.

The book's plot, too, does not lead to a final moment of clarification. Rather, it sets the stage for the sense of epistemological confusion that *The Skin* more overtly thematizes. The concluding chapter of *Kaputt* takes place in Naples, when on August 7, 1943, Malaparte, having traveled from the eastern front back to Italy, reaches the Parthenopean city, described as a "huge pile of debris and bloody rags" (*Kaputt*, 410). A "black, glistening cloud of flies" covers the city, which, disfigured by the bombings, appears eerily empty. A closer look, however, reveals a place teeming with life, where creatures, objects, and debris pile up without any apparent discontinuities. Beings with "horrible deformities" roam Naples: "Some were skeletons clothed in rags, their heads covered with yellow skin stretched tightly over their skulls, their teeth bared by an atrocious grin; some were old men, bald and toothless, with dog faces. There were young girls with monstrously large and swollen heads attached to tiny, fleshless bodies; there were old hags, huge, fat, swollen, with enormous bellies and small shriveled birdlike heads on which the hair stood hard and bristly, like feathers. There were crippled children with ape-like faces; some of them dragged themselves on all fours" (*Kaputt*, 413). These creatures are the "monsters" of Naples: the mutilated, the homeless, the deformed, the insane, "objects of religious idolatry." In a world going ***kaputt***, they are taking over the streets, guided by their leader, "the god." This creature of grotesque and Luciferian features towers over the multitude of monsters as their ruler: "against that background of ruin and death the god proceeded as if across a desert." With a parallelism to Spin's story, these beings seek shelter by heading "into the bowels of the earth, into the subterranean kingdom of Plutonic Naples" to escape the bombings of the city, which took place with increasing frequency over the summer of 1943. This time, however, the descent is led not by an ambassador, but instead by the leader of an infernal legion (*Kaputt*, 415).

Naples is the place in *Kaputt* where reality becomes so deranged as to appear closer to Hell than Earth. This serves the narrative trajectory of the book by allowing it to reach its climax right before the end, which does not carry any sense of resolution—just as the war in 1943 was still far from its conclusion, and was in fact entering, at least for the Italian peninsula, its bloodiest phase. Malaparte's arrival in Naples ends the book with a cliffhanger, by revealing the innermost core of horror to the reader right before closing the narrative.

This narration is taken up in *The Skin*, where Malaparte starts by retelling his time in Naples, a city where the flies have defeated mankind. I here refer to the last phrase of *Kaputt*, where a Neapolitan answers Malaparte's questions concerning the presence of flies in the city by stating that "the flies have won" (*Kaputt*, 428). The presence of the flies is an instance of metonymy, hinting at how the city, representing a world upside-down, now belongs to the dead more than to the living.

Further unwinding this thread, in *The Skin* Malaparte addresses more explicitly the shortcomings of Cartesian reason in a world that resembles Hell more than Earth. In so doing, he also addresses the normalization of the horrifying without, however, implying that a "horrifying" experience is uniformly endured by all. Even in a city going *kaputt* like Naples there can be figures for whom reality is not turning upside-down: they are the soon-to-be victors of the war, Italy's liberators, those whose world and home country have not collapsed—the Americans. Building on these premises, in analyzing *The Skin* I will argue that even when horror seems to be a structural feature of reality, it still remains to an extent subjective.

Malaparte travels to Naples at the end of *Kaputt*, in summer 1943, headed home to his villa in Capri.[29] At that time, Naples was a powder keg: famine was rampant in the city, and the Anglo-American bombings intensified as the war was entering its final stage. Simultaneously, the grip of the Axis forces on the peninsula tightened after the Allied offensive in Sicily began the Italian campaign. Before the situation in Naples collapsed, Malaparte had managed to reach his Casa Malaparte, which he himself had in part designed on a narrow, rocky promontory of Capri. There, he finished writing *Kaputt* in September 1943.

Meanwhile, a few miles from the island, the Four Days of Naples were taking place, and the popular insurrection against the Axis culminated with the Allied forces entering the city on October 1. In November, Malaparte, still in Capri, was arrested by the US Counterintelligence Corps because of his former role as a diplomat and brought back to Naples where he was incarcerated in solitary confinement. On November 30, Colonel Henry H. Cumming took Malaparte out of his prison cell to interrogate him. Malaparte, with one of his typical twists, convinced the American that he could be a valuable asset, and began collaborating with the Public Safety Division of the Allied forces.[30] Eventually reintegrated into the post-armistice Italian army with the rank of captain, Malaparte closely collaborated with Cumming for almost two years, until the American soldier died on July 10, 1945, just a few weeks before he was scheduled to fly back to his home in South Carolina.

This brief biographical digression allows us to understand how, similar to *Kaputt*, *The Skin*, too, plays with history: in this novel as well the distinctions between fact and fiction blur and, tellingly, Malaparte puts the words "history and story [*storia e racconto*]" on its frontispiece to signal the hybrid nature of what follows.[31] The book chronicles Malaparte's time alongside the Allies during the last two years of war, beginning in Naples after his release from prison. *The Skin* is dedicated to the "affectionate memory of Colonel Henry H. Cumming, of the University of Virginia"[32]—the same Cumming who enlisted Malaparte with the American forces. Colonel Cumming also appears as one of the main characters of the book, under the pseudonym of Colonel Jack Hamilton.

Jack Hamilton is a southern gentleman with a soul both innocent and cultivated: he was "an American in the noblest sense of the word," equally passionate about his study of Latin and Greek and the sports he practiced in college. With the candor that, according to Malaparte, can only belong to American undergraduates, Jack had put equal faith "in the hands of Horace, Virgil, Simonides, and Xenophon, and in those of the masseurs of the university gymnasiums." He is a francophile who considers Europe to be "*la banlieue de Paris*," and had written a book on Descartes that helped him obtain tenure at an American university, where Jack spends his time between the lecture halls and the university's fitness center (*Skin*, 17). As a francophile educated in the United States under the spell of European culture, Jack is a Cartesian.[33] As a Cartesian, he finds that the spectacle of Naples going *kaputt* is difficult to reconcile with the clear and distinct ideas he held about the city:

> Although he called himself Cartesian, affecting to put his trust wholly and always in reason and to believe that reason can probe and explain everything, his attitude towards Naples, Italy, and Europe was one of affection tempered both with respect and with suspicion. To him, as to all Americans, Naples had been an unexpected and distressing revelation. He had believed he was setting foot in a world dominated by reason, governed by human conscience; and he had found himself without warning in a mysterious country, where men and the circumstances that make up their lives seemed to be governed not by reason and conscience, but by obscure subterranean forces. (*Skin*, 37–38)

In *The Skin* Naples is the kernel of a world going *kaputt*, where "obscure subterranean forces" challenge the Cartesian subject's belief in their capacity to dominate their surroundings through reason alone. The book stages this confrontation through what Malaparte calls "the plague of Naples" and its effects on the population. Jack arrives in Naples during the first outbreak of this mysterious disease on October 1, 1943, right when the Allied forces enter the city (*Skin*, 7). The disease's most salient trait is that it transforms "human conscience into a horrible, noisome ulcer," as its victims undergo a process of perversion whereby they become betrayers of their loved ones "but never against themselves." This plague leaves the body intact, "but within the integument of the healthy flesh the soul festered and rotted," through a mutation that Malaparte describes, with a couplet of adjectives already found in *Kaputt*, as horrible and piteous (*Skin*, 31–32). Certain zones of the city, where the outbreak reaches its most violent expression, have turned into a "funeral kermis" where the infected abandon themselves to orgiastic celebrations "amid the horrible stench that emanated from the countless hundreds of corpses buried beneath the ruins" (*Skin*, 31).[34] In these zones, Hell seems to have erupted on Earth.

Mentioning Hell is not hyperbolic, for the plague of Naples is of Dantean essence. The sinners in Dante's *Inferno*, as Robert Pogue Harrison argues, all suffer from variously conjugated forms of egoic self-love, which makes Hell "not so much a place as a human condition, or way of being."[35] The same is true for the disease described in *The Skin*. Although in 1943–44 Southern Italy did suffer epidemics of smallpox and typhus, no cases of plague were recorded; indeed, Malaparte's plague is not so much a true disease as a human condition or a way of being. The infected turn into traitors (in Dante's *Inferno* traitors are cast into the deepest circles, close to Lucifer), capable of any abjection and betrayal that will allow them to reap some benefits from the presence of the newly installed Allied forces. There are, however, crucial differences between Dante and Malaparte. Dante considered himself to be a *cantor rectitudinis* (a poet of rectitude) in a cosmos governed by clear and distinct rules; his worldview allowed him to separate good from evil, and the very existence of Hell is symptomatic of the possibility of this division. Conversely, hundreds of years later, Malaparte realizes that a world that is *kaputt* does not offer any sense of reassuring stability; restraining himself from judging, he instead expresses horror and pity as he journeys through this modern Inferno.[36]

The first pages of the book throw the reader, and Jack too, into a reality where the world and its circumstances seem to be uncontrollable. In one of the first scenes, taking place in the cloister of what used to be a leper hospital, Malaparte meets the soldiers whom he and Jack will take command of. They are Italians who fought against the Allied forces up until the armistice of September 8, 1943, and now wear the uniforms of British military personnel they had killed in North Africa—a reversal symptomatic of a world where "making sense" is, on an individual level, a complicated matter. Each of these young men presents a "pale and emaciated [face]; their eyes, which were white and steady, consisted of a moist, opaque substance," and they stare at Malaparte "without blinking." Their hands, holding on to their rifles, are "white and bloodless" and the skin on their fingers flaccid (*Skin*, 9). Their uniforms are stained by black spots of blood. Malaparte is transfixed by the sight of these emaciated figures, forced, regardless of their own personal beliefs, to side with, and fight against, anyone their superiors dictate. All of a sudden, under the pressure of Malaparte's already troubled experience of the present situation, reality cracks: "Suddenly I realized to my horror that those soldiers were dead. They gave out a faint odor of musky cloth, rotten leather, and flesh that had been dried up by the sun. I looked at Colonel Palese, and he was dead too. The voice that proceeded from his lips was watery, cold, glutinous, like the horrible gurgling that issues from a dead man's mouth if you rest your hand on his stomach" (*Skin*, 10). Malaparte himself, rallying the troops, utters with a "horrible gurgling" words that are "muffled, thick, flaccid." One of the soldiers is asked to repeat Malaparte's patriotic speech. With the same gurgling, he responds: "It is our duty to show ourselves worthy of the shame of Italy," thus twisting Malaparte's speech (*Skin*, 10). Right after the soldier finishes speaking, a bloodstain starts expanding below his left armpit, close to his heart. This scene sets the stage for the entire book by presenting the reader with a world that certain of its dwellers must bear without the possibility of mastering, portrayed through deforming descriptions that poke a hole in the fabric of realism to which the book subscribes.

It is fundamental to underscore that, although the setting (fall 1943 in a "liberated" Naples) is the same for all involved, not all of the characters of the novel experience it the same way. Indeed, the American soldiers are strangely immune to the plague of Naples, and can roam around: "pink-faced, calm, and smiling, they moved about in the midst of the plague-stricken mob without contracting the loathsome disease" (*Skin*, 30). Why is this so? Because, I argue, they are the victors: they are there with a purpose, as active agents of a story in which they are the righteous protagonists.

In her *Horrorism: Naming Contemporary Violence*, Italian philosopher Adriana Cavarero distinguishes between "terrorism" and "horrorism": whereas the former sets the attention on an agent's motivations in committing terrible yet spectacular acts, the latter term emphasizes the horrifying state of helplessness of those who suffer the consequences of that very act.[37] Depending on one's circumstances, the same event acquires a different value also from an experiential point of view: to paraphrase Cavarero, behind an act of terrorism there lies also the presence of horrorism, as it takes hold of the life of a victim.

The idea of horrorism seeks to reframe the discussion of violence to emphasize the victims' experiences of horror over the terror intended by the perpetrators, and in so doing it implicitly invites us to side with the former. But an emphasis on the victims' perspective is not a choice available in the face of terrorism only: the Americans' immunity to the plague of Naples invites us to consider that the distinction between victors and defeated, too, in the context of warfare, can lead to a similar experiential divergence. In other words, the phenomenology of the former does not overlap with that of those whose world is *kaputt*: horror is a subjective, contextually constructed experience.

For the Americans, as symbolized by Jack the Cartesian, the situation "makes sense": they disembarked in Sicily and are climbing up the Italian peninsula to defeat the Axis. They know why they are in Naples, and can contextualize why Naples is *kaputt* the way it is. The city was disfigured by the German occupying forces, and now, after having been a battlefield, bears the traces of that captivity. Crucially, the Americans are not in Hell: they are in a city that they themselves liberated. Their phenomenology of the situation is thus flipped: the outward historical context is for them not a source of horror but rather something that prevents them from experiencing that same horror.

Conversely, those whose city has been destroyed, whose houses have been turned into debris, and whose families have been killed—*they* live in Hell and suffer from the plague. If from a broad historical and political perspective their situation too can "make sense" (it can adequately be explained by the succession of events leading to that point), from a personal standpoint their experience of these circumstances is more somber. There are certainly good reasons why the Italian troops are now siding with the Allies, whom they had fought only a few months earlier: the armistice took place, and Italy switched sides. But is this "reason" something that, phenomenologically speaking, "makes sense" for the soldiers gathered in the cloister? Or are they instead subject to a context that, valid as it may be, they must bear without mastering?

The plague and its diverse effects on the city's population highlight the subject-centered nature of horror. They also remind us that situations and contexts, extreme as they may be, are neither neutral nor objective. Even in scenarios such as World War II, Malaparte's plague, in infecting only a specific demographic of the city, reveals the experiential differences that the same setting can promote. Even when horror appears to be structural, it still maintains a subjective strain: one person's forced powerlessness can be someone else's victorious entrance into a city. As suggested previously, Hell is a way of being more than a place.

In Malaparte's account, the winners mistake their contextual status (something potentially mutable) for one of their essential features (hence immutable). Jack is a Cartesian who had landed more on the shores of an abstract idea (his "ideal Cartesian Europe" [*Skin*, 39]) than on a real continent going *kaputt*. The events of Naples, however, start interfering with the image of Europe he had in mind: "But the classic landscape of the Doric columns of the temples of Paestum concealed from his eyes a secret, mysterious Italy. It concealed Naples, that terrible, wonderful prototype of an unknown Europe, situated outside the realm of Cartesian logic—that other Europe of whose existence he had until that day had only a vague suspicion, and whose mysteries and secrets, now that he was gradually probing them, filled him with a wondrous terror" (*Skin*, 39). The mutilations, the suffering, the prostitution, and the famine and diseases he is exposed to in Naples make Jack—and Jack alone, at least among the Americans—question the "reasons" behind what he is witnessing. Malaparte observes that the rest of the Allied soldiers "despised Naples, Italy, and Europe, they despised us because they believed that we alone were responsible for our miseries and misfortunes, our acts of cowardice, our crimes, our perfidies, our infamies" (*Skin*, 37). Conversely, Jack senses that the powerlessness of the Neapolitan people is forced rather than willful: he begins to understand that there are moments when the subject loses their illusory Cartesian pedestal and is shown to be incapable of fully mastering their world.

But ultimately Jack refuses to yield to this darker side of Europe. In French, he utters: "Je crois [. . .] que Naples n'est pas impénétrable à la raison. Je suis cartésien, hélas!" To which Malaparte answers: "Do you think, then, that Cartesian reason can help you, for instance, to understand Hitler? [. . .] Hitler too is an element in the mystery of Europe, because Hitler too belongs to that *other* Europe which Cartesian reason cannot penetrate. Do you think, then, that you can explain Hitler solely with the help of Descartes?" (*Skin*, 40).

Kaputt gave a very early chronicle of the cruelty of the German lieutenants against the population of the occupied territories, particularly the Jews. Was there a "reason" for that cruelty? Or better: did it "make sense"? In *The Skin*, Malaparte challenges the assumption that one can understand any historical event with enough clearness and distinction to make valid inferences regarding its causes and reasons. Because of this, Malaparte writes something that is "history [*storia*]" and "story [*racconto*]" alike: despite the long and complex unfolding of antisemitism and revanchism in Europe, the hi*story* of Hitler, of World War II, and of the Holocaust only "makes sense" retrospectively, when one concocts an explanation around a steady succession of events that lead from World War I to the Weimar Republic and then to the Third Reich. Such a linear, clear, distinct succession of events can be described only in hindsight.

This thinking is elucidated by the work of statistician Nassim Nicholas Taleb. In *The Black Swan*, he refers to the rise of Hitler as what he calls a "black swan" event, which is to say an event with the three following attributes: "First, it is an *outlier*, as it lies outside the realm of regular expectations, because nothing in the past can convincingly point to its possibility. Second, it carries an extreme impact (unlike the bird). Third, in spite of its outlier status, human nature makes us concoct explanations for its occurrence *after* the fact, making it explainable and predictable."[38] In other words, "black swans" are events that frustrate those convinced of their mastery of the world.

To Malaparte's question whether Jack could explain Hitler solely through Descartes, the American responds, again in French, "Je l'explique parfaitement." Malaparte reacts by sharing with him an anecdote about a symposium of German scientists in Heidelberg where the participants, after a long discussion, conclude that "the world can be explained with the aid of reason alone." After this deliberation is reached, an old professor sitting on the other side of the room, who had remained perfectly silent thus far, stands up and asks:

> "You who explain everything—could you tell me how on earth this thing has appeared on my head tonight?" And, slowly removing the silk hat, he revealed a cigar, a genuine Havana, which was projecting from his bald cranium.
>
> "Ah, ah, c'est merveilleux!" said Jack, laughing, "do you mean, then, that Hitler is a Havana cigar?"
>
> "No, I mean that Hitler is *like* that Havana cigar."
>
> "C'est merveilleux! Un cigare!" said Jack; and he added, as though seized by sudden inspiration, "Have a drink, Malaparte." But he corrected himself, and said in French: "Allons boire quelque chose." (*Skin*, 40)

This surreal scene exaggerates in a comical way the essence of the Hitler phenomenon. Hitler is not a cigar, but his success in Germany, his role as the initiator of World War II and the mind behind the Holocaust are *like* the cigar of the anecdote: something that cannot be inferred given a previous context. A cigar, of course, cannot simply grow out of someone's head. But the simile that Malaparte italicizes points at the opacities inherent in the nature of a complex social phenomenon such as the rise of Hitler to power and the unfolding of World War II. These opacities are then made to disappear once one crafts a compelling historical narrative that, in retrospect, integrates a black swan into a paradigm of (again, retrospective) predictability and thus hypothetical controllability.

The Naples of *The Skin* is a world going *kaputt*, and a world going *kaputt* is also "*like* that Havana cigar" for those, unlike Jack, forced to experience it without the possibility of a recontextualization within a satisfactory framework of sense-making; it is something that frustrates desires of predictability and control, an outlier event that must be dealt with before being made sense of. How did the cigar appear on the professor's head? How did Naples become a "funeral kermis"? Why are the dead overtaking the city? "Have a drink, Malaparte," Jack responds, immediately repeating the same phrase in French. The code-switch to French is a corrective because French is the language of Jack's Cartesianism: the language he uses to "make sense" of the presently lived situation through clear and distinct ideas about why he is there, why Naples is in its current state, and so on.

Malaparte seeks to convince Jack about the possibility of outlier events that shatter previous paradigms of sense-making. The nature of such events must also be gauged against someone's contextual understanding of them: a lived situation can be experienced as a negative outlier even if not statistically rare. This makes it possible to develop Taleb's concept of "black swan" by arguing that one can meaningfully talk about "phenomenological black swans." With this expression, I refer to events that are *experienced by someone* as a "black swan": instead of considering an event a statistical outlier insofar as its frequency stands out once analyzed against the backdrop of a broader dataset, a phenomenological "black swan" simply needs to be an outlier for the experience of an individual. In other words, while an event may or may not be a statistical anomaly in a wide-ranging historical context, the subject-centered claim that I am making here is, more narrowly, that a phenomenological "black swan" is an event experienced as anomalous by someone, overarching historical priors notwithstanding.

The horrors of war are not "black swans" in the statistical understanding of the term: atrocities similar to the ones described in *Kaputt* and *The Skin* have characterized war throughout history across nations and geographical regions, and today as well. For this reason, too, there is an intuitive connection, in ordinary language, between horror and war. Yet, a statistically common event can become a world-shattering outlier for someone who, thus far, has not been exposed to anything similar. One need only think about a cancer diagnosis to realize how an event that occurs to a great number of people any given day, and that we cannot rule out of our experiential horizon, can cast a life into a state of profound crisis.

Similarly, for Jack the Cartesian and a great part of the US army, this is the first exposure to the horrors of war, and the reality of Naples *kaputt* troubles their abstract model of the city. In the Parisian diaries that Malaparte writes after the end of World War II, he describes the French philosopher Jean-Paul Sartre as the champion of Cartesianism, here understood as a tendency toward abstraction and clear and distinct reasons over the messiness of real-world circumstances.[39] To Malaparte, however, Sartre is a peculiar kind of Cartesian, one "who has glimpsed the limits of Cartesianism, the insufficiency of reason, and is at the same time afraid of the uncontrollable dark forces that Cartesianism can neither master nor explain."[40] Jack shares the Cartesianism of Malaparte's Sartre, although at this point in the novel he is still distant from the abyss that made the French recoil in horror. Jack's Cartesianism is preserved, as it is part of the phenomenology of the victor: just as people craft their own stories to explain to themselves how and why they got where they are, Jack concocts a compelling set of explanations to "make sense" of the horrors of war.

The victors can make sense of a world that for the victims is upside-down: "all conquerors need to see these things, to convince themselves that they have won the war," Malaparte affirms while describing the "horrible thing" of a young girl putting her virginity on display, allowing the Americans to touch her unbroken hymen. To Malaparte's bleak commentary, Jimmy, another soldier, responds that "even if we had lost the war you wouldn't see things like that in America." According to Malaparte, however, "you would have seen worse things in America if you had lost the war" (*Skin*, 49–51). Here, too, the phenomenology of the victors does not overlap with that of those whose world is *kaputt*.

Given the separation between victims, on the one hand, and perpetrators or conquerors, on the other hand, *The Skin* resolutely sides with the former. Siding with the victims involves bearing testimony to events that may be deemed "impossible" by those unaffected by them. After the introductory chapter on the plague of Naples, the rest of *The Skin* chronicles a set of loosely connected scenes suspended between reportage and hallucination, colored by tints even more disquieting than those of *Kaputt*. While Naples is overtaken by the dead, phosphorus bombs turn Hamburg's citizens into living blazes stuck in the earth from the waist down (*Skin*, 106–7), and hundreds of Jews are crucified upon trees in the forests of Ukraine (*Skin*, 156–64). Are any of these events real? Was a young girl really boiled alive and served as a "siren" at a banquet hosted by an American general to make up for the shortage of fresh fish in Naples (219–21)? Or are all these scenes yet another instantiation of Malaparte's aesthetics of deformation? Such queries raise a question central to this project: should horror be conveyed through factual reportage, or does literature offer a distinct vantage point?

From this perspective, *The Skin* emerges as a phenomenological novel that leverages what Kundera called the "aesthetic intention" of Malaparte's prose to offer an account of what it meant to experience a world going *kaputt*. A scene from the chapter "The Flag" offers a metaliterary reflection on the author's style. Malaparte and Jack are invited to breakfast by a French officer, General Guillaume. The latter introduces the two to a group of soldiers, some of whom have read Malaparte's work and express their skepticism concerning the truth-value of *Kaputt* (*Skin*, 282–83). Malaparte, in response, turns his head to Guillaume and calmly states that "a few moments ago, at this very table, I had the most extraordinary experience of my life," thus seizing the guests' curiosity (*Skin*, 284).

With what at first seems an unnecessary digression, Malaparte evokes the mythical origins of the food they have been eating: sacred ham, noble trout, and propitiatory couscous. After Malaparte's storytelling conjures up this enchanted atmosphere, while describing the couscous, he adds: "I had suddenly become aware that the warm, strong flavor of the mutton had an unpleasant sweetness about it, and that I was chewing a piece of meat that was colder and softer than the rest. I looked at my plate, and was horrified to see a finger appear in the middle of the bran—first one finger, then two, then five, and finally a hand with white nails—a man's hand." The guests are shocked, as Malaparte affirms that his sense of proper etiquette prevented him from saying anything while they were eating to avoid spoiling the gathering. "If you don't believe me," he continues, "look here, on my plate. Do you see all these little bones? They are the knuckles. And these, ranged along the edge of the plate, are the five nails" (*Skin*, 286–87). The breakfast is suddenly interrupted by the sound of cannons, which announce that the US Fifth Army is finally getting ready to enter the city of Rome. Everyone rushes toward the jeeps, and the general excitement compounds Malaparte's and Jack's laughter about the French reaction to the story of the eaten hand:

> "Ah! ah! Bien joué, Malaparte! Un tour formidable!' cried Jack as he ran. "That'll teach them to question the truth of what you say in *Kaputt*!"
>
> "Did you see their expressions? I thought they were all going to be sick!"
>
> "Une sacrée farce, Malaparte! Ah! ah! ah!" cried Jack.
>
> "Did you see how skillfully I had arranged those little ram's bones on the plate? They looked just like the bones of a hand!"
>
> "Ah! ah! ah! merveilleux!" cried Jack as he ran. "It looked just like a hand—the skeleton of a hand!" (*Skin*, 288)

This passage echoes another metaliterary reflection that Malaparte wrote in *Prospettive*, the literary magazine he founded in 1937.[41] There, in a 1939 piece, he comments: "The ideal and moral problems of literature are closely connected with the so-called formal problems, with the problems of expression. It's not just about considering reality in a new way [. . .] but about expressing it in a new way. [. . .] The so-called 'content,' the objective reality, or in more current terms the material, the topic, even the subject itself, have no importance for the purposes of artistic creation."[42] Similar to how Malaparte deceived the group of French soldiers by arranging some mutton bones in a specific way, one of literature's most salient traits lies in the way in which it engages with its content. The remarkable "literary intention" that Kundera saw in Malaparte is part of a project that I here define as phenomenological, and which allows for the expression of reality "in a new way" as far as it does not seek to explain or to "make sense," but instead tries to reveal what it means to experience one's own world going *kaputt*. If properly orchestrated, Malaparte seems to suggest, the rearrangement of some mutton bones can provide an impression of a severed hand.

But a fine balance must be preserved in order to safeguard the disquieting ambiguity of Malaparte's prose. The carefully crafted, looming uncertainty concerning the truth-value of what his writings narrate mirrors the phenomenology of living through events that blur the boundary between possible and impossible. A final passage from *The Skin* strikingly exemplifies this equilibrium between "history [*storia*]" and "story [*racconto*]" that Malaparte sought to achieve.

The chapter "The Rain of Fire" opens with the expressionistic description of a cataclysm: "The sky to the east was scarred by a huge, crimson gash, which tinged the sea blood-red. The horizon was crumbling away, plunging headlong into an abyss of fire. [. . .] A horrifying grinding noise filled the air, like the sound of bones when they are broken and crushed." All of a sudden, a terrible cry pierces the air: "Vesuvius screamed in the night, spitting blood and fire" (*Skin*, 258).[43] The witnesses are "dumb with horror," transfixed by the eruption: "That ghostly Caesar with his dog-like head, sitting on his throne of lava and ashes, cleft the sky with his flame-crowned head, and barked horribly. The pillar of fire that rose from his throat penetrated deep into the celestial vault and vanished into the abyss of heaven. Rivers of blood streamed from his gaping red jaws, and earth, sky and sea trembled" (*Skin*, 265). The city is in a state of mayhem, which, this time, affects the Americans, too: "Lost in a fearsome crowd, which swept them now this way, now that, as it surged to and fro, turning them round and buffeting them like the gale in Dante's Hell, the American soldiers looked as if they too were possessed by a primeval terror and fury. [. . .] They were conquered wretches, victims of the blind fury of nature" (263). Their abstract image of Italy was one of harmony, reason, and domesticated nature. While the events of Naples could undermine this belief—they were the city's liberators, and they could "make sense" of what was going on in the city—now even Jack the Cartesian is forced to reckon with "that vision of hell, and horror, dread and wonder mingled in his wide eyes" (*Skin*, 260).

Horror is the result of an interplay between the subject and contextual, contingent factors. With this scene Malaparte shows that the Americans' seemingly miraculous immunity against the plague of Naples was simply a matter of context: they were immune because they were not victims—and horror, as Cavarero reminds us, implies being, or siding with, the victim. But the upheaval of nature makes a victim of everyone exposed to its power, no matter their role in the war: the eruption of Mount Vesuvius forces the powerlessness of all who, due to physical proximity, cannot experience it, in Kantian terms, as sublime. As argued in chapter 1, if the sublime involves a degree of separation between the subject and an overwhelming event, in a moment of horror what overwhelms directly and negatively affects the perceiving subject, casting their world into crisis.

In terms of the two words present on *The Skin*'s frontispiece, is the eruption that Malaparte describes "history [*storia*]" or "story [*racconto*]"? A reader accustomed to a Malapartian world of living dead and boiled children may glide over this event, taking place a good two hundred fifty pages into the book, as an additional impossible happening, and a distortion of historical facts. And yet, it is based in reality: March 1944 marked the last major eruption of Vesuvius, which destroyed a number of towns in the area, while leaving Naples, as *The Skin* accurately describes, almost untouched. Malaparte's description of the eruption is thus both "*storia*" and "*racconto*": it narrates an almost unbelievable event through a phenomenological account that, via a careful use of the aesthetics of deformation, seeks to convey not only a sequence of facts, but also the experience behind them. To witness one's world collapse is something almost unbelievable, just like the events chronicled in *Kaputt* and *The Skin*.

These epistemological concerns inform Malaparte's aesthetic choices, and not only in regard to his descriptive techniques. Literary prose is the form that Malaparte chooses to retell the experience of living in a context where "possible" and (previously considered) "impossible" events blend together. Through his wartime novels, and chiefly in *The Skin*, Malaparte also wagers his critique of Cartesianism—or at least his understanding thereof, namely, the belief that one can explain and eventually control the circumstances of one's life through reason alone. Why the novel?

Malaparte's literature of testimony depicts a world where facts and fictions lose their clear distinction, as in a chapter of *The Skin* where the sudden presence of the "black wind" announces and accompanies horrifying events such as the crossing of a forest of crucified Jews, the vivisection of Malaparte's dog Febo, or the agony of a young soldier whose belly was torn up by an explosion (*Skin*, 154–89). To be sure, in the context of World War II none of these happenings ought to be dismissed as unbelievable. Yet, echoing again Kundera, Malaparte's texts are charged with an "aesthetic intention so strong, so apparent, that the sensitive reader *automatically* excludes it from the context of accounts brought to bear by historians, journalists, political analysts, memoirists."[44]

The blurring between fact and fiction throughout Malaparte's writings complicates the assessment of the truth-value of what is described on the page in the context of a historical, autobiographical novel rife with extraordinary events. This recalls Tzvetan Todorov's canonical definition of "the fantastic," which concerns the transient hesitation experienced by protagonists and readers alike in choosing a natural or supernatural explanation for a given event—a hesitation primarily triggered by authorial reticence and stylistic artifices.[45] However, whereas Todorov's fantastic accommodates a moment of epistemic resolution that leads to either the uncanny (for a natural explanation) or the marvelous (for a supernatural one), Malaparte depicts a world where events that would normally be ruled out of an ordinary paradigm of sense-making become the norm. The horizon of expectations of the literature of testimony is challenged, similar to how outlier events—Taleb's "black swans," be they statistical or phenomenological—may challenge the nest of predictability and alleged control ruling a life. Extraordinary events become possible, perhaps even plausible, in a context ruled by the horrors of war, not unlike how Jack's abstract image of Italy as a land governed by the discernible, clear, and distinct laws of reason is shattered by the encounter with a context where what he had learned to expect is upended.

Even the Americans eventually experience horror once they face something that cannot be kept at bay: for them as well, the present situation stops "making sense" and simply overwhelms them once Vesuvius erupts. However, Malaparte is careful to not essentialize warfare as a neutral context, identical for everyone experiencing it. From this perspective, the plague of Naples suggests that even when horror appears to be a structural feature of reality, it still maintains a contextual, hence subjective, strain. In order to highlight these differences, Malaparte sides with the victims—those experiencing their forced powerlessness—as he journeys full of pity and horror through a world going *kaputt*. Conveying pity and horror implies a phenomenological perspective that the Italian author filters through a deforming style suspended between *storia* and *racconto*.

For Malaparte, contrary to Colonel Jack, the world was a mysterious place that cannot be fully explained, thus fully domesticated, through reason alone, and in *The Skin* Malaparte describes what we could call an anti-Cartesian Hell. In the next section, conversely, we side with a Cartesian who is cast into Hell: we descend a level deeper into the abyss of World War II, to explore how the self-proclaimed Cartesian Primo Levi described his experience in the "black hole of Auschwitz."[46]

A CARTESIAN IN HELL: PRIMO LEVI

While in 1943 Malaparte began his collaboration with the Allies, Primo Levi was in Northern Italy in the ranks of an anti-fascist partisan group tied to the Partito d'Azione. Shortly after Malaparte was released by the Americans, Levi, on December 13, was captured by a fascist militia and eventually taken to Auschwitz. *Kaputt* and *The Skin* leave out anything related to Malaparte's captivity; Levi's *If This Is a Man*, conversely, begins with the author's arrest. Malaparte was a fascist, he had fought in World War I, and, as a writer and intellectual, he was fluent in the languages of Surrealism and Expressionism. Levi was an Italian Jew, born after World War I in 1919, and, as a chemist, considered much of the writing process to be a controlled matter of separating, weighing, and discerning—skills he learned from his scientific studies.[47]

The differences between their lives and works cannot be overstated. Malaparte did not experience the Lager, and he was not discriminated against by the 1938 Italian racial laws: these facts are decisive differences. Without trying to bridge or overlap two vastly distant experiences, I here study the phenomenology of horror in Levi's account of the Auschwitz concentration camp as another facet of the historical moment analyzed in this chapter: World War II, in particular as an event that seemed to have made horror structural. But even when a situation appears to be under the banner of horror beyond any reasonable doubt, as in Auschwitz, Levi invites us to consider that substantial differences persevere, and undermine the very idea of horror as a univocal or universally accepted category—one that is immediately recognized by anyone who is exposed to something allegedly horrifying.

It is from this perspective that Levi, too, although in very different circumstances from those of Malaparte's Jack, was forced to come to terms with a context that made his Cartesianism collide with a state of affairs that he could not reintegrate into a satisfactory paradigm of rational sense-making. The encounter with the horrors of Auschwitz made Levi reconsider the belief that Cartesianism can provide a stable, secure, and universal vantage point when faced with events of such a nature. Cast in a horrifying world, Levi, as we shall see, invites us to think that the phenomenology of such a place, too, is multilayered, and may not always or only be characterized by horror.

Descartes opens his *Meditations on First Philosophy* with an attempt to differentiate dream from reality: false opinions had previously underpinned his understanding of the world, so much so that it became necessary to "raze everything to the ground and begin again from the original foundations" in order to establish firm and lasting knowledge.[48] If carried out successfully, this process requires only a single iteration: once solid foundations are provided, the reliance on clear and distinct ideas allows us to preserve the edifice of knowledge from errors. But what if these new foundations, too, are revealed to be unfit for dealing with phenomena that seem to undermine the stability of the whole edifice? Are we to start everything anew?

In the first paragraph of *If This Is a Man*, Levi writes that the racial laws forced him to live "in an unrealistic world of my own, a world inhabited by civilized Cartesian phantoms."[49] On the one hand, Levi is here referring to the quakes caused in society by the implementation of a set of racial laws that discriminated against certain categories of Italian citizens on an arbitrary and pseudoscientific basis. These laws impacted only a fraction of the population, and Levi is careful in saying that it is *his* world that underwent a process of derealization, not the world as a whole—just as in Malaparte's Naples the Americans are immune to the plague. On the other hand, in this world, too, Levi finds some "civilized Cartesian phantoms": people who, despite the general breakdown of reality, still hold ideas clear and distinct enough to act in accordance with the norms of reason and civic duty, and not accept the corruption of sense-making introduced by the racial laws. Yet, they are "phantoms": they are on uncertain ontological grounds (on the verge of disappearance given the crackdown of propaganda and policing especially after the Italian armistice) and haunt a place more than inhabit it (they are forced to either dissimulate their beliefs, or live like outlaws).

This last stand of a reality that still, although only precariously, made sense disappears once the military forces of the Italian Social Republic raid the hideout in the Aosta Valley where Levi lived while collaborating with the partisans. He is captured and sent to an internment camp in Italy, with other political dissidents and Jewish families. On February 20, 1944, a contingent of the SS arrives at the camp. They announce that all the Jews will leave the camp, specifying neither the destination nor the reason for their departure. The next morning, the last scaffoldings of Levi's precarious reality crumble to pieces as the Germans start hitting them for no apparent reason: "the thing was so new and senseless that we felt no pain, in either body or spirit. Only a profound astonishment: how can one strike a man without anger?" (*ITIM*, 12). In a world where things make sense, Levi presupposes that hitting someone implies feeling some anger toward that person, but this does not seem to be the case. Attempts at making sense—something a "Cartesian phantom" would do—will accompany Levi through part of his stay in the Lager to which he is transported. Six hundred fifty human beings are crammed into twelve freight wagons, which are locked from the outside. The few slits in the wagons' sides provide some oxygen to the deported (called *Stücke,* "pieces," by the SS); those who by sheer luck are closer to the slits have a better chance of surviving the travel. After four days of attempts, they cease trying to communicate with the "outside world" during the train's stops: "we felt ourselves by now 'on the other side'" (*ITIM*, 14).

The "other side" of what, one may ask? Does the existence of an "other side" undermine the stability that a Cartesian, once set on solid epistemological foundations, supposedly inhabits? The journey to Auschwitz is the first encounter with the goal of the concentration camp, that is, the "demolition" (*ITIM*, 22) or destruction of the human,[50] which underpins what Cavarero considers the most chilling example of twentieth-century horrorism: the Holocaust.[51] The "gigantic biological and social experiment" of the Lager is defined by the forced powerlessness of the interned: this upside-down world is a space where agency is largely stripped from the inhabitants, who are exposed to indifferent and overpowering forces, both embodied (the guards) and not (the rules of the camp) (*ITIM*, 82).

Does this mean that the interned constantly experience horror? In his 1986 collection of essays on the Lager, *The Drowned and the Saved*, Levi describes Auschwitz's everydayness as "boredom punctuated by horror," thus highlighting the oscillating nature of the experience of the inmates.[52] Horror's forced powerlessness is distinct from boredom: whereas boredom mourns the prolongation of an empty present into the future, horror concerns the here and now in its threatening and overwhelming power. In doing so, it presupposes either an element of novelty, or the failure (perhaps, the impossibility) of normalizing, and hence becoming habituated to, the presently lived situation. The journey to Auschwitz and the first encounter with the camp are relevant for a phenomenology of horror insofar as these two events constitute a moment of rupture with what came before: they force the "Cartesian phantoms" to confront what they cannot reintegrate into the ranks of standard (and supposedly stable) sense-making, in a way structurally similar to the derangement of the ordinary that belongs to Malaparte's description of a world going *kaputt*.

Suddenly, the train reaches its destination. The passengers, including those, like Levi, who just a few days ago were still Cartesian phantoms, are now diminished to simple "shadows" (*ITIM*, 15). Several deportees are immediately sent to the gas chambers, some for the "reason" of being women or children, some for no apparent "reason" whatsoever, chosen arbitrarily from among those who exit the wagon in one direction rather than another. A handful of "strange individuals" with emaciated bodies and worn-out suits emerge out of nowhere, take their baggage, and check if anything has been left on the trains. Levi describes this arrival in four sentences: "We looked at one another without a word. It was all incomprehensible and mad, but one thing we had understood. This was the metamorphosis that awaited us. Tomorrow we would be like them" (*ITIM*, 16–17). Amid an incomprehensible situation, Levi still seeks to maintain a minimum of mastery of his environment, although only insofar as he can anticipate, rather than control, the transformation that awaits the new inmates. But this is the last spasm of a Cartesian phantom, and soon enough a general sense of stupefied confusion takes over.

A sense of horrified paralysis is followed by, and interwoven with, the awareness that they will soon undergo an unavoidable metamorphosis. The camp takes over in its overwhelming power; only a few hours in Auschwitz is long enough to make Levi realize the gap between his former world and the one where he now dwells: "This is hell. Today, in our time, hell must be like this. A huge, empty room: we are tired, standing on our feet, and there is a tap that drips and the water cannot be drunk, and we wait for something that will certainly be terrible, and nothing happens and nothing continues to happen. What to think? One cannot think anymore, it's like being dead already. Someone sits down on the floor. The time passes drop by drop" (*ITIM*, 18). Critics have highlighted the numerous parallelisms and intertextualities between Dante's *Commedia* and Levi's work, with Levi taking Dante as a model for his description of the concentration camp.[53] But while he certainly draws from Dante's poem, Levi's account of both Auschwitz and his journey home, narrated in *The Truce*, cannot be classified as a *commedia* insofar as it lacks a positive ending: the horrors of the Lager still haunt him even once he is back in Turin—almost as if Dante had been left out of *Paradise* after having journeyed through *Inferno* and *Purgatory*. Additionally, while Dante recognizes the justness of Hell, Levi is thrown into a world whose unjustness is clearly understood by both the author and the reader.

There is a third and crucial difference between the two authors: whereas *Inferno* "makes sense" in Dante's worldview, Auschwitz casts Levi's sense-making into crisis. Indeed, Levi's phenomenology of Hell, contrary to Dante's, is defined by confusion. Why can the inmates not drink the water dripping from the faucet? Why was the three-year-old Emilia killed as soon as she arrived in Auschwitz (*ITIM*, 16)? Why is a German guard mixing all their shoes ("He's crazy, he's throwing them all together, ninety-six pairs, they'll be unmatched" [*ITIM*, 19])? Why are they given some clothes but then forced to run naked, in the snow, to another building before being allowed to wear them (*ITIM*, 21)? In a moment of thirst, Levi resorts to an icicle that hangs just outside of a window; as soon as he grabs it, a guard takes the icicle away. "'*Warum*?' I asked him in my poor German. '*Hier ist kein Warum*' (there is no why here), he replied, shoving me back inside" (*ITIM*, 25). This most revealing scene stages the demise of a "Cartesian phantom." The possibility of "making sense" is withheld, externally, from the interned: there remains only a new reality that takes over.

In Levi's account, the demolition of the human enacted by the Lager is also underpinned by the impossibility of using previous standards of sense-making to master the current world. Throughout his memoirs of the Holocaust, Levi the chemist and former Cartesian phantom first laments, then resigns himself to this condition: "Everyone, with the exception of those who had already lived through similar experiences, expected to find a world that was terrible but decipherable"; soon enough, however, everyone realizes that this new world, while certainly terrible, is also at its core indecipherable.[54] In little time the subject transitions from reasoning to resignation: "I stopped trying to understand long ago," as Levi writes while reminiscing about his time in the Ka-Be, the grotesque hospital ward of the Lager (*ITIM*, 45). Indeed, according to Levi, the first words of wisdom to learn in the Lager are "not trying to understand" (*ITIM*, 110) since "it is useless to think in the Lager, because events happen for the most part in an unpredictable manner" (*ITIM*, 163).

But the Lager undoubtedly "made sense" to the Nazis. Their confidence in their own reasons is mirrored by the "absurd precision" that characterizes the Germans and the structures they created (*ITIM*, 12). This again highlights the importance of distinguishing the phenomenology of the victim from that of the oppressor.[55] The pity and horror that Malaparte evokes presuppose, at the very least, an empathetic connection with the victim. This choice, which opens up space for an ethics to exist, must be understood in its nonuniversality. At first, Levi struggled to accept the very fact that a place like the Lager could exist: he lived in an unrealistic world, where even his rebellion against the Axis was abstract. Auschwitz, however, made him snap out of this abstraction. Through a collision with a reality that he could not reintegrate with his previous standards of sense-making, he is forced to come to terms with the fact that "monsters" exist in very concrete ways, as they can construct a monstrous world. Moreover, and perhaps most important, Levi also learns that "alongside the logic of Descartes existed the one of the SS."[56]

Soon enough, the deported acknowledge that they have been transformed into those strange figures they had seen after stepping out of the wagons. This mirroring makes Levi realize that, despite his rationalizing efforts, he cannot find a way to adequately describe the change they underwent and its outcome: "Then for the first time we become aware that our language lacks words to express this offense, the demolition of a man" (*ITIM*, 22). We could use the word *kaputt*, first discussed with respect to Malaparte, to describe this demolition—and tellingly, Levi himself encounters this word in an exchange that he considers to be the most atrocious of his entire life, when a Polish nurse tells him coldly and for no reason: "*Du Jude, kaputt. Du schnell Krematorium, fertig* (You Jew, done for. You soon for the crematorium, finished)" (*ITIM*, 46).

The forced powerlessness of the Lager is not enacted only in the realm of sense-making: this demolition of the human is also, of course, physical. This epistemological and corporeal crisis, as in Malaparte's case, affects the aesthetic realm as well. While Levi's dry and composed style greatly differs from Malaparte's ornate expressionism, *If This Is a Man* is interpolated with grotesque descriptions that rupture the realistic fabric of the text. In so doing, Levi resorts to the aesthetics of deformation to describe a world that loses its familiar traits, and instead turns horrifying.

On this point, Hayden White convincingly argued that Levi's "figural realism" endows a number of scenes with a figural power that hints at a phenomenological experience beyond a sequence of facts.[57] Indeed, as Judith Butler notes, building on White's commentary, "the reality communicated consists not only in 'what happened,' but also in that it happened, and that requires language to assert its reality and its force."[58]

Two days in the concentration camp are enough to transform healthy humans into "miserable, sordid puppets" (*ITIM*, 22), who now walk with "with an oddly unnatural, stiff gait, like rigid puppets made only of bones" (*ITIM*, 26). Two weeks are all that is required to radically disfigure the human: "my body is no longer mine: my belly is swollen, my limbs are emaciated, my face is puffy in the morning and hollow in the evening; some of us have yellow skin, others gray" (*ITIM*, 32). Food itself becomes an agent of corruption: the soup that the deported eat is so watery that it swells their bodies, gives all the features "a deformed likeness," and overtaxes the organs within, the liver in particular (*ITIM*, 58). Every so often, the inmates find a clear reflective surface that reveals the magnitude of their disfigurations:

> We are ridiculous and repulsive. Our heads are bald on Monday, and covered by a short light-brown mold by Saturday. We have swollen, yellow faces, permanently marked by the cuts of the hasty barber, and often by bruises and numb sores; our necks are long and knobbly, like plucked chickens. Our clothes are incredibly filthy, stained with mud, grease, and blood: [. . .] my jacket slips off my shoulders as if off a wooden clothes hanger. We are full of fleas, and often scratch ourselves shamelessly; we have to ask to go to the latrine with humiliating frequency. Our wooden clogs are intolerably noisy and are encrusted with alternate layers of mud and regulation grease. (*ITIM*, 136)

The subject's demolition in the concentration camp overlooks ontological boundaries as well: the medical experiments on the living extend to the dead, as the human body is treated as "brute, indifferent matter, useful at best only for industrial purposes."[59] What in Malaparte's books are ambiguous scenes suspended between truth and fiction become real in Levi's account of Auschwitz. The Lager is a heterotopia of uniquely horrifying nature insofar as it negates the suspension of disbelief: contrary to the reluctance with which historians consider Malaparte's narrations, Levi's works inherently resist questioning.[60]

Questioning is what, as we saw, opens Descartes's *Meditations*: more specifically, a form of questioning whose aim is to differentiate once and for all dream from reality. Auschwitz, however, not only legitimates as real what otherwise could be deemed fictional; it also causes dreams and reality to merge into an ontological aberration of opaque and incontrollable nature similar to the one that made Malaparte's Sartre and Jack waver.

Physical and mental horrors characterize the nights of the deported, which lose their restorative properties as they become populated by "shapeless nightmares of unprecedented violence" that in a world still making sense would occur only "during a fever." The inmates wake up "at every moment, frozen with terror" as if someone were shouting at them in a language that, revealingly, is as indecipherable as the concentration camp itself. As soon as they close their eyes again, their minds start fabricating "phantoms and terrible signs." But most horrifying of all is that a day in the

Lager will follow the night—and this lingering awareness is made concrete by the "Wstawać [*get up*]" uttered by the Polish night guard long before dawn. That foreign word forces everyone to wake up, and be once again "exposed to insult, atrociously naked and vulnerable." A new day begins, another day of "boredom punctuated by horror."[61] The guards whose duty is to quickly make everyone leave the barracks with blows and shouts are the first encounter of the day, every day. The deported leave their beds, and upon putting on their stiff, wrongly sized shoes, the wounds covering their feet reopen—"and a new day begins" (*ITIM*, 59–60).

The word "Wstawać" also bookends *The Truce*, which closes with the description of a recurring nightmare that Levi still has almost twenty years after his return to his hometown of Turin following his internment in Auschwitz. The dream starts with a vague sensation of anxiety that creeps into an always different idyllic scene, signaling the unspoken threat of an incumbent menace. Then, "little by little or brutally," everything goes *kaputt*:

> Everything collapses and is destroyed around me, the scene, the walls, the people [. . .]. Everything has now turned into chaos; I am alone at the center of a gray and murky void [. . .]. I am again in the Lager, and nothing outside the Lager was true. The rest was a brief holiday, or a trick of the senses, a dream: the family, nature in flower, the house. Now this internal dream, the dream of peace, is over, and in the external dream, which continues coldly, I hear the sound of a well-known voice: a single word, not imperious, but brief and subdued. It is the dawn command of Auschwitz, a foreign word, feared and expected: get up, "*Wstawać*."[62]

What for Michelstaedter were the night terrors of those whose safety fallacy momentarily cracked and disfigured reality to the point of self-annihilation is for Levi the haunting memory of the Lager as it takes over his present. Whereas the centering of the subject, and in particular the subject's thinking, allowed Descartes to build a more secure epistemological and ontological edifice and distinguish dream from reality, that same centrality of the I turns here into a nightmare. Rather than being composed of clear and distinct elements that the Cartesian subject masters, Levi's world is opaque and chaotic. The last sound heard in the dream is that "foreign word" whose semantics, for Levi, exceeded its denotation:

heard in the concentration camp, "Wstawać" means that the previous day was not a nightmare; heard in Turin, "Wstawać" means that nightmares can be real, no matter how little they "make sense" during the day.

It is indeed difficult to "make sense" of events that are so far beyond what we are accustomed to. The horror of Auschwitz can be read as a phenomenological "black swan" for the subject experiencing it: it is an outlier; it carries extreme impact; it can be rationalized only with hindsight. The Holocaust can be considered a "black swan" from a historical perspective as well: certainly not the first genocide of history, but unprecedented in its magnitude and structure due to the technoscientific advancement and political centralization that, in tandem, allowed for it to happen in the heart of Europe. Historical determinism can pretend to "make sense" of "black swans" only retrospectively. Those who experience these events themselves do not have a vantage point that grants them what Sloterdijk calls "sublime sangfroid": a detached subjectivity that "has the virtue of looking steadfastly at the sun and at death while engaged in its learning process."[63]

But the point is not only about harmonizing phenomenology and historiography (or the impossibility thereof). In one of the last essays in *The Drowned and the Saved*, Levi deals with his embarrassment concerning some of the questions he had been asked about the Holocaust. His uneasiness is not about the experience itself, which he feels compelled to retell. Rather, it arises when his interlocutors ask for "reasons": why did the Holocaust happen in the first place, why did the Jews not escape before it was too late, why were there no rebellions against the Final Solution? Reflecting on these questions, Levi writes that the issue is that they all presuppose some form of inferentiality: "The history of human affairs does not necessarily abide by strict logical models. Not every watershed is necessarily the consequence of a single 'why.' Simplifications are good only for textbooks; there may be many 'whys,' muddled or unknowable if not outright nonexistent. No historian or epistemologist has yet succeeded in proving that human history is a deterministic process."[64] In the last years of his life, Levi grew progressively more pessimistic concerning life and history. In his 1983 essay "The Brute Power," he describes the force that governs them as "perverse," since it "prefers disorder to order, jumble to purity, a tangle to parallelism, rust to iron, a pile to a wall, and stupidity to reason." A certain degree of homeostasis, Levi continues, is our strongest weapon against "the brute power of degradation and of death."[65]

The expression "brute power" comes from Leopardi's 1833 poem of despair, *To Himself.*[66] As seen in chapter 1, Leopardi was skeptical about the possibility of reducing history to a linear system—something that would, in turn, open up the possibility of controlling the uncontrollable and predicting the unpredictable. Reality's complexity and interdependencies make us, at least to some degree, blind to "black swans," and therefore the possibility of being thrown off balance will always be present. For Levi as well, a state of absolute homeostasis is nothing but a fantasy: "human societies are so complex, the parameters in play so many, that this dream will never come true."[67]

The Holocaust shattered the Cartesian dream of absolute homeostasis. While Levi's faith in reason as fallible tool to better comprehend reality never wavers, the former Cartesian phantom now argues that the meaningful patterns that rationalism looks for may not be present in all subjects of analysis. In affirming that rationalism cannot always and fully be extended to a domain such as history, Levi, perhaps unwittingly, amends the overextension of Cartesianism that he seemed to have embraced before Auschwitz, according to which clear and distinct ideas can be formed about any given matter, and thus constitute the basis for valid inferences.

For these reasons Auschwitz could not "make sense" for Levi: a phenomenological outlier, the camp called into question some of the basic assumptions that had ruled Levi's life before 1944. His take also suggests that the Holocaust was not an inevitable occurrence, insofar as inevitability presupposes a form of inferentialism in hindsight. Instead, more modestly and harrowingly, Levi's account of the Lager affirms that Auschwitz was above all horrifying: a "black swan" that made a Cartesian phantom realize that his reason, this time, could not offer a secure footing in the midst of the crisis.

A DECLARATION AGAINST HORROR: CONCLUSION

The Universal Declaration of Human Rights was born out of historical necessity once liberty, dignity, and equality of humankind were shown not to be self-evident concepts. To our ears, this affirmation may sound naïve: we well know that the West engaged in widespread forms of discrimination and colonialism that systematically denied these concepts and thus their self-evidence. This raises the question of what change made the Declaration both possible and necessary.

Malaparte and Levi chronicle their journeys through events that made their worlds go *kaputt*. In the context of this book, they serve as a landmark, a divide after which it became impossible for modernity to believe that it had banished horror from its house. Their works, however, show that horror, even when it appears to be structural, always maintains a subjective strain: as the Americans are not infected by the plague ravaging Malaparte's Naples, so Levi contends that the logic of the SS exists alongside that of Descartes. To be sure, both Jack and, to a different degree, Levi are, strictly speaking, "bad Cartesians": they overextend the reach of Descartes's method beyond the limits established by the French philosopher—that is to say, beyond the sphere of mathematical inference, which rules the quest for truth in the sciences. But bad Cartesianism—one that, in Stephen Toulmin's words, forgets "the distinction between theoretical certainty and practical certitude, and treat[s] mathematical inference as the Royal Road to Truth"[68]—may nevertheless lead to a horrifying shock if taken as a code of conduct, once reality's jaggedness upends the allegedly clear and distinct ideas that seem to rule a life.

The shock that both Malaparte and Levi depict is mediated by the literary nature of their productions. From an aesthetic standpoint, as we saw, Malaparte and Levi use the literary medium to describe their experiences of world collapse: what for Kundera is Malaparte's "aesthetic intention" and for White is Levi's "figural realism" both confront the issue of conveying something that may appear "impossible" for those not directly exposed to it. In so doing, Malaparte and Levi provide a testimony to literature's power in vividly rendering the epistemological and existential crises triggered by the horror that surrounded them; in other words, their literary productions respond to what psychologists David Witherington and Naila deCruz-Dixon identify as the horror-induced "urge to gawk—a compulsory motive to bear witness to something."[69] While horror may indeed leave us speechless as it shatters the assumptions of homeostatic control that underpin our lives, Malaparte and Levi show that literature—with its ability to depart from strict verisimilitude and aesthetically bend our retelling of reality—can provide an outlet for our screams.

Considering this, we can now venture a hypothesis about why World War II led to the Universal Declaration of Human Rights. Horror, as Cavarero reminds us, implies being the victim, or siding with them. And being a victim constitutes a substantial phenomenological difference, although nothing assures us that the victim will not turn into a butcher. During World War II, the West was butcher and victim alike. While its role as the former was nothing new, the first half of the twentieth century made much of the West experience the latter standpoint to a degree that called for *something* to happen. The catastrophes of the epoch became an event (*Ereignis*): a moment of rupture that restructured the world of those affected by it. Perhaps, then, the Universal Declaration of Human Rights was also born out of phenomenological, in addition to historical, necessity, as the West reckoned with the horror it had experienced. The demise of the Cartesian subject—the modern subject par excellence—that Malaparte and Levi stage provides a blueprint of what made the Declaration both possible and necessary.

These two authors confronted an event of such magnitude as to call for a Universal Declaration of Human Rights. The next chapter leaves this landmark of the twentieth century behind and enters the sphere of the personal and the unexceptional to keep investigating the unassuming ways in which horror belongs to ordinary life. With Anna Maria Ortese and Giuseppe Berto we will explore horrors that are widespread, and yet, precisely because of this, also banal and mundane, such as poverty and illness.

FOUR

THE BANALITY OF HORROR: ANNA MARIA ORTESE AND GIUSEPPE BERTO

Arthur Koestler's 1944 essay "The Nightmare That Is a Reality" raises a question that may sound bizarre to our ears: how to convince Americans that the killing of "the total Jewish population of Europe" was taking place during World War II? Today we take the Holocaust as a historical fact, and for good reason. But on January 9, 1944—the day when the *New York Times* published Koestler's essay—the historical facticity of this most horrifying catastrophe was still a matter of debate, and not only for fringe revisionists. The word "Holocaust" had not yet entered the general vocabulary, and, according to data that Koestler quotes, for "nine out of ten average American citizens" the rumors concerning the atrocities perpetrated by the Nazis were "all propaganda lies," of which "they didn't believe a word."[1]

There was, however, a group of people for whom revealing what was happening had become a mission charged with the pathos of urgency. Koestler, a Jew, included himself in this group, which he refers to as "we, the screamers"—a powerful formulation that echoes, only to darken it, the enlightened "We the People" of the Preamble to the US Constitution. Koestler writes that the screamers have desperately been trying to make people believe in the existence of the concentration camps or the mass graves of Poland, but with little success. The screamers may achieve some results when they show their audiences a photo or a film clip, but soon enough most of their listeners "shake themselves, their mental self-defenses begin to work and in a week the shrug of incredulity has returned like a reflex temporarily weakened by a shock." Society may in fact consider those whose defense mechanisms never activate to be "maniacs," individuals who keep shouting despite the generalized incredulity; most likely, Koestler seems to concede, the screamers are people who suffer from a "morbid obsession, whereas the others are healthy and normal."

Koestler's gambit lies in guiding the reader to this viewpoint only to turn it inside out: since maniacs "lose contact with reality and live in a fantasy world," he continues, "perhaps, it is the other way around: perhaps it is we, the screamers, who react in a sound and healthy way to the reality which surrounds us, whereas you are the neurotics who totter about in a screened fantasy world because you lack the faculty to face the facts." The screamers may indeed be those who see reality correctly, with their reaction being commensurate to the horrors that may be dismissed, overlooked, or unseen altogether by those "healthy and normal."

Without equating different historical circumstances, I here argue that Koestler's reflections on the presence of screamers in society—their roles, reasons, and the stigmas they bear—transcend the context of 1944. After having discussed that very context in my previous chapter, I now turn to Anna Maria Ortese and Giuseppe Berto as two screamers whose works expose how horror had not been chased away from society with the end of the war. Their screams are not caused by outlier events as in Malaparte and Levi's cases; on the contrary, my focus will be on Ortese's and Berto's depictions of sources of ordinary horror that are widespread and yet, precisely because of this, also banal and mundane, such as poverty and illness.[2]

I begin with Ortese's 1953 work, *Il mare non bagna Napoli* (literally, "The Sea Does Not Bathe Naples"), or *Neapolitan Chronicles* in the English translation. This collection of short stories and journalistic reportage describes a postwar Naples where the living conditions of part of the population are nothing short of horrifying, even in the absence of extreme circumstances like warfare. Ortese's work describes and seeks to disrupt processes of habituation that rendered tolerable living conditions that must remain unacceptable; in so doing, *Chronicles* enables a reflection on the consequences of normalizing the horrifying, as well as how and why this process may occur. Conversely, with Berto's 1964 autobiographical novel, *Il male oscuro*, translated as *Incubus*,[3] I discuss attempts at making tolerable a situation that inherently seems to resist habituation. Focusing on scenes that describe how Berto's illness provided a recurring source of horror, his work shows how our own self, rather than what lies outside of us, may be enough to turn our existence into a nightmare. This analysis underscores that novelty, the overwhelming, and unpredictability feature prominently in the phenomenology of horror.

Besides furthering my study of ordinary horror in the terms just laid out, this chapter also provides the first comparative study of Ortese and Berto to date, which rests on three overlooked points of contact between the two authors. The first one is lexical: both Ortese and Berto use the expression "*male oscuro*"—"obscure evil" or "obscure disease"—in crucial passages of their works.[4] This overlap allows me to emphasize another feature shared by the two: the common source of their "*male oscuro*." This second link is biographical, and consists of the "neurosis" that both admit suffering from, which compels them to write, respectively, *Chronicles* and *Incubus*—*Il mare* and *Il male*.[5] Moreover, their neurosis alters Ortese's and Berto's relation with their world. This leads to a third point of contact, one connected to the century's literary currents: Ortese's and Berto's complicated relation with neorealism. Both authors subscribe to one of its main tenets, namely, the urgency of bearing witness. But Ortese and Berto also depart from neorealist literature's project of providing a truthful and holistic representation of the world, one that brings together external reality and the human experience of it.[6] Their prose troubles that project, rife as it is with passages that poke a hole in the very fabric of realism, and thus call into question the idea that what is represented *is* reality. For both Ortese and Berto, existence itself possesses opaque and menacing traits, making it something difficult to withstand, decipher, and depict: the aesthetics of deformation deployed by both symbolizes this state of affairs and its at times horrifying nature.

This third point brings us back to Koestler's essay. It is important to emphasize that Koestler does not lament the impossibility of having information circulate: the evolution of means of communication in the twentieth century has provided technologically advanced societies with an information superhighway—the United States was and is inundated with news concerning past and present horrors. But, Koestler asks, what can we do to make sure that the information sticks? In the author's example, a "dog run over by a car upsets our emotional balance and digestion" more than any list of casualties we read in a newspaper. His conclusion: "statistics don't bleed; it is the detail which counts."[7]

The issue Koestler highlights is that of expression, which touches some of the aesthetic concerns that underpin this project's choice of studying horror through literary prose.[8] How might we provide an effective description of facts whose nature is so disturbing that we may shake them off as our defense mechanisms activate? Why does seeing a dog run over by a car upset us more than the news of the violations of human rights taking place on the other side of the world? And, if this is true, what is to be made of it in order to make horrible facts stick?

For Koestler, statistics do not bleed because "we are unable to embrace the total process with our awareness; we can only focus on little lumps of reality":[9] it is the individual story in its messiness and singularity that may seize the listener's attention, the single voice on the stage rather than the chorus in the background. Ortese's and Berto's works echo Koestler's concerns, and are an attempt at making details bleed. This will also allow me to assess the position of their works in relation to neorealism's ethos, goals, and literary techniques.

Beginning with Ortese's short story "A Pair of Eyeglasses," I read *Chronicles* as a repository of the horrors that postwar Italy displayed in plain sight yet that often remained unseen. I then move from the poorest neighborhoods of Naples to the Italy of the economic miracle, turning inward with Berto's *Incubus* to explore the inner workings of a life seized by a mysterious and unsettling disease. Covering a decade of economic growth and increasing national cohesion, this chapter explores some of the widespread, banal, and mundane ways in which horror may belong to existence in peacetime and in the absence of extraordinary circumstances.

SCREAMING THE INTOLERABLE: ANNA MARIA ORTESE

"A Pair of Eyeglasses" introduces Ortese's Naples to her readers through a morning in the life of Eugenia Quaglia, the nearsighted daughter of a family living in poverty. This exquisitely crafted novella centers on the events leading to Eugenia receiving her first pair of eyeglasses. The text opens with Eugenia's awakening, filled with hope as her long-awaited eyewear will be ready that day; it unfolds over the course of a morning busy with errands that take the girl around her neighborhood, and climaxes right before lunchtime, when Eugenia finally wears her new glasses. Once she puts them on, Eugenia suffers from a violent attack of vertigo. "A Pair of Eyeglasses" follows the Aristotelian unities of action, place, and time, and in so doing emphasizes from a formal standpoint its dramatic content.

With this trifold unity set in place, Ortese details Eugenia's living conditions, and through them conjures up a pained ecosystem as the story's background. The opening paragraphs of "A Pair of Eyeglasses" describe the Quaglia family and their mundane discontents: whereas Rosa, Eugenia's mother, is stuck in bed due to her environment-induced arthritis and heart issues, Nunziata, the aunt, complains about a cockroach she has just found in her sleeve. With a gothic touch, we read that Eugenia's bed stands in a corner "which was really a cave, with a low vault of dangling spiderwebs." Dire social circumstances notwithstanding, this opening also reveals Eugenia's excitement, expressed with a "small, calm" voice, about the eyeglasses that she will receive that day (*Chronicles*, 13).

Squalor and wonder coexist all through the story, as two juxtaposed descriptive layers: on the one hand, the narrator's rendition of lives and spaces plagued by poverty, described through a third-person, extradiegetic point of view; on the other hand, Eugenia's partial unawareness of this miserable situation, and, simultaneously, her sense of expectation concerning a world that she will soon see with clarity. The distance between these two standpoints collapses once Eugenia wears her glasses and catches a first glimpse of her pitiful surroundings—with the glasses also functioning as a narrative device that, bringing Eugenia's story to a close, invites the reader to "keep them on" for the rest of the book.[10]

Ortese, however, nuances what might otherwise be a direct connection between wearing glasses and the turmoil that Eugenia experiences at the end of the story. The girl's first time trying them on takes place at the optician's office and, in triggering wonder rather than vertigo, kindles her sense of excitement for a world that had been shrouded by the fog of her shortsightedness. What made Eugenia's experience at the optician's so different from the one in the courtyard of her house?

The scene at the optician's is a flashback, and the only infringement on the story's unity of time. A week earlier Eugenia and her aunt traveled from their poor neighborhood, once called Vicolo della Cupa (literally,

"Somberness Alley") but eventually renamed Via Fratelli Magnoni, to an eyeglasses store in Via Roma, an upscale shopping district today known as Via Toledo. Whereas Eugenia's house is a humid, dusty, and gray environment, the shop is clean and flooded by an emerald light thanks to tinted curtains. Here Eugenia tries a pair of eyeglasses and, amazed, observes on the sidewalk a parade of well-groomed Neapolitan bourgeois and aristocrats, promenading in one of the wealthiest areas of the city. Alongside them, she sees cars and trams painted with shiny colors, and "beautiful" shops, with sparkling windows displaying an abundance of goods (*Chronicles*, 15).

Eugenia's first moments as a person with good vision show her something radically different from the poverty surrounding her household, of which the reader is by this point aware. The girl's full attention is seized by the glamorous scenery, which makes her impenetrable to any stimuli belonging to her "previous" life: her nearsightedness recedes, leaving space to a luminous world disclosed to her eyes for the first time, and she does not hear Aunt Nunziata's unsuccessful attempts at convincing the optician to give them a discount (*Chronicles*, 15).

Since that day, "Eugenia had lived in a kind of rapture, waiting for the blessed glasses that would allow her to see all people and things in their tiny details" (*Chronicles*, 17). Eugenia's world had always been shrouded by the fog of her nearsightedness, where only the faces of her relatives assumed clear contours when they slept together, in the same bed—faces that from up close show "broken yellow teeth" and purulent skins covered with cysts. While her room, "always full of wet laundry, with broken chairs and a stinking toilet," does not resemble in any way what she saw in via Roma, Eugenia clings to the memory of that radiant world she caught a glimpse of at the optician's office, and which she will be able to see again once her eyeglasses are delivered (*Chronicles*, 17).

The narrative follows Eugenia in her mundane chores (she, of course, cannot go to school because she must help her family). Eventually, Mother Rosa comes back home with her daughter's new glasses, and the neighbors gather around Eugenia to witness her initiation into the world of those with clear vision. Expecting to see once again the beauty and the colors that surrounded her in Via Roma, she brings the eyeglasses to her face. Instead, a horrifying vision takes hold of Eugenia's present. For this conclusive climax, while maintaining an omniscient third-person point of view, the narrator shifts to an almost complete internal focalization with the girl's perspective:

> Her legs were trembling, her head was spinning, and she no longer felt any joy. With her white lips she wished to smile, but that smile became a moronic grimace. Suddenly the balconies began to multiply, two thousand, a hundred thousand; the carts piled with vegetables were falling on her; the voices filling the air, the cries, the lashes, struck her head as if she were ill; she turned, swaying, toward the courtyard, and that terrible impression intensified. The courtyard was like a sticky funnel, with the narrow end toward the sky, its leprous walls crowded with derelict balconies; the arches of the basement dwellings black, with the lights bright in a circle around Our Lady of Sorrows; the pavement white with soapy water; the cabbage leaves, the scraps of paper, the garbage and, in the middle of the courtyard, that group of ragged, deformed souls, faces pocked by poverty and resignation, who looked at her lovingly. They began to writhe, to become mixed up, to grow larger. They all came toward her, in the two bewitched circles of the eyeglasses. It was Mariuccia who first realized that the child was sick, and she tore off the glasses, because Eugenia, doubled over and moaning, was throwing up. (*Chronicles*, 32–33)

The world as seen from Eugenia's house in Vicolo della Cupa, does not resemble the one of the optician's office in Via Roma. Ortese's prose throughout "A Pair of Eyeglasses" is realistic, plain, and hypotaxical. Here, as an event (*Ereignis*) restructures Eugenia's experience of the world, the author's style morphs, leans into free indirect speech, and becomes overwhelming through the use of parataxis, accumulation, and deforming descriptors. Objects multiply ("two thousand, a hundred thousand"), and appear to be physically threatening the girl ("the carts piled with vegetables were falling on her"). Eugenia's surroundings turn into an abject scene: the courtyard and the walls that her nearsightedness could not bring into focus are now revealed as slimy and purulent, sprawling with balconies that give an impression of claustrophobia. Those around her begin to realize that the girl is unwell, and get closer to assist her. Yet, the narrating voice, anchored to Eugenia's point of view, describes them as a mass of monstrous creatures, menacingly jerking ahead. Her present now overwhelming and uncontrollable, and her expectations shattered by this horrifying development, Eugenia, bent over, groans and vomits.

"It's always like that, the first time," utters a woman witnessing the scene. Does she mean the first time that someone realizes their surrounding misery, or is she referring to the physical sickness that may be triggered by newly worn glasses? The woman's next sentence compounds this ambiguity: "You mustn't be shocked; little by little one gets used to it [*a poco a poco si abitua*]" leaving suspended the question of *what* she will apparently become used to (*Chronicles*, 33).[11] Will Eugenia become accustomed to her poverty now that she clearly sees it? Is the woman simply referring to wearing eyeglasses? The text provides no answers. Instead, it ends by describing how Eugenia now displays an "old lady's face" (*Chronicles*, 33)—as if abandoning nearsightedness, in her socioeconomic context, also meant relinquishing a juvenile sense of wonder regarding the world.

In chapter 1, I discussed how and why entering a garden can be a horrifying experience. In that page of Leopardi's *Zibaldone* lies a guiding assumption of this project: horror is a contextual experience without a fixed referent. In chapter 2, I analyzed how neither the temporality nor the outcome of horror should be overdetermined; the possibility of its transience coexists with that of its endurance, and presupposing its inherently redemptive or traumatic unfolding risks too narrowly delimiting what horror is and can do. Chapter 3 showed that even when horror appears to be widespread and foundational to a given context, as it was during World War II, this experience does not become universal and instead calls for specific attention to phenomenological distinctions such as those between victims and perpetrators, or conquered and conquerors.

My reading of *Chronicles* further articulates the contextual nature of horror, here with a specific emphasis on ordinary rather than extraordinary circumstances.[12] To evoke an author whom Ortese greatly admired, one is tempted to say that "A Pair of Eyeglasses" stages Eugenia's entrance into her own Leopardian garden. Indeed, the story plays with a double register to affirm the coexistence of horror and wonder, but while the reader is presented with both from the novella's opening paragraphs, Eugenia's true encounter with the squalor of her condition is postponed to the conclusion of the narration. In setting the stage for Eugenia's horrified reaction,

Ortese describes how the same context can provoke two radically different experiences depending on circumstantial elements.

The "little by little one gets used to it [*a poco a poco si abitua*]" that closes "A Pair of Eyeglasses" hints at how it is possible to be living in horrifying conditions without experiencing them as such. To tackle this ostensible paradox, our attention must focus on markers of habituation scattered throughout the story. Examples include the definition of life as a "punishment" (*Chronicles,* 14), or Aunt Nunziata's affirmation that it is better to avoid seeing reality altogether (16). Crucially, the Quaglia family are not affected by the garbage that fills up their spaces; in fact, according to the narrator, they do not even notice it (*Chronicles,* 20). All these markers point to the following conclusion: the inhabitants of Vicolo della Cupa are habituated to these circumstances, rather than being horrified by them. Their habituation is reinforced by socioeconomic structures that solidify their condition as inevitable and inescapable. Conversely, Eugenia's nearsightedness deferred her full encounter with her surroundings. The dramatic nature of this encounter, once it happens, is compounded by the difference between what the girl saw in Via Roma and what she sees in her neighborhood.

Similar to Leopardi's unorthodox take on what can horrify (gardens have not yet fully captured the attention of horror authors), Ortese, too, chooses a rather overlooked topic in canonical works of horror: poverty. Indeed, one wonders why the horror genre has generally shied away from poverty, given its past and ongoing relevance for our societies: what poverty may lack in spectacularity, it provides in concreteness. And concreteness rather than abstraction or lofty feelings is what horror is made of, according to Ortese. In her "Summer Terrors" ("Estivi Terrori"), a short story based on her travels throughout Italy in the 1950s, she writes: "If someone is full of feelings, it means they have long since solved, or never had, financial problems, and thus the horror of living hasn't even touched them, and talking about drama is laughable."[13] The syntagm "horror of living" is a revealing one that, as I will show, recurs in the author's productions, speaking to Ortese's direct and explicit correlation between horror and plausible real-life circumstances, as she relates the former to concrete economic conditions rather than to any typical motifs of the genre.

Discussing concreteness in relation to Ortese leads to debates concerning the author's reception. Much of Ortese's production evokes dreamlike and labyrinthine atmospheres, often removed from reality by several layers of symbolism.[14] This tendency has informed her reception through the various (and all variously unsatisfactory) critical lenses, such as "magical realism," "the fantastic," "the uncanny," and, more recently, "international magic realism."[15] Against this backdrop, the realism of *Chronicles*, featuring two pieces of what today could be called "docufiction" ("A Pair of Eyeglasses" and "Family Interior") and three pieces of journalistic reportage ("The Gold of Forcella," "The Involuntary City," and "The Silence of Reason"), did not go unnoticed, and since its publication in 1953 the volume has led to Ortese's enlistment within the ranks of neorealism.[16]

To be sure, as the Italian critic Giulio Ferroni remarked, Ortese had a "passion for reality."[17] Reality obsessed her—an obsession that led to hatred, as Ortese states in "The 'Sea' As Disorientation," the introductory text that she penned for the 1994 reissue of *Chronicles* by the Italian publishing house Adelphi. In it, looking back at her first book, *Angelic Pains* (*Angelici dolori,* 1937), an eccentric, dreamlike collection of reveries and short stories, Ortese confesses that a "neurosis" has underpinned her production. This neurosis is "metaphysic[al]," and caused by her hatred of reality: "For a very long time, I hated with all my might, almost without knowing it, so-called *reality*: that mechanism of things that arise in time and are destroyed by time." Due to this bleak and pessimistic slant, her work became an object of derision for the "champions of the 'real.'" Indeed, whereas for the rising tide of neorealism "the real" was the object of observations aimed at its betterment, for Ortese it was instead "incomprehensible and ghastly [*incomprensibile e allucinante*]" and thus resisted adequate descriptions (*Chronicles*, 10).

Her "irritation with the real" steadily increased in World War II (*Chronicles*, 10), during which she learned that the word "horror" ought to be connected with existence at large ("And this word: *horror* [. . .] was the last great word I learned regarding universal living.")[18] This ever growing fixation on the most disquieting aspects of human life fed Ortese's neurosis and forced her to eventually express it through her writings on postwar Naples. In the author's words, the city was a mirror of a "universal condition of being torn apart [*lacera condizione universale*]"—a metonymy for what she calls, with a strong Leopardian inflection, "the infinite blindness of life [*la infinita cecità del vivere*]" (*Chronicles*, 10). And it is precisely this broadly understood "life" that she calls into question: rather than plainly acknowledging her existential disquietude, Ortese "cried out [*gridai*]" her irritation against reality (*Chronicles*, 11), here echoing Leopardi's indignation concerning the indifference of existence to the suffering of existent beings. Ortese's metaphysical concern, and neurosis as well, is pulled to a more concrete level by the historical circumstances she was exposed to: postwar Naples was "shattered," just as Malaparte's Naples was *kaputt*, and for Ortese a source of "disorientation [*spaesamento*]" mixed with "horror" (*Chronicles*, 10).

This bleak picture is rendered more complex by Ortese's admission that Naples, despite being in ruins, was a repository of immense resources. Reflecting on the book almost forty years after its publication—a publication that effectively exiled Ortese from Naples due to its brutal and brutally transparent depiction of the city and its intelligentsia—she admits that the "disorientation" she felt was "primarily mine." Indeed, just as a garden can be a source of beauty and suffering alike depending on contextual factors, Ortese, in her writings, depicts *her* Naples: a place full of wonders and horrors, similar to the world that Eugenia, thanks to her glasses, encounters in Via Roma first, and Vicolo della Cupa then. *Chronicles* thus became a screen "on which to project the painful disorientation, the 'dark suffering of life' [*il male oscuro di vivere*], as it came to be called, of the person who had written the book" (*Chronicles*, 11). This does not imply solipsistic inwardness: as will become increasingly clear, there were good reasons for Ortese's horrified screams.

In underlining the personal tone of the book, the preface also reminds us that *Chronicles* is a work of literature. Even in its most journalistic pieces, such as "The Involuntary City," Ortese never puts down the tools of the writer's trade (similar to what Levi does in *If This Is a Man*, as discussed in the previous chapter). Through a careful use of these tools, Ortese's depiction of the misery of Naples is charged with the pathos of her own personal neurosis: from this encounter emerges a book that seeks to convey a sense of bewilderment about a reality that had assumed horrifying traits. In letting her "disorientation" haunt Naples, Ortese also troubles what could be taken as a neorealist text, without, however, distancing herself from the reality that irritated her, hence without drifting, for instance, toward the supernatural or the fantastic. This amphibiousness rendered her an outcast, working beyond and between ruling literary trends, and explains alike the critical successes and discontents of *Chronicles*:

the book, while ostracized by a number of militant critics, particularly from the group centered upon the magazine *Sud,* also won the prestigious Premio Viareggio in 1953.

Chronicles, to evoke a notorious yet fitting adage by American poet Walt Whitman, contains multitudes: it sets a stage upon which extreme dejection and misery coexist with resourcefulness and local flavor. Thus, Ortese's book offers a depiction of Naples that is not unlike Malaparte's: one colored by pain and rage, pity and awe, wonder and horror, highlighting the soundness of using the term "horror" to describe even that which does not belong to extraordinary circumstances, such as poverty and its unspectacular yet widespread nature.

Horror, as Ortese well knew, had not been chased away by the end of the war, and *Chronicles* makes the case that poverty is one of the banal and mundane ordinary horrors that belong to peacetime. This is her invitation, as it were, to keep on wearing Eugenia's glasses, and see reality with renewed clear-sightedness: Ortese's prose and its deformed descriptions of otherwise mundane aspects of life distance themselves from plain realism to affirm a sense of "disorientation" with respect to what must not be normalized. For reasons that will become increasingly clear, especially through my analysis of the final text of *Chronicles*, "The Silence of Reason," this reminder was particularly apt for postwar Naples, and remains valid for today's economically advanced societies as well, where poverty is at times forgotten when not outright ignored.

The following discussion opens with "Family Interior," or "Interno familiare" in the original, the second and last fictional text of *Chronicles*, to explore why an "interior" (*interno* in Italian) can also be an "inferno." Taken together with "A Pair of Eyeglasses," these two texts upend some of the cornerstones of Italianness, such as the household and the family (*casa e famiglia*, as one says in Italian). The discussion then moves to the streets of Naples with "The Gold of Forcella" and "The Involuntary City," where Ortese's reportage sketches a cartography of urban horrors spanning from local pawnshops to the underworlds of Naples homeless shelters.[19] This analysis concludes by touching on "The Silence of Reason," to argue that horror, even when it crawls quite literally on the streets of a city, may go unseen even by those who are supposed to be the most sensitive to it. Through Ortese, the discussion also reflects on processes of habituation and desensitization, raising questions about how a previous exposure to horror does not prefigure anything concerning how we will react to it in the future.

The fact that only one consonant separates the Italian words *inferno* and *interno* likely informed Ortese's choice of the title of the second text of *Chronicles*. After the book's opening novella ended with an invitation to keep Eugenia's glasses on, "Family Interior" is a blueprint of what a normalized, everyday hell may be like in times of peace and in a life not exposed to extraordinary circumstances.

Anastasia Finizio, the protagonist of the second and last fictional piece in *Chronicles*, is a middle-aged woman whose income supports her entire family. Unmarried, Anastasia lives a life characterized by the apathy, coldness, and resignation of someone "on the verge of forty, who, almost without realizing it, had lost every hope of personal happiness" (*Chronicles*, 35). A change, however, occurs on Christmas Eve, when Anastasia is told that Antonio Laurano, a younger man she was once enamored of, is back in Naples after a prolonged absence, and has tasked a common acquaintance to bring Anastasia his "special greeting." The event shakes the depressive indifference coating her life and rekindles the woman's hopes for a different future: after years of sameness, she now experiences "a revival of the imagination she had believed dead, a disorientation [*smarrimento*]" (*Chronicles*, 36).

The word *smarrimento* echoes the *spaesamento* that Ortese, in her 1994 preface, connects with the writing of *Chronicles* and her encounter with postwar Naples, and the two are in fact translated with the same English word by Ann Goldstein and Jenny McPhee: "disorientation." In both cases, this feeling of confusion is tied to a revitalization of imaginative power: it compels Ortese to scream and, in turn, to write *Chronicles*, and for Anastasia it is of similarly ambiguous essence—it is an "obscure" feeling, for sure, but also one rife with hopes about the reasons and consequences of Antonio's reappearance. Yet, Anastasia holds back and, with a sentence that echoes the topic of vision present in Eugenia's story, affirms: "I have no illusions; I look at reality, I do look" (*Chronicles*, 36–37).

Despite Anastasia's self-proclaimed lucid acceptance of her condition, daydreaming about a life where she is not an unmarried woman anymore triggers another change on top of rekindling her imagination: the comparative standpoint offered by this alternate future she now imagines also makes Anastasia see, with new eyes, her current unhappiness, which she had grown accustomed to. Unused to bringing into focus the squalor of her existence beyond her habituation to it, now, as if she wore Eugenia's glasses, the urban landscape that Anastasia glimpses through a window appears to her as "the world's dribbles," with everything soaked by a light "unusual" and "cruel" (*Chronicles*, 38–39). She painfully senses the loss beyond repair of her "health and youth," and captured by this novel attunement to reality, realizes that "her saddest moments were also the most perfectly banal" (*Chronicles*, 40). Indeed, there is no grandeur in Anastasia's *inferno/interno*: just like many other unmarried women in postwar Naples (unmarried also because a considerable fraction of Neapolitan men died in the war or suffered its consequences), she was, and is, alone with her family.

But can being alone with one's own family be horrifying? "Family Interior" suggests that it can be an infernal matter, despite the absence of extreme situations such as physical abuse. Right after Anastasia found her metaphorical pair of glasses in the "feeling as obscure as it was extraordinary" that made her see her life's true colors, she is summoned by her mother (*Chronicles*, 36). To emphasize Anastasia's novel awareness of her condition, Ortese turns to an aesthetics of deformation to introduce the other family members, creating a continuity of abjection between the Finizio family and the Quaglias from the previous text.

The reader thus starts observing the world as it is mediated by Anastasia's "disorientation." Entering the kitchen, she focuses on her Aunt Nana (*nana* means "dwarf" in Italian), busy mopping the floor, bent over, who, in "Anastasia's disturbed gaze" seems "a real monstrosity [*un mostriciattolo*]" with a swollen face and a "putrid-yellow" skin that emphasizes the blackness of her "terrible eyes [. . .] of a woman who hasn't been able to live" (*Chronicles*, 45). In the same room Anastasia's brother Eduardo is shaving: the man is "terribly [*orribilmente*] thin," and, as if seeing him for the first time, she fixates on his back, which now appears to Anastasia as unnaturally oblong, and makes Eduardo resemble a "a half-desiccated spider that sometimes hung from a web." He lived the life of a human being "only in appearance": to Anastasia's eyes, Eduardo is in fact nothing more than "a shadow [*una larva*]" (*Chronicles*, 46).

Further twisting the reassuring stereotypes of family figures, the most horrifying member of the household is Anastasia's mother, Angelina. The narrator describes her by reclaiming an omniscient perspective, thus momentarily stepping away from Anastasia's internal point of view. Rather than dwelling on Angelina's appearance, as with the other members of the Finizio family, Ortese focuses on the mother's deranged psychology, introducing her as someone whose main interest is to humiliate her daughter ("humiliate her, she had to, that was all, humiliate her" [*Chronicles*, 53]). As the protagonist steps into the kitchen, Angelina senses Anastasia's tumultuous state of mind, torn between elation and hopelessness because of Antonio's return. Immediately, the mother looks for a way of mortifying her daughter, whose precarious emotional condition is clear. While making sarcastic and degrading comments about her forty-year-old daughter's marital status and physical appearance, Angelina, in passing, reveals that Antonio is newly engaged. Ortese makes the mother's malicious intent clear: "And she quietly observed her daughter's long face, which had become horribly hard and unpleasant in her efforts to control herself. Signora Finizio's lips lengthened into a very thin smile" (*Chronicles*, 50).

Angelina's revelation about Antonio's romantic life takes place halfway through "Family Interior," and effectively halts its plot. The second half of the story continues the description of a day in the Finizio family, without any significant developments in the protagonist's life: Antonio never shows up, an old neighbor dies, Anastasia keeps attending to her chores, and Angelina continues abusing her. Everything remains suspended in an atmosphere of dusty stillness and habituation—a suffocated scream, as it were.

In contrast to the outlier events described in chapter 3 through the lens of Taleb's "black swans," in postwar Naples hell belongs to everyday life: "There was nothing extraordinary here. Anastasia knew and pitied the young, who were sickly and unemployed, with few ambitions, few dreams, a scant life" (*Chronicles*, 57)—they are, to quote an essay in which Ortese reflects on postwar Italy's socioeconomic conditions, "young people thrown like corpses before society."[20] Anastasia's thoughts, too, after the momentary flickering of earlier that day, transition back to their former status—"calm, cold, inherent, as they had always been" (*Chronicles*, 61). These men's and women's lives only produce "a faint noise" (*Chronicles*, 62), further suggesting the purposelessness of their misery, fated to sterility despite the postwar climate of political militancy and enthusiasm. Indeed, the story ends with the phrase "I'm coming," mechanically uttered by Anastasia (a surrender, almost) as she is again summoned by her mother, without Antonio ever showing up (*Chronicles*, 62).

Where the first story of *Chronicles* culminates with an event that upends Eugenia's world, the narrative fabric of "Family Interior" is homogeneous, with one of the most horrifying elements of Anastasia's life being precisely that nothing changes. A certain homogeneity could be taken, in other contexts, as a positive, even reassuring factor concerning family structures, and "Family Interior," as its title suggests, indeed calls for attention to the inner dynamics of the household. Yet, it does so only to turn them upside-down: the grotesque traits of the Finizio family are exposed, and the mother becomes a monster who, rather than supporting her daughter, perpetuates Anastasia's powerlessness, turning it into habituation as the story's ending suggests.

With "Family Interior," Ortese gives a blueprint of a domestic environment where ordinary and rather banal circumstances underpin the "dark suffering of life [*male oscuro di vivere*]" evoked by the book's preface. The remaining pieces take the reader out onto the streets of the city, with Ortese shifting from narrative fiction to a narrativized reportage on the living conditions of postwar Italy. Anastasia's private interior leads to the city's public exterior, which Ortese explores first in "The Gold of Forcella" and then in "The Involuntary City," with a descent into the city's underbelly, where the lowest social strata live.

Forcella is one of the oldest and most iconic neighborhoods of Naples, deriving its name from its Y-shaped main road (*forcella* is the Italian for "fork," or "forked"). Right in the historic city center and once home to the city's Jewish population, Forcella is a labyrinth of chaotic and narrow streets that organically sprawled over the centuries rather than following planned developments: at the time of Ortese's writing it was a so-called "popular district," where the lower classes lived in close proximity to landmark buildings such as the cathedral.

With the exclusion of its preface and afterword, "The Gold of Forcella" is the shortest piece of the book, and fulfills a bridging role in its structure: it marks the transition from an external narrative point of view to an internal one, as Ortese switches from third- to first-person singular to describe her visit to one of the neighborhood's pawnshops. This switch underlines a second transition, one away from fiction: indeed, "The Gold of Forcella" first appeared as a piece of journalism in 1951 in the Italian magazine *Il Mondo*,[21] to then be republished in *Chronicles*.

In contrast to the purposefully dry tone of most neorealist prose and despite its formal status as reportage, "The Gold of Forcella" makes ample use of the aesthetics of deformation previously encountered in the two short stories that open the book. The tone of the piece is set from its beginning by two different, yet equally grotesque descriptions of Forcella's crowd: the first compares it to a snake that produces a "mournful buzz" by rhythmically inflating and deflating its own body (*Chronicles*, 64); a second, just a few lines afterward, describes the multitude of people teeming on the streets as giving the narrator the impression of looking at a "carpet of flesh" (65). Among these people are women whose faces have been left scarred by smallpox, or mutilated men whose torsos are the only part left of their bodies. Looking back to the previous chapter, they are the "monsters" of Naples that Malaparte depicts in the concluding passages of *Kaputt*, who barely survived the war only to suffer its aftermaths, such as epidemic outbreaks or severe disabilities (*Kaputt*, 415).

With the same dehumanizing reference to spiders that informed the description of Eduardo's emaciated physique in "Family Interior," Forcella's crowd appears "silent as a spider," glued together by a shapeless misery that blends different bodies—bodies that Ortese calls "wretched fabrics [*miseri tessuti*]," with a metonymic use of the Italian word *tessuti* that refers to both the homogeneous fabric of the crowd, and the very skin of a populace scarred by misery (*Chronicles*, 67). The twisting of stereotypes that in the previous text upended the support and love provided by one's family and, in particular, one's mother is here transferred to the customs of the city, with the hanging "sheets for which Naples is well known" replaced by "black hollows [*buchi neri*] in which they were once hung" (*Chronicles*, 66). Similarly, the colorful and joyful buzzing that supposedly belongs to the narrow streets of the city center here turns disquieting: rather than being an indication of liveliness, it becomes symptomatic of a disorderly environment where empty spaces are immediately overrun by "a confused jumble of various items" (*Chronicles*, 66). In this chaotic landscape, children play among piles of trash, unaware of, since habituated to, the horrors that the flaneur-narrator here witnesses and reports through descriptions rife with deforming elements.

But postwar Naples is not a Paris or Berlin where the arcades are still standing, and Ortese's gaze is more pained than that belonging, with more than a tint of voyeurism, to Charles Baudelaire or Walter Benjamin. Ortese is not a flaneur musing about urban life while gently intoxicated by the fumes of alcohol or hashish:[22] as she writes in the book's preface, her goal is less to analyze reality than to scream against it.

Yet, Ortese's wanderings also provide the reader with some insights concerning the social fabric of Forcella. Among the neighborhood's apparently untamable chaos, two forces hold a steady grasp on the population. The first is religion, whose radiant iconography on display in shop windows clashes with the misery of the streets. Ortese writes how "vice and folly" turned the population into "a race devoid of all logic and reason," desperately hanging onto cult-like superstitions that diminish mankind to the status of "a shadow of itself, weak, neurotic, resigned to fear and impudent joy" (*Chronicles*, 67). The grotesque coexistence of earthly poverty and heavenly embellishments is emphasized by the brief, yet disquieting appearance of two "very tall priests, their waxen hands grasping red leather books" (*Chronicles*, 68), who embody the same ontological difference as the American troops that in *The Skin* walk amid the plague-stricken crowds while being immune to the contagion.

The second force ruling Forcella, and the city's poor districts more generally, is a form of sexuality that, unprotected and uncontrolled, makes the population steadily increase while rendering it "even more lifeless," and turns Naples' underbelly into a "dark pit [where] only the fire of sexuality burned bright under an eerie black sky." This second force is entangled with the first: the increasing numbers of newborns, Ortese reports with a sentence intentionally left ambiguous, make "the hearts of the clergy [. . .] swollen with a strange pride and ever stranger hope" (*Chronicles*, 67).

After an overview of the abject conditions of Forcella, the narration leads to a pawnshop, Ortese's destination and the place where the Neapolitan underclass takes out loans, leaving their gold as security (hence the text's title). There, Ortese enters a room with high ceilings hung with spiderwebs, which echoes the gothic opening of "A Pair of Eyeglasses." The space is filled with individuals that she describes as "bodies [*corpi*]" rather than persons, placing the emphasis on their materiality instead of humanity, and also indicating their semblance of living dead more than live creatures (*Chronicles*, 68). Inside, surrounded by a howling crowd, she sees a woman busy convincing those waiting in line to let her pass, since the shop is about to close and she urgently needs money to provide support for her dying eldest son. In truth, however, readers discover that she has been playing the same trick for months, repeatedly deceiving her fellow Neapolitans just to skip the long wait. Although the workers of the pawnshop know this, they too are seized by the apathy that grips Forcella's population, and do nothing to block her from cheating her way through the line (*Chronicles*, 69–70).

This resigned stasis is, however, momentarily broken by the sudden appearance of a brown butterfly—perhaps a moth, symbol of death—that seizes everyone's attention and compels a communal expression of wonder ("'Oh! . . . Oh! . . . Oh! . . .' murmured the crowd"). Their sudden stupor reveals an important facet of their condition: these individuals' apathy is not totalizing, as something that encompasses each and every aspect of their lives; on the contrary, as this display of emotion shows, they are still capable of being affected by the external world. Yet, their surroundings, their horrible poverty, and the apparent inescapability of their condition are elements that they are fully accustomed to, whereas a brown butterfly is a rare sighting in Forcella—so much so that it compels "an old crippled woman [*una vecchia deforme*], her mouth full of bread" to start singing, with this grotesque scene bringing the piece to its end (*Chronicles*, 72).

For the crowd of Forcella's pawnshop the brown butterfly is essentially what Antonio's reappearance was for Anastasia in "Family Interior," or what Eugenia's wearing of her new glasses in "A Pair of Eyeglasses" did: an event that ruptures the apathy of those experiencing it, either in bono or in malo, either as wonder or as horror. The rekindling of these individuals' emotional life clashes with the otherwise resigned habituation to what takes place around them. In this way, Ortese signals that, rather than inherent, their orientation toward the circumstances of their life is contingent and mutable. In other words, not only horror is contextual—its normalization is as well.

Ortese places herself in opposition to apathy, and instead of shrugging off the present state of affairs screams her denunciation of it. She does so with the tools of literary prose, and in particular through the aesthetics of deformation that renders striking what might otherwise be taken as normal, such as Anastasia's brother's thinness or the misery of Forcella's crowds. Via a process of defamiliarization through deformation, Ortese thus positions her narrating voice outside of the sphere of habituation:[23] from this vantage point, she witnesses with horror, and describes accordingly, the impact of poverty on some of the most destitute Neapolitan communities.

Horror is an experience that, before making sense, simply takes over one's present in its overpowering force. In *Chronicles*, this is at play both in form and in content. Regarding the book's content, this dynamic revolves around the characters' uncontrollable reactions to the newfound awareness of their living conditions, as with Eugenia or, in part, Anastasia. Regarding the book's form, it operates in how Ortese describes these circumstances, either as an omniscient narrator in her fictions, or as an eyewitness in her reporting. In both cases the realism of the narrative fabric stops "making sense," gets pierced, and is taken over by scenes where the world assumes disquieting and hallucinatory appearances.

Here too, however, horror maintains a contextual strain: what horrifies Ortese and her characters remains a subjective matter, one that presupposes neither universality nor necessity. Indeed, as Ortese implies, processes of habituation can render people apathetic to what an external and unaccustomed observer may experience as horrifying. Further, the diverse array of horrifying situations to which the characters in *Chronicles* are fully habituated suggests that, given enough time and exposure, such processes of normalization can occur for a great number of scenarios. In other words, habituation can mean that a present situation "takes over" to such an extent that it effectively prevents the possibility of what the sociologist Niklas Luhmann calls "second-order observation"—that is, it prevents a form of observation that endows what is observed with the form of contingency, and the possibility of being different.[24] Ortese highlights the collective forced powerlessness that prolonged poverty imposes, and that compounds poverty's already horrifying nature: a state that ought to be considered exceptional is rendered ordinary, as one grows accustomed to it—be it as an observer or as the one experiencing it.

From the perspective of the history of genres, the denunciation of poverty and the depiction of its effects on the population has been an explicit goal of realism from the nineteenth century onward. Yet this realism was also largely underpinned by the belief that a comprehensive and adequate description of poverty's underpinnings, its causes and effects, would entail its denunciation, and thus hopefully pave the way for society's betterment.

This legacy was taken up by postwar neorealism, and it merged with the progressive political underpinnings of the movement.

Ortese's project runs on a parallel, yet different track: while she accepts and adopts the descriptive thrust of neorealism, her prose leverages deforming aesthetics that trouble the militant side of (neo)realist descriptionism by veering into the grotesque, the hallucinated, and the expressionistic.[25] Her preface to *Chronicles* elucidates the reasons behind this choice: there, Ortese writes that the book is a reaction to the "disorientation" and "horror" she experienced, with an emphasis on the individual nature of her screaming. Contrary to a platform for social change that may be incorporated within a broader political movement, Ortese conceives *Chronicles* as a personal matter and as a "*vision* of the intolerable" rather than as a detached "true measure of things" (*Chronicles*, 191). Ortese considered reality an opaque and menacing matter, difficult to withstand, decipher, and represent—something that provoked in her a neurosis and kindled a contempt for the real, instead of making her desire to wholeheartedly engage with it. It is given these premises that Ortese distanced herself from neorealism's project, while simultaneously being distanced by that very movement.

And yet, although not explicitly militant, Ortese's writings had very tangible repercussions on reality. To illustrate this point, I now turn to "The Involuntary City" and its protagonist: the building complex Granili.

"The Involuntary City" was first published in two parts in the magazine *Il Mondo* in January 1952, with the first one titled, just like the text in *Chronicles*, "The Involuntary City," and the second, "The Horror of Living,"[26] echoing the piece's final sentence. This latter title is significant, as "horror of living" is a syntagm that Ortese uses in "Summer Terrors" to describe the poverty of the city's lowest strata after World War II. The word "horror" itself, too, is a central and recurring one in her production, as this chapter demonstrates.

In Ortese's work horror exists in the absence of extraordinary circumstances such as an armed conflict: to see it, one just needs to look carefully enough. In Eugenia's story Ortese invites us to become sensitive to its presence around us—we too, she seems to suggest, should put on our own pair of eyeglasses. While her interest in horror beyond the horror genre is remarkable, with "The Involuntary City" Ortese deploys one of the most common tropes of the genre only to turn it inside-out: the one of the haunted house. As we shall see, the building that Ortese explores is one haunted by human beings living in horrifying conditions rather than by ghosts.[27]

The title "The Involuntary City" refers to the building complex Granili, as it constituted an urban ecosystem of its own in the heart of Naples, and the text describes Ortese's real journey into it.[28] Built in 1778 under the reign of Ferdinand IV of the Kingdom of Naples, the Granili is a palimpsest of the city's convoluted past: this building complex of monumental size (four 30-meter-tall, structurally similar buildings, for a total of 560 meters in length) was initially an armory and a rope factory. Eventually repurposed as a jail, it became a cholera hospital in the early nineteenth century during an outbreak. In 1846 the Granili was made into a military barracks, thus finding a fixed use until the end of World War II. Although heavily damaged during the conflict, the building stood half-destroyed in postwar Naples and housed in its lower and less damaged floors a multitude of otherwise homeless people.[29]

"The Involuntary City" begins with an impersonal voice that departs from the personal one of the preceding texts. The opening section describes with great accuracy the building's formal aspects, starting from the outside and working inward: details include its size ("around three hundred meters long, between fifteen and twenty meters wide"), the number of windows ("a hundred and seventy-four openings), of the sewage pipes ("eight"), of floors ("there are three floors, plus a ground floor"), and of rooms ("three hundred and forty-eight rooms, all equally high and large"). The absurdly specific nature of this description escalates as Ortese describes the Granili's corridors: their number ("four"), their width ("from seven to eight meters"), their total length ("one kilometer two hundred meters"), and the number of lamps in each ("twenty-eight") plus their power ("each with five candlepower"). Ortese concludes this overview by calculating how many families live there, detailing the number of cubicles in the Granili ("eighty-six doors of private dwellings open, forty-three on the right, forty-three on the left"), the total number of people inside ("three thousand") and of families as well ("five hundred and seventy"), with the average size of these families provided too ("an average of six people per family"). Given all this data, Ortese concludes that "when three, four, or five families live in the same space, it reaches a density of twenty-five or thirty inhabitants per room"—an arithmetic demonstration of the Granili's overcrowdedness, *quod erat demonstrandum* (*Chronicles*, 73–74).

Despite what these first paragraphs may suggest, Ortese is not interested in mathematically proving that the Granili is horrendously overpopulated, nor does she believe that such a proof would provide anything more than a string of data. As her preface to *Chronicles* makes clear, reality was for Ortese incomprehensible, and the list that opens "The Involuntary City" offers the author an opportunity to provide a meta-reflection on this topic. After enumerating the Granili's formal characteristics, Ortese comments on this description's efficacy (or lack thereof) by affirming that "hav[ing] stated in summary fashion some facts about the structure and population of this Neapolitan neighborhood, one realizes that one has expressed almost nothing" (*Chronicles*, 74).

Quantifying something can certainly fulfill many purposes, but, according to Ortese, it does not solve the problem of expression: for her, as for Koestler, statistics do not bleed. Ortese's affirmation indeed touches on a central aesthetic concern of this project: How to best express the subjective and contextual experience of horror? How to make it stick? And do the devices of literary prose offer any specific vantage point? In relation to "The Involuntary City," these questions can be condensed into one: how can one effectively convey the horrifying nature of the Granili?

Ortese argues that truly grasping the Granili phenomenon requires a different approach from data fetishization: "Granili III and IV, one of the most evocative phenomena in the world, and like Southern Italy, dead to the progress of time, should therefore be, rather than described with ingenuous figures by this or that obscure reporter, visited carefully, in all its deformities and absurd horror" (*Chronicles*, 75). Paraphrasing, we could say that she advocates for a phenomenological approach as opposed to a quantitative one that would enumerate the building's characteristics. Instead of counting its rooms, one should step over the threshold that separates the world of the living—Naples, the voluntary city—from the one of the dead, the Granili, the involuntary city.[30] Numbers, Ortese continues, stop being endowed with holy meaning in relation to a context such as the Granili's, where "barometers no longer display any measure; compasses go crazy" (*Chronicles*, 75).

The disorientation caused by the breakdown of the tools used to make sense of our surroundings demands stepping down from the pedestal of the *quod erat demonstrandum*, relying instead on the humbler, subject-centered approach of phenomenological description to address the "deformities and absurd horror" one encounters in the Granili. In this upside-down world, it is the Granili—its ecosystem as an involuntary city, the fact that it really exists—that is more threatening than its dwellers: "The men you meet can't do you any harm: ghosts [*larve*] from a life in which wind and sun existed—these good things they no longer remember. They creep or climb or stagger: that is their way of moving. They speak very little; they are no longer Neapolitans, or anything else. A committee of priests and American scholars, which, days ago, boldly crossed the threshold of that melancholy dwelling [*malinconica Casa*], quickly turned back, with incoherent words and looks" (*Chronicles*, 75). In Ortese's prose, the human beings who live inside the Granili do not walk; instead, they crawl, they sway, they slither. They barely speak. They are not Neapolitans anymore, nor anything else really. In the Italian original the word "house" ("*Casa*") is capitalized, suggesting either its personification or at least an emphasis on the uniqueness and perhaps even aliveness of this building. Ortese knew the horror genre well, and one of her favorite authors was Edgar Allan Poe, whom she "venerated."[31] In order to convey the nature of the Granili, Ortese twists the trope of the haunted house, repurposing it beyond the horror genre.

Instead of ghosts, Ortese's house is haunted by humans who have lost their state of humanity. They are "*larve*," which can be translated as "ghosts," but also as "larva" and "shadow," echoing not only Eduardo's description in "Family Interior" but also how Levi refers to the condition of the inmates in Auschwitz.[32] No longer used to behaving in accordance with the standards of society, these "*larve*" have lost their capacity to be part of it, and an involuntary city was thus founded by the outcasts that Naples, the voluntary city, pushed to its margins. For those who belong to the realm of the officially sanctioned and the humanly civilized, the experience of visiting this involuntary city challenges standard categories of sense-making. This is the case for the priests and the American scholars who enter the Granili and leave shortly thereafter mumbling incoherent words. This, too, is another trope of the horror genre that Ortese twists, one found, for instance, in H. P. Lovecraft, where the encounter with non-Euclidean cities and their eons-old inhabitants often drives the protagonists of his stories insane.[33]

But there are no Lovecraftian, tentacular monsters lurking in the darkness of this building; instead, there is human misery. "The Involuntary

City" emphasizes the contrast between the quantitative and the experiential starting from Ortese's first interaction with the Granili at its entrance: "In front of me, I saw the ground-floor corridor, extending for three hundred meters, but at that moment it seemed an incalculable distance." Still partially connected to the domain of the human, she sees beyond that liminal space "some shadows," moving around the corridor in a seemingly random fashion (*Chronicles*, 76). The sensation of being about to cross a threshold between worlds is emphasized by a focus on Ortese's sense of smell, with "gusts of bitter odor, mainly of toilets, [which] continually reached the threshold, mixed with the darker smell of dampness." For those not habituated to the house, just like Ortese, "it seemed impossible to advance ten meters into that tunnel without fainting" (*Chronicles*, 76).

Upon crossing the building's entrance, Ortese's sight readjusts, albeit slowly, to the surrounding darkness, recalling the topic of vision first introduced in "A Pair of Eyeglasses." Coherent with her invitation to phenomenologically describe the Granili instead of just quantifying it, she begins "making sense" of her surroundings, though her senses begin to unveil a world different from the one she left behind: in this new world, the smell of coffee is intermixed with that of urine, the hair she brushes against is hard rather than soft, and the human body cold rather than warm (*Chronicles*, 76–77).

Just as Dante could not go through Hell without Virgil, Ortese too needs a guide to explore this Neapolitan Inferno. This role is fulfilled by Antonia Lo Savio, but, contrary to the *Divine Comedy*, no details are provided about the connection between guide and pilgrim. While Dante stresses Virgil's noble qualities even as the Latin poet appears to him under the guise of a shadow, Ortese's first description of Lo Savio focuses on her grotesque body and demeanor: "A small woman, completely bloated, like a dying bird, her black hair cascading over a hunchback, and with a lemon-colored face, dominated by a large, pointed nose that hung over a harelip, was combing her hair in front of a fragment of mirror, holding some hairpins between her teeth" (*Chronicles*, 78). Ortese, tempted to flee from that place, explicitly calls Lo Savio "my guide," and states that "behind [her] deplorable forehead, a measure of hope existed." Like the other characters from *Chronicles* who live in apparently untenable circumstances, she displays signs of habituation, but also, sometimes, of hope. It is indeed crucial to emphasize that it is Ortese who is horrified by the Granili, not Lo Savio: while the former is entering a new world, the latter is fully accustomed to the building complex and is the "queen of the house of the dead"—a queen "bloated, horrendous," in whose eyes shines the "knowledge of evil and its extent," and a certain "pleasure needed to confront it," too (*Chronicles*, 80).[34]

Following her, Ortese visits an upside-down world. According to her guide, the building is a place of sorrows where the walls wail. But Ortese, still partly belonging to the realm of standard sense-making, knows that haunted houses do not exist, and is quick to add that "it wasn't the walls, of course, it was the wind, which crept in between the great doors." In a world where things make sense, Ortese is aware that walls cannot wail, and yet, as she continues, "the big structure [*la grande Casa*] really seemed to be shuddering continuously, almost imperceptibly, as if from an internal landslide, from an anguish and dissolution of all the quasi-human material that composed it" (*Chronicles*, 81). The word "*Casa*" is capitalized here as well, once again emphasizing the disquieting nature of this building. Through a careful balance between otherworldly suggestions and steadfast focus on the ordinary horror of abject living conditions, Ortese disconnects the trope of the haunted house from the supernatural by pointing to the concreteness of the "quasi-human material" constituting the edifice. That material is the human beings whose humanity is dissolving and who are turning into shadows unfit for society—the "*larve*" encountered before.

Slowly, almost as if under the influence of her hallucinogenic surroundings, Ortese begins abandoning the realm of standard sense-making that belongs to the outside world: "now the walls appeared wet, corroded, all encrustations and dark drips," with the temporal adverb marking a transition between past and present perception of reality. Having fully crossed the Granili's threshold, Ortese reports, without providing any further explanation, that she glimpsed a woman with a strange growth on her face, one that resembled a red fungus, as she carried a green bottle wrapped up in a napkin "as if it were a child." Further emphasizing the absurdity of what she is exposed to, the narrator hears a voice singing "a sacred hymn in which the goodness of existence was praised," despite the surrounding misery (*Chronicles*, 81).

The structure of the text itself begins to be affected by Ortese's descent into hell. Spatial transitions become sudden and less orderly, as Ortese struggles to adapt to what she is now exposed to: "Strange room" is the lapidary comment that introduces a transition to a new room, where feces are stored in jars scattered all around. Ortese notes the room's number, "258 B," in an attempt at making sense of her surroundings (*Chronicles*, 82)—an attempt that, at this point, the text itself undermines.

In the same room, on a mattress, three rats gnaw on a piece of bread, without any hesitation, as if they have taken over that space from the humans living there. This scene of a defeated humanity snaps Ortese out of her sense of passivity, and momentarily makes her aware of the horror taking place in front of her: "those three animals appeared so sure of being able to gnaw on those crusts of bread, that I had the impression that I was dreaming, or at least contemplating a drawing, of a horrendous truthfulness, that had mesmerized me to the point of making me confuse a representation with life itself" (*Chronicles*, 83). As if spellbound, confused regarding whether she is daydreaming or not, Ortese wonders how what she *sees* can possibly *be*.

Chronicles lingers on the tension between the miserable living conditions of some of its characters and their habituation to their surroundings, which, despite the circumstances, still allows for sparks of enthusiasm and even of joy. In "The Involuntary City" Ortese faces this ostensible paradox firsthand, as she encounters "*larve*" whose material circumstances should make them question the "goodness of existence" that they laud, or the "holy obedience to God's wishes" that they respect (*Chronicles*, 84). But the horror induced by the Granili is Ortese's rather than theirs: where she is dealing with a new context that has cast her world into crisis, for them that same context has become a matter of habituation and is largely normalized.

This normalization, too, is contextual, and the Granili displays a hierarchy of its inhabitants, with those living in the upper floors avoiding any contact with those living below. Those who do not live in the building's basement are convinced that their prosperity, "having no doubt with regard to its stability," is due to their own virtuosity, and if for an "absolutely random circumstance," such as unemployment or a sudden illness, someone from above descends below, they are "sure that in just a short time [they] would move back up to the third floor, or even leave the Granili." But nobody reappears after having entered the black hole of the lower floors: "that man, that family, never returned to the surface, nor did they get out of there entirely, although in the first days it had seemed possible. [. . .] No one rose again, from down there" (*Chronicles*, 88).

Lo Savio, attracted by some unusual noises coming from below, leads Ortese to the depths of the Granili. There, they realize that the sounds are due to the death of Scarpetella, a seven-year-old child who suddenly dropped dead while playing with his friends. The family, as if habituated to such mournful circumstances, stages a funeral whose composure Ortese deems "absurd" given Neapolitans' theatricality and public display of passions (*Chronicles*, 91). But Ortese is quick to realize that "down there no possibility of emotion survived"—in the lowest floors of the Granili not even the death of a young boy can trigger horror: "there was darkness, and nothing else," with habituation turning into apathy, screams of horror and cries of joy into emotional numbness. Lo Savio, too, an otherwise loquacious guide, becomes silent in this earthly, yet equally frozen Giudecca (*Chronicles*, 93).[35]

Ortese's journey through the Granili ends with an encounter with a syphilitic, revisiting the topic of vision that the book introduced with Eugenia's story. The dying man sits in a room full of "people, shadows [*larve*]" with his head reclined; "he was looking up, as if blind, and his body trembled." The man's blindness, whether actual or not, is not only caused by the disease, but also because he has dropped his eyeglasses (*Chronicles*, 98). This is a suggestive detail, one rife with symbolism in a book where the theme of sight is central: in my reading of it, it symbolizes how not wearing glasses allows the Granili's inhabitants, here represented by the syphilitic through a metonymy, to become habituated to their living conditions. Wearing glasses would involve seeing their surroundings with clarity and hence suffering from the same vertigo that struck Eugenia when she first glimpsed the misery of Vicolo della Cupa. In order to live in the Granili, they must normalize that which should remain unacceptable; they must avoid seeing their condition as an external observer would, in order to avoid the same horrified reaction to the Granili that the priests, the American scholars, and Ortese experience upon crossing the threshold of that building.

From this point of view, the habituation to horrible living conditions fosters different yet interrelated effects. On the one hand, it may prevent the possibility of what, as we already saw, Luhmann calls "second-order observation"—that is, an observation that sees the current reality as contingent and capable of being different. In other words, processes of habituations may crystalize as immutable that which ought to be resisted, fought against, and ultimately changed. On the other hand, habituation can become a way of insulating oneself from otherwise untenable conditions, and also a coping mechanism: if one is stuck in a horrible situation, is it necessarily better to keep its horror in plain sight at all times? For those forced to live in the Granili, habituation becomes a way of normalizing the abnormal, and in this way, it turns into a survival mechanism. In different circumstances, Levi, too, talks of his imprisonment in the Lager as "boredom punctuated by horror,"[36] and reminds us that those who faced Medusa for too long became the "drowned," as in those who did not survive the Gorgon's petrifying gaze.[37]

Ortese refrains from judging such processes of habituation among the most destitute parts of the Neapolitan population. Instead, she describes with horror what she sees on the streets of Naples and its underbelly. In so doing, she champions a phenomenological perspective that also fulfills the goal of *Chronicles*, as stated in its introduction: that goal is to scream. Hers is also a scream against inertia, directed, as we shall see particularly in "The Silence of Reason," at shaking off the indifference and habituation of those outside the Granili, those who should be looking at the most disturbing aspects of reality with clear sight and steadfast resolution.

Inertia and horror are explicitly evoked in the concluding sentence of "The Involuntary City": "At the Granili, night was beginning, and the involuntary city was preparing to consume its few goods, in a fever that would last until the following morning, the hour when complaints, surprise, mourning, the moribund horror of living [*l'inerte orrore di vivere*] start again" (*Chronicles*, 98). An inert horror of living is what Ortese describes at great length in *Chronicles*, and her exploration of the Granili is the apex of her Neapolitan journey: in this building complex, especially at its lowest floors, the horrifying exists without it constituting a form of shock for those exposed to it. While Ortese's reaction is certainly one of turmoil, the same cannot be said of those who are habituated to the Granili's living conditions. In contrast to what was analyzed in chapter 3, where some individuals could live in the midst of the horrifying without experiencing it as such given their position as victors or perpetrators, here the contextual nature of this experience is revealed in how becoming accustomed to horror may effectively mean to stop seeing it as such. The expression "*inerte orrore di vivere*" encapsulates this double perspective: while her use of the word "horror" is surely bolstered by ordinary language to describe what goes on in the Granili, Ortese's use of the adjective "*inerte*" suggests that such horror may not cause a commensurate reaction, or may remain latent and dormant, for those who have grown accustomed to it.

These reflections on the contextual nature of horror bring us back, once again, to her book's preface, where Ortese writes that the "disorientation" and "horror" that she projected onto the city are *hers*, rather than existing *in themselves*. Postwar Naples, just like the lives of those who live around Forcella or in the Granili, contained multitudes: for Ortese, however, that multitude was overtaken by *her* "dark suffering of life [*male oscuro di vivere*]." The literary project of *Chronicles* thus becomes a way of doing what the list of the Granili's features that opens "The Involuntary City" could not accomplish: that is, to express Ortese's horror concerning the state of affairs she was exposed to.

It is important to keep in mind that the contextual and subject-centered nature of this experience does not entail solipsistic inwardness: if reality horrifies, there are likely good reasons for it, at least for the subject who experiences reality as such. And these reasons can be widespread characteristics of the external world: they may be exceptional ones, such as an armed conflict, or more mundane ones, such as the poverty and the abject living conditions narrated by Ortese. Without equating two vastly different settings, I contend that structural similarities exist among them, also as they induce in some the necessity to become screamers.

The historical concreteness of *Chronicles*, together with its depiction of ordinary circumstances, reveals how horror haunted Italy even after the end of World War II. To display this horror, Ortese resorts to deforming aesthetics that momentarily depart from realism to convey the nature of what she witnessed. In conjunction, she twists some of the tropes of the horror genre—the haunted house, in particular. Ortese does all this because she wants to make horror stick. She wants to make her readers sensitive to, and aware of, the surrounding horror. But was Ortese successful? Did her scream and its rendition through literary prose reach anywhere beyond the written page?

In January 1952, the president of the newly established Italian republic, Luigi Einaudi, read Ortese's reportage in *Il Mondo*. He was left appalled. Profoundly shocked, Einaudi ordered the immediate demolition of the Granili. He was so impressed by those pages that he asked to be put in contact with the still somewhat unknown author, Anna Maria Ortese. He invited her to dine at the Quirinale, the home of the president of the republic. We know that Ortese was very impressed by Einaudi's erudition, tact, and the way he cut his pears. Today, the area where the Granili stood is part of the harbor of Naples.[38]

Ortese's screams asserted that even in times of peace, horror was present no further than a few blocks away from the city center. But if so, why was it necessary to scream? How could the city be so oblivious to the horrors hiding in plain sight, right on the streets of Naples? These are central concerns for both this chapter and the book at large, transcending the specificities of the analyzed historical context. The piece that bookends *Chronicles* offers Ortese's answer to these questions.

"The Silence of Reason" describes a part of the intellectual milieu of Naples, specifically the one centered on the journal *Sud,* which Ortese herself belonged to. In this concluding text, Ortese targets the Neapolitan intelligentsia that, despite a first phase of postwar liberal and leftist militancy, quickly became habituated to the living conditions of the most destitute Neapolitans. "The Silence of Reason" constitutes an indictment of these intellectuals who grew indifferent to the horrors all around. Simultaneously, in closing the book that "A Pair of Eyeglasses" opened, this concluding piece serves as Ortese's invitation to keep Eugenia's glasses on, and face horror directly rather than maintaining the safe distance of intellectual abstraction.[39]

By the time readers reach the fifth, final, and longest piece of *Chronicles,* they are accustomed to roaming the streets of a Naples that, as seen through Ortese's eyes, assumes disquieting traits. "The Silence of Reason" continues this tendency, describing the Neapolitan crowd as a "snake struck by the sun but not yet dead" that upon closer scrutiny reveals a multitude of "living creatures who dragged themselves along in a continuous motion resembling the actions of someone with a fever, or the nervous mania that possesses certain beings before dying" (*Chronicles,* 104–5).[40] Separated from this crowd stand figures described as exceptionally pale, bent over and twisted (*Chronicles,* 141): they are some of the intellectuals who, after the tide of fascism and World War II had passed, sought to rebuild the foundations of the South upon the soil of reason and conscience. By the early 1950s, this plan showed the "unquestionable evidence of failure" (*Chronicles,* 121).

Ortese's reaction to this failure is to become a screamer. But for many, it triggered a different transformation, making them the pale and scornful figures "full of resignation and fury" that "The Silence of Reason" describes (*Chronicles*, 109). In this text, Luigi Compagnone, a once militant writer now "ensconced in the reaction [*seduto al centro della reazione*]" (*Chronicles*, 125), becomes the archetype of the intellectual who, to paraphrase Koestler, takes the screamers for madmen, and does not react soundly to the horrors in front of his eyes.

Naples, Ortese observes, is indeed rife with "anxiety and horror," although everything appears on the surface "gay and harmonious" (*Chronicles*, 141). In this context, too, just as in Koestler's America, the majority of individuals think and behave differently from the screamers. Alongside the populace pouring from the poorest alleys of the city walk men and women incapable of even noticing who and what surrounds them, oblivious to the misery all around to an extent that prevents them from even feeling "irritation or disgust" (*Chronicles*, 141). With a twisted form of habituation that mirrors, only to pervert, the habituation of the Granili's dwellers to their surroundings, part of the Neapolitan population "had, in order to save themselves, renounced the ability to see the common people [*la plebe*] as living beings" (*Chronicles*, 165). Such an attitude entails the acceptance of some allegedly unmodifiable worldly orders; this, in turn, makes such individuals normalize what is horrible, and should not be naturalized. In Ortese's words, those who turn a blind eye to the surrounding poverty and a deaf ear to the screamers undersign "the age-old habit of respecting nature's orders, accepting from it the enlightenment as well as the horror" (*Chronicles*, 168).

Such passivity is, I argue, what Ortese calls the "silence of reason." Conversely, the voice of reason holds true to the necessity of screaming once faced with situations that should not be tolerated. In postwar Naples, there are good reasons to be horrified: not seeing them, and not reacting properly, is the true madness. For Ortese, it is the insensitive members of the Neapolitan upper class who, in Koestler's terminology, are the true maniacs. In the context of *Chronicles*, "The Silence of Reason" thus raises at least two important issues: is it possible to become insensitive to horror after having gone through World War II? And can a particular mental framework, or a set of beliefs, shield someone from the surrounding horrors?

For Ortese, reason can be silent even where it should find a privileged venue for expression, namely, in the intellectual milieu of the city. As Ortese writes in the concluding pages of the text, "like all monstrosities, Naples had no effect on people who were barely human, and its boundless charms could leave no trace on a cold heart" (*Chronicles*, 185). Not only does Ortese describe, particularly through Compagnone's entourage, a transition from engagement to resignation, she also affirms the necessity of maintaining a posture of phenomenological openness regarding what may horrify rather than resorting to intellectual abstractions as distancing tools. In so doing, Ortese affirms the reasonableness of experience and expression, which are not to be neglected in favor of abstraction and quantification. This directly echoes the first description of the Granili in "The Involuntary City," where a list of the building's features is followed by an invitation to explore it. From this perspective, her description of Naples is, as she writes in the 1994 afterword to *Chronicles*, a "*vision* of the intolerable" rather than a detached "true measure of things" (*Chronicles*, 191).

Ortese here also invites us to consider that reason and horror are not mutually exclusive. The latter does not exist without the former: the question "how can *this* be happening?" is devoid of meaning if not set against the backdrop of a reasonable setting, one that involves a given event casting into crisis our assumptions concerning how things should go, how people should be treated, and so forth.[41] Ortese's appalled reaction when faced with the horrors of postwar Naples goes hand in hand with her indictment of those who do not see how reasonable it is to be horrified and to scream when faced with the miserable living conditions of a number of their fellow Neapolitans.

In a similar vein, in her Leopardian essay "The Virtue of Nothingness" Ortese writes that "man lives in a place 'not of his own'—such is the universe." The universe, she continues, is a "place entirely alien to reason, where reason makes no sense, a hostile place, deep, without light, without signs, without directions, without names."[42] These bleak affirmations are followed by a commentary on the role of reason itself, which should "continuously illuminate everything, it should illuminate disorder and pain."[43] For the author of *Chronicles*, reason should describe rather than prescribe, and be the guiding light of writers, journalists, and artists, too, as well as engineers, legislators, and so forth. Since illumination is for Ortese also a matter of expression, being sensitive to horror involves finding ways to effectively cast some light on what ought to make us pause our gaze, so that the unreasonableness of turning it away is clearly shown. And while Leopardi lifted his head to the starry cosmos and its terrifying silence alongside its indifference to human suffering, Ortese's gaze focuses on the earthly business of material human misery.[44]

Ortese ultimately channels her "dark suffering of life [*male oscuro*]" outward, and in so doing screams the mundane horrors of postwar Naples. But is human misery, in its concreteness, only tied to what lies outside of us? Can horror be ultimately eliminated through a more wealthy and equitable society, one where reason does not go silent? What if the source of someone's "*male oscuro*" lies inside? These questions lead to this chapter's second author, Giuseppe Berto, whose autobiographical novel *Incubus* twists Ortese's scream inward, as its protagonist confronts the horrors that he harbors within.

THE SCREAM WITHIN: GIUSEPPE BERTO

Eleven years after Ortese's *Chronicles* won the Premio Viareggio in 1953, in 1964 Giuseppe Berto's *Il male oscuro* (*Incubus* in translation) was awarded both the Premio Viareggio and the Premio Campiello. Despite the mere decade that separates the publication of the two books, the Italy of 1964 was vastly different from the one of 1953: in 1964 the so-called Italian economic miracle was well underway, and it brought a period of remarkable social, economic, and technological development to the peninsula; the centrist party Democrazia Cristiana gathered a vast consensus, led Italy into NATO, and held steady the reins of power; the Partito Comunista Italiano had become well integrated within the democratic fabric of the country, and, with the labor unions, exerted political influence so that GDP growth would go hand in hand with improvements in the living conditions of workers and the population's lowest social strata. After going through the horrors of World War II and the tumult of the postwar period, the Italian population found itself wealthier than it had ever been: the symbols of this economic effervescence were tangible goods, such as the popular car model Fiat 600, or the refrigerators and washing machines that became increasingly widespread across the population.[45]

The mid- to late 1950s and the 1960s also saw the artistic world move away from the great neorealist season of the 1940s. The return of an interest in more experimental forms of literary expression led to the *neoavan-*

guardia of the Gruppo 63, which brought together writers such as Nanni Balestrini, Umberto Eco, Giorgio Manganelli, and Edoardo Sanguineti. A similar shift took place in the movie industry: Vittorio De Sica's 1952 *Umberto D.* marked a transition from the neorealist phase to the more introspective and existential tones that would flourish in the work of Federico Fellini and Michelangelo Antonioni, with their masterpieces *La dolce vita* and *L'avventura,* both released in 1960.

Berto's authorial trajectory is a blueprint of the trends of the time. His 1947 literary debut with the war novel *The Sky Is Red* [*Il cielo è rosso*], written while he was a prisoner of war in Hereford, Texas, is profoundly influenced by American writers such as John Steinbeck and Ernest Hemingway.[46] But it is only with his 1964 *Incubus,* as a new artistic season was unfolding, that Berto reached his artistic maturity, and surged in both sales and critical acclaim.

Incubus is an autobiographical novel about Berto's neurosis, an illness also triggered by the death of his father. Its style privileges long and convoluted sentences arranged through a patchwork of parataxis and hypotaxis, and closely resembles modernism's stream of consciousness in relying on free association rather than clear and distinct transitions.[47] In Berto's words, however, the main difference between the modernist style championed by James Joyce and his own lies in how *Incubus* is informed by the author's own experience with psychoanalytic therapy,[48] which he began in the 1950s at the peak of his mental issues, and which profoundly affected the book's form and content.[49]

Incubus is a text that turns inward the "dark suffering of life [*male oscuro di vivere*]" that in Ortese was primarily induced by external circumstances such as the war, first, and then postwar Naples living conditions (*Chronicles,* 10). This shift inward also responds to clear material reasons: the economic miracle of the 1950s and 1960s meant that for years Italy's GDP grew at a rate between 5 percent and 8 percent annually, which, in turn, had massive positive effects on the Italian population (in 1963 the unemployment rate was as low as 4.3 percent, a record so far unchallenged). In a country of increasingly widespread economic well-being, and in the absence of extraordinary circumstances, one might have been led to believe that modern life was getting the upper hand in its struggle against horror. But while the latter had at least partly withdrawn from the streets of the cities, it could still wreak havoc in one's own private existence, and for reasons different from the material circumstances that Ortese explicitly connected to what she termed "the horror of living."[50] Through *Incubus*, I consider how illness—be it episodic or chronic, real or imaginary, mental or physical—constitutes one of the most widespread ways in which ordinary horror can erupt in someone's life, and wage an onslaught against its very fabric.

What is, exactly, the "*male oscuro*" that Berto's title refers to? To answer this question we must first take a step back, and consider how his work's main topic, in the words of Italian critic Cesare de Michelis, is "that of the world's evil, of universal evil [*male universale*], for which there is no hope of salvation for humanity."[51] Berto's Leopardian pessimism is a recurring motif in the author's production, and so is a sense of hopelessness concerning mankind's agency with regard to the rulings of existence. The idea of "universal evil" emphasizes the generality of this condition, much like the metaphysics of horror in Leopardi. But unlike the philosophical systematicity of Leopardi's *Zibaldone*, Berto's "*male oscuro*" refers to his *own* illness, as it stems from, and affects, the specific circumstances of his life: it presupposes a turn inward, and in so doing evokes the more introspective ethos of Berto's novel.

Berto himself provides the source of the formulation "*male oscuro*" in the novel's first of three epigraphs, this one taken from Carlo Emilio Gadda's *The Experience of Pain* (*La cognizione del dolore*): "It was the obscure disease [*male oscuro*] whose causes and behavior the histories and laws and the universal disciplines of the great University chairs continue to ignore; and the victim carries it within himself, along the whole blasted descent of a lifetime, heavier every day, untreated" (*Incubus*, i). While "*male universale*" could presuppose a choral expression (like the one of Leopardi's *Broom*, where mankind's "common pact [*social catena*]" collectively braces against Nature),[52] the "*male oscuro*" Gadda refers to is colored by existentialist tints that make it more personal and less socially addressable; as it implies a degree of opacity that resists communal understanding, it is something that one carries within.

The second epigraph, from a letter by Sigmund Freud, clarifies what this entails, underlining the incurable nature of such "*male oscuro*" alongside the suffering that it brings: "What oppresses me cannot be cured: it is my cross and I must bear it, but God knows how my back is bent from the effort" (*Incubus*, i). It is the third epigraph, however, drawn from Aeschylus's *Prometheus*, that highlights why Berto chose to address this topic in a novel: "Painful are these things to relate [*Il racconto è dolore*], but silence too is painful" (*Incubus*, i). As Ortese's irritation against reality made her a screamer, Berto, too, is compelled to find an avenue of expression for something that cannot be borne any longer.

Spanning more than four hundred pages of dense prose, *Incubus* covers a wealth of autobiographical material that, while focusing on the author's neurosis, particularly active from the early 1950s onward, encompasses a wide array of emotions and experiences, some undoubtedly positive. As Berto himself affirms in the book's appendix, *Incubus* "is neither, I hope, a depressing novel nor a boring one."[53] The horror present in Berto's novel, while prominent, is not totalizing and coexists with a plethora of other experiences, suggesting again the unfixed and limited temporality of horror. Coherently, and in accordance with my book's approach of reading for horror scenes in texts not belonging to the eponymous genre, I will focus on passages in which the protagonist suffers horrifying bouts of his disease, in a way that alters how he relates to his surroundings and his own body. Whereas Ortese's *Chronicles* compelled us to reflect on the horrors of poverty, *Incubus* highlights some of the ways in which a horrible illness can suddenly seize control of a life and unravel it.

Illness and horror are at the novel's forefront from its opening passage, where Berto describes the event that will inform the rest of his story and, therefore, underpin his neurosis: the cancer that kills his father. This "horrible cancerous death" is rendered concrete by Berto's description of his father's surgery (*Incubus*, 17). The passage, nestled in a four-page-long paragraph of typical Bertian fashion, narrates in vivid terms the apparition of the tumor: "I saw all these people terribly stained with my father's blood, and as I went forward I also saw the tumor exposed on his belly." The tumor is "big and disgusting and bloody, like the guts of a dead dog set on my father's belly and connected to him indissolubly by a mortal knot"; it is a "fearsome disease" that leaves "his face and skull yellow" (*Incubus*, 23–24). The externalization of his father's "*male oscuro*" effectively triggers Berto's own internalization of the same, and this scene, in the author's words, opens a new and tragic chapter of his life.

It is worth considering that while a deforming register may be used to give the impression of a reality that no longer responds to standard sense-making, here the description of a tumor and its consequences does not need to depart from verisimilitude to come across in all its horror: as explored by oncologist and Pulitzer Prize winner Siddhartha Mukherjee in *The Emperor of All Maladies: A Biography of Cancer*, cancer radically calls into question our capacity to control and successfully react to the circumstances of our life, modern medicine notwithstanding. The awareness that cancer may touch our existence, turn it inside out, and force us to engage in a struggle that we may be bound to lose, is something that nobody can fully rule out despite our efforts at minimizing causes of risk. Cancer stands as one of the purest expressions of ordinary horror: an event inherent to our world and its horizon of expectations (inherent to the very functioning of our organism), and yet something that, once it appears in our life, starts corroding it from within, be it literally through the course of the disease or metaphorically via the specter of possible clinical complications, metastases, or recurrences.

Cancer and other similarly horrible diseases represent a profound shift in everyday life. They tend to be silent, often invisible menaces that can affect anyone, turning the familiar terrain of the body into something almost indefensible. For this reason, too, they intuitively evoke a form of horror that belongs to the ordinary—the unsettling realization that beneath the veneer of normalcy lies the potential for profound disturbance. Something that was once set aside as an unlikely possibility can come to rule a life. But perhaps even more disquietingly, an illness of such kind may also blend horror and the ordinary: everyday actions become infused with the creeping awareness that there is something unsettling happening to us, within us, as the grammar of our daily lives, our experiences, and our existential terrain are all altered.

The idea of "body horror" acquires a different connotation in this context, and in relation to cancer more specifically. Rather than emphasizing the grotesque or disturbing violation of corporeality, as in an external agent disfiguring it, the expression here also refers to how the body itself turns into the source of the horrifying: cancer *is* the body turning against itself, and represents a process of transformation that allows horror to arise from within the standard functioning of an organism. Cancer cells hijack the normal process of mitosis by overriding the regulatory mechanisms that control cell division, leading to unchecked and rapid proliferation. Simultaneously, they evade apoptosis—the programmed cell death meant to eliminate damaged or unnecessary cells. This evasion turns them into "zombie cells," accumulating in the body and forming tumors. This combination of relentless growth and resistance to death enables cancer cells to spread and invade other tissues. Perhaps more than anything else, the sense of horror evoked by this process arises from the body's own fundamental functions going awry: the forced powerlessness I connect to the experience of horror here lies in the fact that our body itself, in its very functioning, is incapable of halting a process of slow, painstaking self-destruction that unfolds right within us. From this perspective, horror also emerges from the breakdown in collaboration and coexistence of the parts that constitute the very fabric of our being: while our body is normally an ecosystem of cooperation, cancer renders that very ecosystem feral. The compounding nature of these elements ensures that, despite our mental defense mechanisms, to see someone being devoured by cancer may raise a creeping doubt, which, in turn, may lead to a newfound awareness of our fragility: if *this* is happening, why could it not happen *to me*?

Indeed, Berto's first reaction to his father's tumor is to think about himself, and whether he, too, will die of cancer (*Incubus*, 24). This anxiety will haunt Berto from this point on, and will, at times, erupt in moments of horror. A first example within the narrative takes place that very day at a movie theater, where Berto goes to seek some distraction. There, he realizes that the screening is in fact raw footage of his father in the surgery room, "with his mortal growth tied to his belly," instead of an actual film. Horrified, Berto leaves the movie theater and runs back to the hospital to make sure that his father is still alive (*Incubus*, 26).

How, and why, did a movie show footage of the tumor removed from the body of Berto's father? *Incubus* features several moments of such ambiguous status, where a hole is poked into the book's realism. These may well be hallucinations triggered by trauma—but more than what they are, I want to reflect on what these moments do. Building on the interrelations between horror and trauma that I traced in chapter 2—where I described "trauma" as an overarching temporal process, beginning with a horrific event that then ramifies through time—I see the departures from realism that Berto deploys as his way of conveying the horror that, however momentary and bound to the rekindling of trauma, seizes his present and casts his world into crisis. In other words, they represent a state of phenomenological crisis that is mirrored by a crisis of the text's aesthetic framework, which bends under the weight of a situation that can no longer be endured.

Berto himself fought in World War II, on the frontlines, where he became "pretty familiar with death" (*Incubus*, 46). And yet, pondering his father's fate, Berto realizes that of every form of death he witnessed, his father's was the cruelest one (*Incubus*, 24). This is a recurring theme in the book: no matter Berto's past experiences, each and every instantiation of the "*male oscuro*" trumps the previous one in (perceived) gravity and intensity, thus calling into question the very possibility of becoming habituated to it. Contrary to some of the Neapolitans in Ortese's *Chronicles*, who were so accustomed to the surrounding misery as to appear oblivious to it, the protagonist of *Incubus* never gets used to the bouts of this disease, and a phenomenology of horror must accordingly be wary of overdetermining its unfolding and consequences.

While the book's structure does not follow a strictly chronological sequence of events and is rife with analepses that address the author's youth, the core of Berto's struggle with his own "*male oscuro*" starts from his father's death in 1953 (incidentally, the year of publication of Ortese's *Chronicles*). A first episode takes place just a few months afterward, when, one day, Berto realizes that the color of his urine is darker than normal. This unexpected occurrence, which Berto takes as a symptom of a catastrophe he is bound to suffer, shakes the foundations of his already precarious psychological stability (*Incubus*, 95–96). He promptly begins his search for a cause, thus starting the epistemological and medical journey into the roots of his "*male oscuro*."

The outcome of several medical exams is a floating kidney diagnosis, which at first Berto takes as a manageable condition. Soon enough, however, a "disaster" crushes his hopes concerning the control he could still exert over his illness: a kind of pain that he describes as monstrous and unfair, something of a "new kind to me, never experienced [. . .] before," forces him to call a doctor in the middle of the night, and undergo another set of examinations (*Incubus*, 103–8). The new results: an ulcer that had been diagnosed in the past has grown to the point of perforating his duodenum, and he must undergo emergency surgery. Lamenting his own impotence ("I am no longer the one who guides the final events of my life" [*Incubus*, 112]), cursing the therapeutic obstinacy that prevents him from dying and instead keeps him in his Leopardian "garden of agonies," he starts thinking that perhaps not even his father had suffered that much (114).[54]

Berto's illness follows a pattern that emphasizes its constant novelty and overwhelming nature, as each new instantiation of his "*male oscuro*" is experienced as worse than the previous one. It never "gets better." On the contrary, it only "gets worse," and there are no coping mechanisms that can help Berto control his reactions, nor a clear way toward habituation. These new episodes are always fresh sources of horror, with their perceived, persistent novelty underpinning their overwhelmingness.

But apart from novelty and overwhelmingness, a compounding factor of distress is that there is also no clear reason for his suffering. A moment of horror may give us pause, prompting us to ask why and how such an event has befallen our life. But what if there is no reason to be found? And would a string of causes and effects provide a secure footing in the midst of a crisis? After Berto's belly is stitched back together post-operation, a nurse informs the bedridden patient that the doctor did not find anything in his stomach. There is no specific clinical explanation for Berto's agonies, and this becomes yet another source of horror—as he writes, "and at this last piece of news I'm in a cold sweat" (*Incubus*, 119–20). Still in search of a reason, the only one that Berto can think of is that the doctors discovered a tumor but decided against operating on it, leaving him with a "fatal cancer sewn back into my stomach" (*Incubus*, 120)—thus echoing his father's fate, worsened by epistemological and clinical opacity as the doctors keep him in the dark regarding his condition. Despite the health care providers' reassurances concerning the groundlessness of this hypothesis, Berto's skepticism persists. The following day the "terrible pains [come] back," and once again Berto is rendered powerless concerning the circumstances of his life (*Incubus*, 122).

Given the perceived novelty and overwhelming nature of each iteration of his "*male oscuro*," this autobiographical novel can then be read as the testimony of Berto's repeated encounters with forces that escape his control, and repeatedly cast his world into crisis. But since the protagonist also cannot find a reason why he suffers from his illness, the text is also the chronicle of Berto's repeated attempts at making sense of something that seems to escape any reason whatsoever.

A floating kidney that turned into an ulcer and then into renal tuberculosis is compounded by the "particularly depressing vicissitudes" that he suffered and still suffers from (*Incubus*, 131). None of this, according to Berto, can be attributed "to destiny or chance or to other forces which in their blindness are impartial or at least without any specific will to harm" (*Incubus*, 131–32)—in other words, there must be a clear and distinct reason, an identifiable cause behind his illness. But every time that some progress is achieved in charting this territory and his "*male oscuro*" starts appearing as something one could deal with, a new, unexpected development takes place.

After two weeks without abdominal cramping, Berto's hopefulness is shattered by a night that brings a "new and particularly calamitous dimension to the rest of my whole life" (*Incubus*, 137). This new instantiation of his illness appears even more inscrutable than all previous ones, and occurs as the protagonist lies in bed, reading crime news in search of inspiration for his writing. Right after having skimmed an article about the suicide of a young girl, Berto suffers from a new crisis:

> I suddenly feel a warm sensation towards the base of my back where there are the five lumbar vertebrae, that is at the very spot which from then on I call for good reasons the suicide spot, and that warmth exactly as if it were warm water suddenly gone mad begins to climb up my spine all along it rather hastily and ends up right in the cerebellum where it produces an inconceivable tumult, all of a sudden I feel overwhelmed with terror, my God this is death I say to myself without thinking that death can't be something so terrifying. (*Incubus*, 139)

Berto tries to stand up, but the sudden movement makes him lose his balance. Lying on the floor, he calls for help, but his dry and semi-paralyzed throat can only utter a "rattling and horrifying shout" (*Incubus*, 140). The pain he suffers from "isn't really pain but a kind of sickness in an immeasurable quantity," which causes an "exorbitant terror" whose cause remains unknown. According to the doctor who eventually visits him, Berto has suffered from a nervous breakdown. This diagnosis does not strike the protagonist as plausible: Berto affirms that "not even in the worst moments of my life when I was about to die" had he undergone anything similar, and therefore a mere mental collapse appears to him an unlikely explanation given the intensity of this most recent episode (*Incubus*, 141).

Once the crisis subsides, Berto reflects on the nature of what he has just experienced: to the exhausted protagonist, the events of the previous night represent the collapse of everything that his ancestors "had achieved along the path of reason" (*Incubus*, 142).[55] That is, if his illness remains untreatable, unknowable, and ultimately a source of horror, then the impression of safety and control over the world and its circumstances provided by modernity must be called into question.

This affirmation can be read in relation to the historical framework that I am proposing in this book, one that connects modernity with a struggle against that which escapes our control—the Cartesian project of becoming masters and possessors of nature. Undeniably, some of the most striking achievements in this regard have taken place in the field of medicine: vaccinations and antibiotics are just two examples of mankind's progressive taming of chance, the contingent, and the ecosystems we interact with.

While this, too, should remind us of the contextual nature of horror, underpinned as it is by the tools we can wield (after the discovery of penicillin, for example, infection became considerably less horrible to deal with), Berto's work shows that against the backdrop of this ever increasing degree of mastery over our surroundings, what renders us powerless constitutes a violent onslaught on the episteme modern individuals are embedded in and therefore used to. In Berto's case, as in many other similar situations, this is also aggravated by the curtain of opacity surrounding the nature of his illness: if modernity's agenda also revolves around dispersing the fog that shrouds the functioning of reality, then it should come as no surprise that dealing with our epistemological limits may cause great distress—especially when this affects our bodies and well-being.

To better understand why Berto believes that his illness and its effects undo reason's achievements, we must consider the phenomenological thickness of dealing with something of the nature of his "*male oscuro*." Novelty, overwhelmingness, opacity, and unpredictability are the four horsemen that make it horrifying: crucially, from a subjective point of view, none of these features exists as an abstract quality in isolation; rather, they are co-constructed by a subject actively interpreting and experiencing their world. In this sense, Berto's "*male oscuro*" emerges as a phenomenological event whose horror is felt through the mutable lens of personal vulnerability and uncertainty, rather than as a fixed ontological category. By insisting on the inwardness of this possible kind of ordinary horror—on its arising not from ruined streets or wartime devastation, but from the private terrain of the mind and body—*Incubus* reveals a landscape of suffering that persists also when external conditions appear for the most part secure, just as in the postwar Italy of the economic miracle.

Such a perspective does not deny the severity of historical horrors, or the possibility of their resurgence; rather, it highlights the existence of an interior battlefield where horror can seize control of a life despite material abundance and social progress. *Incubus* thus invites us to consider the limits of the seemingly inverse and linear correlation between economic prosperity and technological advancement, on the one hand, and existential suffering, on the other hand—something that those of us living in societies where material abundance is widespread are increasingly reckoning with, also as shown by the staggering number of people suffering from mental distress regardless of their material circumstances.

Instead of being able to find solace in modernity's outward achievements—that is, in what societies "had achieved along the path of reason"—Berto grapples with a horror grounded in the unpredictability and uncontrollability of his own body and psyche. This turn inward demands that we reckon with horror not only as a more or less distant wartime memory or a social ill soon to be eradicated, but as an unsettling possibility embedded in the fabric of everyday life. Horror is thus revealed as part of the ordinary, without for this reason being less than phenomenologically extraordinary when it takes hold of a life. Underneath a veneer of stability and normality, there opens "a world of fear into which I risked plunging at any moment without being able to realize the causes which made it happen" (*Incubus*, 142); this world is not always present, to be sure, but it lurks beneath the surface of ordinary life.

When Berto is cast into the "realms of terror and tears" by his illness (*Incubus*, 152), the collapse of his world goes so far as to alter its predictable geometry, further undoing the already damaged "path of reason." This is not merely a metaphorical reference to the aesthetics of deformation *Incubus* repeatedly leverages; it can be taken literally in a scene where a moment of crisis makes the protagonist call into question even the most familiar geometric concepts that underpin a reality of reliable sense-making: "I'm overwhelmed with terror [. . .] trembling and overwhelmed I stand still for a moment with my head in my hands and then pace up and down looking at those horrible tiles on the floor with the frightful designs that aren't straight my God why aren't they straight and now I see clearly that the floor itself isn't level it slopes all off to one side and off to the other, so the straight line no longer exists in any direction help" (*Incubus*, 207). The straight line no longer exists in a world where the "path of reason" has been shown to lead to a dead end. The event (*Ereignis*) of horror restructures Berto's perception of reality, and the collapse of his certainties affects how Berto sees his "*male oscuro*," too: unpredictable in its nature and effects, his disease no longer appears to him as something that follows a logic of consequentiality that would link causes to effects, symptoms to diagnosis. His illness, instead, is something "kind of a *sui generis* [. . .] that might even suddenly disappear if it chose," untreatable because unknowable (*Incubus*, 213). This revelation undermines the very possibility of finding a clear and distinct source for his "*male oscuro*," and thus compounds the forced powerlessness that it brought to Berto's life.

As the story progresses, rather than being cured, Berto's "*male oscuro*" is increasingly externalized, and the reader slowly understands that the book in their hands is the outcome of such a process. This externalization needs an objective correlative—a role in the novel fulfilled by Berto's brain, which also suggests the strong psychological nature of his illness. The beginning of the novel is mirrored by a later scene in which Berto sees "my brain outside my body with all the bloody spirals that brains generally have," reminiscent of the "cancer extracted from the viscera of my father." The brain, however, "isn't death and cancer it is fear of the abyss and darkness beyond death" (*Incubus*, 250). This apparition, too, does not lead to any revelation, but instead reinforces a sense of opacity and powerlessness regarding a future rife with horrors even beyond death. The episode, too, as the reader has come to expect, is described as novel and overwhelming: "I had never felt anything so terrifying [. . .] I never suffered anything that awful before" (*Incubus*, 250–51). But the reader, of course, is not the narrating protagonist, and what the former is now used to is not equivalent to how the latter experiences such events.

The externalization of Berto's "*male oscuro*" acquires further symbolic value once read against the backdrop of the novel's third epigraph: "Painful are these things to relate, but silence too is painful." Externalization becomes connected to expression: to relate is to scream, for the horror within cannot be borne inside any longer. In the end, after having tried morphine and tranquilizers, Berto finds in psychoanalytic therapy, and then in writing, the most effective tools to respond to the illness affecting him. In a structural plot twist that makes the book's content address its form, the writing process itself of the autobiographical novel *Incubus* becomes the most effective treatment available to the protagonist.

Therapy and writing become epistemological tools, ways for Berto to make sense of, and reclaim control over, the overwhelming bouts of his illness. In being so, they both respond to a certain desire "of order, of logic, of clarity" that was upended by the opacity and unpredictability of Berto's disease.[56] All that matters, as the protagonist realizes and, at the same time, confesses near the end of the novel, "is to achieve a serene evaluation of oneself in relation to reality"; while this is "easier said than done," the alternative to screaming is to remain paralyzed (*Incubus*, 372).

Looking back at *Chronicles*, in Ortese's case also writing becomes the preferred way of addressing her neurosis, which she, too, calls "*male oscuro*." But whereas for Ortese such neurosis was largely due to her irritation against reality, and in particular concerning the living conditions of postwar Naples, in Berto's novel it presupposes a degree of inwardness, as it is bound to an illness that for a good part transcends external circumstances.

Their differences notwithstanding, for both authors expression becomes charged with the pathos of existential urgency. But expression, as we saw for Ortese, is a necessity rather than a solution: at times we simply cannot hold back our screams—and Koestler reminds us that nothing guarantees that anyone will pay attention to them. Perhaps rather than the final word, a scream is better understood as a point of departure. This echoes the last page of *Incubus*, where Berto confesses that despite having embraced therapy and writing, he is still ill and most likely will never fully heal; yet, he continues, "I am healed to the extent that I so desperately wanted to heal, that is, I am no longer afraid to write."[57]

The outcome of expression may indeed be precarious and not conclusive, but whereas horror involves powerlessness and paralysis, the outburst of a scream evokes, at a minimum, the desperate desire for agency and action. With great differences in form and content, Ortese and Berto invite us to consider that life, even in the absence of extreme circumstances, can turn horrifying. When this happens, they seem to suggest, screaming may be a necessary first step to keep moving forward.

"WE, THE SCREAMERS": CONCLUSION

In the concluding paragraphs of "The Nightmare That Is a Reality," Koestler reflects on the effects that screamers have on society. He does so by recounting the story of a "well-known London publisher" who organized meetings in the United States to raise awareness concerning the atrocities taking place in Europe. Before each meeting the publisher "used to lock himself up in a room, close his eyes, and imagine in detail, for twenty minutes, that he was one of the people in Poland who were being killed." He would then walk out to the platform and talk, until, after one year, "he collapsed with a nervous breakdown." This man faced the *male oscuro* of his time and exposed it to his audiences. According to Koestler, "one should imitate this example," even at risk of suffering from the same mental collapse that befell the Londoner.[58]

This chapter focused on two authors who, although in contexts vastly different from World War II, became screamers of their times and suffered from a neurosis deeply entangled with their own *male oscuro*. Faced with the ordinary horrors of their lives, Ortese and Berto could not remain silent, and for both expression became a necessity. They addressed this matter from a perspective that remained anchored to the individual rather than leaning toward more choral forms of narration, with their works gesturing toward a reality that is ultimately unknowable, undecipherable, and only partially capable of being improved. While this marks their distance from neorealism, they arguably remain close to the movement's ethos in their desire to bear witness, narrate, and scream.[59]

For both Ortese and Berto, being a writer meant transposing onto the page the most disturbing features of their worlds. But as Koestler reminds us, the screamers' unsettling revelations can trigger in their audiences defense mechanisms that may result in ostracizing those who cannot stay silent. Ortese knew this all too well: as she recalls in her preface to *Chronicles*, her book was "judged to be 'anti-Naples,'" and its crude description of the living conditions of some of city's poorest districts effectively forced the author to leave the Parthenopean city. As Ortese herself writes in a 1980 essay, those who go against the grain, and in moments of generalized hope still stubbornly show how life can turn into a "dump and slaughterhouse," are bound to be attacked as "saboteurs and visionaries."[60]

Berto did not face such harsh personal repercussions due to the more inward-looking nature of his work, but he, too, as De Michelis highlights, "took upon himself [. . .] the task of showing the nature of evil to those who strive not to see it, denouncing its unspeakable horror."[61] Following the path traced by Italo Svevo's *Zeno's Conscience* and Gadda's *The Experience of Pain*, Berto's novel describes how illness remains an overpowering force that can turn a life into a nightmare, and is only partly addressable by societal progress.

Their shared status as screamers is a fourth point of contact between Ortese and Berto, in addition to the three that I highlighted at the start of this chapter. The horrors they describe may lack the spectacularity of those of the eponymous genre, but are undeniably more common and concrete. In the context of *Ordinary Horror,* too, they possess a uniquely disquieting status, given their close proximity to our lives: while few among us are likely to experience (or so we hope) anything comparable to roaming a Europe gone *kaputt* or surviving the daily life of the Lager, can the same be said about the possibility of encountering abject poverty or an overpowering illness? A walk through the downtowns of some of the most prosperous American cities offers a reminder, for those willing to see, of how extraordinary wealth coexists with miserable living conditions. Debilitating diseases, too, are likely presences that haunt our lives, either as we experience them ourselves or deal with them indirectly through our loved ones.

Ortese and Berto are two screamers fit for our time: their works depict horrors that are widespread and often normalized in society, horrors that remain unaddressed also because their exorcism cannot be taken for granted. With deeply unsettling, yet never hopeless or solely bleak prose, they invite us to consider that some of the most disquieting features of our present are those that hide in plain sight, and that we tend to dismiss or minimize: they are the "*mali oscuri*" that fill up the lungs of yesterday's and today's screamers. According to Koestler, we should at least lend our ears to these individuals, who, while coming across as maniacs, may in fact be pointing at horrors that we are still unwilling to accept or even see. Such heightened sensitivity will not immediately lead to a solution, but it will be a step in the direction of awareness, preparedness, and empathy: "Two minutes of this kind of exercise per day, with closed eyes, after reading the morning paper, are at present more necessary to us than physical jerks and breathing the Yogi way. It may even be a substitute for going to church. For as long as there are people on the road and victims in the thicket, divided by dream barriers, this will remain a phony civilization."[62]

FIVE

TO MAKE HORROR CONCRETE: ELENA FERRANTE

I have taught the garden scene from Giacomo Leopardi's *Zibaldone* that opens this book in several classes.[1] Every time, my students' reactions remind me of how unrelatable that passage is for most people. I am told that Leopardi's description of a garden as a horrifying torture chamber overlooks the beauty of the natural world, and that his pessimism is questionable at best: is *everything*—every single thing that exists—evil? Only after a laborious journey through some of the basic assumptions of Leopardi's philosophy do I receive the benefit of the doubt, and we reach the conclusion that his horror-garden can be read as a very specific exploration of something not as neutral as may initially appear.

Nevertheless, my students' reluctance merits consideration. Leopardi's view of that Bolognese garden is indeed alien to most of us. What makes it so distant from our common-sense experience of the world? If a skeptical reader of Leopardi is pressed enough, they might admit that, yes, everything withers and dies; yes, everything is preyed upon by overpowering and somewhat indifferent forces; and yes, the experience of suffering appears to be widespread. However, for many, these would be reluctant concessions at best. It is simply quite implausible to experience a well-tended garden as a torture chamber, especially in springtime, and especially in Italy. Leopardi's description may not strike the reader as very concrete; for many, it represents a rather abstract and counterintuitive philosophical exercise.

In the light of this, it is surprising that the most recent Italian literary sensation—one that has sold more than 15 million copies and been translated into more than forty-five languages, and whose main work has been ranked as the best book of the twenty-first century by the *New York Times*[2]—is anchored to a Leopardian worldview and features a Leopardian protagonist. I am referring to Elena Ferrante's Neapolitan Quartet, published between 2011 and 2014, and to the character of Raffaella Cerullo, better known as Lila, Elena Greco's brilliant friend. As I will show, not only does Ferrante directly refer to the Leopardian garden and to Leopardi more broadly—calling him "the most extraordinary of Italian poets"[3]—but crucially, several key scenes of her own Neapolitan Quartet echo the *Zibaldone*'s garden passage: they depict in horrified terms something that would generally be represented in a significantly more positive light, as when Lila describes the starry sky as a jumble of glass shards adrift in a tar-like substance.

Yet, despite these somewhat off-putting observations, readers consider Ferrante's female characters as extraordinarily relatable, and Ferrante is praised as a clear-sighted and enthralling storyteller of women's lives. Critics and journalists have even referred to a worldwide "Ferrante Fever"—the compulsion that drives people to binge-read Ferrante's novels.[4] What is it, then, that makes Lila's starry sky more relatable than Leopardi's garden?

Italian philosopher Adriana Cavarero, a philosopher read and admired by Ferrante,[5] emphasizes the importance of narrativity in Ferrante's success. For Cavarero, the effectiveness of Ferrante's characters stems from their being built around and through networks of concrete events: "It is the narratable self inserted within the *relationality of concrete situations* that determines the specific, universally appreciated quality of Ferrante's books."[6] Lila's Leopardian description of the starry sky does not just suddenly appear on the page: it follows the tumultuous narration of years of her life, and these fictive events, cast against the backdrop of real historical happenings, underpin its plausibility within Lila's worldview and story. Thanks to the relationality of concrete situations that Cavarero highlights and that form Lila as a narratable character, a reader might find Lila's sky less jarring, and conversely more plausible, than Leopardi's garden, regardless of how both arguably depart from our everyday experience of the natural world. This chapter reconstructs this process and, in so doing, addresses a question that has haunted this book: how can we most effectively convey what may come across as unbelievable, as is the case for many horrifying experiences?

Leopardi's bleakest formulations of his ideas are found in his philosophical diary, the *Zibaldone*, whereas his fictional *Moral Essays* are, in general, of a lighter tone. Ferrante inverts this split: her fiction, of which the Neapolitan Novels constitute the major work, is where readers encounter the most horror-stricken pages, while her essays and letters constitute a more controlled, less visceral set of reflections on horror-adjacent topics. The reasons behind this choice are addressed by Ferrante herself in an exchange with journalist Stefania Scateni, which first appeared in the Italian newspaper *L'Unità*. In answering the interviewer's questions about the crude realism in gendered matters of one of her earlier novels, *The Days of Abandonment*, Ferrante argues that lies, and in particular the lies we tell ourselves, are what dilute "the horrors of our time." The duty of the literary author is to counter this tendency: "When one writes one must never lie. In literary fiction you have to be sincere to the point where it's unbearable, otherwise the pages will be empty" (*FR*, 80).[7]

In other words, and to connect this to Cavarero's passage quoted above, Ferrante argues that the narrative space is where our lives' concrete horrors should be depicted. This recalls Ortese, another author admired by Ferrante, for whom horror is linked to concrete aspects of reality, such as poverty. In Ferrante's case, as in Ortese's, the invitation to pay attention to the ordinary, concrete horrors of the world is ethical as well as aesthetic, responding to the need to display the horrors of our time that we may dismiss or be reluctant to face.

In an email exchange with journalist Nicola Lagioia published in the newspaper *Repubblica*, Ferrante states that, while she finds comfort in narratives where horror is overcome, she does not believe in them: "I'm comforted by stories that emerge through horror to a turning point, stories in which someone is redeemed as confirmation that peace and happiness are possible, or that one can return to a private or public Eden. But I tried to write stories like that, long ago, and I discovered that I didn't believe in them" (*FR*, 373).[8] What seizes Ferrante's attention, and compels her to craft the "relationality of concrete situations" that Cavarero highlights, are "fiction[s] [*finzioni*]" that "arise from a profound crisis of all our illusions," and that bear the traces of "firsthand knowledge of the terrible, and hence an awareness that they *are* unreal, that they will not hold up for long against the collisions" (*FR*, 373).[9] Whereas Leopardi's later work considers the production of illusions a tool that modernity can no longer leverage to engender feelings of greatness and happiness, for Ferrante the shattering of such consolatory illusions and the awareness of their fictive and transitory nature is what sets her storytelling in motion. This takes place through what Ferrante calls "collisions"—collisions, as we shall see, caused by the jaggedness of our lives, which may cause a crisis of one's illusions of stability and control.

Ferrante's literary works depict several moments of crisis. These are moments when her protagonists catch a glimpse of, or sometimes fully plunge into, the "terrible [*tremendo*]" that Ferrante refers to in the passage above. Indeed, Ferrante is attracted to those stories that dwell in horror, rather than those where horror functions as a means for a positive resolution. In her work, a moment of horror is not necessarily something edifying; as I argue in this book, horror does not necessarily possess redemptive qualities.

The word that Ferrante uses to describe these moments is *smarginare*—the "dissolving of boundaries," as the term is commonly translated in English.[10] *Smarginatura* is a fraught, yet well-established matter in Ferrante scholarship, also thanks to authorial emphasis on its importance. Broadly speaking, a moment of *smarginatura* is one when things fall apart. These are moments when someone's reality assumes disquieting traits, and the precarious control exerted over one's world collapses. As Ferrante herself writes, "when shapes lose their contours we take a glimpse into the terrible [*Lo smarginarsi delle forme è un affacciarsi sul tremendo*]" (*FR*, 373).[11]

Smarginatura, I argue, is both the name Ferrante gives to an experience *and* the aesthetics of the retelling of that experience: crucially, in a moment of *smarginatura*, the crumbling of the protagonist's world goes hand in hand with the interpolation of deforming descriptions that depart from Ferrante's usual realism through a distortion of objects and persons. During a moment of *smarginatura*, as we shall see, fireworks can turn into razor-sharp blades, or someone's body and their car may start melting and blending together.

I consider Ferrante's *smarginatura* as a means of narrating the horror her protagonists experience. Critics have, in passing, used the term "horror" and its derivatives to talk about *smarginatura*.[12] From the perspective of ordinary language philosophy this is reassuring, as it suggests an intuitive connection between the horrifying and *smarginatura*. Expanding on this intuitive connection, this chapter provides a first study of how horror and *smarginatura* intersect. Given her explicit coinage of a term to describe this entanglement of aesthetics and phenomenology, I place Ferrante as the culmination of this book's canon of authors: authors who depict the event (*Ereignis*) of horror, beyond the horror genre, through what I term aesthetics of deformation.

This allows for a different contextualization of Ferrante's presence in the Italian canon, offering an alternative to the (legitimate and well-founded) tendency to read her work alongside other female authors or as world literature.[13] It also bypasses speculations related to Ferrante's identity. In accordance with this book's methodology, by taking what we encounter on the page at face value, concerns of authorial authenticity regarding what is narrated become secondary. Instead of declaring the author dead, I more humbly propose to leave the author aside in this analysis of *smarginatura*'s aesthetics and phenomenology.

Indeed, the gendered matters that concern us here are not the authorial ones. They are, more fittingly in the context of this book, those that belong to the written page: they are the gendered, ordinary stories that Ferrante narrates and the gendered, ordinary horrors present in them.[14] Ferrante's books are a compendium of betrayals, crises, rapes, and more. The experiences they depict largely reflect a specific flavor of the horrifying that belongs to contexts where gendered relations are informed by asymmetrical power dynamics. Insofar as one of this book's goals is to explore how horror hides in plain sight in modern societies, this example of the horrifying allows us to study how gendered matters of forced powerlessness were, and to some extent still are, common in postwar Italy, even after women gained the right to vote in 1945, to divorce in 1970, or to abort in 1978.

At the same time, I will argue that Ferrante's work engages with horror beyond gendered matters: Ferrante's *smarginatura* is also informed by a set of authorial reflections on matters more generally tied to human impotence and the limits of the control we can exert over the circumstances of our lives. This engagement with matters of agency or the lack thereof—an engagement overlooked by critics and one that I reconstruct also through her nonfiction—underpins her novels' horror scenes. In unwinding this thread, I establish a dialogue between horror as a gendered matter and horror as a more universal experience, without overlapping the two or eliding the former's specificities, which are central in Ferrante's texts.

The ties between Ferrante and the horror genre have been the subject of in-depth studies. One of the first to blaze this critical trail was Stiliana Milkova, who demonstrated Ferrante's extensive reuse of the horror genre's motifs, ranging from aesthetics and affects like disgust, the abject, and the monstrous to objects like dolls, needles, and sharp tools, and even to actions like eating, chewing, and piercing.[15] But is Ferrantian horror solely a matter of reuse of horror genre tropes? My study argues that horror is a more pervasive and constitutive element of her work, one that almost amounts to a theory of (ordinary) horror. This chapter therefore approaches her work through my book's established phenomenological lens, centering on matters of powerlessness and the stylistic techniques deployed to describe them.

The first two sections of this chapter analyze two key terms in Ferrante's production and their connection to the topic of horror: the first is *smarginatura*, and the second is *frantumaglia*. This is achieved primarily through a character study of Lila, and in particular of what I argue is one of her most defining traits: her genius in maximizing the control she exerts over her life's circumstances despite the patriarchal societal structures of the *rione* (quarter), a control that both *smarginatura* and *frantumaglia* call into question. The third section then delves into what happens to Lila when her resourcefulness is shattered by events she cannot overcome. In the conclusion of this chapter I provide a reading of Lila's disappearance, which serves as the event that opens and closes the Neapolitan Quartet.

With Ferrante, my book continues its journey through the Italian twentieth century and reaches the beginnings of the twenty-first. While chapters 2 through 4 each paired two authors together and established through horror links between writers not typically studied comparatively, I here look back at the foundational figure of this project and reveal what makes Ferrante, perhaps surprisingly, more Leopardian than usually imagined, thus providing the first comprehensive study of Leopardi's influence on Ferrante.[16] These comparative analyses reveal a coherent, yet subterranean thread that courses through modern Italian literature—one that coalesces around a set of aesthetic motifs variously deployed to depict horrifying experiences in different contexts by authors rarely analyzed together. For all of these authors, a crucial, albeit at times implicit, question is how to make horror concrete. This chapter articulates Ferrante's answer.

THE HORROR UNRAVELING: *SMARGINATURA*

Can fireworks be horrifying? According to the eighteenth-century philosopher Edmund Burke, the apparent disorder of firework explosions, with their seemingly infinite profusion of colors, is what makes them magnificent.[17] The magnificent, for Burke, is a source of the sublime, which he defines as "the strongest emotion which the mind is capable of feeling."[18] He also concedes that in the sublime there is a "degree of horror" at play, due to the astonishment that the sublime causes—with astonishment being "that state of the soul in which all its motions are suspended."[19]

The connection of fireworks to the magnificent, to the sublime, to astonishment, and finally, to horror relies on a somewhat convoluted path. One may indeed follow it and understand why the path was traced in the first place, but horror, as with Leopardi's garden, is not the first thing that comes to mind for most people as they enjoy a firework show. In general, fireworks are launched during celebrations, and the spectacle they provide captivates adults and children alike.

An example of a festivity celebrated with fireworks is New Year's Eve. On December 31, 1958, Elena and Lila, the two protagonists of Ferrante's Neapolitan Novels, are with their friends: lightly dressed in order to appeal to their male peers, they stand cold and shivering on a rooftop in Naples—a city where to this day, at the turn of the year, countless people still invest a substantial amount of effort in firework displays. Lila, too, worked on the preparations for the celebration, and yet, for seemingly no reason, her experience of the fireworks turns in a matter of minutes into something horrifying.

The narration of Lila's first substantial episode of *smarginatura* takes place through Elena's words, just like everything else in the Neapolitan Quartet, as she retrospectively retells the story of her brilliant friend. With a phenomenological twist, that night of 1958, everything around Lila suddenly acquires a strange aura, to the point that the contours of her world shatter ("she had the impression that something [. . .] was breaking down the outlines of persons and things and revealing itself"). In the midst of the celebration, Lila "had begun to feel horror." A new, threatening reality starts taking over, as the excited screams and gestures of her friends turn disquieting.[20]

The mutation that Lila's brother undergoes is the most appalling one:

> It was—she told me—as if, on the night of a full moon over the sea, the intense black mass of a storm advanced across the sky, swallowing every light, eroding the circumference of the moon's circle, and disfiguring the shining disk, reducing it to its true nature of rough insensate material. Lila imagined, she saw, she felt—as if it were true—her brother break. Rino, before her eyes, lost the features he had had as long as she could remember [. . .]. There, amid the violent explosions, in the cold, in the smoke that burned the nostrils and the strong odor of sulfur, something violated the organic structure of her brother, exercising over him a pressure so strong that it broke down his outlines, and the matter expanded like a magma, showing her what he was truly made of. Every second of that night horrified her, she had the impression that, as Rino moved, as he expanded around himself, every margin collapsed and her own margins, too, became softer and more yielding. (*BF*, 176–77)

Similar horrific deformations of the human body appeared in the work of Carlo Michelstaedter. Here, too, the narrator clarifies that what we are invited to consider is a matter of phenomenology rather than something that could lead us toward a supernatural explanation of the scene—with the phenomenological thickness of the scene emphasized by the three verbs that open the quotation, and the parenthetical "as if it were true." However, whereas in Michelstaedter the creatures who undergo a process of deformation are anonymous caretakers, here the mutation affects Lila's brother—"the person she loved the most" (*BF*, 90).

What is it that may make a firework show a horrifying spectacle, one that can trigger such turmoil? We learn more about this episode in the fourth volume of the Neapolitan Quartet, *Story of the Lost Child*, when Lila, in 1980, talks for the first time to Elena about the *smarginatura* of 1958's New Year's Eve. There, she confesses that the source of her horror was the color of the fireworks, in particular the green and the purple as they appeared distinctively sharp to Lila's eyes ("the green and the purple especially were razor-like"); this made her fear that they could cut open Rino's skin, and through those wounds would "drip out of him" a second and horrifying brother.[21] The doppelgänger who lives under Rino's skin is a creature that would hurt Lila if she did not immediately push him back inside.

This scene is jarring when read against the backdrop of Ferrante's realism. How can we take it at face value within the nexus of concrete and plausible events that make the Neapolitan Quartet so readable and relatable? What is the purpose of this departure from verisimilitude? Throughout *Ordinary Horror* we have encountered several instances of this literary technique: the interpolation of deforming aesthetics into an otherwise realistic framework to describe horrifying experiences is present, although differently conjugated, in every author discussed thus far. Each time, I emphasized the entanglement of phenomenology and aesthetics: a description may momentarily depart from realistic standards to convey the individual crisis that horror evokes and responds to.

Ferrante's term for these moments and this literary technique is *smarginatura*. *Smarginare* literally means to go beyond the margins, and the word traffics in a semantic field that evokes a certain absence of control concerning the crossing of such borders—aesthetic borders and the borders of our comfort as well. Crucially, the crossing is forced; *smarginare*, in Ferrante's use of the word, is not an exuberant and willed overcoming of fixed structures.[22]

As this first scene suggests, *smarginatura* occurs when the subject is overwhelmed by a present situation. This, in turn, calls into question the limits of their control over the world and its circumstances. The event (*Ereignis*) of *smarginatura* unravels and reshapes the reality experienced by the subject: what was once a known, controlled, and controllable place now turns horrifying. Such a shift is rendered, aesthetically speaking, through a deforming description that momentarily departs from the text's realism. It is important to remember that Lila's *smarginatura* affects only *her* perception of the world; while Elena can sense a certain disquietude coming from her friend, everyone else on the rooftop remains excited by the celebration. With this framework set, we are in a better position to understand the dynamics of this scene, particularly as they involve Rino, the figure most affected by Lila's *smarginatura*.

Lila's beloved brother is an ambivalent character in Ferrante's tetralogy. Just as ambitious as his younger sister, Rino shares Lila's contempt for how their Neapolitan *rione* is ruled by corruption and crime. He is also one of the first to recognize Lila's remarkable intelligence, and, in an act of subversion of the stiff family hierarchies of the time, Rino confronts his parents when they refuse to keep Lila in school and demand that she support the family by working. At the same time, Lila's brother is fully embedded in the neighborhood's patriarchal mores and culture of male violence.

Rino's most striking act of violence directed toward Lila takes place just before New Year's Eve. A disagreement about a shoe model that they were working on to help expand their father's cobbler business results in Rino's sudden fit of rage, which leads him to threaten Lila with a shoe anvil that he almost throws at his sister. Elena, appalled, witnesses this episode and notices a transformation in Rino's features that predates the one Lila will experience on the rooftop. The reader never learns about Lila's recollection of the scene; the narrator simply states that for days after the episode she sounds "a little sad" (*BF*, 165).

The hidden Rino whose appearance Lila worries about on New Year's Eve is the one who was menacingly wielding the shoe anvil, one whose aggressive instincts overpower his love for his sister. The very night of Lila's *smarginatura*, Rino is engaged in an attempt at proving that his group can assert its dominance over the neighborhood, by staging the most impressive firework display. While not violent in itself, this activity ends up emphasizing his masculine violent traits. Rino's attempts at displaying dominance are met by the Solaras, the mafioso family that rules the *rione*. All the members of Rino's group are "cheerful, aggressive, dark figures carried away by the party, the food, the sparkling wine," and they utter "unbearable atrocities," but Rino's frenzy is so palpable that even his already overexcited peers try to calm him down, with no success (*BF*, 85–86). The confrontation between the two groups escalates to the point that the Solaras, once they run out of fireworks, start shooting with a gun to trump their neighbors. Everyone runs back inside except Rino, who is still bent over the railing, raging against the opposing faction, until he is eventually pulled back inside by his sister Lila, who has snapped out of her horror-driven paralysis.

Lila's *smarginatura* is a reaction to a context that escapes her control. Throughout the Neapolitan Quartet, her character develops as one whose actions are largely aimed at maximizing the reach of her control over the world and its circumstances while, in return, minimizing the space of the unexpected and her powerlessness. In a letter, Lila tells Elena about a copper pot that once exploded in her kitchen for no apparent reason. While the causes behind this mystery are never fully clarified, the retelling of the episode to her friend brings Lila to admit that "It's this sort of thing [. . .] that frightens me. More than Marcello [a Solara whose advances she rejected], more than anyone. And I feel that I have to find a solution, otherwise, everything, one thing after another, will break, everything, everything" (*BF*, 229).

Chain reactions beyond her control are what horrify Lila. In the case of the firework display, this translates into her impotence regarding Rino's outbursts of masculine violence, symbolized by the creature living under her brother's skin. These are moments when Lila—the resourceful and brilliant Lila—experiences a form of forced powerlessness, to describe her phenomenology with the definition of horror proposed in this book.

Lila's world is one where gendered violence, or the possibility thereof, is the norm; it is a world where situations may at any time escalate violently. As a woman in such a patriarchal context, the control Lila seeks to exert over her life is inherently precarious. Her marriage, too, is an attempt to overcome these structural limitations and thus exert greater control over the circumstances of her and her family's life: Stefano Carracci, a bully from the *rione* whom she ends up marrying, appears to Lila as a means to escape Marcello Solara's proposals, and, through the money Stefano inherited from his deceased father, as an investor for her family's cobbler shop. However, this attempt is likewise troubled by the very force that Lila sought to overcome: patriarchal violence, this time as exerted by her husband himself, who, during their honeymoon, undergoes a transformation similar to the one that her brother underwent.

This takes place not on a rooftop but in a hotel bedroom, when Stefano realizes that Lila is not going to consent to the consummation of the marriage and thus takes her by force. If Ferrantian horror, as I argue, is tied to powerlessness, the absence of control that rape evokes indeed epitomizes the horrifying. The connection between horror and rape diffuses through the work of thinkers connected to difference feminism, especially Cavarero[23]—thinkers well known to Ferrante and who have influenced her writing, as she discusses in two exchanges with Goffredo Fofi (*FR*, 59, 77). In Ferrante's fiction, the horror of sexual violence connects to *smarginatura* and a specific form of masculine violence. Stefano's rape of Lila is predicated on his projected image of what masculinity means; he tells himself: "be a man, Ste'; either you subdue her now or you will never subdue her; your wife has to learn right away that she is the female and you're the male and therefore she has to obey."[24] As Lila is raped, she starts noticing that her husband's skin is cracking, and from underneath emerges, just as in Rino's case, another figure: "Don Achille was rising from the muck of the neighborhood, feeding on the living matter of his son. The father was cracking his skin, changing his gaze, exploding out of his body" (*SNN*, 41). It is not a doppelgänger this time, but instead Don Achille, Stefano's deceased father, an usurer whose violence and cruelty were well known in the *rione*. Lila makes another attempt at pushing Stefano away while repressing the horror she experiences ("she, as she had always been able to do, repressed her horror" [*SNN*, 41]), but the rape is fully consummated once Lila realizes that Stefano "would certainly kill her" if she kept resisting (*SNN*, 42).

The passage suggests that Lila's familiarity with horror and her tendency to repress it have deep roots in her past. Indeed, Lila's exposure to masculine violence can be traced back to her father, Fernando. Early in the novel, readers learn that in a fit of rage he threw Lila out of a window, breaking her arm as she landed on the asphalt; Lila later associates the feeling of falling with the *smarginatura* she experienced in 1958 (*BF*, 91). Fernando, like Stefano, is presented as a decent man within the context of the *rione*, "a kind, sympathetic man, a hard worker," but he, too, "when he lost his head turned ugly" (*BF*, 81). In the *rione*, masculine violence is embedded in the structure of society and everyday life: just as everyone agrees that "all fathers had fits of anger" (*BF*, 81), a man must learn to "be a man" and assert his will, even if that involves taking his wife by force (*SNN*, 41). But regardless of its societal normalization, experiencing such violence remains horrifying, as is the case for many of the female protagonists of Ferrante's novels.

The horrors lurking beneath the *rione*'s patriarchal norms often involve gendered experiences of forced powerlessness for those who suffer from the violent outbursts of their fathers, husbands, and brothers. These horrors acquire meaning beyond horror-genre motifs such as the monstrous, the grotesque, and the repellent, although Ferrante's deforming descriptions may draw upon such motifs.[25] However, these motifs are not symbols that stand in for something else; rather, they serve to describe the monstrous, grotesque, repellent reality that Ferrante's female characters at times inhabit. Despite *smarginatura*'s departure from realism, and in line with Cavarero's ideas, Ferrante's horror scenes strike us as both plausible and chilling due to the relationality of concrete situations that underpins them. It is through these principles that a firework display can become horrifying. We find the scenes horrifying, in other words, also because we know that similar scenes have happened, are happening, and will happen in the real world as well.

The events of Lila's adolescence and young adulthood are categorized as *smarginatura* only in retrospect. While Ferrante does not reveal when Lila originally coined the term, we know that it is in 1980 that she provides Elena with a full account of the phenomenon and reflects on its broader implications. To gain a better understanding of *smarginatura*, its role in the Neapolitan Quartet, and its connection to the understanding of horror developed in this book, we must first consider the philosophical underpinnings of *smarginatura* and what enables it in the first place: *frantumaglia*.

THE HORROR BENEATH: *FRANTUMAGLIA*

The importance of *frantumaglia* is made clear by a paratextual element of Ferrante's production: the term serves as the title of a collection of Ferrante's essays and interviews spanning 1991 to 2016.[26] Title notwithstanding, a reader looking for a clear and distinct definition of *frantumaglia* will be disappointed: while Ferrante discusses the topic at length and in numerous instances, she does not provide an unambiguous explanation of it. Instead, she piles up a set of reflections, sometimes contradictory in nature. This definitory confusion echoes the essence of what *frantumaglia* is.

Ferrante writes that the term comes from her mother, who used *frantumaglia* ("she pronounced it *frantummàglia*") to describe the state she experienced when torn by contradictory impressions of the same thing. Depressive and mysterious in its nature, *frantumaglia*, in her mother's understanding, "referred to a miscellaneous crowd of things in her head, debris in a muddy water of the brain" (*FR*, 99).

As Ferrante acknowledges, it is now too late to ask her mother what she truly meant by that word. Ferrante thus provides a "catalogue of images, but they have more to do with my problems [Ferrante's] than with hers [her mother's]" (*FR*, 100). *Frantumaglia* is "an unstable landscape, an infinite aerial or aquatic mass of debris that appears to the I, brutally, as its true and unique inner self," but also "the storehouse of a time without the orderliness of a history, a story," and "an effect of the sense of loss, when we're sure that everything that seems to us stable, lasting, an anchor for our life, will soon join that landscape of debris that we seem to see." A landscape, storehouse, and effect alike, *frantumaglia* is connected to matters of perception and expression as well: regarding perception, "*frantumaglia* is to perceive with excruciating anguish the heterogeneous crowd from which we, living, raise our voice, and the heterogeneous crowd into which it is fated to vanish"; regarding expression, "it's only my way of describing the anguish of death, the fear that the capacity to express myself would get stuck—as if the organs of speech had been paralyzed—and everything I'd learned to control, from the first year of life until now, would start fluctuating on its own, dripping or hissing out of a body becoming a thing, a leather sack leaking air and liquids" (*FR*, 100).

Amid this vortex of definitions (Ferrante entitles "Vortexes" the subsection of her essay "La frantumaglia" where these definitions are taken from), some common elements emerge. *Frantumaglia* refers to that which is multiple, as exemplified by Ferrante's use of terms like "landscape," "deposit," "infinite," "everything," or "heterogeneous crowd." However, this is not a positive multitude but one that is or may soon become threatening and overwhelming—much like the troubling, rather than exuberant, crossing of boundaries in *smarginatura*. *Frantumaglia*'s multitude is threatening because it escapes the subject's desire for control over it: Ferrante emphasizes a certain sense of loss and anguish stemming from the awareness that things may break down or fall apart, and eventually they will wither away. This refers both to the inevitability of one's death and, perhaps more important, to the limits of the control we can exert over the circumstances of our lives.

Milkova writes that "to be afflicted with frantumaglia is to acknowledge—and to submit to—the protocols of a universal patriarchy."[27] While Ferrante certainly inflects the topic from a gendered perspective, it is important to also identify the broader implications of *frantumaglia*. The creeping sense of impotence that *frantumaglia* evokes and responds to should first be located at the level of human finitude and the absence of control, before it can be coherently understood in the context of patriarchy and (re)signified in fiction via the specific experiences of the women who populate Ferrante's books.

Ferrante links the instability symptomatic of *frantumaglia* to the history of gender and to the formation of the female Self: "the female 'I,' in particular, with its long history of oppression and repression, tends to shatter as it's tossed around, and to reappear and shatter again, always in an unpredictable way" (*FR*, 322). While this gendered thrust is central, *frantumaglia* is underpinned by a broader set of reflections tied to matters of powerlessness, overwhelmingness, and the absence of control that make it a universal condition. In these regards, *frantumaglia*'s capaciousness becomes clear in an exchange with Turkish journalist Yasemin Çongar, where Ferrante argues that "*frantumaglia* is the part of us that escapes any reduction to words or other shapes, and that in moments of crisis dissolves the entire order within which it seemed to us we were stably inserted" (*FR*, 302).

The verb "to dissolve" is key here, as it brings us back to the topic of *smarginatura*. *Frantumaglia* and *smarginatura*, two crucial terms of Ferrante's work, are interrelated and at times difficult to disentangle, but the use of the verb "to dissolve" in the aforementioned passage, on top of alluding to the semantics of *smarginatura*, may provide some clarity. My contention is that *frantumaglia* is the condition of possibility for *smarginatura*: the former indicates a state of affairs necessary for the latter to erupt into a life. A state of *frantumaglia* may lead to a moment of *smarginatura*: a seemingly stable order of things can dissolve insofar as it is, in its essence, already *frantumato*; when this dissolution takes place in a life, Ferrante resorts to *smarginatura* to describe that experience.

According to Ferrante, the equilibrium that governs everyday life is precarious at best and can be shattered by a vast array of circumstances. This is a topic reminiscent of Levi's discussion of the struggle between the human desire for homeostasis and "the brute power" that governs life, society, and history—with Levi referring to the chaos, fragility, and unpredictability of complex systems as they may yield horrifying outcomes.[28] This also connects to what Taleb calls "black swans": as I argued in chapter 3, our inability to foresee outlier events, be they statistical or phenomenological, is what can make them a trigger for horror, as their emergence can trouble the nest of predictability that rules a life. Ferrante, too, sets forth a similar set of considerations regarding matters of forecasting, unpredictability, and uncertainty, in a way that echoes Michelstaedter's critique of what in chapter 2 I termed the "safety fallacy":

> I am not fond of the technicians of prediction. They work on the past, yet they see only the past that is comfortable to see. Navigating by sight is less progressive and impulsive but more sensible, especially when there are a lot of whirlpools. To me living on the edge of chaos seems inevitable, it's the fate of those who feel—and a writer has no choice but to feel it—the precarious balance of all existences and of all that exists. It's right, and stimulating, to always keep in mind that while on that precipice things still function somewhat, elsewhere nothing functions, and the distant imbalance is the sign of an imminent collapse. (*FR*, 377)

The reasoning that underpins the last sentence of this passage is similar to the one that leads from the awareness of the existence of a single black swan to the discarding of the proposition "all swans are white": if elsewhere things are falling apart, nothing guarantees us that we will be spared the same fate. The chaos Ferrante refers to is the *frantumaglia* that lurks beneath "the precarious balance of all existences and of all that exists"; its collapse is what triggers what she calls *smarginatura*.

The path in Ferrante's corpus that I am tracing shows that her engagement with the concepts of *frantumaglia* and *smarginatura* is capacious, and touches on several aspects of her worldview, in addition to underpinning her narratives. Moreover, the relation of these concepts to matters of impotence and the lack of control operates both in and beyond gendered considerations. Ferrante sketches what appears to be a theory of horror, as she repeatedly employs this term in her work, and connects it to the specific set of experiential underpinnings that I am teasing out.

Focusing on these nonfiction pages of Ferrante's work allows us to appreciate her intellectual engagement with concepts that her stories leverage and are made of, while also unveiling some substantial connections between Ferrante and Leopardi. The first connection is the mixture of stupor and horror regarding the transience and the precariousness of everything that exists. A second overlap is the skepticism they share concerning the technicians of forecasting. For Leopardi, as we saw, nature, history, and society are complex systems that are bound to retain a degree of opacity, making them irreducible to human syntheses. Ferrante shares similar epistemological concerns, as her critique of the "technician of prediction" indicates.

The "technician of prediction" passage above, taken from an interview, is a response to Nicola Lagioia's insistence on the connections between the Neapolitan Quartet and the historical pessimism present in Malaparte's *The Skin*. To point out the similarities between the two Italian writers, Lagioia evokes a passage from *Story of the Lost Child* when Elena, triggered by the violence of Naples and echoing Lila's pessimistic reflections on the topic, provides her own philosophy of history. The excerpt from Ferrante's novel that Lagioia refers to is worth quoting in its entirety:

> Naples was the great European metropolis where faith in technology, in science, in economic development, in the kindness of nature [*nella bontà della natura*], in history that leads of necessity to improvement, in democracy, was revealed, most clearly and far in advance, to be completely without foundation. To be born in that city—I went so far as to write once thinking not of myself but of Lila's pessimism—is useful for only one thing: to have always known, almost instinctively, what today, with endless fine distinctions, everyone is beginning to claim: that the dream of unlimited progress is in reality a nightmare of savagery and death. (*SLC*, 337)

This passage echoes Leopardi's critique of his century's adamant faith in humankind's "*magnificent, progressive destiny* [magnifiche sorti e progressive],"[29] which he most poignantly expresses in the already discussed poem *Broom*—a text that, fittingly, Leopardi composed while in Naples. The poem's pessimism about history extends to mankind's struggle against nature and its cycles of creation and destruction, which succeed one another without any regard for humanity. While the importance of Naples in the two authors' reflections on history may be a coincidence, the Leopardian origins of this passage are suggested by Ferrante's wary mention of "*la bontà della natura.*" In the context of the Italian canon, this phrase evokes Leopardi's conception of Nature as an evil mistress, "*natura matrigna*," exemplified also by the garden passage from his *Zibaldone*.

The idea of nature as something evil may not be a particularly popular one. Ideas, however, can be memorable precisely because of their strangeness. This recalls my students' initial reluctance to subscribe to a perspective that sees an Italian garden in bloom equated to a torture chamber. Students in the United States are, in general, blissfully unaware that an analysis of the role of nature in Leopardi's production is a milestone of Italian education. Given the complexity of Leopardi's take on the topic and its distance from common sense, other than the notions-centered approach taken in Italian education, on quizzes most Italian students resign themselves to repeating what they have read in their schoolbook, without necessarily agreeing (or disagreeing) with Leopardi's ideas.

This time-honored tradition of Italian education is, in fact, experienced by Elena in the second volume of Ferrante's Neapolitan Quartet, *The Story of a New Name*. Elena is taking her *maturità*—the anxiety-inducing, encyclopedic exit exam of the Italian high school system—and one of the prompts is about the role of nature in Leopardi. Elena, like many other Italian students, writes an essay regurgitating some Leopardian passages she has learned by heart, and resorts to a few sentences taken from her Italian literature manual. During the oral component of the *maturità*, one of the examiners asks her to defend the Leopardian pessimism of her essay:

> "Do you really think that nothing is fated to last, not even poetry?"
> "That's what Leopardi thinks."
> "You're sure?"
> "Yes."
> "And what do you think?"
> "I think that beauty is a sham."
> "Like the Leopardian garden?"
> I didn't know anything about Leopardian gardens, but I answered, "Yes. Like the sea on a calm day. Or like a sunset. Or like the sky at night. It's like face powder patted on over the horror. If you take it away, we are left alone with our fear [*restiamo soli col nostro spavento*]." (*SNN*, 323)

For Leopardi, the self-sustenance of existence is underpinned by a blind cycle of creation and destruction that, indifferent to individual suffering, affects each and every sentient being. To showcase the horror of this condition, Leopardi—in the passage referred to in the exchange above, a passage I extensively analyzed in chapter 1—describes a garden in bloom as a torture chamber: in it, bees are flowers' skillful torturers, and a frolicking girl turns into a harbinger of physical destruction for the frail ecosystems she interacts with. Through this estranging perspective, Leopardi aims to show that suffering is not only ubiquitous but in fact necessary for the functioning of existence. Natural beauty, from this perspective, is mask for existence's relentless and violent mechanisms.

Although Elena admits to not knowing much about Leopardi's garden, and is here likely just repeating what she memorized from her literature textbook, the final answer she provides is perfectly Leopardian: by looking at things with unclouded eyes, nature's beauty is revealed to be hiding a world where a blind cycle of creation and destruction rules sentient (and thus suffering) life. The veneer of beauty on top of these mechanisms is the "powder patted over the horror" that Elena evokes, leading her to create her own Leopardian garden—three, in fact: a calm sea, a sunset, and a night sky. If the "powder" is removed, the garden appears as a torture chamber, and one is left horrified.

The horror Elena refers to is the one that *frantumaglia* represents: the fact that underneath a layer of control and beauty lurks that which could at any time erupt and cast someone's world into crisis—the Leopardian torture garden present beneath a garden in bloom. It is the "precarious balance of all existences and of all that exists," as quoted above (*FR* 377), the lingering sense of fragility and powerlessness that *frantumaglia* evokes and responds to. To convey the emotional consequences of this horror once unveiled, Elena crafts her own line instead of quoting Leopardi directly: "we are left alone with our fear," which echoes the entanglement of confusion, dread, and solitude of the notorious "all is mystery except our pain [*arcano è tutto / fuor che il nostro dolor*]"[30]—the most memorable line of Leopardi's "The Last Song of Sappho," a text known to Italian high school students.

While Elena attends high school and there studies Leopardi, Lila starts working after elementary school. Yet, it is in the latter's worldview that Leopardian themes emerge with even greater prominence. I have already discussed a number of structural similarities between Leopardi's garden and Lila's fireworks. And Elena, as previously noted, explicitly invokes "Lila's pessimism" in advancing her take on Naples, history, and progress. Indeed, Lila is the source of many of Elena's ideas (as Elena is painfully aware), and while their friendship remains on purely platonic levels, the Sapphic undertones—a mixture of love and envy—are palpable throughout the four novels.[31] Lila is Elena's Sappho in providing the source of the pessimism that she cyclically, and with explicit mention to her friend, expresses—a Leopardian Sappho to be sure, and more precisely the one of Leopardi's aforementioned poem in which the Greek poetess becomes a champion of philosophical disillusionment and existential pessimism.

The novel's pivotal passage for the constitution of Lila's (and hence Elena's) Leopardianism is a scene that takes place less than one year before

Elena's *maturità* and the writing of her Leopardian essay. The two friends are vacationing in Ischia, during the summer. There, Lila, already married at this point, starts an affair with the university student Nino Sarratore, while Elena fends off the propositions of Nino's friend Bruno Soccavo. One night the four are sitting on the beach, under the starry sky. While Elena, Nino, and Bruno go through their catalog of "trite formulas" of sublime stupor regarding the celestial architecture, Lila sits quietly, and only when the others find themselves with nothing more to say, does she provide her take: "[Lila] said that the spectacle of night frightened her, she saw no structure but only random shards of glass in a blue pitch" (*SNN*, 267).

Two Leopardian intertexts are worth nothing here. First, Lila's pessimistic reflections about the workings of existence are triggered by the starry sky, similar to the case of Leopardi's shepherd in the poem "Night-Song of a Wandering Shepherd in Asia." Second, against the Pythagorean credo of a *musica universalis*, Lila too embraces a Leopardian view of a silent and empty cosmos that "knows nothing of music."[32] Ferrante herself does not shy away from this intertext, and in an essay confesses the Leopardian influence in shaping her vision of the night sky "full of worlds and yet empty."[33]

Just like the Leopardian garden, these too are not particularly commonplace views. Indeed, the starry sky is generally held to be a sublime matter rather than a horrifying one; the "admiration and reverence" for the starry sky expressed by the philosopher of the sublime Immanuel Kant offers a more conventional response compared to the disquietude of Leopardi and Lila.[34] Elena's immediate reaction is one of irritation regarding Lila's implausible take—not only is Elena secretly in love with Lila's new lover, Nino, but she is also annoyed by her friend's habit of "disrupt[ing] with a single remark everything that we had more or less thoughtlessly said" (*SNN*, 267–68). Yet, in just a matter of days, Elena, too, ends up subscribing to a worldview similar to Lila's: "I thought: yes, Lila is right, the beauty of things is a trick, the sky is the throne of fear; I'm alive, now, here, ten steps from the water, and it is not at all beautiful, it's terrifying; along with this beach, the sea, the swarm of animal forms, I am part of the universal terror; at this moment I am the infinitesimal particle through which the fear of every thing becomes conscious of itself" (*SNN*, 289).

What triggered such a drastic change of perspective? That night, Elena comes to acknowledge that "everything in the world was in precarious balance, pure risk," primarily because she is heartbroken by Nino's choice of pursuing Lila instead of her. Sitting on the beach, where a few days before she ridiculed Lila's take on the starry sky, Elena discovers her own Leopardian garden, one in which natural beauty is a cover-up ("beauty is a sham") for a much more disturbing reality, and she herself is part of "the universal terror." Much as Leopardi's garden is generally dismissed by my students, Elena did not subscribe to Lila's sky at first. And yet, a shift in the circumstances of her life makes that very sky horrifying for Elena as well, underscoring again that horror is a subjective and contextual experience without a fixed referent.

Elena's plunge into this horrifying reality becomes totalizing, and takes over her desires as well: "I hope that while I'm sitting here," Elena tells herself, "assassins will arrive out of the night and torture my body" (*SNN*, 289). That night, while Lila and Nino are having their first night of love, Elena's morbid desires materialize in the figure of Nino's father, Domenico Sarratore, who comes looking for her. The man, a vulgar scribbler and womanizer who had molested her a few years earlier, approaches Elena with his usual declarations of love and sexual advances. Elena, stuck in a self-destructive mood, gives herself to the man, on the beach, under the tar-like vault. The intercourse consummated, Elena glances a last time at "the tremendous sky"; in a daze, she leaves Domenico and the horrifying world in which she had dwelt that night, a world where a lurid and aging man took her virginity (*SNN*, 292).

Elena's glimpse of a cosmos where she was an "infinitesimal particle through which the fear of every thing becomes conscious of itself" allowed her to sense the truthfulness of Lila's worldview, one that acknowledges the presence of *frantumaglia* and where horror can suddenly erupt into a life. This awareness does not necessarily translate into living a horrified life. It is important to avoid making general claims about horror's temporality and its effects: if the world horrifies, it does not follow that it remains so indefinitely, nor should we overdetermine this experience's consequences. In the context of a work of fiction, and in this case Ferrante's work, this also means that the presence of horror does not make her novels about horror only. Horror is one of the many experiences that belong to a life, and Ferrante's Neapolitan Novels depict an extraordinary range of experiences over several hundreds of pages. But Ferrante's engagement with horror is not occasional, or simply due to the breadth of her work; instead, it is capacious and widespread, multifaceted and intentional. This is why, among other things, Ferrante's books often read as horrifying, without being for this reason horror books.

As it may happen in our lives, too, the experience of horror can function as a trigger. A parallel exists between Elena Ferrante's predilection for those stories that bear a "firsthand knowledge of the terrible" (*FR*, 373), and her character Elena Greco, who will begin a career as a writer with a book that retells, although anonymized, the sexual intercourse with Domenico Sarratore. The book, once published, meets with considerable critical and public acclaim. However, just as Elena's first reaction to Lila's description of the starry sky was one of irritation intermixed with incredulity, the *rione*'s reaction to Elena's book's sex scene will be one of scorn: to paraphrase T. S. Eliot's *Four Quartets*, neither Elena nor the readers of the *rione* could bear too much reality,[35] especially if the reality described calls into question the one the receiver dwells in (conversely, Elena's book will be read as authentic and hailed as a success by the bourgeois readers of Northern and Central Italy, far removed from the reality of the poorest neighborhoods of Naples).

Horror stories may come across as implausible. This does not only refer to the horror genre, which frequently relies on plots and characters far removed from what we are ready to accept as realistic—spanning protagonists devoid of common-sense instincts of self-preservation, serial killers of superhuman resilience, and fantastical creatures such as vampires and zombies. Horror's implausibility extends to real-life events as well, as seen in the context of World War II and Koestler's "The Nightmare That Is a Reality," which addressed the widespread disbelief in the United States regarding what was taking place for the European Jewish population at that time.[36] More recently, and with explicit reference to gendered horrors, the "believe women" slogan of the #MeToo movement constituted an invitation to overcome incredulity and accept women's allegations of sexual harassment and sexual assault at face value.[37]

While Elena's first novel stirred up a minor scandal in the *rione*, a later book of hers would provoke an even more significant uproar due to its portrayal of the neighborhood's violence and organized crime, inspired by the Solara family. As previously examined, a real text addressing the horrors in postwar Naples was Ortese's 1953 "The Involuntary City," whose depiction of the abject poverty in the city's underbelly incited such scandal among the Neapolitan intelligentsia that it effectively led to the author's banishment from the city. In a 1995 interview—sixteen years before the publication of *My Brilliant Friend*—Ferrante stated, "As for Naples, today I feel drawn above all by the Anna Maria Ortese of 'The Involuntary City.' If I managed again to write about this city, I would try to craft a text that explores the direction indicated there" (*FR*, 59–60). Arguably, the Neapolitan Quartet is the realization of that project: Elena and Lila were born in 1944, and the retelling of their story commences in the early 1950s, when they meet in elementary school, coinciding with the years depicted in Ortese's "The Involuntary City." Moreover, the Granili, the all-too-real haunted house at the center of Ortese's text, was situated just a twenty-minute walk from the *rione* Luzzatti of Ferrante's novels. The *rione*'s adverse reactions to Elena's publications also mirror the scorn that accompanied the release of Ortese's "The Involuntary City." It is even plausible to hypothesize that Ferrante's *smarginatura* finds inspiration in Ortese's style, which frequently incorporates deforming descriptions within a realistic narrative framework to convey the disturbing nature of the subject matter.[38]

We observed that Ortese wrote *Neapolitan Chronicles*, which anthologized "The Involuntary City," due to her need to scream when confronted with a reality that evoked in her bewilderment and horror (*Chronicles*, 9–11). In Ortese's preface to the book, penned in the 1990s, she acknowledged, somewhat apologetically and in response to accusations of the book being "anti-Naples," that the city portrayed through her prose was *her* Naples, a vision of the intolerable deeply influenced by *her* state of mind at the time rather than the true measure of things (*Chronicles*, 191). Elena, too, faces a host of similar issues with regard to her book about the *rione*'s camorra. When she started writing it, Elena was in Florence, and Naples seemed a distant world, heavily mediated by her memories. However, upon returning to Naples, she was suddenly seized by a "mania for reality" that disrupted the balance between facts and fiction she had maintained thus far, inadvertently causing her to lean toward the former (*SLC*, 283). It is only because of the *rione*'s reaction of disbelief that Elena realizes she ultimately wrote something closer to reportage than a novel.

In the depictions of Naples by both Elena and Ortese, the boundaries between facts and fiction are porous. The refusal of many readers to acknowledge the reality portrayed in their works raises a concern previously encountered in Levi and Koestler: how to most effectively convey what may come across as unbelievable? In relation to Ferrante's production, this question also invites us to consider how the reality of *frantumaglia* can most effectively be communicated.

According to Lila, Elena's book about the *rione*'s organized crime is disappointing. She tells Elena: "Things are told or not told: you remained in the middle" (*SLC*, 285). As with her historical and existential pessimism, Elena eventually ends up agreeing with her brilliant friend Lila: "my book," Elena tells herself, "really was bad, and this was because it was well organized, because it was written with obsessive care, because I hadn't been able to imitate the disjointed, unaesthetic, illogical, shapeless banality of things" (*SLC*, 311). Elena's book, according to her own self-critique, does not leave any space for *smarginatura* and fails to adequately represent the *frantumaglia* lurking beneath everyday life—the implicit assumption being that a tightly woven fabric of aesthetic control over a fundamentally disordered reality renders a book untruthful. While this recalls Ferrante's take on the duty of a writer in facing the horrors of the present times, it also refers to Ferrante's stylistics: to compose a text, for the author, is a process where a solid world is swept away by a "convulsive, disintegrating type of writing,"[39] echoing the dynamics between *smarginatura* and *frantumaglia* traced here.

Readers may still hesitate at Elena's sweeping take on the (dis)order of things: is everything that exists—every single thing—a disorderly, deformed, illogical mess? This question mirrors the one I heard numerous times from my students concerning Leopardi's description of a garden and Leopardi's overarching assertion that everything, every single thing, is evil—"*Tutto è male*" (*Zib.* 4174). While structural similarities between the two passages exist, there is also a clear difference: Elena's take is cast against the backdrop of concrete situations that Cavarero identifies as the most important reason for the success of Ferrante's Neapolitan Novels. A concrete element here is Elena's friendship with Lila, who, as the former recalls, had understood since her childhood that the disturbing aspects of the *rione* extend beyond the borders of the neighborhood: "it is not the neighborhood that's sick, it's not Naples, it's the entire earth, it's the universe, or universes."[40] With another Leopardian intertext, this assertion echoes a notorious passage from the *Zibaldone* where it is argued that "the evil is in the order of things [*il male è nell'ordine*]" (*Zib.* 4511).

Elena's negative take on her own work is inspired by her friend Lila, whose pessimistic worldview is made plausible by her personal story—the one that the four volumes of the Neapolitan Quartet retell. At this point in the tetralogy, Lila has gone through episodes of sexual violence, professional exploitation, and various other kinds of trauma.[41] The concrete situations Lila has suffered from justify, at least on an experiential level, the bleakness of her views. Just as we do not (or at least should not) dismiss someone's feelings of grief for the death of their elderly mother just because everyone eventually ages and dies, Lila's proposition can be taken at face value even if we disagree with her arguments throughout the novels regarding life's disorder and instability, and even if we ignore or disagree with the way Ferrante conceptualizes what she terms *frantumaglia*. Conversely, Leopardi's philosophical essays rely primarily on argumentative rather than narrative logic: if one disagrees with some of their foundational assumptions, their entirety is called into question.

In yet another parallel between the two texts, a trajectory similar to the one in Leopardi's *Zibaldone*, where his tone grew increasingly bleak, also occurs with Lila. She starts with fleeting moments of *smarginatura* in her younger years, progresses through an object-specific assessment of *frantumaglia* with her take on the starry sky as an adolescent, and eventually reaches sweeping statements concerning the general (dis)order of things in adulthood. To trace this development, we must now turn to the fourth and final book of Ferrante's tetralogy, *Story of the Lost Child*. In it, Ferrante brings to its apex her tendency to construct stories that push their protagonists to the brink of the abyss—the "terrible" that, as Ferrante tells Nicola Lagioia, a moment of *smarginatura* connects to.

In that same exchange, Ferrante argues that "catching a glimpse of the terrible" is a moment of great risk: "You don't go beyond that; you have to take a step back and, to survive, reenter some good fiction" (*FR*, 373). But what if this does not take place? Lila does not take that step back, and instead remains "at the center of *her* horror" (*SLC*, 331). Her refusal enables an exploration of what it means to face Medusa, the Gorgon whose gaze paralyzed those who crossed it. It also sheds some light on Lila's mysterious end through a comparison with another Leopardian figure, Tristan from the concluding dialogue of the *Moral Essays*.

THE EYE OF HORROR: LILA'S PARALYSIS

While Lila's episodes of *smarginatura* reveal that she is not immune to horror, her character is an embodiment of resilience. Thrown out of a window as a child by her father, she quickly gets up after the fall and asserts that she did not hurt herself. Threatened by her brother and raped by her husband, she consistently finds a way to bounce back and make the most of any situation. From a professional standpoint, Lila's genius enables her to transform her parents' decision to take her out of school into an opportunity to become a successful shoe designer and the driving force behind her father's cobbler shop. Similarly, her time as an exploited worker in a meat factory leads her to learn computer programming and become a software developer at IBM. No matter her awareness of *smarginatura* and its potential repercussions ("That people, even more than things, lost their boundaries and overflowed into shapelessness is what most frightened Lila in the course of her life" [*SNN*, 355]), Lila always retains her ingenuity, which makes her the title character of Ferrante's tetralogy—*My Brilliant Friend*.[42]

But is there a limit to how much one can withstand? Ferrante contends that once we get too close to the "terrible," it becomes necessary to take a step back. Lila, however, always leaps forward: the horrifying events in her life are mere setbacks that she overcomes. Seemingly unstoppable, Lila always succeeds in (re)claiming a degree of control over the circumstances of her life—regardless of these circumstances, whatever happens, and whatever it takes.

This comes to an end in the fourth and final volume of the Neapolitan Quartet. *Story of the Lost Child* introduces, from its early chapters, the idea that not every situation can be overcome. At first, this is not directly thematized in relation to Lila's character development; instead, it emerges in a conversation between Elena and Silvia—with Silvia being a university student who was beaten and raped by a group of neofascists because of her political activism in the far-left group Avanguardia Operaia.

Like Lila, Silvia was one of those who "even in the midst of chaos, [was] always inventing an order and pretending to know exactly where things were going." This, however, changes after she is assaulted right in front of her home. As Silvia tells Elena, "It's so comfortable never to be confused by anything. No infected bedsores, no wound without its stitches, no dark room that frightens you." However, echoing Ferrante's pessimism regarding the possibility of always overcoming the crises we face, Silvia adds, with reference to her recent past, that "at a certain point the trick no longer functions" (*SLC*, 78). Silvia is broken by the assault she suffered: limping and depressed, she reflects on how things may go wrong to an extent that negates the possibility of full recovery and the repurposing of horror into a propelling device.

For Lila, too, in *Story of the Lost Child*, the "trick" Silvia refers to eventually stops working. The objective correlative of this character development is the earthquake that strikes Naples on November 23, 1980. This earthquake, similar to the Vesuvius eruption in Malaparte's *The Skin*, is not merely a fictional event or a device to keep the plot in motion. As Malaparte's book retells a real event that took place in 1944, Ferrante's novel interpolates in its plot a historically accurate cataclysm, one that killed approximately twenty-five hundred people in the Irpinia region and left hundreds of thousands homeless.

Spanning approximately ten pages, the narration of the Irpinia earthquake serves to both develop and deal a shattering blow to Lila's character, while articulating what *smarginatura* is through Lila's coinage of the term. The earthquake confronts Lila with the limits of what I argue is one of her most salient traits: her desire for, and successes in, maximizing control over the circumstances of her life.

Once the earthquake begins, much as Lila tried repressing her horror when raped by her husband during their honeymoon, here too Lila's first reaction is to resist a situation that escapes her control. Pregnant, she stands immobile with her hands around her belly in a protective gesture. Elena initially takes this as an example to follow, and thinks that in this case, too, her brilliant friend's reaction is the one that she should imitate. Yet, as soon as Elena gets closer to Lila, she realizes that this time Lila's actions are not informed by her instincts of mastery; instead, Elena observes that Lila, "always in control of everything, at that moment wasn't in control of anything. She was immobilized by horror, fearful that if I merely touched her she would break" (*SLC*, 171).

Elena realizes that the current event undoes what Lila represents to her. Lila is not immobile because that reaction might allow her to regain a degree of control over her surroundings; on the contrary, she is paralyzed by the horror she is experiencing. While the earthquake takes over Lila's present and reduces her to powerlessness, Elena is still capable of exerting a degree of agency and drags Lila out of her apartment. With a momentary sidestep from the diegesis, Elena's narrative voice comments on the earthquake's immediate and future consequences on the two women's lives: the cataclysm "expelled the habit of stability and solidity, the confidence that every second would be identical to the next, the familiarity of sounds and gestures, the certainty of recognizing them. A sort of suspicion of every form of reassurance took over, a tendency to believe in every prediction of bad luck, and obsessive attention to signs of the brittleness of the world, and it was hard to take control again" (*SLC*, 172).

The newly found awareness of a generalized sense of instability reflects Ferrante's concept of *frantumaglia*, a word not explicitly mentioned here but which diffuses throughout the scene. The earthquake becomes an event that transcends its immediate repercussions: it becomes a sign of the presence and existence of that which cannot be controlled, something that undermines the nest of predictability that allegedly rules a life. This is a phenomenological, rather than an actual, "black swan" event: while earthquakes have indeed been recorded throughout history in the Irpinia region, the experience of one in their lives confronts Elena and Lila with the possibility of unforeseen events that carry a massive impact.

Two important features separate this event from the other horrifying experiences that take place in Lila's life. First, this event is exogenous rather than endogenous: the masculine violence that rules the *rione*, and that caused Lila's episodes of *smarginatura* in her past, is a defining and known feature of her upbringing. Through repeated exposure, Lila knows that in her world outbursts of masculine violence pose a threat to the control she exerts over her life. This does not mean that those are not horrifying moments; it simply means that they are not unforeseeable, and are somewhat already embedded in the nest of predictability that rules her life. Second, because of this epistemological matter—the fact that Lila knows she needs to work around patriarchal structures—she generally succeeded in overcoming the horrors she encountered in her past. The earthquake, however, is something exogenous, and this is her first exposure to it: seismic events of extreme magnitude were not part of her upbringing, contrary to the widespread masculine violence she was exposed to since her youngest years. This, in turn, and in addition to the earthquake's magnitude, affects her phenomenology of the event, and Elena's as well.

Horror turns their world upside down: what is stable becomes unstable, and predictable events are overshadowed by unpredictable ones. The story of Spin in Malaparte's *Kaputt* offers a clear parallel: the dog whose world stopped making sense when he discovered that the banging sounds during the bombardment of Belgrade in 1941 were not caused by the hunting rifles to which he was accustomed. Spin was horrified by something that did not align with his paradigm of sense-making: for him, explosions had thus far meant he was out on a hunting trip, and his first experience of an air raid called into question one of the fundamental assumptions governing his world.[43] For Lila, the earthquake causes a similar shattering, as it represents something she, for the first time, cannot reintegrate into a paradigm of sense-making and controllability. The upheaval caused by this event challenges the defining feature of her character, insofar as her genius consisted for a considerable part in being able to master the circumstances of her life and maximize the degree of control she exerted over them, despite the limitations imposed by life in the *rione*.

Elena notes that the Lila she knew, the one "able to precisely calibrate thoughts, words, gestures, tactics, strategies," was swept away by the earthquake (*SLC*, 173). Lila now resembles "the person I [Elena] had glimpsed [. . .] the night of New Year's Eve," when she, horror-stricken, experienced her first episode of *smarginatura*. Crucially, however, the Lila of 1958 still maintained "some points of contact" with her former self,[44] and indeed she overcame that state of crisis and several other ones in the course of her life. But this time, Lila's crisis is much more profound, and as Elena observes with foresight, "now that other person seemed to have emerged directly from the churning guts of the earth; she bore no resemblance to the friend who a few minutes before I had envied for her ability to choose words deliberately" (*SLC*, 174).

While Elena progressively regains control over herself after the initial, major shake, Lila's status remains precarious, as she no longer appears to "believe in solid connections." Always so careful in her acts and words, Lila utters incoherent sentences and eventually, at the peak of her crisis, coins the term that readers already encountered in the first book of the tetralogy: *smarginatura,* or "dissolving boundaries," in translation. Lila's first use of the term refers to how the surrounding world appears to her eyes: as she recalls, "the car's boundaries were dissolving [*l'auto s'era smarginata*], the boundaries of Marcello, too, at the wheel were dissolving [*anche Mar-*

cello al volante si stava smarginando], the thing and the person were gushing out of themselves, mixing liquid metal and flesh" (*SLC*, 175).

Lila attempts to define *smarginatura*. This effort is met with challenges due not only to Lila's agitation but also to factors inherent to matters of phenomenology: Elena is not experiencing the world in the same way Lila is, because the former has, to a significant degree, overcome the horror that still dominates the latter's present. However, while individual experiences involve a degree of intersubjective opacity, the aestheticization produced by telling, retelling, and imagination allows for a description that, in this case, seeks to convey Lila's subjective turmoil. Indeed, the question is not whether cars and people genuinely start melting from Lila's perspective: in the context of a literary work such as Ferrante's, this is not a propositional formula that involves a truth-value. Instead, it is more sensible to ask what such a description of her experience does, and what purpose it serves in Ferrante's work. A possible answer is that it seeks to depict the horror Lila is affected by, instead of providing an impersonal, indexical, or "neutral" description of the experience itself. In other words, Lila is trying to convey something essential about *her* experience of this event, "the feeling of it," rather than what the experience actually was like (as this would not be possible). From this perspective, *smarginatura*, as discussed in the first section of this chapter, is a matter of both phenomenology and aesthetics, and thus part of the lineage of texts traced in this book: one in which scenes of horror leverage deforming aesthetics within an otherwise realistic narrative framework to convey an experiential twist of massive and negative nature.

Lila continues her comments on *smarginatura* and its underpinnings by stating that she always considered reality a disorderly matter, whose scaffolding constantly ran the risk of collapsing. Although many believe life involves stable and predictable structures, since her childhood Lila has known that "*it was absolutely not like that*," and that given this inherent degree of fragility, she had to stay focused to exert the maximum degree of control possible. The earthquake, however, deals a crushing blow to the presuppositions that underpin this homeostatic project: after it, for Lila, there is "nothing, nothing, nothing about which one can say conclusively: it's like that" (*SLC*, 176, original emphasis).

Her resilience and resourcefulness cease to be that which allows her to overcome any external stressors: "Up to now [. . .] I thought it was a matter of bad moments that came and then passed"—with Lila here referring directly to the events that took place on New Year's Eve in 1958, and reflecting on how her own life has been a constant and thus far successful effort to work around and overcome those events. But Lila confesses that she has always been aware of the precariousness of her triumphs and that beneath a veneer of brilliance lurked the overpowering chaos of *frantumaglia*, which could have erupted at any moment and dismantled her bulwarks of control over the circumstances of her life. Looking back, she reminisces with Elena about the "horror" triggered in her by "the night sky of Ischia," that, sublime to her friends' eyes, evoked in Lila the sensation of crushing in her mouth "rotten eggs, eggs with a greenish-yellow yolk inside the white and inside the shell" (*SLC*, 177).

Just as Leopardi's torture garden is the objective correlative of both his philosophical system and a world that suddenly horrifies, Lila's starry sky, too, was not just the consequence of a transitory mood: as Lila indeed concedes, she was happy that summer ("I was happy, full of love"), and yet that did not shield her from the horrification of that natural spectacle because "my head always finds a chink to peer through, beyond—above, beneath, on the side—where the fear is." For Lila as well, in other words, the figuration of her reality into something more disquieting responds to a set of broader philosophical beliefs. This, too, echoes Leopardi's view regarding the presence, ubiquitous yet subterranean, of horror or the possibility thereof: for both, the fact that human beings are ultimately powerless in the face of finitude and the overpowering, indifferent unfolding of existence constitutes a source of horror, a muffled scream that echoes through each fiber of being, usually imperceptible and yet constantly humming beneath a veneer of silence. "The terror remains," Lila states, "it's always in the crack between one normal thing and the other. It's there waiting, I've always suspected it, and since yesterday evening I've known for certain: nothing lasts" (*SLC*, 177–78).

Elena now fully realizes that Lila's persistent attempts at exerting control over the circumstances of her life are a form of "preventive engineering of persons and things" (*SLC*, 179).[45] Lila's extensive knowledge of the *rione* and its inhabitants, too, responds to this compulsion to maximize the reach of her control and, in turn, minimize her impotence. Lila indeed "knew everything out of pure, simple fear of all that was living or dead" (*SLC*, 168); her genius was also a form of defense against *frantumaglia* she had always been aware of, and whose uncontrollable eruptions she sought to prevent or avoid. Yet, when things fell apart and triggered a moment of *smarginatura*, "Lila lost Lila, chaos seemed [*pareva*] the only truth" (*SLC*, 168).

Crucially, the chaos "seemed" to be the only form of truth, with the choice of this verb emphasizing that we remain anchored to matters of phenomenology: the world stays the same; what matters in those moments is that Lila can no longer keep at bay the awareness that *frantumaglia*, in the end, cannot be fully overcome. I am aware that every time I leave my house, something could fall on my head and injure me, perhaps lethally; yet, in order to live my life, I act as if a nest of safe predictability exists, one that allows me to leave my apartment in the morning without fear that a tile will hit my head as soon as I go outside. After the earthquake, this nest of predictability ceases to rule Lila's life: "the earthquake seemed so terrible to her that each moment now is uncertain, and she would like everything to stand still, even her pregnancy" (*SLC*, 190).

Lila's desire for stasis, however, is left unfulfilled. She eventually gives birth to her daughter, Tina, albeit after a seemingly abnormal delay, as if Lila were trying her best not to deliver her baby. Lila's retelling of her childbirth is colored by her post-earthquake worldview: she wonders, why do we expel from our body something that could otherwise safely stay there, especially when the very act involves a revolt of the body against itself, "until it achieves the most terrible pain possible" (*SLC*, 216)? According to her gynecologist, Lila's childbirth took place under normal and rather effortless circumstances, but her emphasis in retelling her story underscores how painful and complicated the delivery was. Her experience is negatively colored by her lack of control over both the delivery of her baby and the future risks to which her daughter will be exposed.

The tendency in Ferrante's stories' to glimpse the "terrible" that may suddenly erupt into one's life is carried to a point of no return in Lila's case. One day, Lila's beloved newborn Tina disappears under mysterious circumstances and is never to be found again. After this event, Lila's already compromised state suffers another collapse. Without the ability to rely on a nest of safe predictability to inform the most basic aspects of her life, she will from that moment onward leave the house only on rare occasions, with her unwillingness to take any risks whatsoever effectively paralyzing her. Lila, as Elena notes, "remained at the center of *her* horror" (*SLC*, 349, original emphasis).

For Ferrante, there is a threshold of "terrible" that one should avoid crossing, and that, once approached, calls for a step back into "some good fiction" (*FR*, 373). Lila's character development runs in the opposite direction: incapable of taking that step back, she now refuses to move in any way whatsoever. In Lila's world, the fact that a tile may hit me every time I leave my apartment turns from a remote possibility that I bracket on a daily basis into something exceedingly plausible, which demands that I stay inside all the time in order to survive. "You don't go out of the house," Lila once shouts at Elena's daughter, whom she is taking care of for a few days, "outside it's dangerous, outside you'll die" (*SLC*, 355).

The analysis in chapter 2 of horror's varying temporality provides a useful framework here. With Michelstaedter, I considered horror as a moment of shattering soon overcome by the subject, reflecting on its potential transience; with Pirandello, conversely, I delved into horror's potential endurance and how the experience may instead lead to a shattered self. The case of Lila is exemplary insofar as it showcases the coexistence of these two temporalities within the same story: whereas for the most part of her character development, her episodes of *smarginatura* resembled those described by Michelstaedter as temporally limited instantiations of an experience soon overcome, the Lila of *Story of the Lost Child* is someone whose experienced horror produces a lasting rupture in the fabric of her world. But unlike Pirandello's Vitangelo Moscarda, whose acceptance of a life where control over oneself and one's own life is to a great extent relinquished and replaced by a form of immanence that resembles madness in centering on the present only, Lila remains anchored to her approach of "preventive engineering" that clashes against the untamable world fully revealed by the earthquake and Tina's disappearance. Lila's incapacity, impossibility, or unwillingness to change her approach to life prevents her from stepping away from the horror that, as Elena points out, she now dwells in.

In seeking to maximize her control over the world and its circumstances, Lila's character arguably embodies some of the main tenets of modernity's project, as understood in this book in conversation with authors such as Toulmin, Taleb, and Rosa. However, Lila's tendencies, regardless of one's opinion of them, are likely to come across as universally relatable, and not the byproduct of a specific episteme only: who would not be shocked and suffer from the turmoil caused by an earthquake or their daughter's disappearance? From this perspective, perhaps, we have always been modern, although modernity may indeed have led to a generalized overestimation of the control we project over the present and future circumstances of our lives—subjectively speaking and societally as well.

If the quintessential modern subject is one that, to paraphrase Descartes, seeks to become master and possessor of the world and its circumstances, Lila's approach to life champions this perspective. Lila's undoing occurs when *frantumaglia* takes over: these are her moments of *smarginatura*, the ones when "Lila lost Lila" (*SLC*, 168). In other words, in those moments Lila is deprived of her most distinctive characteristic by the encounter with what resists her approach of "preventive engineering" (*SLC*, 179). Her approach postulates that the world is not populated by forces inherently overpowering and removed from the subject's reach; on the contrary, it presupposes that the subject's interactions with such forces can be perfected and eventually lead to their domestication.

Things, however, can fall apart, as they do in Lila's case. What is there to be done in such circumstances? The magnitude of horrifying events can be massive, like the Irpinia earthquake or Tina's disappearance, and in such situations, it appears vital to at least hold onto the hope that moving beyond them is possible. To quote Ferrante, we need to fall back on a "good fiction" to survive the "terrible" (*FR*, 373): that is to say, we need to hold onto the belief that things will get better. But the key word here is "fiction [*finzione*]." What, beyond our hopefulness, can reassure us that we may find a safe harbor in which to withdraw after the horrifying? The fantasy, the story ("*finzione*") we tell ourselves may precisely be that a "good fiction" is possible in the first place. Ferrante leaves this question open.

Horror, as I understand it, is that which resists domestication: an event that forces our powerlessness, casts our world into crisis, and restructures our experience of the present. While it is indeed true that a presently horrifying situation may eventually be integrated into a paradigm of controllability, this future-oriented speculation serves little purpose in a moment of crisis. In horror, what matters is the here and now, and the turmoil that the subject presently undergoes. If this is overcome, the subject leaves the phenomenology of horror to enter another domain. This is the norm: in Levi's recounting of Auschwitz, even in the Lager horror was a somewhat sporadic occurrence in an otherwise vast expanse of fatigue, discomfort, and boredom ("boredom punctuated by horror").[46] But Lila "remained at the center of *her* horror" (*SLC*, 349)—*her* horror, with the authorial emphasis further underlining that it is here a personal matter rather than a blank statement about reality as a whole.

Lila embodies an unusual yet plausible scenario in which an individual endures a relentless state of horror. It is fitting that we encounter Lila's story through Elena's eyes, as Levi's recollections from Auschwitz suggest that those who have experienced such ongoing and profound horror are often unable to recount their own ordeal. As he writes, "those who saw the Gorgon, did not come back to tell, or they came back mute"; they are the "drowned," for whom horror is not a fleeting experience but rather a constant reality.[47]

Although Lila has not faced the atrocities of Auschwitz, she, too, bears the traces of confronting Medusa's gaze, particularly after her daughter's disappearance. Yet, Lila's story does not culminate in her paralysis; instead, it concludes with her mysterious vanishing. The epilogue of Ferrante's Neapolitan Novels circles back to the prologue, where Lila's disappearance is first announced—a narrative event that only becomes comprehensible upon reaching the final installment.

Ferrante deliberately leaves the reasons behind Lila's disappearance largely unexplored, and it is not my aim to unravel this enigma in the conclusion of this chapter. Instead, I propose interpreting Lila's ending as another manifestation of her Leopardian nature, this time drawing upon a character from Leopardi's *Moral Essays* rather than a passage from his *Zibaldone*. In this instance, the reference is to Tristan, the most quintessentially Leopardian character in Leopardi's entire body of work.

HOW TO DISAPPEAR COMPLETELY: CONCLUSION

Interviewed by Elissa Schappell, Ferrante confesses her fascination for those figures who withhold their consent from existence after having fully come to terms with its horrors:

> I have always been fascinated by those people who, faced with a world so full of horrors it can seem intolerable, claim that the human condition is unchangeable, that nature is a monstrous machine, that humanity has produced an endless cycle of inhumanity even when animated by good intentions, and then back away. The problem is not what other

> people do to you. The problem is to stand impotent before the horror that afflicts the majority of people, the most precarious of our fellow human beings. Every day we find ourselves faced with the intolerable, and no promise of utopia—whether it be political, religious, or scientific—is capable of calming us. Each generation is obliged to verify this horror anew for itself, and to discover that it is impotent. So either you take a step forward or you take one back. I'm not talking about suicide. I'm talking about refusing to engage, about removing oneself from the picture. The sentence "No, I will not," when it comes from the depths of the intolerable, seems to me to be weighty sentence, one full of meaning and entirely worth narrating [*tutta da raccontare*]. (*FR*, 338–39)[48]

In connecting horror to a sense of impotence, Ferrante implicitly counterpoises this experience to everything that the resourceful Lila represents: her Cartesian desire to master the world and its circumstances makes of Lila's collision with horror's forced powerlessness a story "entirely worth narrating." Lila's disappearance symbolizes that "No, I will not" referenced in the passage above. This event does not occur unexpectedly. This holds true not only for the reader, who learns about Lila's vanishing in the book's first pages, but also for Elena. As she notes, "[Lila] often expressed the idea of eliminating herself [*cancellarsi*], [. . .] it became a sort of teasing chorus." To Elena, this is not the expression of suicidal intent but rather a sort of "aesthetic project," a rejection of engaging with a reality Lila deems at this point chaotic and sullied (*SLC*, 455). The notion of an "aesthetic project" is connected to Elena's belief that Lila is in fact writing "a book of Neapolitan curiosities" (*SLC*, 448)—or perhaps a novel, one that once published would be "much better" than Elena's (458) and "would endure through time and would be read and reread for hundreds of years" (461–62). But to Elena's insecurity-fueled repeated and oblique queries on the topic, Lila responds, "To write, you have to want something to survive you. I don't even have the desire to live, I've never had it strongly the way you have. If I could eliminate myself now, while we're speaking, I'd be more than happy" (*SLC*, 454).

Lila's attempts at "preventive engineering" made her for the best part of her life the embodiment of resourcefulness and rendered her Elena's brilliant friend. Once broken by the events narrated in *Story of the Lost Child*, she found herself paralyzed "at the center of *her* horror" (*SLC*, 331). However, the final act of her lifelong confrontation with *frantumaglia* leads to a perhaps surprising outcome given Lila's former self: disillusionment. It is better to leave this world without leaving any traces, Lila suggests, and it would be equally desirable to expedite this exit as much as possible.

Lila's flippant yet lucid tone, and her desire for self-erasure, resonate with the bitter sarcasm of Tristan, the protagonist of Leopardi's *Dialogue of Tristan and a Friend*, the concluding piece of his *Moral Essays*. Tristan's pronouncements are also tied to a literary work, one that he published but whose pessimistic and resigned tone regarding human existence and society's progress made it unpalatable to the public and to his interlocutor. Tristan initially claims to have reconsidered his book's pessimism and now agrees with his friend's optimism about the "unlimited perfectibility of man." However, his interlocutor eventually senses Tristan's sarcasm and tells him that his pessimism will cause the book to be read as "little versed in modern philosophy, and little concerned for the progress of civilization and enlightenment." The sarcastic mask now dropped, Tristan turns to a bitter form of disillusionment, arguing that the best fate for his book would be to be burnt, given its eminently unrelatable nature in a society convinced of its happiness and ceaseless progress. Tristan's only desire is death, and his envy is directed solely toward the dead since they are no longer subject to the whims of life.[49]

While Lila, contrary to Tristan, does not explicitly mention death and dying, their attitudes share a rejection of life, and, in their projected outcomes, Lila's desire to erase herself goes hand in hand with Tristan's self-annihilating wishes. Lila's disappearance also enacts Tristan's cancellation of the products of his work: while Lila's book, unlike Tristan's, may exist only in Elena's suspicious and insecure mind, when she disappears not only do all her belongings vanish, but in her craving for absolute erasure Lila also cuts herself out of every photo in the house—a gesture marked by her desire to leave nothing whatsoever behind. And if Tristan's disillusionment is rooted in a philosophical attitude that makes him the quintessential Leopardian character, Lila's position, too, is tied not only to the relationality of concrete situations chronicled in Ferrante's novels but also to a broader authorial conceptual engagement with the (im)possibility of mastering the world and its circumstances. From this perspective, Lila develops in prose several of Ferrante's philosophical remarks found in the author's nonfiction writings, much as Tristan embodies some of Leopardi's philosophical ideas found in his *Zibaldone*.

Can any conclusions be drawn from Lila's story? Her disappearance may be interpreted as an act of rebellion—a withdrawal of consent, so to speak, from the rulings of *frantumaglia*. Is this an assertion of agency and autonomy in the face of a life—specifically in the context of the *rione*, but also more generally—that she now recognizes as unmasterable? Is Lila's vanishing her last stand against the possibility of experiencing the horrors of *smarginatura*? And what of the package containing their long-lost childhood dolls that Elena receives from Lila in the tetralogy's closing pages? Ferrante leaves these questions unanswered. Given phenomenology's focus on description rather than explanation, alongside its approach of attending rather than expanding a text, they will remain unresolved here as well.

This should not be cause for concern; in the end, the value of the analysis presented here lies not in providing definitive answers or complete mastery over the subject matter. As Sloterdijk observes when commenting on the dialectics between concealment and unconcealment in Heidegger's work, "in the clearing, it becomes manifest that not everything is manifest. The manifestation is never complete—and the suspicion against what is veiled and not appearing is in principle never to be put to rest."[50] If chapter 1 emphasized this passage's relevance to phenomenological analysis, we can now circle back to Sloterdijk's reflections to underscore their significance for hermeneutics: while providing some answers, the manifestation of horror and Leopardianism in the Neapolitan Quartet raises a host of new interpretative questions.

In the concluding paragraph of the Neapolitan Novels, Elena states that "real life, when it has passed, inclines toward obscurity, not clarity" (*SLC*, 473). This too, arguably, gestures toward a kind of disillusionment: the clearing we laboriously reach through our experiences and the passing of time remains surrounded by a darkness expanding beyond our mastery, a darkness that, resorting to Ferrantian terminology, bears the signs of *frantumaglia*. Whether Lila's vanishing represents a plunge into that darkness, her withdrawal of consent regarding its presence, or perhaps something else entirely is a matter that Ferrante leaves open, emphasizing the uncontrollable and unpredictable effects of horror's eruption into a life, even for someone whose genius is defined by surmounting the insurmountable and defying the undefiable.

CODA
ARE HORROR STORIES REAL?

A few years ago, I was in Italy visiting my family. My US visa stamp had recently expired, and since getting one generally requires being outside the United States, I decided to take advantage of a stay in my home country to complete this routine process. I gathered all the required material and sent everything off, including my passport, to the American consulate in Milan.

A few weeks passed without any news. Then, on a hot July afternoon, I received a phone call from the consulate: the issuance of my visa had been halted. Further instructions would follow via email. I immediately asked for clarification, but the voice on the other side of the phone said they were a simple intermediary: the order to halt my visa issuance had come directly from mainland America. The consulate did not have any access to additional information, and even if they did, my anonymous interlocutor added, they were not allowed to disclose anything: I was simply going to receive a form to fill out and send back in a matter of days. With a knot in my throat, I tried explaining that most of my life—my job, my relations, my belongings—was at that point in the United States, and that I needed to get back to the country as soon as possible. "Please try to remain calm," the consulate's employee told me, "and provide us, to the best of your capacity, with all the necessary information."

I hung up, and in a matter of seconds I received an email from a governmental address with a document attached, Form DS-5535. The form asked me to disclose all my social media handles, and provide the details (address, date, duration of my stay, source of funds) of every place where I had spent one night or more outside of Italy over the past fifteen years. I typed the name of the form into a search engine and learned that a DS-5535 is what begins a process of "heightened screening and vetting" for visa applicants who "may aid, support, or commit violent, criminal, or terrorist acts."[1] Browsing the web, I also learned that the process focuses on individuals with ties to countries whose diplomatic relations with the United States are fraught, such as Iran, North Korea, or Yemen. As someone who had never traveled outside of Europe or North America, and whose closest exposure to terrorism had been, at least as far as I could tell, through some characters of Russian nineteenth-century novels, I found myself at a loss for words. As I kept searching for more information—as I kept trying to make sense of what was happening—I discovered that the vetting process could take several months, if not years, and that a fraction of those affected by it never had their visas issued.

It all felt so absurd. How could this be happening, and why was it happening to me? My university's international affairs office shared my disbelief: it was exceedingly rare that an Italian without a complex travel history was selected for this vetting process. In the span of a phone call, my life plunged into crisis. My room felt oppressive, the summer heat unbearable, my head spun: it was as if I had been stripped of the future that I had created for myself, and thrown into a world where I was preyed upon by overpowering, anonymous forces that could dispose of me at will.[2]

A few weeks later, however, the problem evaporated: without any explanation from any of the agencies involved, I was notified of the successful renewal of my visa, and was allowed to return to the United States. To this day, I do not know why the vetting process took place. Though it felt utterly horrifying as I was living it, this is now an anecdote that never fails to shock and entertain my interlocutors.

By that summer, I had been thinking about horror for some time. And horrifying events, such as seeing my father die of cancer in a matter of months, were not absent from my recent past. Every time something of such a nature happened, it always left me paralyzed and in a state of turmoil: I never got better at dealing with horrible experiences, despite my familiarity with them both in theory and in practice. I wondered: shouldn't the study of something make us better at dealing with it? Shouldn't my research give me access to some tools to make sense of horrifying situations in a way that allowed me to exert some control over my response to similar events? This, clearly, was not happening, and I began questioning my ruminations on the topic, as they did not seem to provide me with anything useful to better handle those episodes.

But perhaps that was the point. Perhaps, I thought, horror is exactly that which cannot be controlled—the experience of forced powerlessness, the blow that we cannot parry. Control runs against horror, and the two are mutually exclusive: if I can exert a degree of control over a situation in a way that prevents my world from being unraveled by it, I find myself in a different phenomenological territory from that of horror. I may be afraid, disgusted, shocked, or scared—but horror is something that throws us into a state of crisis and confronts us with the limits of our control more profoundly than a jump scare does in forcing a sudden physical reaction.[3] We do not "get better" at dealing with horror, and this is precisely the point. To be sure, we may get better at dealing with a particular situation that has horrified us in the past, but as soon as that happens it ceases to be a horrifying matter and becomes something else.

This perspective does justice to the inexhaustible sources of horror as well as their devastating, ever fresh impact. It does not, however, lead to the reassuring conclusion that we can learn a great deal from this experience. Whereas anxiety, for Martin Heidegger, "discloses, primordially and directly, the world as world,"[4] or boredom, according to Walter Benjamin, is "the dream bird that broods the egg of experience,"[5] horror, I believe, stands as a negative outlier, an experience that resists redemptive readings. Horror may be considered one of those ugly feelings, in the words of Sianne Ngai, that are obstructed, noncathartic, and difficult to mobilize toward clear political or ethical goals.[6] But if Ngai's ugly feelings tend to be lower intensity, prolonged, and often suspended affects, horror's intensity and overwhelming nature, alongside its varying temporality, make it operate differently. Perhaps more than an ugly feeling, horror should be considered a vehement passion: something that, to paraphrase Philip Fisher, disrupts the ordinary flow of experience, and commands our attention to something happening in the present, prior to any integrative acts that may make us regain our wits. But while for Fisher such passions compel and impel our actions,[7] horror, conversely, engulfs the subject in a generalized state of impotence.

Horror undoes the subject—their control over the world and its circumstances, and sense-making as well. It is no coincidence that questions such as "how can this be happening to me?" or "how is this possible?" come to mind as we are left horrified.[8] In part, this suggests the inadequate nature of realism to make sense of this experience: something seems impossible until the moment we are faced with it, as the event (*Ereignis*) of horror reorders and centers the world anew, be it just momentarily.

Such rupture evokes the aesthetics of deformation that I identify as a technique to depict horror beyond the horror genre: if the unimaginable is happening in our life, a realistic descriptive framework may not be sufficient to convey the qualia of this experience. But this should not make us rely on the supernatural to address horror's magnitude. For this reason, I made realism this book's method of analysis: ordinary language philosophy and phenomenology's commitment to the given underpin *Ordinary Horror*'s commitment to the ethos of realism, against the implausible, if not outright impossible, happenings typical of the genre.

A commitment to realism also responds to a desire for sobriety in how we address events whose nature may make us err on the side of the excessive or the unspeakable. With a similar desire to describe Medusa's true appearance, Hannah Arendt wrote about the banality of evil to characterize Adolf Eichmann's actions in orchestrating the Holocaust, as they were carried out with unremarkable obedience to the directives of his superiors, and to the law as well, rather than with ideological fervor or overt malice. Arendt's *Eichmann in Jerusalem* revealed that the emperor had no clothes: against the grandiosity of Evil, she pointed out evil's harrowing banality—something that once shown became immediately apparent, and indeed formulaic. To reactivate a quotation by Wittgenstein already present in this book's introduction, at times "the aspects of things that are most important for us are hidden because of their simplicity and familiarity. (One is unable to notice something—because it is always before one's eyes.) [. . .] We fail to be struck by what, once seen, is most striking and most powerful."[9]

This book's goal, too, is to direct attention to something hiding in plain sight: that horror lurks in our lives, and literature as well. If Arendt made us sensitive to the banality of evil, my aim has been to point our attention to the ordinariness of horror: on the one hand, we use the *word* "horror" in daily life more broadly than we do for the extreme situations that define the genre; on the other hand, the *experience* of horror is itself ordinary—

potential and incipient in many familiar situations. From this starting point, first addressed in my introduction, *Ordinary Horror* developed a taxonomy of this experience, reflected on its presence in modernity, and analyzed its depictions in literature.

Being attentive to ordinary horror makes texts readable in new ways. While I traced its substantial presence in a host of Italian authors, *Ordinary Horror* proposes a blueprint for further inquiries. Just like Austin's method, mine too is a "*first* word" rather than an attempt at closing a conversation.[10] My phenomenological slant made me focus on how texts register horror and describe its effects; alternative, complementary approaches are possible, such as those that focus on voicing an explicit protest against ordinary horrors and seek to repair them. Similarly, whereas I focused on what I have termed "aesthetics of deformation" to connect this experience's qualia with its rendition in literary texts, one could also analyze instantiations of the opposite, when aesthetics and phenomenology do not go hand in hand, and horrifying events are narrated with chilling detachment. Moreover, while my five chapters cover a wealth of sources of horror, the pervasiveness of this experience in our world calls for an expansion of our field of vision and thus of scholarly analyses. My visa horror story is just an example of how situations not thoroughly covered in this book may lead to the forced powerlessness that I connect to horror—other examples range from climate change to atomic warfare, from artificial intelligence doomsday scenarios to pandemics.[11] In a similar vein, *Ordinary Horror* is also an invitation to reflect on this experience in other traditions and media.

No matter the open-ended nature of the present study, one point should be clear: horror does not need implausible situations or events to fully manifest itself. This experience, or the possibility thereof, haunts our lives and, by extension, our artistic productions. This is an unsettling realization, one that the spectacular motifs typical of the genre, alongside modernity's comforts and veneer of predictability, may have dulled us to. Indeed, to echo the concluding sentence of chapter 1, who truly believes in horror tales? Yet, while we may not encounter the extraordinary situations of art-horror in our daily lives, shifting our attention to ordinary horror reveals a new vista that demands we challenge our incredulity. This shift in perspective, argued throughout this book, makes it possible to affirm the veracity of an otherwise questionable claim: horror stories are real, and we ought to be afraid.

NOTES

Introduction

1. H. P. Lovecraft, who died in 1937, was included in the Library of America in 2005. The biographical works of S. T. Joshi are a crucial point of reference for Lovecraft's canonization. Alongside these, contemporary materialist and realist philosophies, such as object-oriented ontology and speculative realism, have shown remarkable interest in Lovecraft's work: see Harman, *Weird Realism: Lovecraft and Philosophy*; Botting, "More Things: Horror, Materialism and Speculative Weirdism"; and Peak, "Horror of the Real: H. P. Lovecraft's Old Ones and Contemporary Speculative Philosophy."

2. For an analysis of this new-wave of art-horror cinema, see Church, *Post-Horror: Art, Genre, and Cultural Elevation*.

3. A watershed moment for horror studies was the publication in 1990 of Noël Carroll's *The Philosophy of Horror: Or, Paradoxes of the Heart*. Today, horror studies is a burgeoning field that encompasses a wide range of methodologies ranging from the psychoanalytic approach of Barbara Creed's *The Monstrous-Feminine: Film, Feminism, Psychoanalysis* to the evolutionary social sciences approach of Mathias Clasen's *Why Horror Seduces*. Alongside a more traditionally scholarly interest in the topic of horror, there exists a sprawling and intriguing galaxy of general-interest works on the topic, which cuts across media and ranges from podcasts such as *Horror Vanguard* to para-academic books, such as Jon Greenaway's *Capitalism: A Horror Story*.

4. For these now canonical interpretations of the genre and more, two useful points of departure are Ken Gelder's *The Horror Reader* and Darryl Jones's *Sleeping with the Lights On: The Unsettling Story of Horror*. It is important to emphasize that while zombies and vampires are fictional inventions with roots in folklore, the figure of the witch occupies a more fraught terrain—both symbolic and historical.

Witches were real in the sense that real people, most often women, were accused of witchcraft and persecuted for it. Yet, like vampires and zombies, the witch has also become a durable cultural figure—fictionalized, mythologized, and repeatedly reimagined, especially within the horror genre. On the richness of the figure of the witch within and beyond the horror genre, see at least Creed, *The Monstrous-Feminine: Film, Feminism, Psychoanalysis*, 73–83; and Federici, *Caliban and the Witch: Women, the Body and Primitive Accumulation*, 163–218.

5. There are, of course, exceptions to the focus on horror as a genre only. The two most notorious ones are Julia Kristeva's *Powers of Horror* and Adriana Cavarero's *Horrorism*. While the former concerns itself more with the category of abjection rather than horror in itself, I will return to the latter in chapter 3. David C. Witherington and Naila V. deCruz-Dixon's recent and excellent "The Nature of Horror" analyzes this experience within psychological science, and focuses on horror's connections with gawking, immobilization, and dynamics of social engagement. Another helpful overview of the phenomenon of horror beyond the horror genre is found in Koloskov, "Beyond the Reach: Horror and Phenomenal Life." Koloskov claims that horror's essential feature consists in its unintelligibility. While connected to my focus on powerlessness as horror's constitutive feature, my emphasis on the ordinary, articulated in the following section of this introduction, substantially diverges from Koloskov's analysis. A focus on horror beyond the horror genre has also enabled the exploration of its presence in classical antiquity, providing some fascinating reflections on horror's presence in art canonically considered to be elevated contra the horror genre's traditional status as a low-brow form of entertainment: Thumiger and Kazantzidis, *Horror in Classical Antiquity and Beyond: Body, Affect, Concepts*.

6. Carroll, *The Philosophy of Horror*, 12.

7. Robert Solomon's "Real Horror" is an important predecessor to my work, especially for its emphasis or real-life matters, the role of helplessness in shaping this experience, and the absence of pleasure in it. At the same time, Solomon's essay-length analysis takes a cognitivist slant, different from the phenomenological and aesthetic approach of my book, rooted as it is in ordinary language philosophy. My focus on literary texts, moreover, makes the use of the adjective "real" fraught in relation to the subject matter. The aesthetic mediation literary texts involve makes me prefer to use the word "ordinary," insofar as ordinary horrors can meaningfully signify both real-life scenarios and the literary, fictional renditions of such scenarios.

8. Jonathan Crane made one of the first attempts at bridging the horror genre with the ordinary matters of everyday life, unlinking the genre's critical reception from overly binding connections with the unconscious and the repressed: "In irrevocably linking horror to the unconscious we dismiss, all too hastily, the possibility that horror films have something to say about popular epistemology, about the status of contemporary community, or about the fearsome power of modern technology," Crane, *Terror and Everyday Life*, 29. "New horror films refuse to entertain

the unconscious as they, instead, offer meaningless death in response to the terrors of everyday life" (39). With a distinct focus on the horror genre, Marc Olivier's *Household Horror* also connects horror to the ordinary, and ordinary household objects more specifically, through an approach rooted in object-oriented ontology.

9. Filippo Contesi takes a different path, and in "The Affective Nature of Horror" argues that no fundamental difference exists between "real horror" and "artistic horror" (37). This claim has been challenged by Witherington and deCruz-Dixon in "The Nature of Horror," 142–43.

10. Wittgenstein, *Philosophical Investigations*, §123.

11. Austin, "A Plea for Excuses," 180. In addressing the possible objection that Austin's "we" is inherently exclusionary, Toril Moi writes: "The usual rejoinder is to reject the 'we' as normative, as an attempt to tell others what they *must* say. But this 'we' is neither an order nor an empirical claim. It is, rather, an *invitation* to the reader to test something for herself, to see if she can see what I see. If she can't, we can try to figure out why. The claims of ordinary language philosophy are invitations to a conversation, invitations to do philosophy together," Moi, *Revolution of the Ordinary*, 18.

12. Austin, "A Plea for Excuses," 182.

13. Austin, "A Plea for Excuses." As Stanley Cavell reminds us, the analysis carried forth in ordinary language philosophy is not a substitute for the empirical methods typically employed to collect sociolinguistic data about the use of certain words. Instead, Cavell emphasizes how ordinary language philosophy asks how we recognize when an expression is apt, off-base, or ambiguous, based on the reflective awareness of our day-to-day way of living (hence the idea of "linguistic phenomenology"), not on a survey of frequency counts or large data sets: "He [Austin] is asking something which can be answered by remembering what is said and meant, or by trying out his own response to an imagined situation." Cavell, *Must We Mean What We Say?* 59.

14. Austin, "A Plea for Excuses," 185.

15. Felski, *The Limits of Critique*, 14–51.

16. Felski, *Uses of Literature*, 23.

17. While Felski focuses on "recognition" as a mode of aesthetic identification, this concept resonates with Moi's discussion of "acknowledgment" (derived from Stanley Cavell). For Moi, to acknowledge a text is to respond to its claims upon us—to treat it not merely as an object of knowledge to be dissected, but as a voice that demands an ethical response. Moi, *Revolution of the Ordinary*, 196–221. Literary texts can be a powerful way to acknowledge the horror lurking in the world; on the topic, see in particular chapters 3 and 4 of my book.

18. Moi, *Revolution of the Ordinary*, 181.

19. Moi, *Revolution of the Ordinary*, 182.

20. One could, of course, start questioning whether the word "horror" can be meaningfully applied to the Holocaust. But as soon as I start questioning this connection—one most people would agree with—then nothing else holds anymore,

and we would need to call into question our shared image of the world in its entirety (that is, an image that involves meaningfully and reliably applying the word "horror" to genocide). Wittgenstein addresses the destructive and ultimately sterile nature of such radical skepticism in *On Certainty*, where he composes a nest of reflections that centers on the following proposition: "If I wanted to doubt the existence of the earth long before my birth, I should have to doubt all sorts of things that stand fast for me." Wittgenstein, *On Certainty*, §234. See also §225–54.

21. Wittgenstein, *Philosophical Investigations*, §116: "What *we* do is to bring words back from their metaphysical to their everyday use."

22. Putnam, "12 Philosophers: And Their Influence on Me," 107.

23. Wittgenstein, *Philosophical Investigations*, §129.

24. The topic is referenced throughout the *Philosophical Investigations*. For an overview and its applicability to literary studies, see Moi, *Revolution of the Ordinary*, 49–54.

25. A possible objection is that I may be overlooking the tension between ordinary language, on the one hand, and the extraordinary, poetically heightened use of language literary texts, on the other—that is, the presence in literary texts of what Roman Jakobson termed "literariness." While I do not believe that literary texts necessarily rely on an extraordinary use of language, the question of literariness is just in appearance related to the claims I advance in my book. I am not implying that literary texts themselves are ordinary in their linguistic form or effect. Rather, I invoke ordinary language as a methodological tool or heuristic, which allows me to identify, group together, and analyze the phenomena represented in the sources I study, not as a descriptor of their linguistic qualities per se. I have already begun addressing this tension between ordinary and extraordinary with the example that opened this introduction, and will return to it in chapter 3.

26. Moi, *Revolution of the Ordinary*, 53.

27. On the role of narratives in structuring our emotional lives and self-understanding, and hence on the connections between stories and everydayness, see Goldie, *The Mess Inside: Narrative, Emotion, and the Mind*.

28. I here draw from the Heideggerian concept of "world." For Heidegger, "world" is not simply a collection of physical objects, but the meaningful context within which Dasein operates—it is not a mere backdrop for human activity but a dynamic, relational network of significance in which Dasein finds itself immersed and through which it interprets and understands its own being. In writing about the world-forming powers of the Greek temple, Heidegger states that the "temple work [. . .] structures and simultaneously gathers around itself the unity of paths and relations in which birth and death, disaster and blessing, victory and disgrace, endurance and decline acquire for the human being the shape of its destiny. The all-governing expanse of these open relations is the world of this historical people," Heidegger, "The Origin of the Work of Art," 20–21.

29. Husserl, *Logical Investigations*, 168. It is at times forgotten that this maxim is also explicitly taken up by Heidegger: "The term 'phenomenology' expresses a

maxim that can be formulated: 'To the things themselves!'" Heidegger, *Being and Time*, 24.

30. Readers might find counterintuitive, if not outright contradictory, the establishment of a methodological dialogue between Husserl's radical bracketing of immediacy through *epoché* and ordinary language philosophy's direct focus on everyday immediacy. However, my goal is not to equate these two approaches but to highlight their shared analytical stance toward the ordinary as a meaningful starting point for philosophical investigation. Françoise Dastur clarifies Husserl's method in terms particularly relevant to my approach: "This *epoché*, this suspension of the ontological validity that things have for us in daily life is, according to Husserl, what indicates in a decisive manner the access to the philosophical attitude. But this does not amount to the philosopher turning away from the real world in order to access a celestial world of eternal essences. On the contrary, one lets things appear as they are given as phenomena in the natural attitude which is ours in daily life. In this way, one becomes attentive to their modes of appearing and givenness. What Husserl calls 'phenomenological reduction' does not permit one to escape from the sensible to an intelligible world. It does not permit a movement of becoming into the stability of ideal essences." Dastur, "Phenomenology of the Event: Waiting and Surprise," 180. Otherwise said, Husserl's method, like that of ordinary language philosophy, insists on focusing on, and returning to, the complexity and, potentially, disruptive nature of what appears immediately and ordinarily.

31. Moi, "A Wittgensteinian Phenomenology of Criticism," 47–48.

32. For a different take on horror's phenomenology, one that primarily draws from Maurice Merleau-Ponty and Emmanuel Levinas, see Trigg, *The Thing. A Phenomenology of Horror*. Trigg's evocative book remains centered on the horror genre, focusing on the notion of the unhuman phenomenology: "a phenomenology that runs against the notion that description is a guarantor of truth [. . .] a genuine alien phenomenology in that it is concerned with the limits of alterity rather than simply replacing subjects with objects" (6). While *The Thing*'s central thesis is that "*the horror of the cosmos is essentially the horror of the body*" (12), my work is anchored to the earthly matters evoked by our ordinary use of the word horror and its derivatives. Akin to Trigg's work in focusing on how horror signals the limits of human's epistemology is Eugene Thacker's "horror trilogy": *In the Dust of This Planet*, *Starry Speculative Corpse*, and *Tentacles Longer Than Night*. Thacker relates horror to "the paradoxical thought of the unthinkable," which he argues finds its privileged expression in supernatural horror (Thacker, *In the Dust of This Planet*, 2). Horror, for Thacker, is "*a non-philosophical attempt to think about the world-without-us philosophically*" (9). With a similar emphasis on epistemological matters, and for a useful distinction between horror, on the one hand, and the weird and the eerie, on the other hand, see also Fisher, *The Weird and the Eerie*.

33. For Heidegger's most thorough discussion of *Ereignis*, see Heidegger, *Contributions to Philosophy (of the Event)* and, subsequently, Heidegger, *The Event*. Both

sources are composed of private and fragmented ponderings not initially intended for publication. One of the clearest and most cohesive overviews of *Ereignis* is provided in Vallega-Neu, "Ereignis: The Event of Appropriation."

34. Neumann, "'Being Tied to Experience': Towards a Subjective Account of the Phenomenology of the Event," 21.

35. Dastur, "Phenomenology of the Event: Waiting and Surprise," 182.

36. On the topic, especially in relation to negative events, see Dastur, "Phenomenology of the Event," 185.

37. Heidegger, *Contributions to Philosophy (of the Event)*, 14–15. It is important to note that Heidegger primarily, but not only, speaks of shock in terms of wonder. However, I here follow Peter Sloterdijk's intuition in coloring this shock with darker tonalities. In intersecting the sense of wonder that underpins Heidegger's *Ereignis* with the horrifying nature of the twentieth century, Sloterdijk writes: "Such wonder, beyond the question concerning the reasons for what is discretely wondrous, bends over the abyss of 'the wonder of all wonders,' *that* beings are. For the historian of ideas it is obvious that the ontological intensification of wonder must have a connection to the catastrophic distortions of life in the era of cosmopolitan civil war—it provides the existentiell foundation for the breakthrough into modern revisions of the world-picture. If twentieth-century wonder changed its colors to alienation and horror, this is because the convulsions of the age have spread into the innermost recesses of philosophical discourse." Sloterdijk, *Not Saved: Essays after Heidegger*, 91.

38. Jean-Paul Sartre provides a powerful description of how phenomenological analysis connects to the vibrancy of the real world: "The philosophy of transcendence throws us on to the highway, in the midst of dangers, under a dazzling light. [. . .] Husserl has restored to things their horror and their charm. He has restored to us the world of artists and prophets: frightening, hostile, dangerous, and with its havens of mercy and love. [. . .] Outside, in the world, among others. It is not in some hiding-place that we will discover ourselves; it is on the road, in the town, in the midst of the crowd, a thing among things, a human among humans." Sartre, "Intentionality: A Fundamental Idea of Husserl's Phenomenology," 5.

39. Jauss, "Literary History As a Challenge to Literary Theory"; Iser, *The Act of Reading: A Theory of Aesthetic Response*. For an overview of affective responses to the horror genre, see Hick, "Horror and Its Affects." While Hick's essay is not fully embedded in the framework of affect theory, this approach has become an important one for horror studies. My approach partially intersects with affect theory by foregrounding the affective shock of horror and its power to rearrange one's sense of reality, but differs by rooting analysis in ordinary language and phenomenological description rather than in prediscursive intensities or large-scale affective frameworks as they are affected by systemic forces.

40. If Peter Brooks invited scholars and beyond to read for the plot (Brooks, *Reading for the Plot*), this approach focuses on scenes instead. While obviously influenced by the long history of close-reading, and my training as a philologist, the

attentiveness of my approach to what is present in specific loci of a text, on the surface level, is in part inspired by Marcus and Best's "Surface Reading: An Introduction." Turning back to this introduction's previous section, my approach also echoes theirs insofar as I focus on what a text gives the reader at face-value, rather than excavating a page for deeper or repressed cues. On the debate of surface versus depth, a balanced and sober stance, also as it critically engages with previously mentioned works by Felski and Moi, is found in Landy, "In Praise of Depth: or, How I Learned to Stop Worrying and Love the Hidden."

41. Love, "Close But Not Deep: Literary Ethics and the Descriptive Turn."

42. Moi, "A Wittgensteinian Phenomenology of Criticism," 51.

43. My chapters nuance and develop the distinctions between aesthetics of deformation and these descriptive techniques. I here understand "aesthetics" as the specific formal and stylistic techniques an author uses to render an experience and, potentially, produce an effect in the reader. My choice of talking about aesthetics of deformation instead of, for instance, the grotesque is tied to a desire to connect the phenomenology of the event and aesthetics in the ways addressed by this introduction, along with a respect for the localism of reading for scenes. Relatedly, certain descriptive techniques adjacent to the aesthetics of deformation maintain a historical specificity that would be cumbersome to transpose to other historical periods, or authors typically not connected with that specific current (see, for instance, my discussion of Expressionism in chapter 2). For a different approach to the aesthetics of horror beyond the horror genre, one that draws from German sources, see Bohrer, *Die Ästhetik des Schreckens: Die pessimistische Romantik und Ernst Jüngers Frühwerk*.

44. Dastur emphasizes the element of surprise in the Heideggerian notion of event: "Against all expectation, even if it has been partially expected and anticipated, such is in fact the 'essence' of the event. Based on this we could say without paradox that it is an 'impossible possible.' The event, in its internal contradiction, is the impossible which happens, in spite of everything, in a terrifying or marvelous manner. It always comes to us by surprise, or from that side whence, precisely, it was not expected." Dastur, "Phenomenology of the Event: Waiting and Surprise," 183.

45. Adorno and Horkheimer, *Dialectic of Enlightenment*, 1.

46. Cavarero recently returned to the topic of horror and horrorism also as it concerns horror's contemporary hypervisibility and normalization: "We witness today a permanent broadcasting of horror scenes enabled by the ease of their mechanical reproduction. [. . .] One can speculate that today's measure of our inhumanity, not unlike that of the German bystanders witnessing the Shoah with inexpressive gazes, is linked precisely to the inability to feel shame. Not because we pretend not to see, but because they hypervisibility of horror clouds our eyes," "'Destroy Your Sight with a New Gorgon': Mass Atrocity and the Phenomenology of Horror," 140–41.

47. Sloterdijk, *What Happened in the Twentieth-Century?* 56.

48. This is a minimum definition of horror that I reach via an eidetic reduction that I primarily conduct in chapter 1. This definition will be nuanced and complexified throughout *Ordinary Horror*; experiences are, of course, impossible to encapsulate in a single sentence, yet I find it productive to offer a definition of horror to anchor this experience to a phenomenological core. In thus defining horror, I am in part inspired by Ann Radcliffe, who famously distinguished between horror and terror in the following terms: "Terror and horror are so far opposite, that the first expands the soul, and awakens the faculties to a high degree of life; the other contracts, freezes, and nearly annihilates them." Radcliffe, "On the Supernatural in Poetry," 403. While Radcliffe's account of horror remains anchored to this rather minute mention, in my reflections on the topic I draw inspiration from it: the forced powerlessness that, in my understanding of it, horror evokes and responds to, echoes the paralysis that Radcliffe argues is the central characteristic of this experience. More recently, the immobilization and helplessness horror evokes and responds to have been addressed in Witherington and deCruz-Dixon, "The Nature of Horror," 138–40. While my analysis of horror's phenomenology departs from premises similar to theirs, also when it comes to horror's gawking impulse, I emphasize that it is not any state of helpfulness whatsoever that characterizes horror: it must be a state of *forced* powerlessness—that is, one that is not consensual, and instead an imposition (be it by an agent or an impersonal situation). Moreover, whereas Witherington and deCruz-Dixon focus on horror's violations of dynamics of social engagement, I instead focus on how this experience restructures one's subjective experience of reality, and thus provide a related, yet very distinct development of horror's phenomenology.

49. Descartes, "Discourse on Method," 35.

50. Toulmin, *Cosmopolis*, 5–44. On the same topic, see also Toulmin, *Return to Reason*, 1–82. Toulmin first developed this thesis as early as 1990 in his *Cosmopolis*, where he traces the intellectual history of this phenomenon and highlights its relevance for the foundation of modernity's episteme. His 2003 *Return to Reason* develops philosophically the matters discussed in *Cosmopolis*, and distinguishes between a modern form of rationalism, convinced of the possibility of expanding mathematical inference to social domains, and the concept of reasonableness, which is to say a form of skeptical pragmatism in dealing with complex phenomena as exemplified by a thinker like Montaigne.

51. Taleb, *Antifragile*, 108.

52. Rosa, *The Uncontrollability of the World*, 38.

53. Beyond the names I reference in my introduction, this shift in episteme has been subject of extensive analyses, especially concerning the idea of disenchantment, ranging from Max Weber's *The Protestant Ethic and the Spirit of Capitalism* and *The Sociology of Religion* to Charles Taylor's *Sources of the Self* and *A Secular Age*. I unwind this thread throughout *Ordinary Horror*, and in particular in chapters 1 and 2.

54. I take solutionism to be the tendency of recasting a complex phenomenon

into a technical problem for which a technical solution exists. I draw this term and idea from Morozov, *To Click Everything Click Here: The Folly of Technological Solutionism*.

55. On the topic, see Cerulo, *Never Saw It Coming: Cultural Challenges to Envisioning the Worst*. I will return to Cerulo's book in chapter 1.

56. Habermas, "Modernity: An Unfinished Project," 45.

57. A partial exception is Orazio Labbate's *L'orrore letterario*, which teases out the *orrore* present in works not part of the horror genre, although in an essayistic more than systematic fashion. Focusing on Italian cinema leads to different results, since horror is central in the production of notorious Italian directors such as Mario Bava, Dario Argento, and Lucio Fulci; on the topic of Italian horror cinema, see, among others, Venturini, *Horror italiano*.

58. Aloisi and Camilletti, "Introduction," 2. Another helpful source to navigate the intricacies connecting the modern episteme (and its darker sides) to Italian modernity is Stefano Serafini's *Gothic Italy*, which provides a fascinating overview of how the gothic affected the project of Italian nation-building in the decades immediately following Italy's unification in 1861.

59. On the topic, see Capra and Malvestio, "Horror and *orrore*: A Canon Hiding in Plain Sight."

60. In the aftermath of World War II, Gianfranco Contini's *Italie magique* paved the way for the study of the fantastic in the Italian canon, although this path remained then mostly unbeaten for several decades. In recent years, the intersection of the fantastic, but also the gothic and the weird with the Italian canon has garnered substantial attention. Among the most notable contributions, see Lazzarin, *L'ombre et la forme. Du fantastique italien au XXe siècle*; Camilletti, *Italia lunare*; Malvestio and Serafini, *Italian Gothic*; Malvestio, "New Italian Weird? Definizioni della letteratura italiana del soprannaturale nel nuovo millennio"; Serafini, *Gothic Italy*.

Chapter 1

1. Leopardi, *Zibaldone*, 4175–77. I here refer to the pagination of the autograph, in parenthesis, as is customary practice regarding the *Zibaldone* (abbreviated as *Zib.*). Further citations in this discussion are given parenthetically in the text. On Leopardi's stay in Bologna, and in particular on the development of his materialism while there, see Bazzocchi, ed., *Leopardi e Bologna. Atti del Convegno di studi per il secondo centenario Leopardiano*.

2. See, among others, these two passages from the *Zibaldone*: "I do not believe much of what Montesquieu says, *Dialogue de Sylla et d'Eucrate*, especially on pp. 293–95, to explain the character and actions of Sulla. He makes the common mistake of believing that people start off with a plan of action and follow it through, when our nature, composed of a hundred passions, is always a mass of contradictions, with first one passion then another gaining the upper hand. And people constantly change their ideas about which aim is better than another or, where the

aim remains the same, about the means of achieving it" (*Zib.* 135). "Both the cheerful and the melancholic (whether they are two thinkers and philosophers, or one philosopher at two different times and in two different states) are very sure that they are seeing the truth, and have convincing reasons for their belief" (*Zib.* 1690–91).

3. Husserl, *Ideas Pertaining to a Pure Phenomenology and to a Phenomenological Philosophy,* 214.

4. Sartre, "Intentionality: A Fundamental Idea of Husserl's Phenomenology," 5.

5. I here emend Caesar and D'Intino's translation, which renders "*orribile*" as "awful."

6. Kant, *Critique of Judgement*, 75–164.

7. Descartes, "Discourse on the Method," 35.

8. Following a different yet related critical path, Fabio Camilletti wrote a number of fascinating studies on Leopardi's proximity to the atmospheres characteristic of the gothic and the uncanny especially as they relate to the post-Enlightenment episteme: Camilletti, *Leopardi's Nymphs. Grace, Melancholy, and the Uncanny*; "Leopardi's Night (T)errors, the Uncanny, and the 'Old Wives Tale'"; "'Dietro le porte.' 'Lo spavento notturno' di Giacomo Leopardi, i terrori della notte e la morte in culla tra 'errori popolari' e nosologia medica." On the topic, see also Camilletti and Scialanga, eds., *Lessico Leopardiano 2024. La paura*.

9. Wittgenstein, *Tractatus Logico-Philosophicus*, 68.

10. On Leopardi's critique of religion, see *Zib.* 364, 416, 420, 431, 1342, 1620, 1644–45. See also Martinelli, *Leopardi tra Leibniz e Locke. Alla ricerca di un orientamento e di un fondamento*, 196–99; and Girolami, *L'antiteodicea. Dio, dei, religione nello "Zibaldone" di Giacomo Leopardi*, 51–59.

11. Leopardi, *The Moral Essays*, 99. The noun "*Natura*" is one of the most actively and diversely employed words in Leopardi's lexicon: it means at times "state of nature," at times "the general order of things," at times "the world"—and it is for the most part conceptually opposed to reason. Leopardi's "*Natura*" is at first a benign mother who then, with the intensification of his pessimism, turns into a malign goddess, careless about the fate of mankind she created, tormenting every living being with a need for happiness which is destined to remain unsatisfied. On the relation between nature and mankind's (un)happiness, see *Zib.* 4517.

12. Leopardi, *The Moral Essays*, 104.

13. Leopardi, *The Moral Essays*, 104.

14. Pascal, *Pensées*, 131.

15. I here draw from Sloterdijk, *Not Saved: Essays after Heidegger*, 91. On the topic of horror and the monstrous in Sloterdijk, see Capra, "Staying with the Darkness: Peter Sloterdijk's Anthropotechnics for the Digital Age."

16. These are all topics that recur throughout Leopardi's production, and the interested reader can rely on the editorial index of Caesar and D'Intino's *Zibaldone* translation.

17. Just a few examples: Leopardi's *Paralipomeni della Batracomiomachia* is a

satirical poem that depicts a war between frogs and mice as an allegory for the fraught Neapolitan political situation of 1820–21, and in particular the failed liberal revolution against the Bourbonic government. Leopardi's most famous love poem is *To Silvia*. For Leopardi's interest in astronomy, see his sprawling *Storia dell'astronomia*, which he wrote at the age of fifteen. His 1824 *Discorso sopra lo stato presente dei costumi degl'Italiani* is a treatise on the mores and the character of the Italian society. Finally, on Leopardi and philology, in lieu of referencing a specific reflection on the topic among the many that he penned over the years, I recommend that the interested reader consult Timpanaro, *La filologia di Giacomo Leopardi*.

18. Leopardi, *Canti*, 107. To provide another example of how Leopardi's highly dysphoric system accommodates the possibility of more positive tonalities, consider how Paul Hamilton finds in Leopardi's *Infinity* a way of sidestepping some of Kant's epistemological conundrums regarding the interrelations of imagination, the imponderable, empirical data, and reason: "Imagination, now failing in that epistemological task, going under, returns us to the inchoate with the unusual pleasure arising from being able to show what it cannot say. Instead of the Kantian pain of empirical failure from which we must be rescued by a higher faculty, Leopardi's infinite, because tailored to no higher intelligence and yet answering with such perfection to what it cannot do, is peculiarly sweet." Hamilton, *Orientation in European Romanticism*, 244.

19. Sartre, *Nausea*, 126–35.

20. Sloterdijk, *Not Saved: Essays after Heidegger*, 129.

21. On the topic of suicide in Leopardi, see, to begin with, Bertolio, "Suicidio." See also Rolfs, *The Last Cross: A History of the Suicide Theme in Italian Literature*, 98–108.

22. "Only one remedy remains: Distraction. This consists in the greatest possible amount of activity, of action, which is to occupy and satiate the developed faculties and the life of the mind. In this way the feeling of this tendency will be either interrupted, or as it were blacked out, confused, its voice smothered and suffocated, eclipsed" (*Zib.* 4187).

23. Kant, *Critique of Judgment*, 90.

24. Kant, *Critique of Judgment*, 91.

25. Kant, *Critique of Judgment*, 94.

26. Heidegger, "The Point of Reference," 4.

27. Leopardi did write about dysphoric emotions such as terror or fear. For a study of this topic from a primarily lexical perspective, see Camilletti and Scialanga, *Lessico Leopardiano 2024. La paura*. My study of horror in Leopardi, coherent with how I approach the topic in this book, intends to draw the (horrifying) conclusions of his philosophy, rather than excavating his use of this specific term.

28. "Now in just the same way the irresistibility of the might of nature forces upon us the recognition of our physical helplessness as beings of nature, but at the same time reveals a faculty of judging ourselves as independent of nature, and

discovers a pre-eminence above nature that is the foundation of a self-preservation of quite another kind from that which may be assailed and brought into danger by external nature." Kant, *Critique of Judgment*, 92.

29. Burke, *A Philosophical Enquiry into the Sublime and Beautiful*, 57.

30. Kant, *Critique of Judgement*, 78–90.

31. Leopardi, *Canti*, 297. I emend Galassi's translation, by rendering the original "*orror*" as "horror" instead of "fear."

32. See at least Luporini, *Leopardi progressivo;* and Negri, *Lenta ginestra.*

33. Taleb, *Antifragile*, 108.

34. Leopardi, *Canti*, 291, emphasis in original.

35. Cerulo, *Never Saw It Coming: Cultural Challenges to Envisioning the Worst*, 234.

36. "*Computisteria*" is a word hardly translatable into English. In their translation of the *Zibaldone*, Caesar and D'Intino translate "*computisteria*" as "accounting." Their translation, however, does not evoke the deep history of computation that leads from the premodern world to the modern computer, and that is present in the semantic root of "*computisteria.*" For this reason I decided to leave the word here untranslated.

37. Leibniz, *The Art of Controversies*, 266.

38. Capra, "Una realtà zibaldonica. Attualità e inattualità della *Proposta di premi fatta dall'Accademia dei Sillografi.*"

39. On solutionism, see Morozov, *To Save Everything, Click Here: The Folly of Technological Solutionism.* On Leopardi and technological solutionism, see Capra, "Torquato Tasso o GPT-3?" 105–19.

40. Leopardi, *The Moral Essays*, 55.

41. Dewey, *The Quest for Certainty: A Study of the Relation of Knowledge and Action.*

42. Leopardi, *Canti*, 307.

43. Leopardi, *Canti*, 309.

44. This, of course, does not mean that Leopardi is uninterested in the sublime. On the contrary, scholars have repeatedly underlined the importance of the sublime in Leopardi's work. See, among others, Bodei, *Leopardi e la filosofia*, 63–95; and Gaetano, *Giacomo Leopardi e il sublime.*

45. On the topic, see Severino, *Il nulla e la poesia. Alla fine dell'età della tecnica: Leopardi*, alongside *Cosa arcana e stupenda* and *In viaggio con Leopardi. La partita sul destino dell'uomo.*

46. The following, closely related passage from the *Zibaldone* echoes this reflection: "It seems that only what does not exist, the negation of being, nothingness, can be limitless, and that infinity is substantially the same as nothingness" (*Zib.* 4178).

47. "The origin of a profound sense of unhappiness, or the development of what is called sensibility, usually comes from the lack or the loss of great and vivid illusions" (*Zib.* 231).

48. A momentous encounter during the years of Leopardi's education was the one with the French philosopher Pierre Bayle, whose skepticism and general suspicion regarding the ability of reason to deliver certain knowledge about the world left a profound trace on Leopardi's production: "Bayle's dictum, that reason is an instrument of destruction rather than construction, applies very well and in fact goes back to what I think I observed elsewhere, namely that the progress of the human spirit since the renaissance, especially in these most recent times, has consisted and continues all the time to consist mainly, not in the discovery of positive truths, but substantially of negative ones. It consists, in other words, in knowing the falsity of what in the more or less distant past was thought to be certain, or else our ignorance about what we thought we knew" (*Zib.* 4192). On the topic, see De Liguori, "Da Teofrasto a Stratone, L'itinerario filosofico di Giacomo Leopardi"; and Damiani, *L'impero della ragione. Studi Leopardiani*, 83–104.

49. Readers of H. P. Lovecraft will recognize familiar overtones in Leopardi's idea that truth is nothing necessarily desirable: "The most merciful thing in the world, I think, is the inability of the human mind to correlate all its contents. We live on a placid island of ignorance in the midst of black seas of infinity, and it was not meant that we should voyage far. The sciences, each straining in its own direction, have hitherto harmed us little; but some day the piecing together of dissociated knowledge will open up such terrifying vistas of reality, and of our frightful position therein, that we shall either go mad from the revelation or flee from the deadly light into the peace and safety of a new dark age." Lovecraft, *Tales*, 167. The echoes between Leopardi and Lovecraft are substantial, although they remain an understudied topic. For a mention of Lovecraft in the context of a Leopardian essay, see Camilletti, "Leopardi avec Sade. Impotence and jouissance in 'La ginestra,'" 213. Cipriani's "Exploring Alienation and Knowledge" offers a more sustained, though still embryonic, first comparative analysis of the two authors. For Cipriani, "while both authors acknowledge the indifference of the cosmos, their responses to this reality diverge significantly. Lovecraft's cosmicism presents a bleak vision where knowledge leads to despair and isolation, reflecting a profound existential crisis. In contrast, Leopardi's cosmic pessimism recognizes the cruelty of existence while advocating for ethical engagement and human solidarity" (297).

50. Friedrich Nietzsche too, a reader and admirer of Leopardi, will argue for a similar philosophical stance: Kain, "Nietzsche, Truth, and the Horror of Existence."

51. Other than the already referenced works by Severino, see, among others, Folin, *Leopardi e l'imperfetto nulla;* and Carrera, "The Consistency of Nothingness: Leopardi's Struggle with 'solido nulla.'"

52. Leopardi, *Lettere*, 230–231. Translations from Leopardi's *Lettere* are mine.

53. Leopardi, *Lettere*, 243–44.

54. Eliot, *The Complete Poems and Plays*, 172.

55. Leopardi, *Lettere*, 244.

56. Leopardi, *Lettere*, 244.

57. “The more Leopardi’s notion of nothingness becomes complex, the more it comes close to being dangerously inconsistent.” Carrera, “The Consistency of Nothingness,” 152.

58. “The horror and fear man has, on the one hand, of nothingness and, on the other hand, *of eternity* appear everywhere” (*Zib.* 644).

59. See, for instance, Leopardi’s poems *To Ahriman* and *To Himself.*

60. Leopardi, *Canti*, 235.

61. The idea of limit is central in Leopardi’s production. As a point of departure on this topic, see Aloisi, “Limite/Confine.”

Chapter 2

1. Heller, *Edvard Munch: The Scream*, 107. See also Schwenger, “Phenomenology of the Scream.”

2. Harrison, *1910: The Emancipation of Dissonance*, 3.

3. On the looming sense of crisis of the period, see Burrow, *The Crisis of Reason: European Thought, 1848–1914* and Harrison, *1910*. The Leopardian quote comes from Leopardi, *Canti*, 291, emphasis in original.

4. On how the horrors of World War I, and warfare more generally, would influence horror films and literature, see Poole, *Wasteland: The Great War and the Origins of Modern Horror.*

5. Sloterdijk, *Not Saved*, 91.

6. I here echo the notorious formulation that opens Adorno and Horkheimer’s *Dialectic of Enlightenment*, 1.

7. Contini, “Espressionismo letterario.”

8. On Michelstaedter and Expressionism, see Harrison, *1910*, 8–9, 124–25, 160–62; and Bini, *Carlo Michelstaedter and the Failure of Language*, 192–254. See also Campailla, “Espressionismo e filosofia della contestazione in Michelstaedter,” 103–31; and Portinari, “Deserto con poesia.” On Pirandello and Expressionism, see Corsinovi, *Pirandello e l’espressionismo*; Bini, “Pirandello, Michelstaedter e l’Espressionismo.”

9. See Cangiano, “Modernism and Rhetoric: Pirandello and Michelstaedter”; Perli, “La vita e la forma. Michelstaedter e Pirandello,” 25–37. See also Salsano, *Michelstaedter tra D’Annunzio, Pirandello e il mondo della vita.*

10. “Necrologio di Carlo Michelstaedter.”

11. Papini, “Un suicidio metafisico.” More recently, see Brianese, *L’arco e il destino. Interpretazione di Michelstaedter*, 65–96.

12. Bini, *Carlo Michelstaedter and the Failure of Language*, 255–68. Another hypothesis is that Michelstaedter had contracted syphilis, and that this played a fundamental role in his suicide; on the topic, see Pradella, *110. Carlo Michelstaedter e il tempo della verità.*

13. See in particular Harrison, “The Michelstaedter Enigma.”

14. Harrison, “The Michelstaedter Enigma,” 133.

15. See primarily Leopardi’s *Dialogue between Plotinus and Porphyry.* On the

topic of suicide in Leopardi, a helpful lexical overview is provided by Bertolio, "Suicidio."

16. No critical contribution on Michelstaedter can overlook the philosophical thrust of his work. Besides the aforementioned scholarship on the author, on this topic specifically see also Cerruti, *Carlo Michelstaedter*; De Monticelli, *Il richiamo della persuasione. Lettere a Carlo Michelstaedter*; Fortunato, *La protesta e l'impossibile. Cinque saggi su Michelstaedter*; Garin, "Postilla: Carlo Michelstaedter."

17. Michelstaedter, *Persuasion and Rhetoric*, 11. Further citations of this work, abbreviated as *PR*, will be given parenthetically in the text.

18. See, for instance, Michelstaedter's late letters: Michelstaedter, *Epistolario*, 407, 441. His earlier letters, too, constitute an important testimony of this struggle; for instance, the one he sends to his sister in 1906, where Michelstaedter already voices depressive tendencies (165).

19. In arguing for the present-centered nature of horror, I am also inspired by Hans Ulrich Gumbrecht's reflections on the concept of presence: Gumbrecht, *Production of Presence: What Meaning Cannot Convey.*

20. Heidegger, *Being and Time*, 231–46.

21. On Michelstaedter's reflections on death, with emphasis on how they connect to Heidegger's, see Brianese, *L'arco e il destino*, 149–92.

22. Michelstaedter was indeed by no means a stranger to more directly artistic forms of writing, with a production including poems, aphorisms, literary dialogues, and short stories; on the topic, see Campailla, *Pensiero e poesia di Carlo Michelstaedter*; Bini, *Carlo Michelstaedter and the Failure of Language*, 101–91; Harrison, *1910*, 122–25; Perli, *Oltre il deserto. Poetica e teoretica di Michelstaedter*; Pistelli, *Carlo Michelstaedter. Poesia e ansia di assoluto.* He also mastered to a high level the art of painting, and produced a number of expressionist sketches that are thoroughly addressed in Bini, *Carlo Michelstaedter and the Failure of Language*, 192–254.

23. And yet, he was painfully aware of how his work was not likely to change anyone's mind. As he writes at the outset of *Persuasion and Rhetoric*, "I know I am talking because I'm talking, but I also know I shall not persuade anyone, and this is dishonesty; but rhetoric ἀναγκάζει με ταῦτα δρᾶν βίᾳ, 'forcibly compels me to do things'" (*PR*, 4).

24. Original emphasis. I add a second "well" at the beginning of this translation to preserve the repetition present in the original.

25. The philosophical proximity between Michelstaedter and the phenomenological tradition has been a topic of in-depth studies, which have gone so far as to suggest Michelstaedter's direct influence on Heidegger: Vašek, *Schein und Zeit: Martin Heidegger und Carlo Michelstaedter.*

26. Leopardi features in the authorial preface of *Persuasion and Rhetoric* as one of the figures in history who already carried forth the instances Michelstaedter presents in his book (*PR*, 4). According to the curators of the English translation of *Persuasion and Rhetoric*, among the modern authors, Leopardi, for Michelstaedter, "had the clearest and most profound impact" (*PR*, xxii). Other than Leopardi's

name repeatedly appearing in his writings, Michelstaedter also wrote a handful of marginal notes on his copies of Leopardi's work; on the topic, see Campailla, *Scrittori giuliani*, 51–64. Schopenhauer, too, frequently appears in Michelstaedter's work, sometimes in dialogue with Leopardi himself: Michelstaedter, *Opere*, 839–40. Michelstaedter also proposed to the eminent Italian critic Benedetto Croce a translation of Schopenhauer's *World As Will and Representation*, which Croce rejected: Michelstaedter, *Epistolario*, 277–78.

27. Trauma studies developed for the most part in the 1990s, and relied on Freudian theory to study experiences so extreme and negative as to challenge the limits of language, memory, and meaning. Two crucial points of departure on the topic are Caruth, *Unclaimed Experience: Trauma, Narrative and History;* and LaCapra, *Writing History, Writing Trauma*. Ruth Leys's *Trauma: A Genealogy* also investigates the conceptual history of trauma, and emphasizes the theoretical oscillations between different paradigms in scholarly discussions. For a recent overview of the field with specific emphasis on literary studies, see Kurtz, ed., *Trauma and Literature*.

28. On the topic, see Mandel, *Against the Unspeakable: Complicity, the Holocaust, and Slavery in America;* and Trezise, "Unspeakability," plus *Witnessing Witnessing*, 40–62.

29. Davis and Meretoja, "Introduction to Literary Trauma Studies," 3–4.

30. Davis and Meretoja, "Introduction to Literary Trauma Studies," 1.

31. Harrison, *1910*, 122.

32. Emmanuel Levinas wrote evocative pages on horror, the night, and depersonalization (see, in particular, Levinas, *Existence and Existents*, 57–74). According to him, "in horror a subject is stripped of his subjectivity, of his power to have private existence. The subject is depersonalized. 'Nausea,' as a feeling for existence, is not yet a depersonalization; but horror turns the subjectivity of the subject, his particularity qua *entity*, inside out. It is a participation in the *there is*, in the *there is* which returns in the heart of every negation, in the *there is* that has 'no exits.' It is, if we may say so, the impossibility of death, the universality of existence even in its annihilation." (61). While my approach to horror differs greatly from Levinas's, his reflections on how this experience drains the subject from within could productively be used to read Michelstaedter's horror scenes. I thank one of the anonymous readers of my manuscript for having brought this connection to my attention. It must also be noted that Levinas's work has also been productively applied to the analysis of the horror genre: on the topic, see at least Trigg, *The Thing*, 46–59; and Burke, *The Ethics of Horror*.

33. I here emend the translation by restoring the authorial third-person plural in lieu of the second-person singular in the first sentence of the quotation.

34. I here emend the translation by restoring the authorial third-person singular in lieu of the second-person singular.

35. I emend the translation of "un pranzo abbondante," and render it "abundant lunch" instead of "abundant dinner."

36. Leopardi, *Canti*, 297.

37. On the topic see Cangiano, *The Wreckage of Philosophy: Carlo Michelstaedter and the Limits of Bourgeois Thought*, 20–21. On Michelstaedter's biography, see Franchi, *Una disperata speranza. Profilo biografico di Michelstaedter.*

38. Toulmin, *Cosmopolis*.

39. Conti and Silei, *Breve storia dello stato sociale*.

40. Beniger, *The Control Revolution: Technological and Economic Origins of the Information Society*, vi.

41. On the topic, see also Fressoz, *L'apocalypse joyeuse. Une histoire du risque technologique*.

42. Cangiano's book on Michelstaedter provides a thorough and valuable overview of how this young philosopher's thinking intersected with, but also diverged from, some of the most important philosophical currents of his time, in particular when it comes to societal processes of rationalization and atomization: Cangiano, *The Wreckage of Philosophy: Carlo Michelstaedter and the Limits of Bourgeois Thought*.

43. On Pirandello's biography and its role in his production, see Andreoli, *Diventare Pirandello. L'uomo e la maschera*.

44. Pirandello, *The Late Mattia Pascal*, 139. I emend the translation of "*strappo*," and render it as "tear" instead of "a little hole."

45. Pirandello, *The Late Mattia Pascal*, 140.

46. As a point of departure regarding *On Humor*, see Pedullà, "Humor."

47. "Life is a continual flux which we try to stop, to fix in stable and determined forms [. . .]. The forms in which we seek to stop, to fix in ourselves this constant flux, are the concepts, the ideals with which we would like consistently to copy, all the fictions we create for ourselves, the conditions, the state in which we tend to stabilize ourselves" (Pirandello, *On Humor*, 137).

48. Cangiano, "Modernism and Rhetoric: Pirandello and Michelstaedter," 184.

49. Pirandello, *On Humor*, 137.

50. Pirandello, *On Humor*, 138. The translators render the Italian "*orrida*" as "dreadful," which I emend to "horrid."

51. Pedullà emphasizes the expressionistic thrust of *On Humor*: "from this Pirandello emerges expressionism—that is to say, the language among those of the historical avant-garde that came out on top. With its invitation to decompose, disorder, and sow discord, *On Humor* sets down the basis for a narrative model that, mixing linguistic registers, extracts a glow of emotions that never would have existed if incompatible words had not been rubbed together to create sparks in the form of heartbreaking ideas" (Pedullà, "Humor," 153).

52. Pirandello describes *umorismo* (humor) as "the feeling of the opposite," and distinguishes it from the comic, defining the latter as "perception of the opposite": while the comic elicits laughter through incongruity, the humorous reveals deeper, often tragic, layers of reality beneath the surface, prompting reflection and empathy rather than mere amusement. Pirandello, *On Humor*, 113.

53. Pirandello, *On Humor*, 138.

54. Harrison, *Essayism: Conrad Musil & Pirandello*, 87–120, 189–215. See also Subialka, "Modernity."

55. Pirandello, *One, No One, and One Hundred Thousand*, 22.

56. Pirandello, *One, No One, and One Hundred Thousand*, 31.

57. Pirandello, *One, No One, and One Hundred Thousand*, 19.

58. Pirandello, *One, No One, and One Hundred Thousand*, 140–41.

59. On the topic of horror in Pirandello, Pietro Frassica writes: "As for the term 'horror', present even in his earliest works, it must be said that it takes on a thematic meaning that, while colored from time to time with different nuances, converges in the intolerance of sexuality as physical abandonment." Frassica, *A Marta Abba per non morire*, 32. My translation.

60. Caputi, *Pirandello and the Crisis of Modern Consciousness*.

61. Pupo, *Interviste a Pirandello. "Parole da dire, uomo, agli altri uomini,"* 527. My translation. On the relevance of the theme of suicide in Pirandello, see Harrison, "Suicide."

Chapter 3

1. United Nations, "Universal Declaration of Human Rights."

2. Franco Baldasso brings them together under the label of World War II Italian testimonial literature: Baldasso, *Against Redemption*, 180.

3. I provided a first overview of Malaparte's and Levi's flawed yet productive understanding of Cartesianism in Capra, "Descartes at War: Curzio Malaparte and Primo Levi."

4. This is not surprising: notoriety and misinterpretation often run hand in hand, and as early as in Voltaire's writings trenchant judgments appear, which cherry-pick elements of Descartes's philosophy while leaving aside others. On the topic, see Jolley, "The Reception of Descartes' Philosophy," 393.

5. Descartes, "Discourse on the Method," 35.

6. Malaparte, *Opere scelte*, 727–28. All translations from "The Mad Rifle" are mine, as the English translation of *Kaputt* inexplicably expunges this crucial section. The English translation that I will be using for my discussion of the rest of the book is Malaparte, *Kaputt*. Further citations of this work will be given parenthetically in the text.

7. "Spin was a hunting dog, and war, everyone knows, is a hunting game where men are both hunters and prey." Malaparte, *Opere scelte*, 731.

8. Malaparte, *Opere scelte*, 729.

9. Malaparte, *Opere scelte*, 729. On the topic of military technology in Malaparte, see Baldasso, "Curzio Malaparte and the Tragic Understanding of Modern History."

10. Malaparte, *Opere scelte*, 731.

11. Malaparte, *Opere scelte*, 730.

12. "Minister Mameli and the officials of the Legation, pale and anxious, surely

knew what they were sitting there waiting for, while smoking one cigarette after another." Malaparte, *Opere scelte*, 731.

13. Malaparte, *Opere scelte*, 732.

14. Malaparte, *Opere scelte*, 733.

15. Malaparte, *Opere scelte*, 743.

16. On Malaparte's life and work, the most important reference is Serra, *Malaparte. Vite e leggende*, recently translated in English as *Malaparte: A Biography.* See also Martellini, *Invito alla lettura di Curzio Malaparte.* Malaparte has become in recent years the object of substantial critical interest, in Italy and beyond: some contributions include Baldasso, *Curzio Malaparte, la letteratura crudele. Kaputt, La pelle, e la caduta della civiltà europea*; De Paulis, *Curzio Malaparte. Il trauma infinito della Grande Guerra*; Baglivo et al., eds., *Curzio Malaparte e la ricerca dell'identità europea.* See also the *Cahier de l'Herne* dedicated to the author: De Paulis, ed., *Curzio Malaparte.*

17. See Serra, *Malaparte*, 288–307.

18. Malaparte, *Opere scelte,* 429. Malaparte draws this explanation from the *Meyer Konversations-Lexicon,* a German encyclopedia Malaparte quotes in *Kaputt*'s authorial preface. The English translation of *Kaputt* expunges this quote, so I here rely on the Italian original.

19. On Malaparte's style, see Baglivo, "Una poetica dell'immaginazione. Il realismo magico di Curzio Malaparte"; and Panella, *L'estetica dello choc. La scrittura di Curzio Malaparte tra esperimenti narrativi e poesia.*

20. A dialogue with Prince Eugen opens *Kaputt* (7). On the historicity of their encounter, see Serra, *Malaparte*, 319.

21. Serra, *Malaparte*, 340.

22. Gheorghiu, "The Iași Pogrom in Curzio Malaparte's *Kaputt*: Between History and Fiction." Gheorghiu concludes that Malaparte was likely not in Iași during the days of the pogrom and that his account is a literary testimony derived from other sources, such as the Italian consul Sartori.

23. Kundera, "*The Skin*: Malaparte's Arch-Novel," 161.

24. On the project of controlling the uncontrollable as a feature of Western modernity, see, for a sociological and phenomenological perspective, Rosa, *The Uncontrollability of the World.* On the "dreams of rationality," see Toulmin's chapter on the topic in Toulmin, *Return to Reason*, 67–82.

25. Horror, central throughout the text, is also at times juxtaposed to, and intermixed with, other feelings, such as pity (*Kaputt*, 91, 142), wonder (159), shame (18, 21), or disgust (425).

26. Malaparte, *Opere scelte*, 837. The English translation of *Kaputt* expunges this passage.

27. On the (im)possibility of communicating pain, see Scarry, *The Body in Pain: The Making and Unmaking of the World*; and in particular, with reference to warfare, 60–157. In *The Body in Pain*, Scarry affirms that "the objectlessness, the complete absence of referential content, almost prevents it [embodied pain] from being

rendered in language [. . .]. But it is also its objectlessness that may give rise to imagining." Imagining, for Scarry, is a "ground of last resort" but also a "visionary solution" that makes up for unacceptable or incomprehensible objects in the natural world, such as Malaparte's white light. This "visionary solution" is ambivalent, at once "creation" and "wounding," at once alleviation of pain via its projection onto symbolic objects, yet also betrayal of the body's suffering through the overwhelming power of such symbolic objects (161–63).

28. Malaparte's flawed understanding of Cartesianism likely made of the French philosopher the champion of this tendency—on the topic, see Malaparte, *Diary of a Foreigner in Paris*, 52; and Capra, "Descartes at War: Curzio Malaparte and Primo Levi," 111–20. On whether Cartesianism programmatically seeks to untether reason from emotion, or only temporarily as a methodological negation, see Damasio, *Descartes' Error*, 127–64, 223–44; and, more generally, Brown, *Descartes and the Passionate Mind*.

29. "I wanted to go home, I wanted to go to Capri, to my lonely house high above the sea" (*Kaputt*, 408).

30. Serra, *Malaparte*, 329.

31. Malaparte, *Opere scelte*, 965. Translation is mine, as these words from the frontispiece are absent from the English version that I will be using,

32. Malaparte, *The Skin*, 3. Further references to this work will be given parenthetcially in the text.

33. On Malaparte's philosophical intertexts and interests, see Orsucci, *Il "giocoliere d'idee." Malaparte e la filosofia*.

34. I emend the translation of "lezzo orrendo" as "frightful stench" to "horrible stench."

35. Harrison, "Preface," viii.

36. It must be said, however, that Malaparte assumes at times a moralistic stance in relation to society's customs, as becomes especially clear in his *Diary of a Foreigner in Paris*.

37. Cavarero, *Horrorism*, 29–32.

38. Taleb, *The Black Swan*, xxii.

39. For a philosophical analysis of modernity's tendencies of privileging abstract reasoning, see Toulmin, *Return to Reason*, 14–46.

40. Malaparte, *Diary of a Foreigner in Paris*, 57. On Malaparte's stay in France, see also Thiret, "L'influenza perenne. Malaparte francese." On Sartre's *Nausea* as the book of a "rationalist in revolt," see Harrison, *Forests*, 145–48.

41. In the late 1930s, *Prospettive* was a rare cosmopolitan window into Europe for an increasingly sealed Italy. With it, Malaparte and the other contributors introduced their readers to the works of authors such as Rilke, Joyce, Pound, and Heidegger. On the journal *Prospettive*, see Martellini, *Le "Prospettive" di Malaparte*.

42. Malaparte, "Prigione gratis," 4. In this piece, Malaparte argues that Soviet literature stopped at the level of content, and overlooked the question of how that

content ought to be expressed. In so doing, he writes, "Soviet literature is, thus, nothing but a literature of bourgeois content and expression" (4). Translations from "Prigione gratis" are mine.

43. I emend the translation of "scricchiolio orrendo" from "dreadful grinding noise" to "horrible grinding noise."

44. Kundera, "The Skin: Malaparte's Arch-Novel," 161.

45. "The fantastic occupies the duration of this uncertainty [. . .]. The fantastic is that hesitation experienced by a person who knows only the laws of nature, confronting an apparently supernatural event" (Todorov, *The Fantastic*, 25).

46. This is the title of one of Levi's essays: Levi, "The Black Hole of Auschwitz."

47. Levi's writing practices are described in his essay "Ex-Chemist." On Levi's life and work, see Belpoliti, *Primo Levi: An Identikit*. On Levi's complex identity, and how this complexity affected his literary production, see Harrowitz, *Primo Levi and the Identity of a Survivor*. For a curated critical overview of Levi's work, see Gordon, ed., *The Cambridge Companion to Primo Levi*.

48. Descartes, "Meditations on First Philosophy," 59.

49. Primo Levi, *If This Is a Man*, 9. Further references to this work (abbreviated as *ITIM*) will be given parenthetically in the text.

50. "To destroy a man is difficult, almost as difficult as to create one: it wasn't easy, it wasn't quick, but you Germans have succeeded" (*ITIM*, 143). Stefano Bellin offers a Derridean reading of the same topic in "Specters of Levi: Shame and the Deconstruction of the Human."

51. Cavarero, *Horrorism*, 33–46.

52. Levi, *The Drowned and the Saved*, 2515.

53. On the topic of Levi, Dante, and Hell, see Ferme, "Translating the Babel of Horror: Primo Levi's Catharsis through Language in the Holocaust Memoir *Se questo è un uomo*"; Portnoff, "Levi's Auschwitz and Dante's Hell"; Kay, "Primo Levi, Dante, and Language in Auschwitz."

54. Levi, *The Drowned and the Saved*, 2431.

55. Levi addresses this point in his "The Grey Area." In the essay, he acknowledges the existence of a zone of grayness in the life of the Lager where clear distinctions between good and evil became blurred (hence the essay's title), such as for prisoners who, to varying degrees and under different levels of coercion, collaborated with their oppressors in exchange for preferential treatment or survival advantages. Yet, Levi maintains that this awareness must not overshadow or erase the distinction between victims and perpetrators—that is, the distinction between those who were forced by the necessity of survival, on the one hand, and those whose horrific acts responded to ulterior reasons such as their sadism or desire for power, on the other. Levi writes: "There has been much discussion of this mimesis, the identification, imitation, or trading of roles between oppressor and victim. This is not virgin territory: assertions of all kinds have been made, true and invited, disturbing and banal, insightful and stupid. On the contrary, it is a field that has been clumsily plowed, trampled, and ravaged. When the film direc-

tor Liliana Cavani was asked to explain briefly the meaning of a fine but mendacious film of hers, *The Night Porter* (1973), she stated, 'We are all victims or murderers and we accept these roles voluntarily. Only Sade and Dostoyevsky really understood this.' She added that she believed that 'in every environment, in every relationship, there is victim-tormentor dynamic more or less clearly expressed and generally experienced on an unconscious level.' I am no expert on the unconscious or the inner depths, but I do know that there are few experts, and that those few are more cautious. I do not know, nor am I particularly interested in knowing, whether a murderer is lurking deep within me, but I do know that I was an innocent victim and not a murderer. I know that murderers existed, and not just in Germany, and that they still exist, retired or on active duty, and that confusing them with their victims is a moral disease, an aesthetic license, or a sinister sign of complicity. Above all, it is a precious service rendered (intentional or not) to the deniers of truth." Levi, *The Drowned and the Saved*, 2439–40.

56. Levi, *The Drowned and the Saved*, 2516. In his *Periodic Table*, a short story collection he publishes in 1975, Levi writes the following about his Cartesianism and Cartesianism's project of exerting control over the world and its circumstances: "We began to study physics together, and Sandro was amazed when I tried to explain to him some of the ideas I confusedly cultivated at that time. That the nobility of Man, acquired in a hundred centuries of trial and error, consisted in making himself master of matter, and that I had enrolled in Chemistry because I wished to keep faith with this nobility. That to conquer matter is to understand it, and understanding matter is necessary in order to understand the universe and ourselves; and that the Periodic Table of Mendeleev, which in those very weeks we were laboriously learning to sort out, was therefore a poem, loftier and more solemn than all the poems we had absorbed in high school: if you thought carefully, it even had rhymes! That, if he was seeking the bridge, the missing link, between the world of papers and the world of things, he needn't look far: it was there, in Autenrieth, in these smoky laboratories of ours, and in our future occupation" (786–87).

57. White, "Figural Realism in Witness Literature."

58. Butler, "Primo Levi for the Present," 285.

59. Levi, *The Drowned and the Saved*, 2501.

60. On Levi's intricate relation with fiction and testimony, see Mariani, *Primo Levi e Anna Frank. Tra testimonianza e letteratura.*

61. Levi, *The Drowned and the Saved*, 2515.

62. Levi, *The Truce*, 397–98.

63. Sloterdijk, *What Happened in the Twentieth-Century?* 57.

64. Levi, *The Drowned and the Saved*, 2522.

65. Levi, "The Brute Power," 2630.

66. Leopardi, *Canti*, 235: "Disdain yourself now, nature, the brute / hidden power that rules to common harm, / and the boundless vanity of all."

67. Levi, "The Brute Power," 2632. On the topic of homeostasis, modernity, and rationalism, see Toulmin, *Return to Reason*, 48–49.

68. Toulmin, *Return to Reason*, 44.

69. Witherington and deCruz-Dixon, "The Nature of Horror," 141–42.

Chapter 4

1. Koestler, "The Nightmare That Is a Reality."

2. It goes without saying that very little is banal for the person experiencing a "banal" instantiation of the horrifying. Here, "banal" must be understood as closely connected to "widespread"—something that society and its members accept as inherent, and thus consider unremarkable. The word "banal" also presents a substantial Arendtian undertone, which I will address in this book's coda.

3. The formulation "*male oscuro*" does not easily lend itself to the English language: it means at once "obscure/dark evil," "obscure/dark disease," or "obscure/dark ill," evoking an existential and clinical undertone at once. Given the difficulties in rendering "*male oscuro*" in translation, I will retain the Italian term.

4. Ortese, *Neapolitan Chronicles*, 11: "*Chronicles* was only a screen, though not entirely illusory, on which to project the painful disorientation, the 'dark suffering of life' [*male oscuro*], as it came to be called, of the person who had written the book." Further references to this work will be given parenthetically in the text. In Berto's case we find the formulation in his book's title, *Il male oscuro*. The translation that I will be using of Berto's novel is William Weaver's (Berto, *Incubus*). Further references to this work, under the English title, will be given parenthetically in the text. The only exception, when I will be providing my own translations, is when I quote from *Il male oscuro*'s "Appendice," which is not included in Weaver's version.

5. "Evident in it [*Chronicles*] are all the signs of an authentic neurosis" (*Chronicles*, 10); "I came down with neurosis" (Berto, *Il male oscuro*, 415).

6. The debates around neorealism are sprawling, and reaching a definition of what neorealism was is no small task. In his *Italian Neorealism: A Cultural History*, Charles Leavitt provides a compelling and comprehensive overview of the debates around the topic, including how this current brought together the documentary and descriptive ethos of nineteenth-century realism with the more introspective, existential tonalities of modernism: Leavitt, *Italian Neorealism: A Cultural History*, 14–48.

7. On the topic of stories versus statistics, and on how stories may stick more decisively than statistics, see Graeber, Roth, and Zimmermann, "Stories, Statistics, and Memory."

8. What I am terming here "the question of expression" is also at the core of neorealism. Consider what Calvino writes in this regard in his 1964 preface to his 1947 neorealist novel *The Path to the Spiders' Nest*: "It was as clear as day to us that the stories that were told were simply raw material: the explosive charge of freedom which inspired young writers in those days resided not so much in their urge to provide documentary information, as in the urge to *express*. Express what? Ourselves, life's rough taste which we had just experienced, the many things we

thought we know or were, and perhaps really did know and really were at that time"; Calvino, *The Path to the Spiders' Nest*, 9. I will return to this topic later in the chapter.

9. Koestler, "The Nightmare That Is a Reality."

10. On the topic of vision in Ortese's *Neapolitan Chronicles*, see Re, "Invisible Sea: Anna Maria Ortese's *Il mare non bagna Napoli*"; and Re, "'Clouds in Front of My Eyes': Ortese's Poetics of the Gaze in 'Un paio di occhiali' and *Il mare non bagna Napoli*."

11. I emend the translation of "*a poco a poco si abitua*" from "one gets used to them" to "one gets used to it."

12. Readers may wonder how an extraordinary happening can be addressed via ordinary language philosophy. But the point here is not about ordinary versus extraordinary circumstances, but about how the word "horror" is used in ordinary language, hence ordinary life—and warfare, an extraordinary circumstance for certain parts of the globe in the present time, can surely be described as horrifying in ordinary language.

13. Ortese, "Estivi terrori," 33. My translation. It is worth noting that Ortese did experience poverty throughout her life: on her biography, see Clerici, *Apparizione e visione. Vita e opere di Anna Maria Ortese*. On the topic of poverty and its horrors in Ortese's *Chronicles*, see Baldi, "Infelicità senza desideri. 'Il mare non bagna Napoli' di Anna Maria Ortese." Baldi's work on Ortese's short stories led to his 2010 monograph on the author: Baldi, *La meraviglia e il disincanto. Studi sulla narrativa breve di Anna Maria Ortese*. On the topic of poverty, see in particular Baldi, *La meraviglia e il disincanto*, 11–72.

14. See, among many other examples, her novel *Alonso e i visionari*, or short stories such as "Il monaciello di Napoli."

15. On the topic, see Ghezzo, "Introduction: Anna Maria Ortese and the Red-Footed Angel."

16. See the recent overview on neorealist narrative in Re, "Neorealist Narrative: Experience and Experiment." Re rightly nuances Ortese's position within the ranks of neorealism (112). See also de Gasperin, *Loss and the Other in the Visionary Work of Anna Maria Ortese*, 106–50; and Seno, *Anna Maria Ortese. Un avventuroso realismo*.

17. Ferroni, *Passioni del Novecento*, 156. My translation.

18. Ortese, *Corpo celeste*, 74: "And this word: *horror*, although, in my experience at that time, only of historical and social origin, was the last great word I learned regarding universal living. [. . .] Finally, here is the Horror: I mean the recurring period of great killings at the popular level—people against people, man against man—which then inevitably end in peace, in which only justice for the dead—that is, their resurrection—is no longer possible." Translations from *Corpo celeste* are mine.

19. I borrow the suggestive formulation "urban horror" from Erin Huang, who uses it in discussing a different context (China) through a different medium (cinema): Huang, *Urban Horror: Neoliberal Post-Socialism and the Limits of Visibility*.

20. Ortese, *Corpo celeste*, 34–35.

21. Ortese, "La plebe regina."

22. On Ortese and the topic of *flânerie,* see Baldi, *La meraviglia e il disincanto*, 52–56. On the role of wandering in relation to the city in the author's production, see Baldi, "Cities 'Paved with Casualties': Ortese's Journeys through Urban Modernity."

23. Ortese's concerns here echo the ones formalized in 1917 by Viktor Shklovsky's concept of *ostranenie*, or "defamiliarization": Shklovsky, "Art, As Device." Whereas Shklovsky left the outcome of *ostranenie* open-ended, I here focus on those instances when a defamiliarizing description is used to convey the horror experienced by a given subject—a horror of a subjective kind, and hence shrouded by the fog of intersubjective opacity. The aesthetics of deformation provides an outlet to signal the phenomenological shift that occurs when the world horrifies.

24. Luhmann, "Second-Order Observation."

25. The intersection of neorealism and deforming aesthetics is a topic worth of more in-depth analysis. Consider what Italo Calvino writes about it, in his preface to *The Path to the Spiders' Nests*: "If Italian literature and art had missed out on expressionism after the First World War, it made up for it at the end of the Second. Perhaps the correct label for that artistic epoch in Italy ought to be 'Neo-expressionism' rather than 'Neo-realism.' The distortions operated by the expressionist lens in this novel are projected on to the faces of those who had been my closest comrades. I was at pains to turn them into caricatures, to make them unrecognizable, 'negative,' because I could write poetically only about 'negativity.'" Calvino, *The Path to the Spiders' Nests*, 13.

26. Ortese, "La città involontaria"; and Ortese, "L'orrore di vivere."

27. Both "The Gold of Forcella" and "The Involuntary City" underscore the labyrinthine nature of Naples, a quality that incubates the horrors Ortese chronicles. In *Gothic Italy,* Serafini discusses the labyrinth motif in relation to the urban ecosystem of Naples in nineteenth-century Italian literature, linking it to the poverty of the city's underbelly and the trope of the gothic haunted mansion (33–37). In this context, Matilde Serao's 1884 *Il ventre di Napoli* serves as a crucial touchstone, constituting, in both form and content, a significant precursor to Ortese's *Neapolitan Chronicles.*

28. I refer from here onward only to the complete text as published in *Chronicles.*

29. On the history of the Granili, see Giordano, *Ferdinando Fuga a Napoli. L'Albergo dei Poveri, il Cimitero delle 366 fosse, i Granili*, 102–15; di Mauro, "La fabbrica dei Granili e la Casina Cinese."

30. It is here worth alluding to how horror's forced powerlessness may result in a deactivation of the will, with this deactivation evoking the adjective "involuntary" present in the title of Ortese's text.

31. Clerici, *Apparizione e visione*, 64.

32. "We were lying in a world of dead men and phantoms [*larve*]. The last trace

of civilization had vanished around and inside us. The work of bestial degradation, begun by the Germans in triumph, had been brought to its conclusion by the Germans in defeat" (*ITIM*, 164).

33. This trope appears in some of Lovecraft's most notorious stories, such as "The Nameless City," "The Call of Cthulhu," or "At the Mountains of Madness."

34. In chapter 1, I discussed how a collapse of distance can transfigure something into a horrifying matter. Here it is precisely Ortese's previous distance from the Granili that allows her to experience the building as horrifying. A similar dynamic may have underpinned the first encounter with the Granili of some of its inhabitants—inhabitants now habituated to the Granili's horrors as that initial collapse of distance belonged to their past rather than her present phenomenology. Otherwise said, being in the Granili becomes an event (*Ereignis*) only for those not yet accustomed to the building.

35. In Dante's *Inferno*, the Giudecca is the innermost zone of the ninth circle of Hell, closest to Lucifer and entirely frozen. This area punishes traitors to their benefactors by encasing them completely in ice, rendering them immobile and silent. In the Granili, the only exception to this generalized stasis is Scarpetella's sister, who, tellingly, had left the Granili to live elsewhere. The father complains with the priest about the girl's screams by saying "That girl is shameless [. . .] she left home without a thought for us. We asked her for help in our need, and she answered that she no longer had parents. Now she's in a state because of her poor brother" (*Chronicles*, 92).

36. Levi, *The Drowned and the Saved*, 2515.

37. "Let me repeat that we, the survivors, are not the true witnesses. This is a troublesome notion that I became aware of gradually by reading other people's memoirs and rereading my own years later. We survivors are an anomalous and negligible minority. We are the ones who, because of our transgressions, ability, or luck, did not touch bottom. The ones who did, who saw the Gorgon, did not come back to tell, or they came back mute. But it is they, the '*Muselmänner*,' the drowned, the witnesses to everything—they are the ones whose testimony would have had a comprehensive meaning. They are the rule, we are the exception." Levi, *The Drowned and the Saved*, 2468.

38. Clerici, *Apparizione e visione*, 231–32.

39. For a historical overview of the tendency of considering theoretical abstraction and logical deduction superior to other modes of analysis, see Toulmin, *Return to Reason*, 29–46.

40. This description echoes the one we encountered in Malaparte, where he described Naples as a shimmering and homogeneous cloud of black flies that, upon closer scrutiny, revealed a city teeming with life, where humans and debris piled up without apparent discontinuities (*Kaputt*, 413).

41. On the topic, see Smith, "Rational Horror."

42. Ortese, *Corpo celeste*, 102.

43. Ortese, *Corpo celeste*, 103.

44. Ortese's admiration for Leopardi bordered on a kind of affection, as is made clear by the epithet "fabulous young person [*giovane favoloso*]" she coins in one of her essays to describe him: Ortese, *Da Moby Dick all'Orsa Bianca*, 11. For Ortese, Leopardi was "the only authentic voice of Italian literature, after Dante"; Ortese, *Corpo celeste*, 98.

45. See Castronovo, *L'Italia del miracolo economico*.

46. Berto self-assesses his own relation to the American tradition in Berto, "L'inconsapevole approccio," 24–48, 58–74.

47. On *Incubus*'s style, see Dottore, *La forma della coscienza. Il male oscuro di Giuseppe Berto*.

48. Piancastelli, *Giuseppe Berto*, 7.

49. On the topic, see Vita, *"Un fulgorato scoscendere." L'opera narrativa di Giuseppe Berto*, 109–75. See also Vettori, *Giuseppe Berto. La passione della scrittura*, 75–121.

50. Ortese, *Estivi terrori*, 33.

51. De Michelis, "Umanità di Berto," 105. My translation. On the topic, see also Vettori, "La predestinazione al male nell'opera di Giuseppe Berto."

52. Leopardi, *Canti*, 297.

53. Berto, *Il male oscuro*, 419. My translation, as Weaver's edition does not include this authorial appendix.

54. Weaver incorrectly translates *"abbandonarmi nel mio orto di agonia"* as "abandoning me to my agony in the garden", which I here emend.

55. Weaver translates *"erano riusciti a raggiungere sulla via del raziocinio"* as "had made in the field of ratiocination," which I here emend.

56. Berto, *Il male oscuro*, 417.

57. Berto, *Il male oscuro*, 420.

58. Koestler, "The Nightmare That Is a Reality."

59. On the topic, see also Schwenger, "Phenomenology of the Scream." Berto reflects on his own relation to neorealism in Berto, "L'inconsapevole approccio," 74–80. Berto's early neorealism, in the words of the author, is deeply tied to a sense of guilt (96).

60. Ortese, *Corpo celeste*, 31.

61. De Michelis, "Umanità di Berto," 116.

62. Koestler, "The Nightmare That Is a Reality."

Chapter 5

1. *Zib.* (4174–77). See chapter 1 of this book for my analysis of the scene.

2. "The 100 Best Books of the 21st Century."

3. Ferrante, *Incidental Inventions*, 40.

4. Bullaro and Love, "Beyond the Margins: 'Ferrante Fever' and Italian Female Writing."

5. Ferrante, *Frantumaglia: A Writer's Journey*, 330. Further references to this work, cited as *FR*, will be given parenthetically in the text.

6. Pinto, Milkova, and Cavarero, "Storytelling Philosophy and Self Writing—Preliminary Notes on Elena Ferrante: An Interview with Adriana Cavarero," 247.

7. I emend Ann Goldstein's translation of the second part of this sentence, where she renders "*pena la vacuità delle pagine*" as "where you suffer the emptiness of the pages."

8. I emend Goldstein's translation by pluralizing the noun "stories," plural in the Italian original but singular in her version.

9. Goldstein translates "*tremendo*" as "terror," which I emend into "terrible."

10. *Marginare* is the verbalized form of the noun *margine* ("margin" or "edge"). In Italian, the prefix *s-* generally indicates a reversal or a privation: *gonfiare* (to inflate) becomes *sgonfiare* (to deflate). *Smarginare* thus evokes a sense of crossing or breaking margins.

11. Translation modified. Goldstein's translation reads: "When shapes lose their contours, we see what most terrifies us."

12. Alessia Ricciardi writes that *smarginatura* names Lila's "horror at the decomposition of physical reality itself" (Ricciardi, *Finding Ferrante: Authorship and the Politics of World Literature*, 16). See also Milkova, *Elena Ferrante As World Literature*, 39, where she connects *smarginatura* to "Lila's horrifying perception of her brother's disintegration" in discussing a scene I will focus on later in this chapter.

13. Ricciardi, *Finding Ferrante*; Milkova, *Elena Ferrante As World Literature*.

14. On the topic of traumatic events and narrative, with particular emphasis on gendered matters, see, among others, Brison, *Aftermath: Violence and the Remaking of the Self*. For a discussion of how horror intersects with trauma, see my chapter 2.

15. Milkova, "Mothers, Daughters, Dolls: On Disgust in Elena Ferrante's *La Figlia Oscura*." See also Pinto, *Elena Ferrante: poetiche e politiche della soggettività*, 37–48.

16. Carlotta Moro briefly discusses Ferrante's engagement with Giacomo Leopardi, in particular as Ferrante's "ecological poetics" relate to Leopardi's: Moro, "Breaking Out of the Cage of Anthropocentrism: Ecofeminism in Elena Ferrante's Neapolitan Quartet and Other Essays," 304–5.

17. Burke, *A Philosophical Enquiry into the Sublime and Beautiful*, 78.

18. Burke, *A Philosophical Enquiry into the Sublime and Beautiful*, 39.

19. Burke, *A Philosophical Enquiry into the Sublime and Beautiful*, 58.

20. Ferrante, *My Brilliant Friend*, 90. Further references to this work, cited as *BF*, will be given parenthetically in the text.

21. Ferrante, *Story of the Lost Child*, 176–77. Further references to this work, cited as *SLC*, will be given parenthetically in the text.

22. On the topic, see at least De Rogatis, *Elena Ferrante. Parole chiave*, 87–91. See also Sarah Chihaya's essay on unforming and deforming in Ferrante's work, in Sarah Chihaya et al., *The Ferrante Letters: An Experiment in Collective Criticism*, 123–51. According to Milkova, *smarginatura* can be considered the fundamental

narratological device of the Neapolitan Novels: Milkova, *Elena Ferrante As World Literature*, 38–43.

23. While Cavarero's *Horrorism* does not dedicate an individual chapter to rape in the specific, the presence of this most horrifying act haunts the book also as a "side-effect" of other acts of horrorism, such as warfare or torture: Cavarero, *Horrorism*, 55, 61.

24. Ferrante, *The Story of a New Name*, 41. Further references to this work, cited as *SNN*, will be given parenthetically in the text.

25. See, for instance, early in the tetralogy, the description of Don Achille as a Frankenstein-like patchwork of different materials (*BF*, 26–29).

26. I refer here to Ferrante, *Frantumaglia*. On the topic, see also De Rogatis, *Elena Ferrante. Parole chiave*, 103–9. It is worth mentioning that the other collection of nonfiction writings Ferrante published is entitled *In the Margins*, which echoes the noun *smarginatura*: Ferrante, *In the Margins: On the Pleasures of Reading and Writing*.

27. Milkova, *Elena Ferrante As World Literature*, 28.

28. Levi, "The Brute Power."

29. Leopardi, *Canti*, 291, original emphasis. Ferrante's passage also echoes the historical pessimism of Adorno and Horkheimer's *Dialectic of Enlightenment*, and Benjamin's "Theses on the Philosophy of History." Ricciardi explores the Benjaminian thrust of Ferrante's philosophy of history: "If the Neapolitan Quartet reflects a particular historical outlook, it would have to be the withering critique of the 'homogenous empty time' of modernity that Benjamin advances in 'On the Concept of History.'" Ricciardi, *Finding Ferrante*, 137.

30. Leopardi, *Canti*, 87.

31. On the topic, see Jill Richards, "The Queer Counterfactual," in Chihaya et al., *The Ferrante Letters*, 178–206.

32. Leopardi, *The Moral Essays*, 71.

33. Ferrante, *Incidental Inventions*, 40. The original passage reads: "*cielo notturno zeppo di mondi e tuttavia vuoto*." Goldstein expunges "*tuttavia vuoto*" in her translation of this passage, which I here restore. In her translation she also puts this sentence in quotation marks, giving the impression of a direct quote from Leopardi—the quotation marks are, however, absent in the Italian original.

34. Kant, *Critique of Practical Reason*, 133. On the analysis of the Kantian sublime in relation to horror, see my chapter 1.

35. Eliot, *The Complete Poems and Plays*, 172: "Go, go, go, said the bird: human kind / Cannot bear very much reality."

36. Koestler, "The Nightmare That Is a Reality."

37. This may come with substantial perils, such as the looming specter of false or manipulative accusations. Rather than advocating for the full and unconditional acceptance as truthful of any horrifying story whatsoever, my point, and, I believe, Koestler's, is to be aware that horrible events may come across as implausible. A possible initial reaction of incredulity must thus be taken into account as

we try to make sense of such events, in particular when they present ethical and social conundrums.

38. A first attempt at connecting Ortese and Ferrante with reference to the former's descriptive techniques and the latter's *smarginatura* is in Atkinson, "Shattered Vision: From Anna Maria Ortese to Elena Ferrante." Tiziana De Rogatis connects the magical realism she sees in Ortese's work with Ferrante's style: De Rogatis, *Elena Ferrante. Parole chiave*, 35.

39. Ferrante, *In the Margins*, 51.

40. Ferrante, *Those Who Leave and Those Who Stay*, 28.

41. Ferrante's novels surely lend themselves to be read through the critical lens of trauma studies. See, in particular, Caffè, "Global Feminism and Trauma in Elena Ferrante's Saga *My Brilliant Friend*."

42. It is debatable whether the title refers to Lila or Elena. While Lila indeed calls Elena her "brilliant friend" in the first book of the series (*BF*, 312), that very book's construction lends credit to the hypothesis that the brilliant friend is Lila. Ultimately, Ferrante leaves the matters ambiguous, and this should not be considered an issue: Elena is Lila's brilliant friend, and Lila is Elena's brilliant friend. On the topic, see Chihaya et al., *The Ferrante Letters*, 30.

43. Malaparte, *Opere scelte*, 727–43.

44. This is my translation of "alcuni punti di contatto" from the original—Goldstein expunges this crucial sentence.

45. I here emend Goldstein's translation of "*ingegneria preventiva sulle persone e sulle cose*" as "defensive manipulation of persons and things."

46. Levi, *The Drowned and the Saved*, 2515.

47. Levi, *The Drowned and the Saved*, 2469.

48. I here emend Goldstein's translation, which renders the Italian "*a me pare una frase densa, carica di senso, e tutta da raccontare*" as "seems to be weighty, full of meaning, with everything to recount."

49. Leopardi, *The Moral Essays*, 220, 224–25.

50. Sloterdijk, *Not Saved: Essays after Heidegger*, 129.

Coda

1. "Memorandum of March 6, 2017."

2. Bureaucratic systems are not the only contexts where we deal with impersonal, anonymous, and frequently overpowering forces. For a fascinating analysis of how large digital networks challenge the limits of our control, see Auerbach, *Meganets*.

3. On how horror differs from adjacent experiences such as disgust or fear, other than my reflections throughout *Ordinary Horror*, see Solomon, "Real Horror," 235–43.

4. Heidegger, *Being and Time*, 175.

5. Benjamin, "The Storyteller: Reflections on the Work of Nikolai Leskov," 56.

6. Ngai, *Ugly Feelings*, 3–6.

7. Fisher, *The Vehement Passions*, 21.

8. On horror's inconceivability, see Witherington and deCruz-Dixon, "The Nature of Horror," 144–47.

9. Wittgenstein, *Philosophical Investigations*, §129.

10. Austin, "A Plea for Excuses," 185.

11. In this book I avoid future or speculative scenarios, and remain anchored to the specificities of the Italian case (an atomic bomb never exploded in Italy, for instance). Yet, the framework for the study of horror beyond the horror genre that I propose could be fruitfully applied to such scenarios as well. Horror and the thinking of the catastrophe go hand in hand: on this topic two useful places of departure, one anchored to the Italian context and the atomic threat, the other to the catastrophe on a planetary scale, are Mariani, *Italian Literature in the Nuclear Age;* and Dupuy, *How to Think about Catastrophe: Towards a Theory of Enlightened Doomsaying.*

BIBLIOGRAPHY

Aloisi, Alessandra. "Limite/Confine." In *Lessico Leopardiano 2014*, edited by Novella Bellucci, Franco D'Intino, and Stefano Gensini, 65–72. Rome: Sapienza Università Editrice, 2014.

Aloisi, Alessandra, and Fabio Camilletti. "Introduction." In *Archaeology of the Unconscious: Italian Perspectives*, edited by Alessandra Aloisi and Fabio Camilletti, 1–12. New York: Routledge, 2020.

Andreoli, Annamaria. *Diventare Pirandello. L'uomo e la maschera*. Milan: Mondadori, 2020.

Arendt, Hannah. *Eichmann in Jerusalem: A Report on the Banality of Evil*. Translated by Amos Elon. London: Penguin Classics, 2006.

Atkinson, Sarah. "Shattered Vision: From Anna Maria Ortese to Elena Ferrante." In *Ferrante Unframed: Authorship, Reception and Feminist Praxis in the Works of Elena Ferrante*, edited by Costanza Barchiesi and Roberta Cauchi-Santoro, 101–13. Florence: Società Editrice Fiorentina, 2021.

Auerbach, David B. *Meganets: How Digital Forces beyond Our Control Commandeer Our Daily Lives and Inner Realities*. New York: PublicAffairs, 2023.

Austin, J. L. "A Plea for Excuses." In *Philosophical Papers*, edited by J. O. Urmson and G. J. Warnock, 175–204. Oxford: Oxford University Press, 1979.

Baglivo, Beatrice, ed. *Curzio Malaparte e la ricerca dell'identità europea*. Chambéry: Presses universitaires Université Savoie Mont Blanc, 2020.

Baglivo, Beatrice. "Una poetica dell'immaginazione. Il realismo magico di Curzio Malaparte." In *Anti-Mimesis. Le poetiche antimimetiche in Italia (1930–1980)*, edited by Andrea Gialloreto and Srecko Jurisic, 135–57. Novate Milanese: Prospero editore, 2021.

Baldasso, Franco. *Against Redemption: Democracy, Memory, and Literature in Post-Fascist Italy*. New York: Fordham University Press, 2022.

Baldasso, Franco. "Curzio Malaparte and the Tragic Understanding of Modern History." *Annali d'Italianistica* 35 (2017): 279–303.

Baldasso, Franco. *Curzio Malaparte la letteratura crudele.* Kaputt, La pelle *e la caduta della civiltà europea.* Rome: Carocci, 2019.

Baldi, Andrea. "Cities 'Paved with Casualties': Ortese's Journeys through Urban Modernity." In *Anna Maria Ortese: Celestial Geographies*, edited by Gian Maria Annovi and Flora Ghezzo, 78–111. Toronto: University of Toronto Press, 2015.

Baldi, Andrea. "Infelicità senza desideri. *Il mare non bagna Napoli* di Anna Maria Ortese." *Italica* 77, no. 1 (2000): 81–104.

Baldi, Andrea. *La meraviglia e il disincanto. Studi sulla narrativa breve di Anna Maria Ortese.* Naples: Loffredo University Press, 2010.

Bazzocchi, Marco Antonio, ed. *Leopardi e Bologna. Atti del Convegno di studi per il secondo centenario Leopardiano (Bologna, 18–19 Maggio 1998).* Florence: L. S. Olschki, 1999.

Bellin, Stefano. "Specters of Levi: Shame and the Deconstruction of the Human." In *Attraversamenti culturali. Cinema, letteratura, musica e arti visuali nell'Italia contemporanea*, edited by Simona Wright and Fulvio Santo Orsitto, 109–18. Florence: Cesati, 2016.

Belpoliti, Marco. *Primo Levi: An Identikit.* Translated by Clarissa Botsford. London: Seagull Books, 2022.

Beniger, James R. *The Control Revolution: Technological and Economic Origins of the Information Society.* Cambridge, MA: Harvard University Press, 1986.

Benjamin, Walter. "The Storyteller: Reflections on the Work of Nikolai Leskov." In *The Storyteller Essays*, translated by Tess Lewis, 48–73. New York: New York Review Books, 2019.

Benjamin, Walter. "Theses on the Philosophy of History." In *Illuminations*, translated by Harry Zohn, 253–64. New York: Schocken Books, 1988.

Berto, Giuseppe. "L'inconsapevole approccio." In Giuseppe Berto, *Le opere di Dio*, 1–96. Milan: BUR, 2014.

Berto, Giuseppe. *Incubus.* Translated by William Weaver. New York: Knopf, 1966.

Berto, Giuseppe. *Il male oscuro.* Milan: Rizzoli, 2006.

Bertolio, Giuseppe. "Suicidio." In *Lessico Leopardiano 2016*, edited by Novella Bellucci, Franco D'Intino, and Stefano Gensini, 129–31. Rome: Sapienza Università Editrice, 2016.

Best, Stephen, and Sharon Marcus. "Surface Reading: An Introduction." *Representations* 108, no. 1 (November 1, 2009): 1–21.

Bini, Daniela. *Carlo Michelstaedter and the Failure of Language.* Gainesville: University Press of Florida, 1992.

Bini, Daniela. "Pirandello, Michelstaedter e l'Espressionismo." In *Pirandello e le avanguardie*, edited by Enzo Lauretta, 173–82. Agrigento: Centro nazionale di studi pirandelliani, 1999.

Bodei, Remo. *Leopardi e la filosofia.* Milan: Mimesis, 2022.

Bohrer, Karl Heinz. *Die Ästhetik des Schreckens. Die pessimistische Romantik und Ernst Jüngers Frühwerk*. Munich: C. Hanser, 1978.

Botting, Fred. "More Things: Horror, Materialism and Speculative Weirdism." *Horror Studies* 3, no. 2 (September 26, 2012): 281–303.

Brianese, Giorgio. *L'arco e il destino. Interpretazione di Michelstaedter*. Milan: Mimesis, 2010.

Brison, Susan J. *Aftermath: Violence and the Remaking of a Self*. Princeton: Princeton University Press, 2023.

Brooks, Peter. *Reading for the Plot: Design and Intention in Narrative*. Cambridge, MA: Harvard University Press, 1992.

Brown, Deborah J. *Descartes and the Passionate Mind*. Cambridge, UK: Cambridge University Press, 2006.

Bullaro, Grace Russo, and Stephanie V. Love. "Beyond the Margins: 'Ferrante Fever' and Italian Female Writing." In *The Works of Elena Ferrante: Reconfiguring the Margins*, edited by Grace Russo Bullaro and Stephanie V. Love, 1–12. New York: Palgrave Macmillan, 2016.

Burke, Edmund. *A Philosophical Enquiry into the Sublime and Beautiful*. New York: Routledge Classics, 2008.

Burke, Michael J. *The Ethics of Horror: Spectral Alterity in Twenty-first-century Horror Film*. Lanham, MD: Lexington Books, 2024.

Burrow, J. W. *The Crisis of Reason: European Thought, 1848–1914*. New Haven: Yale University Press, 2002.

Butler, Judith. "Primo Levi for the Present." In *Re-figuring Hayden White*, edited by Ewa Domańska and Hans Kellner, 282–303. Stanford: Stanford University Press, 2009.

Caffè, Emanuela. "Global Feminism and Trauma in Elena Ferrante's Saga *My Brilliant Friend*." *MLN* 136, no. 1 (2021): 32–53.

Calvino, Italo. *The Path to the Spiders' Nest*. Translated by Archibald Colquhoun and Martin McLaughlin. Hopewell: Ecco Press, 1998.

Camilletti, Fabio. "'Dietro le porte.' 'Lo spavento notturno' di Giacomo Leopardi, i terrori della notte e la morte in culla tra 'errori popolari' e nosologia medica." *Quaderni d'italianistica* 43, no. 1 (January 26, 2023): 101–15.

Camilletti, Fabio. *Italia lunare. Gli anni Sessanta e l'occulto*. Oxford: Peter Lang, 2018.

Camilletti, Fabio. "Leopardi avec Sade: Impotence and Jouissance in 'La Ginestra.'" In *Ten Steps: Critical Inquiries on Leopardi*, edited by Fabio Camilletti and Paola Cori, 205–25. Oxford: Peter Lang, 2015.

Camilletti, Fabio. "Leopardi's Night (T)Errors, the Uncanny, and the 'Old Wives Tale.'" In *Archaeology of the Unconscious: Italian Perspectives*, 67–85. New York: Routledge, 2020.

Camilletti, Fabio. *Leopardi's Nymphs: Grace, Melancholy, and the Uncanny*. Leeds, UK: Legenda, 2013.

Camilletti, Fabio, and Giulia Scialanga, eds. *Lessico Leopardiano 2024. La paura*. Rome: Sapienza Università Editrice, 2024.

Campailla, Sergio. "Espressionismo e filosofia della contestazione in Michelstaedter." In *Scrittori giuliani*. Bologna: Pàtron, 1980.

Campailla, Sergio. *Pensiero e poesia di Carlo Michelstaedter*. Bologna: Pàtron, 1973.

Cangiano, Mimmo. "Modernism and Rhetoric: Pirandello and Michelstaedter." *ENTHYMEMA* 19 (December 31, 2017): 176–94.

Cangiano, Mimmo. *The Wreckage of Philosophy: Carlo Michelstaedter and the Limits of Bourgeois Thought*. Toronto: University of Toronto Press, 2018.

Capra, Andrea. "Descartes at War: Curzio Malaparte and Primo Levi." *MLN* 139, no. 1 (2024): 108–31.

Capra, Andrea. "'Je Suis Cartésien, Hélas!' Malaparte e Descartes." In *Curzio Malaparte e la cultura europea. Cartografia dei palinsesti letterari*, edited by Maria Pia De Paulis, 259–70. Florence: Franco Cesati Editore, 2022.

Capra, Andrea. "Una realtà zibaldonica. Attualità e inattualità della *Proposta di premi fatta dall'Accademia dei Sillografi*." *Cahiers d'études italiennes* 40 (2025).

Capra, Andrea. "Staying with the Darkness: Peter Sloterdijk's Anthropotechnics for the Digital Age." *Angelaki* 26, no. 1 (January 2, 2021): 124–41.

Capra, Andrea. "To Dissolve and to Shatter: The Role of Horror in Elena Ferrante." *Italian Quarterly* 61, no. 239/240 (2024): 88–109.

Capra, Andrea. "Torquato Tasso o GPT-3? Giacomo Leopardi e la 'computisteria' del mondo." *Il Verri* 79 (2022): 105–19.

Capra, Andrea, and Marco Malvestio. "Horror and *orrore*: A Canon Hiding in Plain Sight." *Italian Quarterly* 61, no. 239/240 (2024): 1–12.

Caputi, Anthony. *Pirandello and the Crisis of Modern Consciousness*. Urbana: University of Illinois Press, 1988.

Carrera, Alessandro. "The Consistency of Nothingness: Leopardi's Struggle with 'solido nulla.'" In *The Movement of Nothingness: Trust in the Emptiness of Time*, edited by Daniel M. Price and Ryan J. Johnson. Aurora: Davies Group Publishers, 2013.

Carroll, Noël. *The Philosophy of Horror: Or, Paradoxes of the Heart*. New York: Routledge, 1990.

Caruth, Cathy. *Unclaimed Experience: Trauma, Narrative, and History*. Baltimore: Johns Hopkins University Press, 2016.

Castronovo, Valerio. *L'Italia del miracolo economico*. Rome: Laterza, 2010.

Cavarero, Adriana. "'Destroy Your Sight with a New Gorgon': Mass Atrocity and the Phenomenology of Horror." In *Emotions and Mass Atrocity: Philosophical and Theoretical Explorations*, edited by Johannes Lang and Thomas Brudholm, 123–41. Cambridge, UK: Cambridge University Press, 2018.

Cavarero, Adriana. *Horrorism: Naming Contemporary Violence*. Translated by William McCuaig. New York: Columbia University Press, 2011.

Cavell, Stanley. *Must We Mean What We Say? A Book of Essays*. Cambridge, UK: Cambridge University Press, 2015.

Cerruti, Marco. *Carlo Michelstaedter*. Milan: Mursia, 1967.

Cerulo, Karen A. *Never Saw It Coming: Cultural Challenges to Envisioning the Worst*. Chicago: University of Chicago Press, 2006.

Chihaya, Sarah, Merve Emre, Katherine Hill, and Juno Jill Richards. *The Ferrante Letters: An Experiment in Collective Criticism*. New York: Columbia University Press, 2020.

Church, David. *Post-Horror: Art, Genre, and Cultural Elevation*. Edinburgh: Edinburgh University Press, 2021.

Cipriani, Enrico. "Exploring Alienation and Knowledge: A Comparative Study of H. P. Lovecraft and Giacomo Leopardi." *Dialogoi. Rivista di studi comparatistici* 11 (2024): 293–98.

Clasen, Mathias. *Why Horror Seduces*. Oxford: Oxford University Press, 2017.

Clerici, Luca. *Apparizione e visione. Vita e opere di Anna Maria Ortese*. Milan: Mondadori, 2002.

Contesi, Filippo. "The Affective Nature of Horror." In *Cultural Approaches to Disgust and the Visceral*, edited by Max Ryynänen, Heidi Kosonen, and Susanne Ylönen, 31–43. New York: Routledge, 2022.

Conti, Fulvio. *Breve storia dello stato sociale*. Rome: Carocci, 2013.

Contini, Gianfranco. "Espressionismo letterario." In *Ultimi esercizi ed elzeviri*, 41–106. Turin: Einaudi, 1988.

Contini, Gianfranco. *Italie magique*. Paris: Editions des Portes de France, 1946.

Il corriere friulano. "Necrologo di Carlo Michelstaedter." October 18, 1910.

Corsinovi, Graziella. *Pirandello e l'espressionismo. Analogie culturali e anticipazioni espressive nella prima narrativa*. Genoa: Tilgher, 1979.

Crane, Jonathan Lake. *Terror and Everyday Life: Singular Moments in the History of the Horror Film*. Thousand Oaks, CA: Sage, 1994.

Creed, Barbara. *The Monstrous-Feminine: Film, Feminism, Psychoanalysis*. New York: Routledge, 2023.

Damasio, Antonio. *Descartes' Error: Emotion, Reason, and the Human Brain*. New York: Penguin, 2005.

Damiani, Rolando. *L'impero della ragione. Studi Leopardiani*. Ravenna: Longo, 1994.

Dastur, Françoise. "Phenomenology of the Event: Waiting and Surprise." *Hypatia* 15, no. 4 (2000): 178–89.

Davis, Colin, and Hanna Meretoja. "Introduction to Literary Trauma Studies." In *The Routledge Companion to Literature and Trauma*, edited by Colin Davis and Hanna Meretoja, 1–8. New York: Routledge, 2020.

De Gasperin, Vilma. *Loss and the Other in the Visionary Work of Anna Maria Ortese*. Oxford: Oxford University Press, 2014.

De Liguori, Girolamo. "Da Teofrasto a Stratone. L'itinerario filosofico di Giacomo Leopardi." *Quaderni materialisti* 3, no. 4 (2005): 195–223.

De Michelis, Cesare. "Umanità di Berto." *Studi novecenteschi* 36, no. 77 (2009): 99–117.

De Monticelli, Roberta. *Il richiamo della persuasione. Lettere a Carlo Michelstaedter*. Genoa: Marietti, 1988.

De Paulis, Maria Pia, ed. *Curzio Malaparte*. Paris: Éditions de l'Herne, 2018.

De Paulis, Maria Pia. *Curzio Malaparte. Il trauma infinito della Grande Guerra*. Florence: Franco Cesati Editore, 2019.

De Rogatis, Tiziana. *Elena Ferrante. Parole chiave*. Rome: Edizioni e/o, 2018.

Descartes, René. "Discourse on Method." In *Discourse on Method and Meditations on First Philosophy*, translated by Donald A. Cress, 1–44. Indianapolis: Hackett Publishing, 1999.

Descartes, René. "Meditations on First Philosophy." In *Discourse on Method and Meditations on First Philosophy*, translated by Donald A. Cress, 47–103. Indianapolis: Hackett Publishing, 1999.

Dewey, John. *The Quest for Certainty: A Study of the Relation of Knowledge and Action*. New York: Capricorn, 1960.

Di Mauro, Marco. "La fabbrica dei Granili e la Casina Cinese." *Napoli nobilissima. Rivista di arti, filologia, e storia* 3 (2002): 215–22.

Dottore, Paola. *La forma della coscienza. Il male oscuro di Giuseppe Berto*. Castelfranco Veneto: Biblioteca dei Leoni, 2014.

Dupuy, Jean-Pierre. *How to Think about Catastrophe: Toward a Theory of Enlightened Doomsaying*. East Lansing: Michigan State University Press, 2022.

Eliot, T. S. *The Complete Poems and Plays*. London: Faber and Faber, 1969.

Federal Register. "Memorandum of March 6, 2017: Implementing Immediate Heightened Screening and Vetting of Applications for Visas and Other Immigration Benefits, Ensuring Enforcement of All Laws for Entry into the United States, and Increasing Transparency among Departments and Agencies of the Federal Government and for the American People." April 3, 2017. https://www.federalregister.gov/documents/2017/04/03/2017-06702/implementing-immediate-heightened-screening-and-vetting-of-applications-for-visas-and-other.

Federici, Silvia. *Caliban and the Witch: Women, the Body and Primitive Accumulation*. New York: Autonomedia, 2004.

Felski, Rita. *The Limits of Critique*. Chicago: University of Chicago Press, 2015.

Felski, Rita. *Uses of Literature*. Malden, MA: Wiley-Blackwell, 2008.

Ferme, Valerio. "Translating the Babel of Horror: Primo Levi's Catharsis through Language in the Holocaust Memoir *Se questo è un uomo*." *Italica* 78, no. 1 (2001): 53–73.

Ferrante, Elena. *Frantumaglia: A Writer's Journey*. Translated by Ann Goldstein. New York: Europa Editions, 2016.

Ferrante, Elena. *Incidental Inventions*. Translated by Ann Goldstein. New York: Europa Editions, 2019.

Ferrante, Elena. *In the Margins: On the Pleasures of Reading and Writing*. Translated by Ann Goldstein. New York: Europa Editions, 2022.

Ferrante, Elena. *My Brilliant Friend*. Translated by Ann Goldstein. New York: Europa Editions, 2012.

Ferrante, Elena. *The Story of a New Name*. Translated by Ann Goldstein. New York: Europa Editions, 2013.

Ferrante, Elena. *The Story of the Lost Child*. Translated by Ann Goldstein. New York: Europa Editions, 2015.

Ferrante, Elena. *Those Who Leave and Those Who Stay*. Translated by Ann Goldstein. New York: Europa Editions, 2014.

Ferroni, Giulio. *Passioni del Novecento*. Rome: Donzelli, 1999.

Fisher, Mark. *The Weird and the Eerie*. London: Repeater, 2017.

Fisher, Philip. *The Vehement Passions*. Princeton: Princeton University Press, 2002.

Folin, Alberto. *Leopardi e l'imperfetto nulla*. Venice: Marsilio, 2001.

Fortunato, Marco. *La protesta e l'impossibile. Cinque saggi su Michelstaedter*. Milan: Mimesis, 2013.

Franchi, Gian Andrea. *Una disperata speranza. Profilo biografico di Carlo Michelstaedter*. Milan: Mimesis, 2014.

Frassica, Pietro. *A Marta Abba per non morire. Sull'epistolario inedito tra Pirandello e la sua attrice*. Milan: Mursia, 1991.

Fressoz, Jean-Baptiste. *L'Apocalypse joyeuse. Une histoire du risque technologique*. Paris: Éditions du Seuil, 2020.

Gaetano, Raffaele. *Giacomo Leopardi e il sublime. Archeologia e percorsi di una idea estetica*. Soveria Mannelli: Rubbettino, 2002.

Garin, Eugenio. "Postilla: Carlo Michelstaedter." In *Intellettuali del XX secolo*, 96–104. Rome: Editori riuniti, 1974.

Gelder, Ken, ed. *The Horror Reader*. New York: Routledge, 2000.

Gheorghiu, Mihai Dinu. "The Iaşi Pogrom in Curzio Malaparte's Kaputt: Between History and Fiction." In *Local History, Transnational Memory in the Romanian Holocaust*, edited by Valentina Glajar and Jeanine Teodorescu, 47–56. New York: Palgrave Macmillan US, 2011.

Ghezzo, Flora. "Introduction: Anna Maria Ortese and the Red-Footed Angel." In *Anna Maria Ortese: Celestial Geographies*, edited by Flora Ghezzo and Gian Maria Annovi, 3–31. Toronto: University of Toronto Press, 2015.

Giordano, Paolo. *Ferdinando Fuga a Napoli. L'Albergo dei Poveri, il Cimitero delle 366 fosse, i Granili*. Lecce: Edizioni del Grifo, 1997.

Girolami, Patrizia. *L'antiteodicea. Dio, dèi, religione nello "Zibaldone" di Giacomo Leopardi*. Florence: L. S. Olschki, 1995.

Goldie, Peter. *The Mess Inside: Narrative, Emotion, and the Mind*. Oxford: Oxford University Press, 2012.

Gordon, Robert S. C. ed. *The Cambridge Companion to Primo Levi*. Cambridge, UK: Cambridge University Press, 2007.

Gordon, Robert S. C. *Primo Levi's Ordinary Virtues: From Testimony to Ethics*. Oxford: Oxford University Press, 2001.

Graeber, Thomas, Christopher Roth, and Florian Zimmermann. "Stories, Statistics, and Memory." *The Quarterly Journal of Economics* 139, no. 4 (November 1, 2024): 2181–2225.

Greenaway, Jon. *Capitalism: A Horror Story.* New York: Repeater, 2024.

Gumbrecht, Hans Ulrich. *Production of Presence: What Meaning Cannot Convey.* Stanford: Stanford University Press, 2003.

Habermas, Jürgen. "Modernity: An Unfinished Project." In *Habermas and the Unfinished Project of Modernity: Critical Essays on the Philosophical Discourse of Modernity,* edited by Maurizio Passerin d'Entrèves and Seyla Benhabib, 38–55. Cambridge, UK: Polity Press, 1996.

Hamilton, Paul. *Orientation in European Romanticism: The Art of Falling Upwards.* Cambridge, UK: Cambridge University Press, 2022.

Harman, Graham. *Weird Realism: Lovecraft and Philosophy.* Winchester, UK: Zero Books, 2012.

Harrison, Robert Pogue. *Forests: The Shadow of Civilization.* Chicago: University of Chicago Press, 1993.

Harrison, Robert Pogue. "Preface." In *Purgatorio,* by Dante Alighieri, translated by D. M. Black, vii–xii. New York: New York Review Books, 2021.

Harrison, Thomas. *Essayism: Conrad, Musil and Pirandello.* Baltimore: Johns Hopkins University Press, 1992.

Harrison, Thomas. "The Michelstaedter Enigma." *Differentia: Review of Italian Thought* 18, no. 8 (1999): 125–41.

Harrison, Thomas. *1910: The Emancipation of Dissonance.* Berkeley: University of California Press, 1996.

Harrison, Thomas. "Suicide." In *Pirandello in Context,* edited by Patricia Gaborik, 266–72. Cambridge, UK: Cambridge University Press, 2024.

Harrowitz, Nancy. *Primo Levi and the Identity of a Survivor.* Toronto: University of Toronto Press, 2017.

Heidegger, Martin. *Being and Time.* Translated by Joan Stambaugh. Albany: SUNY Press, 2010.

Heidegger, Martin. *Contributions to Philosophy (of the Event).* Translated by Richard Rojcewicz and Daniela Vallega-Neu. Bloomington: Indiana University Press, 2012.

Heidegger, Martin. *The Event.* Translated by Richard Rojcewicz. Bloomington: Indiana University Press, 2012.

Heidegger, Martin. "The Origin of the Work of Art." In *Off the Beaten Track,* translated by Julian Young and Kenneth Haynes, 1–56. Cambridge, UK: Cambridge University Press, 2002.

Heidegger, Martin. "The Point of Reference." In *Bremen and Freiburg Lectures. Insight Into That Which Is and Basic Principles of Thinking,* translated by Andrew J. Mitchell, 3–4. Bloomington: Indiana University Press, 2012.

Heller, Reinhold. *Edvard Munch: The Scream.* New York: Viking Press, 1973.

Hick, Darren Hudson. "Horror and Its Affects." *The Journal of Aesthetics and Art Criticism* 80, no. 2 (March 1, 2022): 140–50.

Horkheimer, Max, and Theodor W. Adorno. *Dialectic of Enlightenment.* Translated by Edmund Jephcott. Stanford: Stanford University Press, 2007.

Huang, Erin Y. *Urban Horror: Neoliberal Post-socialism and the Limits of Visibility.* Durham, NC: Duke University Press Books, 2020.

Husserl, Edmund. *General Introduction to Pure Phenomenology.* Translated by Fred Kersten. The Hague: Martinus Nijhoff, 1982.

Husserl, Edmund. *Logical Investigations.* Translated by J. N. Findlay. 2 vols. New York: Routledge, 1970.

Iser, Wolfgang. *The Act of Reading: A Theory of Aesthetic Response.* Baltimore: Johns Hopkins University Press, 1980.

Jauss, Hans Robert. "Literary History as a Challenge to Literary Theory." Translated by Elizabeth Benzinger. *New Literary History* 2, no. 1 (1970): 7–37.

Jolley, Nicholas. "The Reception of Descartes' Philosophy." In *The Cambridge Companion to Descartes,* edited by John Cottingham, 393–423. Cambridge, UK: Cambridge University Press, 1992.

Jones, Darryl. *Horror: A Very Short Introduction.* Oxford: Oxford University Press, 2021.

Joshi, S. T. *H. P. Lovecraft: A Life.* West Warwick, UK: Necronomicon Press, 1996.

Joshi, S. T. *I Am Providence: The Life and the Times of H. P. Lovecraft.* New York: Hippocampus Press, 2010.

Kain, Philip J. "Nietzsche, Truth, and the Horror of Existence." *History of Philosophy Quarterly* 23, no. 1 (2006): 41–58.

Kant, Immanuel. *Critique of Judgement.* Translated by James Creed Meredith. Oxford: Oxford University Press, 2009.

Kant, Immanuel. *Critique of Practical Reason.* Translated by Mary Gregor. Cambridge, UK: Cambridge University Press, 1997.

Kay, Tristan. "Primo Levi, Dante, and Language in Auschwitz." *Modern Language Review* 117, no. 1 (2022): 66–100.

Koestler, Arthur. "The Nightmare That Is a Reality." *The New York Times,* January 9, 1944.

Koloskov, Daniil. "Beyond the Reach: Horror and Phenomenal Life." *Journal of the British Society for Phenomenology* 55, no. 4 (October 1, 2024): 394–407.

Kristeva, Julia. *Powers of Horror: An Essay on Abjection.* Translated by Leon Roudiez. New York: Columbia University Press, 1982.

Kundera, Milan. "The Skin: Malaparte's Arch-Novel." In *Encounter,* translated by Linda Asher, 155–78. New York: Harper, 2010.

Kurtz, J. Roger, ed. *Trauma and Literature.* Cambridge, UK: Cambridge University Press, 2018.

Labbate, Orazio. *L'orrore letterario.* Rome: Italo Svevo, 2022.

LaCapra, Dominick. *Writing History, Writing Trauma.* Baltimore: Johns Hopkins University Press, 2014.

Landy, Joshua. "In Praise of Depth: Or, How I Stopped Worrying and Learned to Love the Hidden." *New Literary History* 1, no. 51 (2020): 145–76.

Lazzarin, Stefano. *L'ombre et la forme. Du fantastique italien au XXe siècle.* Caen: Presses universitaires de Caen, 2004.

Leavitt, Charles L., IV. *Italian Neorealism: A Cultural History*. Toronto: University of Toronto Press, 2020.

Leibniz, Gottfried Wilhelm. *The Art of Controversies*. Translated by Marcelo Dascal. Dordrecht: Springer, 2006.

Leopardi, Giacomo. *Canti*. Translated by Jonathan Galassi. New York: Farrar, Straus and Giroux, 2012.

Leopardi, Giacomo. *Lettere*. Edited by Rolando Damiani and Mario Andrea Rigoni. Milan: Mondadori, 2006.

Leopardi, Giacomo. *The Moral Essays*. Translated by Patrick Creagh. New York: Columbia University Press, 1983.

Leopardi, Giacomo. *Poesie e prose*. 2 vols. Milan: Mondadori, 1987.

Leopardi, Giacomo. *Zibaldone*. Edited by Michael Caesar and Franco D'Intino. New York: Farrar, Straus and Giroux, 2015.

Levi, Primo. "The Black Hole of Auschwitz." In *The Complete Works of Primo Levi*, edited by Ann Goldstein, translated by Alessandra Bastagli and Francesco Bastagli, 3: 2752–55. London: Penguin Classics, 2015.

Levi, Primo. "The Brute Power." In *The Complete Works of Primo Levi*, edited by Ann Goldstein, translated by Alessandra Bastagli and Francesco Bastagli, 3: 2629–33. London: Penguin Classics, 2015.

Levi, Primo. *The Drowned and the Saved*. In *The Complete Works of Primo Levi*, edited by Ann Goldstein, translated by Michael F. Moore, 3: 2405–2574. London: Penguin Classics, 2015.

Levi, Primo. "Ex-Chemist." In *The Complete Works of Primo Levi*, edited by Ann Goldstein, translated by Antony Shugaar, 3: 2023–25. London: Penguin Classics, 2015.

Levi, Primo. *If This Is a Man*. In *The Complete Works of Primo Levi*, edited by Ann Goldstein, translated by Stuart Woolf, 1: 5–205. London: Penguin Classics, 2015.

Levi, Primo. *The Periodic Table*. In *The Complete Works of Primo Levi*, edited and translated by Ann Goldstein, 2: 749–946. London: Penguin Classics, 2015.

Levi, Primo. *The Truce*. In *The Complete Works of Primo Levi*, edited and translated by Ann Goldstein, 1: 207–398. London: Penguin Classics, 2015.

Levinas, Emmanuel. *Existence and Existents*. Translated by Alphonso Lingis. The Hague: Martinus Nijhoff, 1978.

Leys, Ruth. *Trauma: A Genealogy*. Chicago: University of Chicago Press, 2000.

Love, Heather. "Close But Not Deep: Literary Ethics and the Descriptive Turn." *New Literary History* 41, no. 2 (2010): 371–91.

Lovecraft, H. P. *Tales*. New York: Library of America, 2005.

Luhmann, Niklas. "Second-Order Observation." In *Risk: A Sociological Theory*, 219–31. New York: de Gruyter, 1993.

Luporini, Cesare. *Leopardi progressivo*. Rome: Riuniti, 1980.

Malaparte, Curzio. *Diary of a Foreigner in Paris*. Translated by Stephen Twilley. New York: New York Review Books, 2020.

Malaparte, Curzio. *Kaputt*. Translated by Cesare Foligno. New York: New York Review Books, 2005.

Malaparte, Curzio. *Opere scelte*. Edited by Luigi Martellini. Milan: Mondadori, 1997.

Malaparte, Curzio. "Prigione Gratis." *Prospettive* 10 (December 15, 1939): 3–6.

Malaparte, Curzio. *The Skin*. Translated by David Moore. New York: New York Review Books, 2013.

Malvestio, Marco. "New Italian Weird? Definizioni della letteratura italiana del soprannaturale nel nuovo millennio." *The Italianist* 41, no. 1 (January 2, 2021): 116–31.

Malvestio, Marco, and Stefano Serafini, eds. *Italian Gothic*. Edinburgh: Edinburgh University Press, 2023.

Mandel, Naomi. *Against the Unspeakable: Complicity, the Holocaust, and Slavery in America*. Charlottesville: University of Virginia Press, 2007.

Mariani, Maria Anna. *Italian Literature in the Nuclear Age: A Poetics of the Bystander*. Oxford: Oxford University Press, 2023.

Mariani, Maria Anna. *Primo Levi e Anna Frank. Tra testimonianza e letteratura*. Rome: Carocci, 2018.

Martellini, Luigi. *Invito alla lettura di Curzio Malaparte*. Milan: Mursia, 1977.

Martellini, Luigi. *Le "Prospettive" di Malaparte*. Naples: Edizioni scientifiche italiane, 2014.

Martinelli, Bortolo. *Leopardi tra Leibniz e Locke. Alla ricerca di un orientamento e di un fondamento*. Rome: Carocci, 2003.

Michelstaedter, Carlo. *Epistolario*. Milan: Adelphi, 1993.

Michelstaedter, Carlo. *Opere*. Florence: Sansoni, 1958.

Michelstaedter, Carlo. *Persuasion and Rhetoric*. Translated by Russell Scott Valentino, Cinzia Sartini Blum, and David J. Depew. New Haven: Yale University Press, 2004.

Milkova, Stiliana. *Elena Ferrante As World Literature*. New York: Bloomsbury Academic, 2021.

Milkova, Stiliana. "Mothers, Daughters, Dolls: On Disgust in Elena Ferrante's *La figlia oscura*." *Italian Culture* 31, no. 2 (September 1, 2013): 91–109.

Moi, Toril. *Revolution of the Ordinary: Literary Studies after Wittgenstein, Austin, and Cavell*. Chicago: University of Chicago Press, 2017.

Moi, Toril. "A Wittgensteinian Phenomenology of Criticism." In *Wittgenstein and Literary Studies*, edited by John Gibson and Robert Chodat, 41–61. Cambridge, UK: Cambridge University Press, 2023.

Moro, Carlotta. "Breaking Out of the Cage of Anthropocentrism: Ecofeminism in Elena Ferrante's *Neapolitan Quartet* and Other Essays." *Romance Studies* 41, no. 4 (October 2, 2023): 303–19.

Morozov, Evgeny. *To Save Everything, Click Here: The Folly of Technological Solutionism*. New York: PublicAffairs, 2014.

Mukherjee, Siddhartha. *The Emperor of All Maladies: A Biography of Cancer*. New York: Scribner, 2010.

Negri, Antonio. *Lenta ginestra. Saggio sull'ontologia di Giacomo Leopardi.* Milan: Mimesis, 2023.

Neumann, Daniel. "'Being Tied to Experience': Towards a Subjective Account of the Phenomenology of the Event." *Continental Philosophy Review* 56, no. 1 (March 1, 2023): 21–40.

The New York Times. "The 100 Best Books of the 21st Century." July 8, 2024.

Ngai, Sianne. *Ugly Feelings.* Cambridge, MA: Harvard University Press, 2005.

Olivier, Marc. *Household Horror: Cinematic Fear and the Secret Life of Everyday Objects.* Bloomington: Indiana University Press, 2020.

Orsucci, Andrea. *Il "giocoliere d'idee." Malaparte e la filosofia.* Pisa: Edizioni della Normale, 2015.

Ortese, Anna Maria. "La città involontaria." *Il Mondo,* January 12, 1952.

Ortese, Anna Maria. *Corpo celeste.* Milan: Adelphi, 1997.

Ortese, Anna Maria. *Da Moby Dick all'Orsa Bianca. Scritti sulla letteratura e sull'arte.* Milan: Adelphi, 2011.

Ortese, Anna Maria. *Estivi terrori.* Rome: Pellicanolibri, 1987.

Ortese, Anna Maria. *Neapolitan Chronicles.* Translated by Ann Goldstein and Jenny McPhee. New York: New Vessel Press, 2018.

Ortese, Anna Maria. "L'orrore di vivere." *Il Mondo,* January 19, 1952.

Ortese, Anna Maria. "La plebe regina." *Il Mondo,* October 6, 1951.

Panella, Giuseppe. *L'estetica dello choc. La scrittura di Curzio Malaparte tra esperimenti narrativi e poesia.* Florence: Clinamen, 2014.

Papini, Giovanni. "Un suicidio metafisico." *Il Resto del Carlino,* November 5, 1910.

Pascal, Blaise. *Pensées.* Paris: Garnier, 1964.

Peak, David. "Horror of the Real: H. P. Lovecraft' s Old Ones and Contemporary Speculative Philosophy." In *Diseases of the Head,* edited by Matt Rosen, 163–80. Santa Barbara, CA: Punctum Books, 2020.

Pedullà, Walter. "Humor." In *Pirandello in Context,* edited by Patricia Gaborik, 147–54. Cambridge, UK: Cambridge University Press, 2024.

Perli, Antonello. *Oltre il deserto. Poetica e teoretica di Michelstaedter.* Ravenna: Giorgio Pozzi Editore, 2009.

Perli, Antonello. "La vita e la forma. Michelstaedter e Pirandello." *Lettore di Provincia* 105 (1999): 25–37.

Piancastelli, Corrado. *Giuseppe Berto.* Florence: La nuova Italia, 1970.

Pinto, Isabella. *Elena Ferrante. Poetiche e politiche della soggettività.* Milan: Mimesis, 2020.

Pinto, Isabella, Stiliana Milkova, and Adriana Cavarero. "Storytelling Philosophy and Self Writing—Preliminary Notes on Elena Ferrante: An Interview with Adriana Cavarero." *Narrative* 28, no. 2 (2020): 236–49.

Pirandello, Luigi. *The Late Mattia Pascal.* Translated by William Weaver. New York: New York Review Books, 2004.

Pirandello, Luigi. *One, No One, and One Hundred Thousand.* Translated by William Weaver. Las Vegas: Spurl Editions, 2018.

Pirandello, Luigi. *On Humor.* Translated by Antonio Illiano and Daniel P. Testa. Chapel Hill: University of North Carolina Press, 1974.

Pistelli, Maurizio. *Carlo Michelstaedter. Poesia e ansia di assoluto.* Rome: Donzelli, 2009.

Poole, W. Scott. *Wasteland: The Great War and the Origins of Modern Horror.* Berkeley, CA: Counterpoint, 2019.

Portinari, Folco. "Deserto con poesia." *La Stampa*, October 3, 1987.

Portnoff, Sharon. "Levi's Auschwitz and Dante's Hell." *Society* 46, no. 1 (January 1, 2009): 76–84.

Pradella, Chiara. *110. Carlo Michelstaedter e il tempo della verità.* Rome: Ensemble, 2020.

Pupo, Ivan, ed. *Interviste a Pirandello. "Parole da dire, uomo, agli altri uomini."* Soveria Mannelli: Rubbettino, 2002.

Putnam, Hilary. "12 Philosophers: And Their Influence on Me." *Proceedings and Addresses of the American Philosophical Association* 82, no. 2 (2008): 101–15.

Radcliffe, Ann. "On the Supernatural in Poetry." In *The Italian*, 395–406. Oxford: Oxford University Press, 2017.

Re, Lucia. "'Clouds in Front of My Eyes': Ortese's Poetics of the Gaze in 'Un paio di occhiali' and *Il mare non bagna Napoli.*" In *Anna Maria Ortese: Celestial Geographies*, edited by Gian Maria Annovi and Flora Ghezzo, 35–77. Toronto: University of Toronto Press, 2015.

Re, Lucia. "Invisible Sea: Anna Maria Ortese's *Il mare non bagna Napoli.*" *California Italian Studies* 3, no. 1 (2012): 1–34.

Re, Lucia. "Neorealist Narrative: Experience and Experiment." In *The Cambridge Companion to the Italian Novel*, edited by Peter Bondanella and Andrea Ciccarelli. Cambridge, UK: Cambridge University Press, 2006.

Ricciardi, Alessia. *Finding Ferrante: Authorship and the Politics of World Literature.* New York: Columbia University Press, 2021.

Rolfs, Daniel. *The Last Cross: A History of the Suicide Theme in Italian Literature.* Ravenna: Longo, 1981.

Rosa, Hartmut. *The Uncontrollability of the World.* Translated by James C. Wagner. Cambridge, UK: Polity Press, 2020.

Salsano, Roberto. *Michelstaedter tra D'Annunzio, Pirandello e il mondo della vita.* Rome: Bulzoni, 2012.

Sartre, Jean-Paul. "Intentionality: A Fundamental Idea of Husserl's Phenomenology." *Journal of the British Society for Phenomenology* 1, no. 2 (January 1, 1970): 4–5.

Sartre, Jean-Paul. *Nausea.* Translated by Lloyd Alexander. New York: New Directions, 2013.

Scarry, Elaine. *The Body in Pain: The Making and Unmaking of the World.* Oxford: Oxford University Press, 1987.

Schwenger, Peter. "Phenomenology of the Scream." *Critical Inquiry* 40, no. 2 (January 2014): 382–95.

Seno Reed, Cosetta. *Anna Maria Ortese. Un avventuroso realismo*. Ravenna: Longo, 2013.

Serafini, Stefano. *Gothic Italy: Crime, Science, and Literature after Unification, 1861–1914*. Toronto: University of Toronto Press, 2024.

Serra, Maurizio. *Malaparte: A Biography*. Translated by Stephen Twilley. New York: New York Review Books, 2025.

Serra, Maurizio. *Malaparte. Vite e leggende*. Venice: Marsilio, 2012.

Severino, Emanuele. *Cosa arcana e stupenda*. Milan: Rizzoli, 2006.

Severino, Emanuele. *In viaggio con Leopardi. La partita sul destino dell'uomo*. Milan: Rizzoli, 2015.

Severino, Emanuele. *Il nulla e la poesia. Alla fine dell'età della tecnica: Leopardi*. Milan: Rizzoli, 2021.

Shklovsky, Viktor. "Art, As Device." Translated by Alexandra Berlina. *Poetics Today* 36, no. 3 (September 1, 2015): 151–74.

Sloterdijk, Peter. *Not Saved: Essays after Heidegger*. Translated by Ian Alexander Moore and Christopher Turner. Cambridge, UK: Polity Press, 2016.

Sloterdijk, Peter. *What Happened in the Twentieth Century? Towards a Critique of Extremist Reason*. Translated by Christopher Turner. Cambridge, UK: Polity Press, 2018.

Smith, Steven J. "Rational Horror." *Philosophy Today* 27, no. 4 (1983): 307–16.

Solomon, Robert C. "Real Horror." In *Dark Thoughts. Philosophical Reflections on Cinematic Horror*, edited by Steven Jay Schneider and Daniel Shaw, 230–59. Lanham, MD: Scarecrow Press, 2003.

Subialka, Michael. "Modernity." In *Pirandello in Context*, edited by Patricia Gaborik, 227–34. Cambridge, UK: Cambridge University Press, 2024.

Taleb, Nassim Nicholas. *Antifragile: Things That Gain from Disorder*. New York: Random House, 2014.

Taleb, Nassim Nicholas. *The Black Swan. The Impact of the Highly Improbable*. New York: Random House, 2010.

Taylor, Charles. *A Secular Age*. Cambridge, MA: Harvard University Press, 2007.

Taylor, Charles. *Sources of the Self: The Making of the Modern Identity*. Cambridge, MA: Harvard University Press, 1992.

Thacker, Eugene. *In the Dust of This Planet*. Winchester, UK: Zero Books, 2011.

Thacker, Eugene. *Starry Speculative Corpse*. Winchester, UK: Zero Books, 2015.

Thacker, Eugene. *Tentacles Longer Than Night*. Winchester, UK: Zero Books, 2015.

Thiret, Jean-Claude. "L'influenza perenne. Malaparte francese." In *Malaparte scrittore d'Europa. Atti del convegno (Prato 1987) e altri contributi*, edited by Gianni Grana and Vittoria Baroncelli, 135–46. Prato: Mazorati, 1991.

Thumiger, Chiara, and George Kazantzidis, eds. *Horror in Classical Antiquity and Beyond: Body, Affect, Concepts*. London: Bloomsbury Academic, 2025.

Timpanaro, Sebastiano. *La filologia di Giacomo Leopardi*. Rome: Laterza, 1997.

Todorov, Tzvetan. *The Fantastic. A Structural Approach to a Literary Genre*. Translated by Richard Howard. Cleveland: Press of Case Western Reserve University, 1973.

Toulmin, Stephen. *Cosmopolis: The Hidden Agenda of Modernity.* Chicago: University of Chicago Press, 1992.

Toulmin, Stephen. *Return to Reason.* Cambridge, MA: Harvard University Press, 2003.

Trezise, Thomas. "Unspeakable." *The Yale Journal of Criticism* 14, no. 1 (2001): 39–66.

Trezise, Thomas. *Witnessing Witnessing: On the Reception of Holocaust Survivor Testimony.* New York: Fordham University Press, 2013.

Trigg, Dylan. *The Thing: A Phenomenology of Horror.* Winchester, UK: Zero Books, 2014.

Tulchinsky, Igor, and Christopher E. Mason. *The Age of Prediction: Algorithms, AI, and the Shifting Shadows of Risk.* Cambridge, MA: MIT Press, 2023.

United Nations. "Universal Declaration of Human Rights." https://www.un.org/en/about-us/universal-declaration-of-human-rights.

Vallega-Neu, Daniela. "Ereignis: The Event of Appropriation." In *Martin Heidegger: Key Concepts,* edited by Bret W. Davis, 140–54. Durham, UK: Acumen Publishing, 2009.

Vašek, Thomas. *Schein und Zeit: Martin Heidegger und Carlo Michelstaedter: Auf den Spuren einer Enteignung.* Berlin: Matthes and Seitz Berlin, 2019.

Venturini, Simone. *Horror italiano.* Rome: Donzelli, 2014.

Vettori, Alessandro. *Giuseppe Berto. La passione della scrittura.* Venice: Marsilio, 2013.

Vettori, Alessandro. "La predestinazione al male nell'opera di Giuseppe Berto." *Forum Italicum* 36, no. 2 (September 1, 2002): 316–38.

Vita, Saverio. *"Un fulgorato scoscendere." L'opera narrativa di Giuseppe Berto.* Ravenna: Giorgio Pozzi Editore, 2021.

Weber, Max. *The Protestant Ethic and the Spirit of Capitalism.* Translated by Stephen Kalberg. Oxford: Oxford University Press, 2011.

Weber, Max. *The Sociology of Religion.* Translated by Ephraim Fischoff. Boston: Beacon Press, 1969.

White, Hayden. "Figural Realism in Witness Literature." *Parallax* 10, no. 1 (January 1, 2004): 113–24.

Witherington, David C., and Naila V. deCruz-Dixon. "The Nature of Horror." *Emotion Review* 17, no. 3 (2025): 137–52.

Wittgenstein, Ludwig. *On Certainty.* Translated by Denis Paul and G. E. M. Anscombe. New York: Harper and Row, 1972.

Wittgenstein, Ludwig. *Philosophical Investigations.* Translated by P. M. S. Hacker and Joachim Schulte. Malden, MA: Wiley-Blackwell, 2009.

Wittgenstein, Ludwig. *Tractatus Logico-Philosophicus.* Translated by Michael Beaney. Oxford: Oxford University Press, 2023.

INDEX

Figures are designated with italicized page numbers

Printed and bound by CPI Group (UK) Ltd, Croydon, CR0 4YY

Printed and bound by CPI Group (UK) Ltd, Croydon, CR0 4YY

13/08/2026

14941844-0006